# Lecture Notes in Computer Science          **9039**

*Commenced Publication in 1973*
Founding and Former Series Editors:
Gerhard Goos, Juris Hartmanis, and Jan van Leeuwen

## Editorial Board

More information about this series at http://www.springer.com/series/7408

Susanne Graf · Mahesh Viswanathan (Eds.)

# Formal Techniques for Distributed Objects, Components, and Systems

35th IFIP WG 6.1 International Conference, FORTE 2015
Held as Part of the 10th International Federated Conference
on Distributed Computing Techniques, DisCoTec 2015
Grenoble, France, June 2–4, 2015
Proceedings

 Springer

*Editors*
Susanne Graf
Université Grenoble Alpes / VERIMAG
Grenoble
France

Mahesh Viswanathan
University of Illinois at Urbana-Champaign
Urbana, Illinois
USA

ISSN 0302-9743      ISSN 1611-3349 (electronic)
Lecture Notes in Computer Science
ISBN 978-3-319-19194-2      ISBN 978-3-319-19195-9 (eBook)
DOI 10.1007/978-3-319-19195-9

Library of Congress Control Number: 2015939161

LNCS Sublibrary: SL2 – Programming and Software Engineering

Springer Cham Heidelberg New York Dordrecht London

Printed on acid-free paper

Springer International Publishing AG Switzerland is part of Springer Science+Business Media
(www.springer.com)

# Foreword

The 10th International Federated Conference on Distributed Computing Techniques (DisCoTec) took place in Montbonnot, near Grenoble, France, during June 2–5, 2015. It was hosted and organized by INRIA, the French National Research Institute in Computer Science and Control. The DisCoTec series is one of the major events sponsored by the International Federation for Information Processing (IFIP). It comprises three conferences:

- COORDINATION, the IFIP WG6.1 International Conference on Coordination Models and Languages.
- DAIS, the IFIP WG6.1 International Conference on Distributed Applications and Interoperable Systems.
- FORTE, the IFIP WG6.1 International Conference on Formal Techniques for Distributed Objects, Components and Systems.

Together, these conferences cover a broad spectrum of distributed computing subjects, ranging from theoretical foundations and formal description techniques to systems research issues.

Each day of the federated event began with a plenary keynote speaker nominated by one of the conferences. The three invited speakers were Alois Ferscha (Johannes Kepler Universität, Linz, Austria), Leslie Lamport (Microsoft Research, USA), and Willy Zwaenepoel (EPFL, Lausanne, Switzerland).

Associated with the federated event were also three satellite workshops, that took place on June 5, 2015:

- The 2nd International Workshop on Formal Reasoning in Distributed Algorithms (FRIDA), with a keynote speech by Leslie Lamport (Microsoft Research, USA).
- The 8th International Workshop on Interaction and Concurrency Experience (ICE), with keynote lectures by Jade Alglave (University College London, UK) and Steve Ross-Talbot (ZDLC, Cognizant Technology Solutions, London, UK).
- The 2nd International Workshop on Meta Models for Process Languages (MeMo).

Sincere thanks go to the chairs and members of the Program and Steering Committees of the involved conferences and workshops for their highly appreciated efforts. Organizing DisCoTec was only possible thanks to the dedicated work of the Organizing Committee from INRIA Grenoble-Rhône-Alpes, including Sophie Azzaro, Vanessa Peregrin, Martine Consigney, Alain Kersaudy, Sophie Quinton, Jean-Bernard Stefani, and the excellent support from Catherine Nuel and the people at Insight Outside. Finally, many thanks go to IFIP WG6.1 for sponsoring this event, and to INRIA Grenoble-Rhône-Alpes and its Director Patrick Gros for their support and sponsorship.

Alain Girault
DisCoTec 2015 General Chair

## DisCoTec Steering Committee

# Preface

This volume contains the proceedings of FORTE 2015, the 35th IFIP International Conference on Formal Techniques for Distributed Objects, Components and Systems. This conference was organized as part of the 10th International Federated Conference on Distributed Computing Techniques (DisCoTec) and was held in Grenoble, France between June 2–4, 2015.

The FORTE conference series represents a forum for fundamental research on theory, models, tools, and applications for distributed systems. The conference encourages contributions that combine theory and practice, and that exploit formal methods and theoretical foundations to present novel solutions to problems arising from the development of distributed systems. FORTE covers distributed computing models and formal specification, testing, and verification methods. The application domains include all kinds of application-level distributed systems, telecommunication services, Internet, embedded and real-time systems, as well as networking and communication security and reliability.

We received a total of 53 full paper submissions for review. Each submission was reviewed by at least three members of the Program Committee. Based on high-quality reviews, and a thorough (electronic) discussion by the Program Committee, we selected 15 papers for presentation at the conference and for publication in this volume.

Leslie Lamport (Microsoft Research) was keynote speaker of FORTE 2015. Leslie received the Turing Award in 2013. He is known for his seminal contributions in distributed systems. He has developed algorithms, formal models, and verification methods for distributed systems. Leslie's keynote lecture was on Temporal Logic of Actions.

We would like to thank all those who contributed to the success of FORTE 2015: the authors, for submitting high-quality work to FORTE 2015; the Program Committee and the external reviewers, for providing constructive, high-quality reviews, an efficient discussion, and a fair selection of papers; the invited speaker for an inspiring talk; and, of course, all the attendees of FORTE 2015. We are also grateful to the DisCoTec General Chair, Alain Girault, Organization Chair, Jean-Bernard Stefani, and all members of their local organization team. The EasyChair conference management system facilitated PC discussions, and the preparation of these proceedings. Thank You.

June 2015

Susanne Graf
Mahesh Viswanathan

# Organization

## Program Committee Chairs

| | |
|---|---|
| Susanne Graf | VERIMAG & CNRS, Grenoble, France |
| Mahesh Viswanathan | University of Illinois at Urbana-Champaign, USA |

## Program Committee Members

| | |
|---|---|
| Erika Abraham | RWTH Aachen University, Germany |
| Luca Aceto | Reykjavik University, Iceland |
| S. Akshay | IIT Bombay, India |
| Paul Attie | American University of Beirut, Lebanon |
| Rohit Chadha | University of Missouri, USA |
| Rance Cleaveland | University of Maryland, USA |
| Frank de Boer | CWI, Amsterdam, The Netherlands |
| Borzoo Bonakdarpour | McMaster University, Ontario, Canada |
| Michele Boreale | Università degli Studi di Firenze, Italy |
| Stephanie Delaune | CNRS & ENS Cachan, France |
| Wan Fokkink | Vrije Universiteit Amsterdam, The Netherlands |
| Gregor Goessler | Inria Grenoble, France |
| Gerard Holzmann | Jet Propulsion Laboratory, Pasadena, CA, USA |
| Alan Jeffrey | Alcatel-Lucent Bell Labs, USA |
| Petr Kuznetsov | Telecom ParisTech, France |
| Ivan Lanese | University of Bologna/INRIA, Italy |
| Kim Larsen | University of Aalborg, Denmark |
| Antonia Lopes | University of Lisbon, Portugal |
| Stephan Merz | LORIA & INRIA Nancy, France |
| Catuscia Palamidessi | INRIA Saclay, France |
| Alan Schmitt | IRISA & INRIA Rennes, France |

## Steering Committee

| | |
|---|---|
| Erika Abraham | RWTH Aachen, Germany |
| Dirk Beyer | University of Passau, Germany |
| Michele Boreale | Università degli Studi di Firenze, Italy |
| Einar Broch Johnsen | University of Oslo, Norway |
| Frank de Boer | CWI, Amsterdam, The Netherlands |
| Holger Giese | University of Potsdam, Germany |
| Catuscia Palamidessi | INRIA, Saclay, France |
| Grigore Rosu | University of Illinois at Urbana-Champaign, USA |
| Jean-Bernard Stefani | INRIA, Grenoble, France (Chair) |
| Heike Wehrheim | University of Paderborn, Germany |

# Additional Reviewers

Agrawal, Shreya
Astefanoaei, Lacramioara
Azadbakht, Keyvan
Bauer, Matthew
Bettini, Lorenzo
Bezirgiannis, Nikolaos
Bracciali, Andrea
Bresolin, Davide
Castellani, Ilaria
Corzilius, Florian
Dalsgaard, Andreas Engelbredt
Dang, Thao
Della Monica, Dario
Demangeon, Romain
Denielou, Pierre-Malo
Di Giusto, Cinzia
Dokter, Kasper
Enea, Constantin
Fehnker, Ansgar
Foshammer, Louise
Francalanza, Adrian
Franco, Juliana
Griffith, Dennis
Guha, Shibashis
Henrio, Ludovic
Herbreteau, Frédéric
Hirsch, Martin
Höfner, Peter
Jongmans, Sung-Shik T.Q.
Kemper, Stephanie
Kini, Dileep
Laurent, Mounier

Lenglet, Sergueï
Loreti, Michele
Mandel, Louis
Marques, Eduardo R.B.
Martins, Francisco
Massink, Mieke
Mateescu, Radu
Mezzina, Claudio Antares
Najm, Elie
Ober, Iulian
Padovani, Luca
Peressotti, Marco
Pessaux, François
Phawade, Ramchandra
Poulsen, Danny Bøgsted
Prisacariu, Cristian
Pérez, Jorge A.
Quinton, Sophie
Ravi, Srivatsan
Reniers, Michel
Rezine, Ahmed
S. Krishna
Sangnier, Arnaud
Serbanescu, Vlad Nicolae
Sirjani, Marjan
Tapia Tarifa, Silvia Lizeth
Tiezzi, Francesco
Trivedi, Ashutosh
Valencia, Frank
Wognsen, Erik Ramsgaard
Xue, Bingtian

# Contents

# Security

# Efficient Verification Techniques

# Ensuring Properties
# of Distributed Systems

# Types for Deadlock-Free Higher-Order Programs

Luca Padovani[✉] and Luca Novara

Dipartimento di Informatica, Università di Torino, Torino, Italy
luca.padovani@di.unito.it

**Abstract.** Type systems for communicating processes are typically studied using abstract models – *e.g.*, *process algebras* – that distill the communication behavior of programs but overlook their structure in terms of functions, methods, objects, modules. It is not always obvious how to apply these type systems to structured programming languages. In this work we port a recently developed type system that ensures *deadlock freedom* in the $\pi$-calculus to a higher-order language.

## 1 Introduction

In this article we develop a type system that guarantees well-typed programs that communicate over channels to be free from deadlocks. Type systems ensuring this property already exist [7,8,10], but they all use the $\pi$-calculus as the reference language. This choice overlooks some aspects of concrete programming languages, like the fact that programs are structured into compartmentalized blocks (*e.g.*, functions) within which only the local structure of the program (the body of a function) is visible to the type system, and little if anything is know about the exterior of the block (the callers of the function). The structure of programs may hinder some kinds of analysis: for example, the type systems in [7,8,10] enforce an ordering of communication events and to do so they take advantage of the nature of $\pi$-calculus processes, where programs are flat sequences of communication actions. How do we reason on such ordering when the execution order is dictated by the reduction strategy of the language rather than by the syntax of programs, or when events occur within a function, and nothing is known about the events that are supposed to occur after the function terminates? We answer these questions by porting the type system in [10] to a higher-order functional language.

To illustrate the key ideas of the approach, let us consider the program

$$\langle \text{send}\, a\, (\text{recv}\, b) \rangle \mid \langle \text{send}\, b\, (\text{recv}\, a) \rangle \tag{1.1}$$

consisting of two parallel threads. The thread on the left is trying to send the message received from channel $b$ on channel $a$; the thread on the right is trying to do the opposite. The communications on $a$ and $b$ are mutually dependent, and the program is a deadlock. The basic idea used in [10] and derived from [7,8] for detecting deadlocks is to assign each channel a number – which we call *level* – and to verify that channels are used in order according to their levels. In (1.1) this mechanism requires $b$ to have smaller level than $a$ in the leftmost thread, and $a$ to have a smaller level than $b$ in the rightmost thread. No level assignment can simultaneously satisfy both constraints. In order to perform these checks with a type system, the first step is to attach levels to

ⓒ IFIP International Federation for Information Processing 2015
S. Graf and M. Viswanathan (Eds.): FORTE 2015, LNCS 9039, pp. 3–18, 2015.
DOI: 10.1007/978-3-319-19195-9_1

channel types. We therefore assign the types $![int]^m$ and $?[int]^n$ respectively to $a$ and $b$ in the leftmost thread of (1.1), and $?[int]^m$ and $![int]^n$ to the same channels in the rightmost thread of (1.1). Crucially, distinct occurrences of the same channel have types with opposite polarities (input ? and output !) and equal level. We can also think of the assignments $send : \forall \iota.![int]^\iota \to int \to unit$ and $recv : \forall \iota.?[int]^\iota \to int$ for the communication primitives, where we allow polymorphism on channel levels. In this case, the application $send\ a\ (recv\ b)$ consists of two subexpressions, the partial application $send\ a$ having type $int \to unit$ and its argument $recv\ b$ having type $int$. Neither of these types hints at the I/O operations performed in these expressions, let alone at the levels of the channels involved. To recover this information we pair types with *effects* [1]: the effect of an expression is an abstract description of the operations performed during its evaluation. In our case, we take as effect the level of channels used for I/O operations, or $\bot$ in the case of pure expressions that perform no I/O. So, the judgment

$$b : ?[int]^n \vdash recv\ b : int\ \&\ n$$

states that $recv\ b$ is an expression of type $int$ whose evaluation performs an I/O operation on a channel with level $n$. As usual, function types are decorated with a *latent effect* saying what happens when the function is applied to its argument. So,

$$a : ![int]^m \vdash send\ a : int \to^m unit\ \&\ \bot$$

states that $send\ a$ is a function that, applied to an argument of type $int$, produces a result of type $unit$ and, in doing so, performs an I/O operation on a channel with level $m$. By itself, $send\ a$ is a pure expression whose evaluation performs no I/O operations, hence the effect $\bot$. Effects help us detecting dangerous expressions: in a *call-by-value* language an application $e_1e_2$ evaluates $e_1$ first, then $e_2$, and finally the body of the function resulting from $e_1$. Therefore, the channels used in $e_1$ must have smaller level than those occurring in $e_2$ and the channels used in $e_2$ must have smaller level than those occurring in the body of $e_1$. In the specific case of $send\ a\ (recv\ b)$ we have $\bot < n$ for the first condition, which is trivially satisfied, and $n < m$ for the second one. Since the same reasoning on $send\ b\ (recv\ a)$ also requires the symmetric condition ($m < n$), we detect that the parallel composition of the two threads in (1.1) is ill typed, as desired.

It turns out that the information given by latent effects in function types is not sufficient for spotting some deadlocks. To see why, consider the function

$$f \stackrel{def}{=} \lambda x.(send\ a\ x;\ send\ b\ x)$$

which sends its argument $x$ on both $a$ and $b$ and where ; denotes sequential composition. The level of $a$ (say $m$) should be smaller than the level of $b$ (say $n$), for $a$ is used before $b$ (we assume that communication is synchronous and that $send$ is a potentially blocking operation). The question is, what is the latent effect that decorates the type of $f$, of the form $int \to^h unit$? Consider the two obvious possibilities: if we take $h = m$, then

$$\langle recv\ a \rangle \mid \langle f\ 3;\ recv\ b \rangle \tag{1.2}$$

is well typed because the effect $m$ of $f\ 3$ is smaller than the level of $b$ in $recv\ b$, which agrees with the fact that $f\ 3$ is evaluated *before* $recv\ b$; if we take $h = n$, then

$$\langle recv\ a;\ f\ 3 \rangle \mid \langle recv\ b \rangle \tag{1.3}$$

is well typed for similar reasons. This is unfortunate because both (1.3) and (1.2) reduce to a deadlock. To flag both of them as ill typed, we must refine the type of $f$ to $\text{int} \to^{m,n}$ unit where we distinguish the smallest level of the channels that *occur* in the body of $f$ (that is $m$) from the greatest level of the channels that *are used* by $f$ when $f$ is applied to an argument (that is $n$). The first annotation gives information on the channels in the function's closure, while the second annotation is the function's latent effect, as before. So (1.2) is ill typed because the effect of $f$ 3 is the same as the level of $b$ in recv $b$ and (1.3) is ill typed because the effect of recv $a$ is the same as the level of $f$ in $f$ 3.

In the following, we define a core multithreaded functional language with communication primitives (Section 2), we present a basic type and effect system, extend it to address recursive programs, and state its properties (Section 3). Finally, we briefly discuss closely related work and a few extensions (Section 4). *Proofs and additional material can be found in long version of the paper, on the first author's home page.*

## 2 Language Syntax and Semantics

In defining our language, we assume a synchronous communication model based on linear channels. This assumption limits the range of systems that we can model. However, asynchronous and structured communications can be encoded using linear channels: this has been shown to be the case for binary sessions [5] and for multiparty sessions to a large extent [10, technical report].

We use a countable set of *variables* $x$, $y$, ..., a countable set of *channels* $a$, $b$, ..., and a set of constants k. *Names* $u$, ... are either variables or channels. We consider a language of *expressions* and *processes* as defined below:

$$ e \;::=\; \text{k} \mid u \mid \lambda x.e \mid ee \qquad\qquad P,Q \;::=\; \langle e \rangle \mid (va)P \mid P \mid Q $$

Expressions comprise constants k, names $u$, abstractions $\lambda x.e$, and applications $e_1 e_2$. We write _ for unused/fresh variables. Constants include the unitary value (), the integer numbers $m$, $n$, ..., as well as the primitives fix, fork, new, send, recv whose semantics will be explained shortly. Processes are either threads $\langle e \rangle$, or the restriction $(va)P$ of a channel $a$ with scope $P$, or the parallel composition $P \mid Q$ of processes.

The notions of free and bound names are as expected, given that the only binders are $\lambda$'s and $v$'s. We identify terms modulo renaming of bound names and we write fn($e$) (respectively, fn($P$)) for the set of names occurring free in $e$ (respectively, in $P$).

The reduction semantics of the language is given by two relations, one for expressions, another for processes. We adopt a *call-by-value* reduction strategy, for which we need to define *reduction contexts* $\mathscr{E}$, ... and *values* v, w, ... respectively as:

$$ \mathscr{E} \;::=\; [\,] \mid \mathscr{E}e \mid v\mathscr{E} \qquad\qquad \text{v,w} \;::=\; \text{k} \mid a \mid \lambda x.e \mid \text{send v} $$

The reduction relation $\longrightarrow$ for expressions is defined by standard rules

$$ (\lambda x.e)\text{v} \longrightarrow e\{\text{v}/x\} \qquad\qquad \text{fix } \lambda x.e \longrightarrow e\{\text{fix } \lambda x.e/x\} $$

and closed under reduction contexts. As usual, $e\{e'/x\}$ denotes the capture-avoiding substitution of $e'$ for the free occurrences of $x$ in $e$.

**Table 1.** Reduction semantics of expressions and processes

$$\langle\mathscr{E}[\text{send } a \text{ v}]\rangle \mid \langle\mathscr{E}'[\text{recv } a]\rangle \xrightarrow{a} \langle\mathscr{E}[()]\rangle \mid \langle\mathscr{E}'[\text{v}]\rangle \qquad \langle\mathscr{E}[\text{fork v}]\rangle \xrightarrow{\tau} \langle\mathscr{E}[()]\rangle \mid \langle\text{v}()\rangle$$

$$\frac{}{\langle\mathscr{E}[\text{new}()]\rangle \xrightarrow{\tau} (va)\langle\mathscr{E}[a]\rangle} \; a \notin \text{fn}(\mathscr{E}) \qquad \frac{e \longrightarrow e'}{\langle e \rangle \xrightarrow{\tau} \langle e' \rangle}$$

$$\frac{P \xrightarrow{\ell} P'}{P \mid Q \xrightarrow{\ell} P' \mid Q} \qquad \frac{P \xrightarrow{\ell} Q}{(va)P \xrightarrow{\ell} (va)Q} \; \ell \neq a \qquad \frac{P \xrightarrow{a} Q}{(va)P \xrightarrow{\tau} Q} \qquad \frac{P \equiv \xrightarrow{\ell} \equiv Q}{P \xrightarrow{\ell} Q}$$

The reduction relation of processes (Table 1) has *labels* $\ell, \ldots$ that are either a channel name $a$, signalling that a communication has occurred on $a$, or the special symbol $\tau$ denoting any other reduction. There are four base reductions for processes: a communication occurs between two threads when one is willing to send a message v on a channel $a$ and the other is waiting for a message from the same channel; a thread that contains a subexpression $\text{fork v}$ spawns a new thread that evaluates $\text{v}()$; a thread that contains a subexpression $\text{new}()$ creates a new channel; the reduction of an expression causes a corresponding $\tau$-labeled reduction of the thread in which it occurs. Reduction for processes is then closed under parallel compositions, restrictions, and structural congruence. The restriction of $a$ disappears as soon as a communication on $a$ occurs: in our model channels are *linear* and can be used for one communication only; structured forms of communication can be encoded on top of this simple model (see Example 2 and [5]). Structural congruence is defined by the standard rules rearranging parallel compositions and channel restrictions, where $\langle()\rangle$ plays the role of the inert process.

We conclude this section with two programs written using a slightly richer language equipped with `let` bindings, conditionals, and a few additional operators. All these constructs either have well-known encodings or can be easily accommodated.

*Example 1 (parallel Fibonacci function).* The `fibo` function below computes the $n$-th number in the Fibonacci sequence and sends the result on a channel c:

```
1    fix λfibo.λn.λc.if n ≤ 1 then send c n
2                    else let a = new() and b = new() in
3                         (fork λ_.fibo (n - 1) a);
4                         (fork λ_.fibo (n - 2) b);
5                         send c (recv a + recv b)
```

The fresh channels a and b are used to collect the results from the recursive, parallel invocations of `fibo`. Note that expressions are intertwined with I/O operations. It is relevant to ask whether this version of `fibo` is deadlock free, namely if it is able to reduce until a result is computed without blocking indefinitely on an I/O operation. ∎

*Example 2 (signal pipe).* In this example we implement a function `pipe` that forwards signals received from an input stream x to an output stream y:

```
1    let cont = λx.let c = new() in (fork λ_.send x c); c in
2    let pipe = fix λpipe.λx.λy.pipe (recv x) (cont y)
```

Note that this pipe is only capable of forwarding handshaking signals. A more interesting pipe transmitting actual data can be realized by considering data types such as records and sums [5]. The simplified realization we consider here suffices to illustrate a relevant family of recursive functions that interleave actions on different channels.

Since linear channels are consumed after communication, each signal includes a *continuation channel* on which the subsequent signals in the stream will be sent/received. In particular, cont x sends a fresh continuation c on x and returns c, so that c can be used for subsequent communications, while pipe x y sends a fresh continuation on y after it has received a continuation from x, and then repeats this behavior on the continuations. The program below connects two pipes:

```
3    let a = new() and b = new() in
4       (fork λ_.pipe a b); (fork λ_.pipe b (cont a))
```

Even if the two pipes realize a cyclic network, we will see in Section 3 that this program is well typed and therefore deadlock free. Forgetting cont on line 4 or not forking the send on line 1, however, produces a deadlock.                        ∎

## 3  Type and Effect System

We present the features of the type system gradually, in three steps: we start with a monomorphic system (Section 3.1), then we introduce level polymorphism required by Examples 1 and 2 (Section 3.2), and finally recursive types required by Example 2 (Section 3.3). We end the section studying the properties of the type system (Section 3.4).

### 3.1  Core Types

Let $\mathbb{L} \stackrel{\text{def}}{=} \mathbb{Z} \cup \{\bot, \top\}$ be the set of *channel levels* ordered in the obvious way ($\bot < n < \top$ for every $n \in \mathbb{Z}$); we use $\rho, \sigma, \dots$ to range over $\mathbb{L}$ and we write $\rho \sqcap \sigma$ (respectively, $\rho \sqcup \sigma$) for the *minimum* (respectively, the *maximum*) of $\rho$ and $\sigma$. *Polarities* $p, q, \dots$ are non-empty subsets of $\{?, !\}$; we abbreviate $\{?\}$ and $\{!\}$ with ? and ! respectively, and $\{?, !\}$ with #. *Types* $t, s, \dots$ are defined by

$$t, s \quad ::= \quad \mathsf{B} \mid p[t]^n \mid t \to^{\rho, \sigma} s$$

where *basic types* $\mathsf{B}, \dots$ include unit and int. The type $p[t]^n$ denotes a channel with polarity $p$ and level $n$. The polarity describes the operations allowed on the channel: ? means input, ! means output, and # means both input and output. Channels are linear resources: they can be used once according to each element in their polarity. The type $t \to^{\rho, \sigma} s$ denotes a function with domain $t$ and range $s$. The function has level $\rho$ (its closure contains channels with level $\rho$ or greater) and, when applied, it uses channels with level $\sigma$ or smaller. If $\rho = \top$, the function has no channels in its closure; if $\sigma = \bot$, the function uses no channels when applied. We write $\to$ as an abbreviation for $\to^{\top, \bot}$, so $\to$ denotes pure functions not containing and not using any channel.

Recall from Section 1 that levels are meant to impose an order on the use of channels: roughly, the lower the level of a channel, the sooner the channel must be used. We extend the notion of level from channel types to arbitrary types: basic types have level $\top$ because there is no need to use them as far as deadlock freedom is concerned; the level of functions is written in their type. Formally, the level of $t$, written $|t|$, is defined as:

$$|B| \overset{\text{def}}{=} \top \qquad |p[t]^n| \overset{\text{def}}{=} n \qquad |t \rightarrow^{\rho,\sigma} s| \overset{\text{def}}{=} \rho \qquad\qquad (3.1)$$

Levels can be used to distinguish *linear types*, denoting values (such as channels) that *must* be used to guarantee deadlock freedom, from *unlimited types*, denoting values that have no effect on deadlock freedom and *may* be disregarded. We say that $t$ is *linear* if $|t| \in \mathbb{Z}$; we say that $t$ is *unlimited*, written $\text{un}(t)$, if $|t| = \top$.

Below are the type schemes of the constants that we consider. Some constants have many types (constraints are on the right); we write $\text{types}(k)$ for the *set of* types of $k$.

| | | | |
|---|---|---|---|
| $()$ : unit | $\texttt{fix} : (t \rightarrow t) \rightarrow t$ | $\texttt{new} : \text{unit} \rightarrow \#[t]^n$ | $n < |t|$ |
| $n$ : int | $\texttt{fork} : (\text{unit} \rightarrow^{\rho,\sigma} \text{unit}) \rightarrow \text{unit}$ | $\texttt{recv} : ?[t]^n \rightarrow^{\top,n} t$ | $n < |t|$ |
| | | $\texttt{send} : ![t]^n \rightarrow t \rightarrow^{n,n} \text{unit}$ | $n < |t|$ |

The type of $()$, of the numbers, and of $\texttt{fix}$ are ordinary. The primitive $\texttt{new}$ creates a fresh channel with the full set $\#$ of polarities and arbitrary level $n$. The primitive $\texttt{recv}$ takes a channel of type $?[t]^n$, blocks until a message is received, and returns the message. The primitive itself contains no free channels in its closure (hence the level $\top$) because the only channel it manipulates is its argument. The latent effect is the level of the channel, as expected. The primitive $\texttt{send}$ takes a channel of type $![t]^n$, a message of type $t$, and sends the message on the channel. Note that the partial application $\texttt{send } a$ is a function whose level and latent effect are both the level of $a$. Note also that in $\texttt{new}$, $\texttt{recv}$, and $\texttt{send}$ the level of the message must be greater than the level of the channel: since levels are used to enforce an order on the use of channels, this condition follows from the observation that a message cannot be used until *after* it has been received, namely after the channel on which it travels has been used. Finally, $\texttt{fork}$ accepts a thunk with arbitrary level $\rho$ and latent effect $\sigma$ and spawns the thunk into an independent thread (see Table 1). Note that $\texttt{fork}$ is a pure function with no latent effect, regardless of the level and latent effect of the thunk. This phenomenon is called *effect masking* [1], whereby the effect of evaluating an expression becomes unobservable: in our case, $\texttt{fork}$ discharges effects because the thunk runs in parallel with the code executing the $\texttt{fork}$.

We now turn to the typing rules. A *type environment* $\Gamma$ is a finite map $u_1 : t_1, \ldots, u_n : t_n$ from names to types. We write $\emptyset$ for the empty type environment, $\text{dom}(\Gamma)$ for the domain of $\Gamma$, and $\Gamma(u)$ for the type associated with $u$ in $\Gamma$; we write $\Gamma_1, \Gamma_2$ for the union of $\Gamma_1$ and $\Gamma_2$ when $\text{dom}(\Gamma_1) \cap \text{dom}(\Gamma_2) = \emptyset$. We also need a more flexible way of combining type environments. In particular, we make sure that every channel is used linearly by distributing different polarities of a channel to different parts of the program. To this aim, following [9], we define a partial *combination* operator $+$ between types:

$$t + t \overset{\text{def}}{=} t \qquad\qquad\qquad \text{if } \text{un}(t)$$
$$p[t]^n + q[t]^n \overset{\text{def}}{=} (p \cup q)[t]^n \quad \text{if } p \cap q = \emptyset \qquad\qquad (3.2)$$

that we extend to type environments, thus:

$$\Gamma + \Gamma' \overset{\text{def}}{=} \Gamma, \Gamma' \qquad\qquad\qquad \text{if } \text{dom}(\Gamma) \cap \text{dom}(\Gamma') = \emptyset$$
$$(\Gamma, u : t) + (\Gamma', u : s) \overset{\text{def}}{=} (\Gamma + \Gamma'), u : t + s \qquad\qquad (3.3)$$

For example, we have $(x : \text{int}, a : ![\text{int}]^n) + (a : ?[\text{int}]^n) = x : \text{int}, a : \#[\text{int}]^n$, so we might have some part of the program that (possibly) uses a variable $x$ of type int along with channel $a$ for sending an integer and another part of the program that uses the same channel $a$ but this time for receiving an integer. The first part of the program would be typed in the environment $x : \text{int}, a : ![\text{int}]^n$ and the second one in the environment $a : ?[\text{int}]^n$. Overall, the two parts would be typed in the environment $x : \text{int}, a : \#[\text{int}]^n$ indicating that $a$ is used for both sending *and* receiving an integer.

We extend the function $|\cdot|$ to type environments so that $|\Gamma| \stackrel{\text{def}}{=} \bigsqcap_{u \in \text{dom}(\Gamma)} |\Gamma(u)|$ with the convention that $|\emptyset| = \top$; we write $\text{un}(\Gamma)$ if $|\Gamma| = \top$.

**Table 2.** Core typing rules for expressions and processes

---

**Typing of expressions**

[T-NAME]
$$\frac{}{\Gamma, u : t \vdash u : t \& \bot} \quad \text{un}(\Gamma)$$

[T-CONST]
$$\frac{}{\Gamma \vdash k : t \& \bot} \quad \text{un}(\Gamma) \quad t \in \text{types}(k)$$

[T-FUN]
$$\frac{\Gamma, x : t \vdash e : s \& \rho}{\Gamma \vdash \lambda x.e : t \to^{|\Gamma|, \rho} s \& \bot}$$

[T-APP]
$$\frac{\Gamma_1 \vdash e_1 : t \to^{\rho, \sigma} s \& \tau_1 \qquad \Gamma_2 \vdash e_2 : t \& \tau_2}{\Gamma_1 + \Gamma_2 \vdash e_1 e_2 : s \& \sigma \sqcup \tau_1 \sqcup \tau_2} \quad \begin{array}{l} \tau_1 < |\Gamma_2| \\ \tau_2 < \rho \end{array}$$

**Typing of processes**

[T-THREAD]
$$\frac{\Gamma \vdash e : \text{unit} \& \rho}{\Gamma \vdash \langle e \rangle}$$

[T-PAR]
$$\frac{\Gamma_1 \vdash P \qquad \Gamma_2 \vdash Q}{\Gamma_1 + \Gamma_2 \vdash P \mid Q}$$

[T-NEW]
$$\frac{\Gamma, a : \#[t]^n \vdash P}{\Gamma \vdash (va)P}$$

---

We are now ready to discuss the core typing rules, shown in Table 2. Judgments of the form $\Gamma \vdash e : t \& \rho$ denote that $e$ is well typed in $\Gamma$, it has type $t$ and effect $\rho$; judgments of the form $\Gamma \vdash P$ simply denote that $P$ is well typed in $\Gamma$.

Axioms [T-NAME] and [T-CONST] are unremarkable: as in all substructural type systems the unused part of the type environment must be unlimited. Names and constants have no effect ($\bot$); they are evaluated expressions that do not use (but may contain) channels.

In rule [T-FUN], the effect $\rho$ caused by evaluating the body of the function becomes the latent effect in the arrow type of the function and the function itself has no effect. The level of the function is determined by that of the environment $\Gamma$ in which the function is typed. Intuitively, the names in $\Gamma$ are stored in the *closure* of the function; if any of these names is a channel, then we must be sure that the function is eventually used (*i.e.*, applied) to guarantee deadlock freedom. In fact, $|\Gamma|$ gives a slightly more precise information, since it records the smallest level of all channels that occur in the body of the function. We have seen in Section 1 why this information is useful. A few examples:

– the identity function $\lambda x.x$ has type $\text{int} \to^{\top, \bot} \text{int}$ in any unlimited environment;
– the function $\lambda \_.a$ has type $\text{unit} \to^{n, \bot} ![\text{int}]^n$ in the environment $a : ![\text{int}]^n$; it contains channel $a$ with level $n$ in its closure (whence the level $n$ in the arrow), but it does not use $a$ for input/output (whence the latent effect $\bot$); it is nonetheless well typed because $a$, which is a linear value, is returned as result;
– the function $\lambda x.\text{send } x\ 3$ has type $![\text{int}]^n \to^{\top, n} \text{unit}$; it has no channels in its closure but it performs an output on the channel it receives as argument;

- the function $\lambda x.(\texttt{recv}\ a + x)$ has type $\texttt{int} \to^{n,n} \texttt{int}$ in the environment $a : ?[\texttt{int}]^n$; note that neither the domain nor the codomain of the function mention any channel, so the fact that the function has a channel in its closure (and that it performs some I/O) can only be inferred from the annotations on the arrow;
- the function $\lambda x.\texttt{send}\ x\ (\texttt{recv}\ a)$ has type $![\texttt{int}]^{n+1} \to^{n,n+1} \texttt{unit}$ in the environment $a : ![\texttt{int}]^n$; it contains channel $a$ with level $n$ in its closure and performs input/output operations on channels with level $n + 1$ (or smaller) when applied.

Rule [T-APP] deals with applications $e_1 e_2$. The first thing to notice is the type environments in the premises for $e_1$ and $e_2$. Normally, these are exactly the same as the type environment used for the whole application. In our setting, however, we want to distribute polarities in such a way that each channel is used for exactly one communication. For this reason, the type environment $\Gamma_1 + \Gamma_2$ in the conclusion is the combination of the type environments in the premises. Regarding effects, $\tau_i$ is the effect caused by the evaluation of $e_i$. As expected, $e_1$ must result in a function of type $t \to^{\rho,\sigma} s$ and $e_2$ in a value of type $t$. The evaluation of $e_1$ and $e_2$ may however involve blocking I/O operations on channels, and the two side conditions make sure that no deadlock can arise. To better understand them, recall that reduction is *call-by-value* and applications $e_1 e_2$ are evaluated *sequentially from left to right*. Now, the condition $\tau_1 < |\Gamma_2|$ makes sure that any I/O operation performed during the evaluation of $e_1$ involves only channels whose level is smaller than that of the channels occurring free in $e_2$ (the free channels of $e_2$ must necessarily be in $\Gamma_2$). This is enough to guarantee that the functional part of the application can be fully evaluated without blocking on operations concerning channels that occur *later* in the program. In principle, this condition should be paired with the symmetric one $\tau_2 < |\Gamma_1|$ making sure that any I/O operation performed during the evaluation of the argument does not involve channels that occur in the functional part. However, when the argument is being evaluated, we know that the functional part has already been reduced a value (see the definition of reduction contexts in Section 2). Therefore, the only really critical condition to check is that no channels involved in I/O operations during the evaluation of $e_2$ occur in the *value* of $e_1$. This is expressed by the condition $\tau_2 < \rho$, where $\rho$ is the level of the functional part. Note that, when $e_1$ is an abstraction, by rule [T-FUN] $\rho$ coincides with $|\Gamma_1|$, but in general $\rho$ may be greater than $|\Gamma_1|$, so the condition $\tau_2 < \rho$ gives better accuracy. The effect of the whole application $e_1 e_2$ is, as expected, the combination of the effects of evaluating $e_1$, $e_2$, and the latent effect of the function being applied. In our case the "combination" is the greatest level of any channel involved in the application. Below are some examples:

- $(\lambda x.x)\ a$ is well typed, because both $\lambda x.x$ and $a$ are pure expressions whose effect is $\bot$, hence the two side conditions of [T-APP] are trivially satisfied;
- $(\lambda x.x)\ (\texttt{recv}\ a)$ is well typed in the environment $a : ?[\texttt{int}]^n$: the effect of $\texttt{recv}\ a$ is $n$ (the level of $a$) which is smaller than the level $\top$ of the function;
- $\texttt{send}\ a\ (\texttt{recv}\ a)$ is ill typed in the environment $a : \#[\texttt{int}]^n$ because the effect of evaluating $\texttt{recv}\ a$, namely $n$, is the same as the level of $\texttt{send}\ a$;
- $(\texttt{recv}\ a)\ (\texttt{recv}\ b)$ is well typed in the environment $a : ?[\texttt{int} \to \texttt{int}]^0, b : ?[\texttt{int}]^1$. The effect of the argument is $1$, which is *not* smaller than the level of the environment $a : ?[\texttt{int} \to \texttt{int}]^0$ used for typing the function. However, $1$ is smaller than $\top$, which

is the level of the *result* of the evaluation of the functional part of the application. This application would be illegal had we used the side condition $\tau_2 < |\Gamma_1|$ in [T-APP].

The typing rules for processes are standard: [T-PAR] splits contexts for typing the processes in parallel, [T-NEW] introduces a new channel in the environment, and [T-THREAD] types threads. The effect of threads is ignored: effects are used to prevent circular dependencies between channels used within the *sequential* parts of the program (*i.e.*, within expressions); circular dependencies that arise between *parallel* threads are indirectly detected by the fact that each occurrence of a channel is typed with the same level (see the discussion of (1.1) in Section 1).

## 3.2 Level Polymorphism

Looking back at Example 1, we notice that `fibo n c` may generate two recursive calls with two corresponding fresh channels a and b. Since the `send` operation on c is blocked by `recv` operations on a and b (line 5), the level of a and b must be smaller than that of c. Also, since expressions are evaluated left-to-right and `recv a + recv b` is syntactic sugar for the application `(+) (recv a) (recv b)`, the level of a must be smaller than that of b. Thus, to declare `fibo` well typed, we must allow different occurrences of `fibo` to be applied to channels with different levels. Even more critically, this form of level polymorphism of `fibo` is necessary *within* the definition of `fibo` itself, so it is an instance of *polymorphic recursion* [1].

The core typing rules in Table 2 do not support level polymorphism. Following the previous discussion on `fibo`, the idea is to realize level polymorphism by *shifting* levels in types. We define level shifting as a type operator $\Uparrow^n$, thus:

$$\Uparrow^n \mathsf{B} \overset{\text{def}}{=} \mathsf{B} \qquad \Uparrow^n p[t]^m \overset{\text{def}}{=} p[\Uparrow^n t]^{n+m} \qquad \Uparrow^n(t \to^{\rho,\sigma} s) \overset{\text{def}}{=} \Uparrow^n t \to^{n+\rho,n+\sigma} \Uparrow^n s \qquad (3.4)$$

where $+$ is extended from integers to levels so that $n + \top = \top$ and $n + \bot = \bot$. The effect of $\Uparrow^n t$ is to shift all the finite level annotations in $t$ by $n$, leaving $\top$ and $\bot$ unchanged.

Now, we have to understand in which cases we can use a value of type $\Uparrow^n t$ where one of type $t$ is expected. More specifically, when a value of type $\Uparrow^n t$ can be passed to a function expecting an argument of type $t$. This is possible if the function has level $\top$. We express this form of level polymorphism with an additional typing rule for applications:

[T-APP-POLY]
$$\frac{\Gamma_1 \vdash e_1 : t \to^{\top,\sigma} s \mathbin{\&} \tau_1 \qquad \Gamma_2 \vdash e_2 : \Uparrow^n t \mathbin{\&} \tau_2 \qquad \tau_1 < |\Gamma_2|}{\Gamma_1 + \Gamma_2 \vdash e_1 e_2 : \Uparrow^n s \mathbin{\&} (n+\sigma) \sqcup \tau_1 \sqcup \tau_2 \qquad \tau_2 < \top}$$

This rule admits an arbitrary mismatch $n$ between the level the argument expected by the function and that of the argument supplied to the function. The type of the application and the latent effect are consequently shifted by the same amount $n$.

Soundness of [T-APP-POLY] can be intuitively explained as follows: a function with level $\top$ has no channels in its closure. Therefore, the only channels possibly manipulated by the function are those contained in the argument to which the function is applied or channels created within the function itself. Then, the fact that the argument has level

$n + k$ rather than level $k$ is completely irrelevant. Conversely, if the function has channels in its closure, then the absolute level of the argument might have to satisfy specific ordering constraints with respect to these channels (recall the two side conditions in [T-APP]). Since level polymorphism is a key distinguishing feature of our type system, and one that accounts for much of its expressiveness, we elaborate more on this intuition using an example. Consider the term

$$\texttt{fwd} \overset{\text{def}}{=} \lambda x.\lambda y.\texttt{send } y \ (\texttt{recv } x)$$

which forwards on $y$ the message received from $x$. The derivation

$$
\cfrac{
\cfrac{
\cfrac{\vdots}{y : ![\text{int}]^1 \vdash \texttt{send } y : \text{int} \rightarrow^{1,1} \text{unit} \,\&\, \bot} \; \text{[T-APP]}
\qquad
\cfrac{\vdots}{x : ?[\text{int}]^0 \vdash \texttt{recv } x : \text{int} \,\&\, 0} \; \text{[T-APP]}
}{
\cfrac{
x : ?[\text{int}]^0, y : ![\text{int}]^1 \vdash \texttt{send } y \ (\texttt{recv } x) : \text{unit} \,\&\, 1
}{
\cfrac{
x : ?[\text{int}]^0 \vdash \lambda y.\texttt{send } y \ (\texttt{recv } x) : ![\text{int}]^1 \rightarrow^{0,1} \text{unit} \,\&\, \bot
}{
\vdash \texttt{fwd} : ?[\text{int}]^0 \rightarrow ![\text{int}]^1 \rightarrow^{0,1} \text{unit} \,\&\, \bot
} \; \text{[T-FUN]}
} \; \text{[T-FUN]}
} \; \text{[T-APP]}
}
$$

does *not* depend on the absolute values 0 and 1, but only on the level of $x$ being smaller than that of $y$, as required by the fact that the send operation on $y$ is blocked by the recv operation on $x$. Now, consider an application $\texttt{fwd } a$, where $a$ has type $?[\text{int}]^2$. The mismatch between the level of $x$ (0) and that of $a$ (2) is not critical, because all the levels in the derivation above can be *uniformly shifted up* by 2, yielding a derivation for

$$\vdash \texttt{fwd} : ?[\text{int}]^2 \rightarrow ![\text{int}]^3 \rightarrow^{2,3} \text{unit} \,\&\, \bot$$

This shifting is possible because $\texttt{fwd}$ has no free channels in its body (indeed, it is typed in the empty environment). Therefore, using [T-APP-POLY], we can derive

$$a : ?[\text{int}]^2 \vdash \texttt{fwd } a : ![\text{int}]^3 \rightarrow^{2,3} \text{unit} \,\&\, \bot$$

Note that $(\texttt{fwd } a)$ is a function having level 2. This means that $(\texttt{fwd } a)$ is *not* level polymorphic and can only be applied, through [T-APP], to channels with level 3. If we allowed $(\texttt{fwd } a)$ to be applied to a channel with level 2 using [T-APP-POLY] we could derive

$$a : \#[\text{int}]^2 \vdash \texttt{fwd } a \ a : \text{unit} \,\&\, 2$$

which reduces to a deadlock.

*Example 3.* To show that the term in Example 1 is well typed, consider the environment

$$\Gamma \overset{\text{def}}{=} \texttt{fibo} : \text{int} \rightarrow ![\text{int}]^0 \rightarrow^{\top,0} \text{unit}, \texttt{n} : \text{int}, \texttt{c} : ![\text{int}]^0$$

In the proof derivation for the body of $\texttt{fibo}$, this environment is eventually enriched with the assignments $\texttt{a} : \#[\text{int}]^{-2}$ and $\texttt{b} : \#[\text{int}]^{-1}$. Now we can derive

$$
\cfrac{
\cfrac{\vdots}{\Gamma \vdash \texttt{fibo } (\texttt{n} - 2) : ![\text{int}]^0 \rightarrow^{\top,0} \text{unit} \,\&\, \bot} \; \text{[T-APP]}
\qquad
\cfrac{}{a : ![\text{int}]^{-2} \vdash a : ![\text{int}]^{-2} \,\&\, \bot} \; \text{[T-NAME]}
}{
\Gamma, a : ![\text{int}]^{-2} \vdash \texttt{fibo } (\texttt{n} - 2) \ a : \text{unit} \,\&\, -2
} \; \text{[T-APP-POLY]}
$$

where the application `fibo (n - 2) a` is well typed despite the fact that `fibo (n - 2)` expects an argument of type $![\text{int}]^0$, while a has type $![\text{int}]^{-2}$. A similar derivation can be obtained for `fibo (n - 1) b`, and the proof derivation can now be completed.                                                                    ∎

### 3.3   Recursive Types

Looking back at Example 2, we see that in a call `pipe x y` the channel `recv x` is used in the same position as x. Therefore, according to [T-APP-POLY], `recv x` must have the same type as x, up to some shifting of its level. Similarly, channel c is both sent on y and then used in the same position as y, suggesting that c must have the same type as y, again up to some shifting of its level. This means that we need recursive types in order to properly describe x and y.

Instead of adding explicit syntax for recursive types, we just consider the possibly infinite trees generated by the productions for $t$ shown earlier. In light of this broader notion of types, the inductive definition of type level (3.1) is still well founded, but type shift (3.4) must be reinterpreted coinductively, because it has to operate on possibly infinite trees. The formalities, nonetheless, are well understood.

It is folklore that, whenever infinite types are *regular* (that is, when they are made of finitely many distinct subtrees), they admit finite representations either using type variables and the familiar $\mu$ notation, or using systems of type equations [4]. Unfortunately, a careful analysis of Example 2 suggests that – at least in principle – we also need *non-regular* types. To see why, let a and c be the channels to which (`recv x`) and (`cont y`) respectively evaluate on line 2 of the example. Now:

- x must have smaller level than a since a is received from x (*cf.* the types of `recv`).
- y must have smaller level than c since c is sent on y (*cf.* the types of `send`).
- x must have smaller level than y since x is used in the functional part of an application in which y occurs in the argument (*cf.* line 2 and [T-APP-POLY]).

Overall, in order to type `pipe` in Example 2 we should assign x and y the types $t^n$ and $s^n$ that respectively satisfy the equations

$$t^n = ?[t^{n+2}]^n \qquad s^n = ![t^{n+3}]^{n+1} \tag{3.5}$$

Unfortunately, these equations do not admit regular types as solutions. We recover typeability of `pipe` with regular types by introducing a new type constructor

$$t \quad ::= \quad \cdots \quad | \quad \lceil t \rceil^n$$

that wraps types with a pending shift: intuitively $\lceil t \rceil^n$ and $\Uparrow^n t$ denote the same type, except that in $\lceil t \rceil^n$ the shift $\Uparrow^n$ on $t$ is pending. For example, $\lceil ?[\text{int}]^0 \rceil^1$ and $\lceil ?[\text{int}]^2 \rceil^{-1}$ are both possible wrappings of $?[\text{int}]^1$, while $\text{int} \to^{0,\perp} ![\text{int}]^0$ is the unwrapping of $\lceil \text{int} \to^{1,\perp} ![\text{int}]^1 \rceil^{-1}$. To exclude meaningless infinite types such as $\lceil \lceil \lceil \cdots \rceil^n \rceil^n \rceil^n$ we impose a *contractiveness condition* requiring every infinite branch of a type to contain infinite occurrences of channel or arrow constructors. To see why wraps help finding regular representations for otherwise non-regular types, observe that the equations

$$t^n = ?[\lceil t^n \rceil^2]^n \qquad s^n = ![\lceil \lceil t^{n+1} \rceil^2 \rceil^2]^{n+1} \tag{3.6}$$

denote – up to pending shifts – the same types as the ones in (3.5), with the key difference that (3.6) admit regular solutions and therefore finite representations. For example, $t^n$ could be finitely represented as a familiar-looking $\mu\alpha.?\lceil\lceil\alpha\rceil^2\rceil^n$ term.

We should remark that $\lceil t\rceil^n$ and $\Uparrow^n t$ are *different* types, even though the former is morally equivalent to the latter: wrapping is a type *constructor*, whereas shift is a type *operator*. Having introduced a new constructor, we must suitably extend the notions of type level (3.1) and type shift (3.4) we have defined earlier. We postulate

$$|\lceil t\rceil^n| \overset{\text{def}}{=} n + |t| \qquad \Uparrow^n \lceil t\rceil^m \overset{\text{def}}{=} \lceil\Uparrow^n t\rceil^m$$

in accordance with the fact that $\lceil\cdot\rceil^n$ denotes a pending shift by $n$ (note that $|\cdot|$ extended to wrappings is well defined thanks to the contractiveness condition).

We also have to define introduction and elimination rules for wrappings. To this aim, we conceive two constants, wrap and unwrap, having the following type schemes:

$$\text{wrap} : \Uparrow^n t \to \lceil t\rceil^n \qquad \text{unwrap} : \lceil t\rceil^n \to \Uparrow^n t$$

We add wrap v to the value forms. Operationally, we want wrap and unwrap to annihilate each other. This is done by enriching reduction for expressions with the axiom

$$\text{unwrap (wrap v)} \longrightarrow \text{v}$$

*Example 4.* We suitably dress the code in Example 2 using wrap and unwrap:

```
1    let cont = λx.let c = new() in (fork λ_.send x (wrap c)); c in
2    let pipe = fix λpipe.λx.λy.pipe (unwrap (recv x)) (cont y)
```

and we are now able to find a typing derivation for it that uses regular types. In particular, we assign cont the type $s^n \to s^{n+2}$ and pipe the type $t^n \to s^n \to^{n,\top}$ unit where $t^n$ and $s^n$ are the types defined in (3.6). Note that cont is a pure function because its effects are masked by fork and that pipe has latent effect $\top$ since it loops performing recv operations on channels with increasing level. Because of the side conditions in [T-APP] and [T-APP-POLY], this means that pipe can only be used in tail position, which is precisely what happens above and in Example 2.    ∎

## 3.4   Properties

To formulate subject reduction, we must take into account that linear channels are *consumed* after communication (last but one reduction in Table 1). This means that when a process $P$ communicates on some channel $a$, $a$ must be removed from the type environment used for typing the residual of $P$. To this aim, we define a partial operation $\Gamma - \ell$ that removes $\ell$ from $\Gamma$, when $\ell$ is a channel. Formally:

**Theorem 1 (Subject Reduction).** *If* $\Gamma \vdash P$ *and* $P \overset{\ell}{\longrightarrow} Q$, *then* $\Gamma - \ell \vdash Q$ *where* $\Gamma - \tau \overset{\text{def}}{=} \Gamma$ *and* $(\Gamma, a : \#[t]^n) - a \overset{\text{def}}{=} \Gamma$.

Note that $\Gamma - a$ is undefined if $a \notin \text{dom}(\Gamma)$. This means that well-typed programs never attempt at using the same channel twice, namely that channels in well-typed programs are indeed *linear channels*. This property has important practical consequences, since it allows the efficient implementation (and deallocation) of channels [9].

Deadlock freedom means that *if* the program halts, then there must be no pending I/O operations. In our language, the only halted program without pending operations is (structurally equivalent to) $\langle() \rangle$. We can therefore define deadlock freedom thus:

**Definition 1.** *We say that P is* deadlock free *if* $P \xrightarrow{\tau}^* Q \not\rightarrow$ *implies* $Q \equiv \langle() \rangle$.

As usual, $\xrightarrow{\tau}^*$ is the reflexive, transitive closure of $\xrightarrow{\tau}$ and $Q \not\rightarrow$ means that $Q$ is unable to reduce further. Now, every well-typed, closed process is free from deadlocks:

**Theorem 2 (Soundness).** *If* $\emptyset \vdash P$, *then P is deadlock free.*

Theorem 2 may look weaker than desirable, considering that every process $P$ (even an ill-typed one) can be "fixed" and become part of a deadlock-free system if composed in parallel with the diverging thread $\langle \mathtt{fix}\ \lambda x.x \rangle$. It is not easy to state an interesting property of well-typed *partial programs* – programs that are well typed in uneven environments – or of *partial computations* – computations that have not reached a stable (*i.e.*, irreducible) state. One might think that well-typed programs eventually use all of their channels. This property is false in general, for two reasons. First, our type system does not ensure termination of well-typed expressions, so a thread like $\langle \mathtt{send}\ a\ (\mathtt{fix}\ \lambda x.x) \rangle$ never uses channel $a$, because the evaluation of the message diverges. Second, there are threads that continuously generate (or receive) new channels, so that the set of channels they own is never empty; this happens in Example 2. What we can prove is that, *assuming* that a well-typed program does not internally diverge, then *each* channel it owns is eventually used for a communication or is sent to the environment in a message. To formalize this property, we need a labeled transition system describing the interaction of programs with their environment. *Labels* $\pi, \dots$ of transitions are defined by

$$\pi ::= \ell \mid a?e \mid a!v$$

and the transition relation $\xrightarrow{\pi}$ extends reduction with the rules

$$\frac{a \notin \mathrm{bn}(\mathscr{C})}{\mathscr{C}[\mathtt{send}\ a\ v] \xrightarrow{a!v} \mathscr{C}[()]} \qquad \frac{a \notin \mathrm{bn}(\mathscr{C}) \qquad \mathrm{fn}(e) \cap \mathrm{bn}(\mathscr{C}) = \emptyset}{\mathscr{C}[\mathtt{recv}\ a] \xrightarrow{a?e} \mathscr{C}[e]}$$

where $\mathscr{C}$ ranges over *process contexts* $\mathscr{C} ::= \langle \mathscr{E} \rangle \mid (\mathscr{C} \mid P) \mid (P \mid \mathscr{C}) \mid (\nu a)\mathscr{C}$. Messages of input transitions have the form $a?e$ where $e$ is an arbitrary expression instead of a value. This is just to allow a technically convenient formulation of Definition 2 below. We formalize the assumption concerning the absence of internal divergences as a property that we call *interactivity*. Interactivity is a property of *typed processes*, which we write as pairs $\Gamma \mathbin{;} P$, since the messages exchanged between a process and the environment in which it executes are not arbitrary in general.

**Definition 2 (Interactivity).** *Interactivity is the largest predicate on well-typed processes such that* $\Gamma \mathbin{;} P$ *interactive implies* $\Gamma \vdash P$ *and:*

1. *P has no infinite reduction* $P \xrightarrow{\ell_1} P_1 \xrightarrow{\ell_2} P_2 \xrightarrow{\ell_3} \cdots$, *and*
2. *if* $P \xrightarrow{\ell} Q$, *then* $\Gamma - \ell \mathbin{;} Q$ *is interactive, and*

3. *if* $P \overset{a!v}{\longmapsto} Q$ *and* $\Gamma = \Gamma', a : ![t]^n$, *then* $\Gamma'' \, \S \, Q$ *is interactive for some* $\Gamma'' \subseteq \Gamma'$, *and*

4. *if* $P \overset{a?x}{\longmapsto} Q$ *and* $\Gamma = \Gamma', a : ?[t]^n$, *then* $\Gamma'' \, \S \, Q\{v/x\}$ *is interactive for some* $v$ *and* $\Gamma'' \supseteq \Gamma'$ *such that* $n < |\Gamma'' \setminus \Gamma'|$.

Clause (1) says that an interactive process does not internally diverge: it will eventually halt either because it terminates or because it needs interaction with the environment in which it executes. Clause (2) states that internal reductions preserve interactivity. Clause (3) states that a process with a pending output on a channel $a$ *must* reduce to an interactive process after the output is performed. Finally, clause (4) states that a process with a pending input on a channel $a$ *may* reduce to an interactive process after the input of a particular message $v$ is performed. The definition looks demanding, but many conditions are direct consequences of Theorem 1. The really new requirements besides well typedness are *convergence* of $P$ (1) and the *existence* of $v$ (4). It is now possible to prove that well-typed, interactive processes eventually use their channels.

**Theorem 3 (Interactivity).** *Let* $\Gamma \, \S \, P$ *be an interactive process such that* $a \in \mathsf{fn}(P)$. *Then* $P \overset{\pi_1}{\longmapsto} P_1 \overset{\pi_2}{\longmapsto} \cdots \overset{\pi_n}{\longmapsto} P_n$ *for some* $\pi_1, \ldots, \pi_n$ *such that* $a \notin \mathsf{fn}(P_n)$.

## 4   Concluding Remarks

We have demonstrated the portability of a type system for deadlock freedom of $\pi$-calculus processes [10] to a higher-order language using an *effect system* [1]. We have shown that *effect masking* and *polymorphic recursion* are key ingredients of the type system (Examples 1 and 2), and also that latent effects must be paired with one more annotation – the function level. The approach may seem to hinder program modularity, since it requires storing levels in types and levels have global scope. In this respect, level polymorphism (Section 3.2) alleviates this shortcoming of levels by granting them a relative – rather than absolute – meaning at least for non-linear functions.

Other type systems for higher-order languages with session-based communication primitives have been recently investigated [6,14,2]. In addition to safety, types are used for estimating bounds in the size of message queues [6] and for detecting memory leaks [2]. Since binary sessions can be encoded using linear channels [5], our type system can address the same family of programs considered in these works with the advantage that, in our case, well-typed programs are guaranteed to be deadlock free also in presence of session interleaving. For instance, the `pipe` function in Example 2 interleaves communications on two different channels. The type system described by Wadler [14] is interesting because it guarantees deadlock freedom without resorting to any type annotation dedicated to this purpose. In his case the syntax of (well-typed) programs prevents the modeling of cyclic network topologies, which is a necessary condition for deadlocks. However, this also means that some useful program patterns cannot be modeled. For instance, the program in Example 2 is ill typed in [14].

The type system discussed in this paper lacks compelling features. *Structured data types* (records, sums) have been omitted for lack of space; an extended technical report [13] and previous works [11,10] show that they can be added without issues. The same goes for *non-linear channels* [10], possibly with the help of dedicated accept and `request` primitives as in [6]. *True polymorphism* (with level and type variables) has also been studied in the technical report [13]. Its impact on the overall type system is significant, especially because level and type constraints (those appearing as side conditions in the type schemes of constants, Section 3.1) must be promoted from the metatheory to the type system. The realization of level polymorphism as type shifting that we have adopted in this paper is an interesting compromise between impact and flexibility. Our type system can also be relaxed with *subtyping*: arrow types are contravariant in the level and covariant in the latent effect, whereas channel types are invariant in the level. Invariance of channel levels can be relaxed refining levels to *pairs* of numbers as done in [7,8]. This can also improve the accuracy of the type system in some cases, as discussed in [10] and [3]. It would be interesting to investigate which of these features are actually necessary for typing concrete functional programs using threads and communication/synchronization primitives.

*Type reconstruction* algorithms for similar type systems have been defined [11,12]. We are confident to say that they scale to type systems with arrow types and effects.

**Acknowledgments.** The authors are grateful to the reviewers for their detailed comments and useful suggestions. The first author has been supported by Ateneo/CSP project SALT, ICT COST Action IC1201 BETTY, and MIUR project CINA.

# References

1. Amtoft, T., Nielson, F., Nielson, H.: Type and Effect Systems: Behaviours for Concurrency. Imperial College Press (1999)
2. Bono, V., Padovani, L., Tosatto, A.: Polymorphic Types for Leak Detection in a Session-Oriented Functional Language. In: Beyer, D., Boreale, M. (eds.) FMOODS/FORTE 2013. LNCS, vol. 7892, pp. 83–98. Springer, Heidelberg (2013)
3. Carbone, M., Dardha, O., Montesi, F.: Progress as compositional lock-freedom. In: Kühn, E., Pugliese, R. (eds.) COORDINATION 2014. LNCS, vol. 8459, pp. 49–64. Springer, Heidelberg (2014)
4. Courcelle, B.: Fundamental properties of infinite trees. Theor. Comp. Sci. 25, 95–169 (1983)
5. Dardha, O., Giachino, E., Sangiorgi, D.: Session types revisited. In: PPDP 2012, pp. 139–150. ACM (2012)
6. Gay, S.J., Vasconcelos, V.T.: Linear type theory for asynchronous session types. J. Funct. Program. 20(1), 19–50 (2010)
7. Kobayashi, N.: A type system for lock-free processes. Inf. and Comp. 177(2), 122–159 (2002)
8. Kobayashi, N.: A new type system for deadlock-free processes. In: Baier, C., Hermanns, H. (eds.) CONCUR 2006. LNCS, vol. 4137, pp. 233–247. Springer, Heidelberg (2006)
9. Kobayashi, N., Pierce, B.C., Turner, D.N.: Linearity and the pi-calculus. ACM Trans. Program. Lang. Syst. 21(5), 914–947 (1999)
10. Padovani, L.: Deadlock and Lock Freedom in the Linear $\pi$-Calculus. In: CSL-LICS 2014, pp. 72:1–72:10. ACM (2014), http://hal.archives-ouvertes.fr/hal-00932356v2/
11. Padovani, L.: Type Reconstruction for the Linear $\pi$-Calculus with Composite and Equi-Recursive Types. In: Muscholl, A. (ed.) FOSSACS 2014. LNCS, vol. 8412, pp. 88–102. Springer, Heidelberg (2014)

12. Padovani, L., Chen, T.-C., Tosatto, A.: Type Reconstruction Algorithms for Deadlock-Free and Lock-Free Linear $\pi$-Calculi. In: Holvoet, T., Viroli, M. (eds.) COORDINATION 2015. LNCS, vol. 9037, pp. 85–100. Springer, Heidelberg (2015)
13. Padovani, L., Novara, L.: Types for Deadlock-Free Higher-Order Concurrent Programs. Technical report, Università di Torino (2014), http://hal.inria.fr/hal-00954364
14. Wadler, P.: Propositions as sessions. In: ICFP 2012, pp. 273–286. ACM (2012)

# On Partial Order Semantics for SAT/SMT-Based Symbolic Encodings of Weak Memory Concurrency

Alex Horn[✉] and Daniel Kroening

University of Oxford, Oxford, UK
alex.horn@cs.ox.ac.uk

**Abstract.** Concurrent systems are notoriously difficult to analyze, and technological advances such as weak memory architectures greatly compound this problem. This has renewed interest in partial order semantics as a theoretical foundation for formal verification techniques. Among these, symbolic techniques have been shown to be particularly effective at finding concurrency-related bugs because they can leverage highly optimized decision procedures such as SAT/SMT solvers. This paper gives new fundamental results on partial order semantics for SAT/SMT-based symbolic encodings of weak memory concurrency. In particular, we give the theoretical basis for a decision procedure that can handle a fragment of concurrent programs endowed with least fixed point operators. In addition, we show that a certain partial order semantics of relaxed sequential consistency is equivalent to the conjunction of three extensively studied weak memory axioms by Alglave et al. An important consequence of this equivalence is an asymptotically smaller symbolic encoding for bounded model checking which has only a quadratic number of partial order constraints compared to the state-of-the-art cubic-size encoding.

## 1  Introduction

Concurrent systems are notoriously difficult to analyze, and technological advances such as weak memory architectures as well as highly available distributed services greatly compound this problem. This has renewed interest in partial order concurrency semantics as a theoretical foundation for formal verification techniques. Among these, *symbolic techniques* have been shown to be particularly effective at finding concurrency-related bugs because they can leverage highly optimized decision procedures such as SAT/SMT solvers. This paper studies partial order semantics from the perspective of SAT/SMT-based symbolic encodings of weak memory concurrency.

Given the diverse range of partial order concurrency semantics, we link our study to a recently developed unifying theory of concurrency by Tony Hoare et al. [1]. This theory is known as *Concurrent Kleene Algebra* (CKA) which is an algebraic concurrency semantics based on quantales, a special case of the

This work is funded by a gift from Intel Corporation for research on Effective Validation of Firmware and the ERC project ERC 280053.

S. Graf and M. Viswanathan (Eds.): FORTE 2015, LNCS 9039, pp. 19–34, 2015.
DOI: 10.1007/978-3-319-19195-9_2

fundamental algebraic structure of idempotent semirings. Based on quantales, CKA combines the familiar laws of the sequential program operator (;) with a new operator for concurrent program composition ($\parallel$). A distinguishing feature of CKA is its exchange law $(\mathcal{U} \parallel \mathcal{V}); (\mathcal{X} \parallel \mathcal{Y}) \subseteq (\mathcal{U}; \mathcal{X}) \parallel (\mathcal{V}; \mathcal{Y})$ that describes how sequential and concurrent composition operators can be interchanged. Intuitively, since the binary relation $\subseteq$ denotes program refinement, the exchange law expresses a divide-and-conquer mechanism for how concurrency may be sequentially implemented on a machine. The exchange law, together with a uniform treatment of programs and their specifications, is key to unifying existing theories of concurrency [2]. CKA provides such a unifying theory [3,2] that has practical relevance on proving program correctness, e.g. using rely/guarantee reasoning [1]. Conversely, however, pure algebra cannot refute that a program is correct or that certain properties about every program always hold [3,2,4]. This is problematic for theoretical reasons but also in practice because todays software complexity requires a diverse set of program analysis tools that range from proof assistants to automated testing. The solution is to accompany CKA with a mathematical model which satisfies its laws so that we can *prove* as well as *disprove* properties about programs.

One such well-known model-theoretical foundation for CKA is Pratt's [5] and Gischer's [6] partial order model of computation that is constructed from *labelled partially ordered multisets* (pomsets). Pomsets generalize the concept of a string in finite automata theory by relaxing the total ordering of the occurrence of letters within a string to a partial order. For example, $a \parallel a$ denotes a pomset that consists of two unordered events that are both labelled with the letter $a$. By partially ordering events, pomsets form an integral part of the extensive theoretical literature on so-called 'true concurrency', e.g. [7,8,9,10,5,6], in which pomsets strictly generalize Mazurkiewicz traces [11], and prime event structures [10] are pomsets enriched with a conflict relation subject to certain conditions. From an algorithmic point of view, the complexity of the *pomset language membership* (PLM) problem is NP-complete, whereas the pomset language containment (PLC) problem is $\Pi_2^p$-complete [12].

Importantly, these aforementioned theoretical results only apply to star-free pomset languages (without fixed point operators). In fact, the decidability of the equational theory of the pomset language closed under least fixed point, sequential and concurrent composition operators (but without the exchange law) has been only most recently established [13]; its complexity remains an open problem [13]. Yet another open problem is the decidability of this equational theory together with the exchange law [13]. In addition, it is still unclear how theoretical results about pomsets may be applicable to formal techniques for finding concurrency-related bugs. In fact, it is not even clear how insights about pomsets may be combined with most recently studied language-specific or hardware-specific concurrency semantics, e.g. [14,15,16,17].

These gaps are motivation to reinvestigate pomsets from an algorithmic perspective. In particular, our work connects pomsets to a SAT/SMT-based bounded model checking technique [18] where shared memory concurrency is symbolically encoded as partial orders. To make this connection, we adopt pomsets as *partial strings* (Definition 1) that are ordered by a refinement relation (Definition 3) based on Ésik's notion of *monotonic bijective morphisms* [19]. Our partial-string model then follows from the standard Hoare powerdomain construction where sets of partial strings are downward-closed with respect to monotonic bijective morphism (Definition 4). The relevance of this formalization for the modelling of weak memory concurrency (including data races) is explained through several examples. Our main contributions are as follows:

1. We give the theoretical basis for a decision procedure that can handle a fragment of *concurrent programs endowed with least fixed point operators* (Theorem 2). This is accomplished by exploiting a form of periodicity, thereby giving a mechanism for reducing a countably infinite number of events to a finite number. This result particularly caters to partial order encoding techniques that can currently only encode a finite number of events due to the deliberate restriction to quantifier-free first-order logic, e.g. [18].

2. We then interpret a particular form of weak memory in terms of certain downward-closed sets of partial strings (Definition 11), and show that our interpretation is equivalent to the conjunction of three fundamental weak memory axioms (Theorem 3), namely 'write coherence', 'from-read' and 'global read-from' [17]. Since all three axioms underpin extensive experimental research into weak memory architectures [20], *Theorem 3 gives denotational partial order semantics a new practical dimension*.

3. Finally, we prove that there exists an *asymptotically smaller quantifier-free first-order logic formula* that has only $O(N^2)$ partial order constraints (Theorem 4) compared to the state-of-the-art $O(N^3)$ partial order encoding for bounded model checking [18] where $N$ is the maximal number of reads and writes on the same shared memory address. This is significant because $N$ can be prohibitively large when concurrent programs frequently share data.

The rest of this paper is organized into three parts. First, we recall familiar concepts on partial-string theory (§ 2) on which the rest of this paper is based. We then prove a least fixed point reduction result (§ 3). Finally, we characterize a particular form of relaxed sequential consistency in terms of three weak memory axioms by Alglave et al. (§ 4).

## 2   Partial-String Theory

In this section, we adapt an axiomatic model of computation that uses partial orders to describe the semantics of concurrent systems. For this, we recall familiar concepts (Definition 1, 2, 3 and 4) that underpin our mathematical model of CKA (Theorem 1). This model is the basis for subsequent results in § 3 and § 4.

**Definition 1 (Partial String).** *Denote with $E$ a nonempty set of events. Let $\Gamma$ be an alphabet. A partial string $p$ is a triple $\langle E_p, \alpha_p, \preceq_p \rangle$ where $E_p$ is a subset of $E$, $\alpha_p \colon E_p \to \Gamma$ is a function that maps each event in $E_p$ to an alphabet symbol in $\Gamma$,*

$e_0$     $e_2$     **Fig. 1.** A partial string $p = \langle E_p, \alpha_p, \preceq_p \rangle$ with events $E_p = \{e_0, e_1, e_2, e_3\}$ and
$\downarrow$     $\downarrow$     the labelling function $\alpha_p$ satisfying the following: $\alpha_p(e_0) = {}'r_0 := [b]_{\text{acquire}}'$,
$e_1$     $e_3$     $\alpha_p(e_1) = {}'r_1 := [a]_{\text{none}}'$, $\alpha_p(e_2) = {}'[a]_{\text{none}} := 1'$ and $\alpha_p(e_3) = {}'[b]_{\text{release}} := 1'$

and $\preceq_p$ is a partial order on $E_p$. Two partial strings $p$ and $q$ are said to be **disjoint** whenever $E_p \cap E_q = \emptyset$. A partial string $p$ is called **empty** whenever $E_p = \emptyset$. Denote with $\mathsf{P}_f$ the set of all **finite partial strings** $p$ whose event set $E_p$ is finite.

Each event in the universe $E$ should be thought of as an occurrence of a computational step, whereas letters in $\Gamma$ describe the computational effect of events. Typically, we denote a partial string by $p$, or letters from $x$ through $z$. In essence, a partial string $p$ is a partially-ordered set $\langle E_p, \preceq_p \rangle$ equipped with a labelling function $\alpha_p$. A partial string is therefore the same as a *labelled partial order* (lpo), see also Remark 1. We draw finite partial strings in $\mathsf{P}_f$ as inverted Hasse diagrams (e.g. Fig. 1), where the ordering between events may be interpreted as a happens-before relation [8], a fundamental notion in distributed systems and formal verification of concurrent systems, e.g. [16,17]. We remark the obvious fact that the empty partial string is unique under component-wise equality.

*Example 1.* In the partial string in Fig. 1, $e_0$ happens-before $e_1$, whereas both $e_0$ and $e_2$ happen concurrently because neither $e_0 \preceq_p e_2$ nor $e_2 \preceq_p e_0$.

We abstractly describe the control flow in concurrent systems by adopting the sequential and concurrent operators on labelled partial orders [9,5,6,19,21].

**Definition 2 (Partial String Operators).** *Let $x$ and $y$ be disjoint partial strings. Let* $x \parallel y \triangleq \langle E_{x\parallel y}, \alpha_{x\parallel y}, \preceq_{x\parallel y} \rangle$ *and* $x; y \triangleq \langle E_{x;y}, \alpha_{x;y}, \preceq_{x;y} \rangle$ *be their **concurrent** and* ***sequential composition**, respectively, where* $E_{x\parallel y} = E_{x;y} \triangleq E_x \cup E_y$ *such that, for all events $e, e'$ in $E_x \cup E_y$, the following holds:*

- $e \preceq_{x\parallel y} e'$ *exactly if* $e \preceq_x e'$ *or* $e \preceq_y e'$,
- $e \preceq_{x;y} e'$ *exactly if* $(e \in E_x$ *and* $e' \in E_y)$ *or* $e \preceq_{x\parallel y} e'$,
- $\alpha_{x\parallel y}(e) = \alpha_{x;y}(e) \triangleq \begin{cases} \alpha_x(e) & \text{if } e \in E_x \\ \alpha_y(e) & \text{if } e \in E_y. \end{cases}$

For simplicity, we assume that partial strings can be always made disjoint by renaming events if necessary. But this assumption could be avoided by using coproducts, a form of constructive disjoint union [21]. When clear from the context, we construct partial strings directly from the labels in $\Gamma$.

*Example 2.* If we ignore labels for now and let $p_i$ for all $0 \leq i \leq 3$ be four partial strings which each consist of a single event $e_i$, then $(p_0; p_1) \parallel (p_2; p_3)$ corresponds to a partial string that is isomorphic to the one shown in Fig. 1.

To formalize the set of all possible happens-before relations of a concurrent system, we rely on Ésik's notion of monotonic bijective morphism [19]:

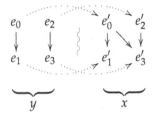

Fig. 2. Two partial strings $x$ and $y$ such that $x \sqsubseteq y$ provided all the labels are preserved, e.g. $\alpha_x(e'_0) = \alpha_y(e_0)$

**Definition 3 (Partial String Refinement).** *Let $x$ and $y$ be partial strings such that $x = \langle E_x, \alpha_x \preceq_x \rangle$ and $y = \langle E_y, \alpha_y, \preceq_y \rangle$. A **monotonic bijective morphism** from $x$ to $y$, written $f: x \to y$, is a bijective function $f$ from $E_x$ to $E_y$ such that, for all events $e, e' \in E_x$, $\alpha_x(e) = \alpha_y(f(e))$, and if $e \preceq_x e'$, then $f(e) \preceq_y f(e')$. Then $x$ **refines** $y$, written $x \sqsubseteq y$, if there exists a monotonic bijective morphism $f: y \to x$ from $y$ to $x$.*

*Remark 1.* Partial words [9] and pomsets [5,6] are defined in terms of isomorphism classes of lpos. Unlike lpos in pomsets, however, we study partial strings in terms of monotonic bijective morphisms [19] because isomorphisms are about sameness whereas the exchange law on partial strings is an inequation [21].

The purpose of Definition 3 is to disregard the identity of events but retain the notion of 'subsumption', cf. [6]. The intuition is that $\sqsubseteq$ orders partial strings according to their determinism. In other words, $x \sqsubseteq y$ for partial strings $x$ and $y$ implies that all events ordered in $y$ have the same order in $x$.

*Example 3.* Fig. 2 shows a monotonic bijective morphism from a partial string as given in Fig. 1 to an $N$-shaped partial string that is almost identical to the one in Fig. 1 except that it has an additional partial order constraint, giving its $N$ shape. One well-known fact about $N$-shaped partial strings is that they cannot be constructed as $x; y$ or $x \parallel y$ under any labelling [5]. However, this is not a problem for our study, as will become clear after Definition 4.

Our notion of partial string refinement is particularly appealing for symbolic techniques of concurrency because the monotonic bijective morphism can be directly encoded as a first-order logic formula modulo the theory of uninterpreted functions. Such a symbolic partial order encoding would be fully justified from a computational complexity perspective, as shown next.

**Proposition 1.** *Let $x$ and $y$ be finite partial strings in $\mathsf{P}_f$. The **partial string refinement** (PSR) problem — i.e. whether $x \sqsubseteq y$ — is NP-complete.*

*Proof.* Clearly PSR is in NP. The NP-hardness proof proceeds by reduction from the PLM problem [12]. Let $\Gamma^*$ be the set of strings, i.e. the set of finite partial strings $s$ such that $\preceq_s$ is a total order (for all $e, e' \in E_s, e \preceq_s e'$ or $e' \preceq_s e$). Given a finite partial string $p$, let $\mathfrak{L}_p$ be the set of all strings which refine $p$; equivalently, $\mathfrak{L}_p \triangleq \{s \in \Gamma^* \mid s \sqsubseteq p\}$. So $\mathfrak{L}_p$ denotes the same as $L(p)$ in [12, Definition 2.2].

Let $s$ be a string in $\Gamma^*$ and $P$ be a pomset over the alphabet $\Gamma$. By Remark 1, fix $p$ to be a partial string in $P$. Thus $s$ refines $p$ if and only if $s$ is a member of $\mathcal{L}_p$. Since this membership problem is NP-hard [12, Theorem 4.1], it follows that the PSR problem is NP-hard. So the PSR problem is NP-complete.     □

Note that a single partial string is not enough to model mutually exclusive (nondeterministic) control flow. To see this, consider a simple (possibly sequential) system such as if $*$ then P else Q where $*$ denotes nondeterministic choice. If the semantics of a program was a single partial string, then we need to find exactly one partial string that represents the fact that P executes or Q executes, but never both. To model this, rather than using a conflict relation [10], we resort to the simpler Hoare powerdomain construction where we lift sequential and concurrent composition operators to *sets* of partial strings. But since we are aiming (similar to Gischer [6]) at an *over-approximation of concurrent systems*, these sets are downward closed with respect to our partial string refinement ordering from Definition 3. Additional benefits of using the downward closure include that program refinement then coincides with familiar set inclusion and the ease with which later the Kleene star operators can be defined.

**Definition 4 (Program).** *A **program** is a downward-closed set of finite partial strings with respect to $\sqsubseteq$; equivalently $\mathcal{X} \subseteq P_f$ is a program whenever $\downarrow_\sqsubseteq \mathcal{X} = \mathcal{X}$ where $\downarrow_\sqsubseteq \mathcal{X} \triangleq \{y \in P_f \mid \exists x \in \mathcal{X} : y \sqsubseteq x\}$. Denote with $\mathbb{P}$ the family of all programs.*

Since we only consider systems that terminate, each partial string $x$ in a program $\mathcal{X}$ is finite. We reemphasize that the downward closure of such a set $\mathcal{X}$ can be thought of as an over-approximation of all possible happens-before relations in a concurrent system whose instructions are ordered according to the partial strings in $\mathcal{X}$. Later on (§ 4) we make the downward closure of partial strings more precise to model a certain kind of relaxed sequential consistency.

*Example 4.* Recall that $N$-shaped partial strings cannot be constructed as $x;y$ or $x \parallel y$ under any labelling [5]. Yet, by downward-closure of programs, such partial strings are included in the over-approximation of all the happens-before relations exhibited by a concurrent system. In particular, according to Example 3, the downward-closure of the set containing the partial string in Fig. 1 includes (among many others) the $N$-shaped partial string shown on the right in Fig. 2. In fact, we shall see in § 4 that this particular $N$-shaped partial string corresponds to a data race in the concurrent system shown in Fig. 3.

It is standard [6,21] to define $0 \triangleq \varnothing$ and $1 \triangleq \{\bot\}$ where $\bot$ is the (unique) empty partial string. Clearly 0 and 1 form programs in the sense of Definition 4. For the next theorem, we lift the two partial string operators (Definition 2) to programs in the standard way:

**Definition 5 (Bow Tie).** *Given two partial strings $x$ and $y$, denote with $x \bowtie y$ either concurrent or sequential composition of $x$ and $y$. For all programs $\mathcal{X}, \mathcal{Y}$ in $\mathbb{P}$ and partial string operators $\bowtie$, $\mathcal{X} \bowtie \mathcal{Y} \triangleq \downarrow_\sqsubseteq \{x \bowtie y \mid x \in \mathcal{X} \text{ and } y \in \mathcal{Y}\}$ where $\mathcal{X} \parallel \mathcal{Y}$ and $\mathcal{X}; \mathcal{Y}$ are called **concurrent** and **sequential program composition**, respectively.*

By denoting programs as sets of partial strings, we can now define Kleene star operators $(-)^{\|}$ and $(-)^{;}$ for iterative concurrent and sequential program composition, respectively, as least fixed points ($\mu$) using set union ($\cup$) as the binary join operator that we interpret as the nondeterministic choice of two programs. We remark that this is fundamentally different from the pomsets recursion operators in ultra-metric spaces [22]. The next theorem could be then summarized as saying that the resulting structure of programs, written $\mathfrak{S}$, is a partial order model of an algebraic concurrency semantics that satisfies the CKA laws [1]. Since CKA is an exemplar of the universal laws of programming [2], we base the rest of this paper on our partial order model of CKA.

**Theorem 1.** *The structure* $\mathfrak{S} = \langle \mathbb{P}, \subseteq, \cup, 0, 1, ;, \| \rangle$ *is a complete lattice, ordered by subset inclusion (i.e.* $\mathcal{X} \subseteq \mathcal{Y}$ *exactly if* $\mathcal{X} \cup \mathcal{Y} = \mathcal{Y}$*), such that* $\|$ *and* $;$ *form unital quantales over* $\cup$ *where* $\mathfrak{S}$ *satisfies the following:*

$$(\mathcal{U} \| \mathcal{V}); (\mathcal{X} \| \mathcal{Y}) \subseteq (\mathcal{U}; \mathcal{X}) \| (\mathcal{V}; \mathcal{Y}) \qquad \mathcal{X} \cup (\mathcal{Y} \cup \mathcal{Z}) = (\mathcal{X} \cup \mathcal{Y}) \cup \mathcal{Z}$$

$$\mathcal{X} \cup \mathcal{X} = \mathcal{X} \qquad \mathcal{X} \cup 0 = 0 \cup \mathcal{X} = \mathcal{X}$$

$$\mathcal{X} \cup \mathcal{Y} = \mathcal{Y} \cup \mathcal{X} \qquad \mathcal{X} \| \mathcal{Y} = \mathcal{Y} \| \mathcal{X}$$

$$\mathcal{X} \| 1 = 1 \| \mathcal{X} = \mathcal{X} \qquad \mathcal{X}; 1 = 1; \mathcal{X} = \mathcal{X}$$

$$\mathcal{X} \| 0 = 0 \| \mathcal{X} = 0 \qquad \mathcal{X}; 0 = 0; \mathcal{X} = 0$$

$$\mathcal{X} \| (\mathcal{Y} \cup \mathcal{Z}) = (\mathcal{X} \| \mathcal{Y}) \cup (\mathcal{X} \| \mathcal{Z}) \qquad \mathcal{X}; (\mathcal{Y} \cup \mathcal{Z}) = (\mathcal{X}; \mathcal{Y}) \cup (\mathcal{X}; \mathcal{Z})$$

$$(\mathcal{X} \cup \mathcal{Y}) \| \mathcal{Z} = (\mathcal{X} \| \mathcal{Z}) \cup (\mathcal{Y} \| \mathcal{Z}) \qquad (\mathcal{X} \cup \mathcal{Y}); \mathcal{Z} = (\mathcal{X}; \mathcal{Z}) \cup (\mathcal{Y}; \mathcal{Z})$$

$$\mathcal{X} \| (\mathcal{Y} \| \mathcal{Z}) = (\mathcal{X} \| \mathcal{Y}) \| \mathcal{Z} \qquad \mathcal{X}; (\mathcal{Y}; \mathcal{Z}) = (\mathcal{X}; \mathcal{Y}); \mathcal{Z}$$

$$\mathcal{P}^{\|} = \mu \mathcal{X}. 1 \cup (\mathcal{P} \| \mathcal{X}) \qquad \mathcal{P}^{;} = \mu \mathcal{X}. 1 \cup (\mathcal{P}; \mathcal{X}).$$

*Proof.* The details are in the accompanying technical report of this paper [21].

By Theorem 1, it makes sense to call 1 in structure $\mathfrak{S}$ the $\bowtie$-**identity program** where $\bowtie$ is a placeholder for either $;$ or $\|$. In the sequel, we call the binary relation $\subseteq$ on $\mathbb{P}$ the **program refinement relation**.

## 3   Least Fixed Point Reduction

This section is about the least fixed point operators $(-)^{;}$ and $(-)^{\|}$. Henceforth, we shall denote these by $(-)^{\bowtie}$. We show that under a certain finiteness condition (Definition 7) the program refinement problem $\mathcal{X}^{\bowtie} \subseteq \mathcal{Y}^{\bowtie}$ can be reduced to a bounded number of program refinement problems without least fixed points (Theorem 2). To prove this, we start by inductively defining the notion of iteratively composing a program with itself under $\bowtie$.

**Definition 6** (*$n$-iterated-$\bowtie$-program-composition*). *Let* $\mathbb{N}_0 \triangleq \mathbb{N} \cup \{0\}$ *be the set of non-negative integers. For all programs* $\mathcal{P}$ *in* $\mathbb{P}$ *and non-negative integers* $n$ *in* $\mathbb{N}_0$, $\mathcal{P}^{0 \cdot \bowtie} \triangleq 1 = \{\bot\}$ *is the* $\bowtie$-*identity program and* $\mathcal{P}^{(n+1) \cdot \bowtie} \triangleq \mathcal{P} \bowtie \mathcal{P}^{n \cdot \bowtie}$.

Clearly $(-)^{\bowtie}$ is the limit of its approximations in the following sense:

**Proposition 2.** *For every program $\mathcal{P}$ in $\mathbb{P}$, $\mathcal{P}^{\bowtie} = \bigcup_{n \geq 0} \mathcal{P}^{n \cdot \bowtie}$.*

**Definition 7 (Elementary Program).** *A program $\mathcal{P}$ in $\mathbb{P}$ is called **elementary** if $\mathcal{P}$ is the downward-closed set with respect to $\sqsubseteq$ of some finite and nonempty set $\mathcal{Q}$ of finite partial strings, i.e. $\mathcal{P} = \downarrow_{\sqsubseteq} \mathcal{Q}$. The set of elementary programs is denoted by $\mathbb{P}_\ell$.*

An elementary program therefore could be seen as a machine-representable program generated from a finite and nonempty set of finite partial strings. This finiteness restriction makes the notion of elementary programs a suitable candidate for the study of decision procedures. To make this precise, we define the following unary partial string operator:

**Definition 8 ($n$-repeated-$\bowtie$ Partial String Operator).** *For every non-negative integer $n$ in $\mathbb{N}_0$, $x^{0 \cdot \bowtie} \triangleq \perp$ is the empty partial string and $x^{(n+1) \cdot \bowtie} \triangleq x \bowtie x^{n \cdot \bowtie}$.*

Intuitively, $p^{n \cdot \bowtie}$ is a partial string that consists of $n$ copies of a partial string $p$, each combined by the partial string operator $\bowtie$. This is formalized as follows:

**Proposition 3.** *Let $n \in \mathbb{N}_0$ be a non-negative integer. Define $[0] \triangleq \emptyset$ and $[n+1] \triangleq \{1, \ldots, n+1\}$. For every partial string $x$, $x^{n \cdot \bowtie}$ is isomorphic to $y = \langle E_y, \alpha_y, \preceq_y \rangle$ where $E_y \triangleq E_x \times [n]$ such that, for all $e, e' \in E_x$ and $i, i' \in [n]$, the following holds:*

- *if '$\bowtie$' is '$\|$', then $\langle e, i \rangle \preceq_y \langle e', i' \rangle$ exactly if $i = i'$ and $e \preceq_x e'$,*
- *if '$\bowtie$' is ';', then $\langle e, i \rangle \preceq_y \langle e', i' \rangle$ exactly if $i < i'$ or ($i = i'$ and $e \preceq_x e'$),*
- *$\alpha_y(\langle e, i \rangle) = \alpha_x(e)$.*

**Definition 9 (Partial String Size).** *The **size** of a finite partial string $p$, denoted by $|p|$, is the cardinality of its event set $E_p$.*

For example, the partial string in Fig. 1 has size four. It is obvious that the size of finite partial strings is non-decreasing under the $n$-repeated-$\bowtie$ partial string operator from Definition 8 whenever $0 < n$. This simple fact is important for the next step towards our least fixed point reduction result in Theorem 2:

**Proposition 4 (Elementary Least Fixed Point Pre-reduction).** *For all elementary programs $\mathcal{X}$ and $\mathcal{Y}$ in $\mathbb{P}_\ell$, if the $\bowtie$-identity program $1$ is not in $\mathcal{Y}$ and $\mathcal{X} \subseteq \mathcal{Y}^{\bowtie}$, then $\mathcal{X} \subseteq \bigcup_{n \geq k \geq 0} \mathcal{Y}^{k \cdot \bowtie}$ where $n = \left\lfloor \frac{\ell_x}{\ell_y} \right\rfloor$ such that $\ell_x \triangleq \max \{|x| \mid x \in \mathcal{X}\}$ and $\ell_y \triangleq \min \{|y| \mid y \in \mathcal{Y}\}$ is the size of the largest and smallest partial strings in $\mathcal{X}$ and $\mathcal{Y}$, respectively.*

*Proof.* Assume $\mathcal{X} \subseteq \mathcal{Y}^{\bowtie}$. Let $x \in P_f$ be a finite partial string. We can assume $x \in \mathcal{X}$ because $\mathcal{X} \neq 0$. By assumption, $x \in \mathcal{Y}^{\bowtie}$. By Proposition 2, there exists $k \in \mathbb{N}_0$ such that $x \in \mathcal{Y}^{k \cdot \bowtie}$. Fix $k$ to be the smallest such non-negative integer. Show $k \leq \left\lfloor \frac{\ell_x}{\ell_y} \right\rfloor$ (the fraction is well-defined because $\mathcal{X}$ and $\mathcal{Y}$ are nonempty and $1 \notin \mathcal{Y}$). By downward closure and definition of $\sqsubseteq$ in terms of a one-to-one correspondence, it suffices to consider that $x$ is one of a (not necessarily unique) longest partial strings in $\mathcal{X}$, i.e. $|x'| \leq |x|$ for all $x' \in \mathcal{X}$; equivalently, $|x| = \ell_x$.

If $|x| = 0$, set $k = 0$, satisfying $1 = \mathcal{X} \subseteq \mathcal{Y}^{k \cdot \bowtie} = 1$ and $k \leq n = 0$ as required. Otherwise, since the size of partial strings in a program can never decrease under the $k$-iterated program composition operator $\bowtie$ when $0 < k$, it suffices to consider the case $x \sqsubseteq y^{k \cdot \bowtie}$ for some shortest partial string $y$ in $\mathcal{Y}$. Since $E_{y^{k \cdot \bowtie}}$ is the Cartesian product of $E_y$ and $[k]$, it follows $|x| = k \cdot |y|$. Since $|x| \leq \ell_{\mathcal{X}}$ and $\ell_y \leq |y|$, $k \leq \lfloor \frac{\ell_{\mathcal{X}}}{\ell_y} \rfloor$. By definition $n = \lfloor \frac{\ell_{\mathcal{X}}}{\ell_y} \rfloor$, proving $x \in \bigcup_{n \geq k \geq 0} \mathcal{Y}^{k \cdot \bowtie}$.  □

Equivalently, if there exists a partial string $x$ in $\mathcal{X}$ such that $x \notin \mathcal{Y}^{k \cdot \bowtie}$ for all non-negative integers $k$ between zero and $\lfloor \frac{\ell_{\mathcal{X}}}{\ell_y} \rfloor$, then $\mathcal{X} \not\subseteq \mathcal{Y}^{\bowtie}$. Since we are interested in decision procedures for program refinement checking, we need to show that the converse of Proposition 4 also holds. Towards this end, we prove the following left $(-)^{\bowtie}$ elimination rule:

**Proposition 5.** *For every program $\mathcal{X}$ and $\mathcal{Y}$ in $\mathbb{P}$, $\mathcal{X}^{\bowtie} \subseteq \mathcal{Y}^{\bowtie}$ exactly if $\mathcal{X} \subseteq \mathcal{Y}^{\bowtie}$.*

*Proof.* Assume $\mathcal{X}^{\bowtie} \subseteq \mathcal{Y}^{\bowtie}$. By Proposition 2, $\mathcal{X} \subseteq \mathcal{X}^{\bowtie}$. By transitivity of $\subseteq$ in $\mathbb{P}$, $\mathcal{X} \subseteq \mathcal{Y}^{\bowtie}$. Conversely, assume $\mathcal{X} \subseteq \mathcal{Y}^{\bowtie}$. Let $i, j \in \mathbb{N}_0$. By induction on $i$, $\mathcal{X}^{i \cdot \bowtie} \bowtie \mathcal{X}^{j \cdot \bowtie} = \mathcal{X}^{(i+j) \cdot \bowtie}$. Thus, by Proposition 2 and distributivity of $\bowtie$ over least upper bounds in $\mathbb{P}$, $\mathcal{X}^{\bowtie} \bowtie \mathcal{X}^{\bowtie} = \mathcal{X}^{\bowtie}$, i.e. $(-)^{\bowtie}$ is idempotent. This, in turn, implies that $(-)^{\bowtie}$ is a closure operator. Therefore, by monotonicity, $\mathcal{X}^{\bowtie} \subseteq (\mathcal{Y}^{\bowtie})^{\bowtie} = \mathcal{Y}^{\bowtie}$, proving that $\mathcal{X}^{\bowtie} \subseteq \mathcal{Y}^{\bowtie}$ is equivalent to $\mathcal{X} \subseteq \mathcal{Y}^{\bowtie}$.  □

**Theorem 2 (Elementary Least Fixed Point Reduction).** *For all elementary programs $\mathcal{X}$ and $\mathcal{Y}$ in $\mathbb{P}_\ell$, if the $\bowtie$-identity program $1$ is not in $\mathcal{Y}$, then $\mathcal{X}^{\bowtie} \subseteq \mathcal{Y}^{\bowtie}$ is equivalent to $\mathcal{X} \subseteq \bigcup_{n \geq k \geq 0} \mathcal{Y}^{k \cdot \bowtie}$ where $n = \lfloor \frac{\ell_{\mathcal{X}}}{\ell_y} \rfloor$ such that $\ell_{\mathcal{X}} \triangleq \max \{ |x| \mid x \in \mathcal{X} \}$ and $\ell_y \triangleq \min \{ |y| \mid y \in \mathcal{Y} \}$ is the size of the largest and smallest partial strings in $\mathcal{X}$ and $\mathcal{Y}$, respectively.*

*Proof.* By Proposition 5, it remains to show that $\mathcal{X} \subseteq \mathcal{Y}^{\bowtie}$ is equivalent to $\mathcal{X} \subseteq \bigcup_{n \geq k \geq 0} \mathcal{Y}^{k \cdot \bowtie}$ where $n = \lfloor \frac{\ell_{\mathcal{X}}}{\ell_y} \rfloor$. The forward and backward implication follow from Proposition 4 and 2, respectively.  □

From Theorem 2 follows immediately that $\mathcal{X}^{\bowtie} \subseteq \mathcal{Y}^{\bowtie}$ is decidable for all elementary programs $\mathcal{X}$ and $\mathcal{Y}$ in $\mathbb{P}_\ell$ because there exists an algorithm that could iteratively make $O(|\mathcal{X}| \times |\mathcal{Y}|^n)$ calls to another decision procedure to check whether $x \sqsubseteq y$ for all $x \in \mathcal{X}$ and $y \in \mathcal{Y}^{k \cdot \bowtie}$ where $n \geq k \geq 0$. However, by Proposition 1, each iteration in such an algorithm would have to solve an NP-complete subproblem. But this high complexity is expected since the PLC problem is $\Pi_2^p$-complete [12].

**Corollary 1.** *For all elementary programs $\mathcal{X}$ and $\mathcal{Y}$ in $\mathbb{P}$, if $|x| = |y|$ for all $x \in \mathcal{X}$ and $y \in \mathcal{Y}$, then $\mathcal{X}^{\bowtie} \subseteq \mathcal{Y}^{\bowtie}$ is equivalent to $\mathcal{X} \subseteq \mathcal{Y}$.*

We next move on to enriching our model of computation to accommodate a certain kind of relaxed sequential consistency.

## 4  Relaxed Sequential Consistency

For efficiency reasons, all modern computer architectures implement some form of weak memory model rather than sequential consistency [23]. A defining characteristic of weak memory architectures is that they violate interleaving semantics unless specific instructions are used to restore sequential consistency. This section fixes a particular interpretation of weak memory and studies the mathematical properties of the resulting partial order semantics. For this, we separate memory accesses into synchronizing and non-synchronizing ones, akin to [24]. A synchronized store is called a *release*, whereas a synchronized load is called an *acquire*. The intuition behind release/acquire is that prior writes made to other memory locations by the thread executing the release become visible in the thread that performs the corresponding acquire. Crucially, the particular form of release/acquire semantics that we formalize here is shown to be equivalent to the conjunction of three weak memory axioms (Theorem 3), namely 'write coherence', 'from-read' and 'global read-from' [17]. Subsequently, we look at one important ramification of this equivalence on *bounded model checking* (BMC) techniques for finding concurrency-related bugs (Theorem 4).

We start by defining the alphabet that we use for identifying events that denote synchronizing and non-synchronizing memory accesses.

**Definition 10 (Memory access alphabet).** *Define* $\langle LOAD \rangle \triangleq \{none, acquire\}$, $\langle STORE \rangle \triangleq \{none, release\}$ *and* $\langle BIT \rangle \triangleq \{0, 1\}$. *Let* $\langle ADDRESS \rangle$ *and* $\langle REG \rangle$ *be disjoint sets of **memory locations** and **registers**, respectively. Let* $load\_tag \in \langle LOAD \rangle$ *and* $store\_tag \in \langle STORE \rangle$. *Define the set of **load** and **store** labels, respectively:*

$$\Gamma_{\text{load, } load\_tag} \triangleq \{load\_tag\} \times \langle REG \rangle \times \langle ADDRESS \rangle$$

$$\Gamma_{\text{store, } store\_tag} \triangleq \{store\_tag\} \times \langle ADDRESS \rangle \times \langle BIT \rangle$$

*Let* $\Gamma \triangleq \Gamma_{\text{load,none}} \cup \Gamma_{\text{load,acquire}} \cup \Gamma_{\text{store,none}} \cup \Gamma_{\text{store,release}}$ *be the **memory access alphabet**. Given* $r \in \langle REG \rangle$, $a \in \langle ADDRESS \rangle$ *and* $b \in \langle BIT \rangle$, *we write* '$r := [a]_{load\_tag}$' *for the label* $\langle load\_tag, r, a \rangle$ *in* $\Gamma_{\text{load, } load\_tag}$; *similarly,* '$[a]_{store\_tag} := b$' *is shorthand for the label* $\langle store\_tag, a, b \rangle$ *in* $\Gamma_{\text{store, } store\_tag}$.

*Let* $x$ *be a partial string and* $e$ *be an event in* $E_x$. *Then* $e$ *is called a **load** or **store** if its label,* $\alpha_x(e)$, *is in* $\Gamma_{\text{load, } load\_tag}$ *or* $\Gamma_{\text{store, } store\_tag}$, *respectively. A load or store event* $e$ *is a **non-synchronizing memory access** if* $\alpha_x(e) \in \Gamma_{\text{none}} \triangleq \Gamma_{\text{load,none}} \cup \Gamma_{\text{store,none}}$; *otherwise, it is a **synchronizing memory access**. Let* $a \in \langle ADDRESS \rangle$ *be a memory location. An **acquire on** $a$ is an event* $e$ *such that* $\alpha_x(e) = $ '$r := [a]_{acquire}$' *for some* $r \in \langle REG \rangle$. *Similarly, a **release on** $a$ is an event* $e$ *labelled by* '$[a]_{release} := b$' *for some* $b \in \langle BIT \rangle$. *A **release** and **acquire** is a release and acquire on some memory location, respectively.*

*Example 5.* Fig. 3 shows the syntax of a program that consists of two threads $T_1$ and $T_2$. This concurrent system can be directly modelled by the partial string

| Thread $T_1$ | Thread $T_2$ |
|---|---|
| $r_0 := [b]_{\text{acquire}}$ | $[a]_{\text{none}} := 1$ |
| $r_1 := [a]_{\text{none}}$ | $[b]_{\text{release}} := 1$ |

**Fig. 3.** A concurrent system $T_1 \parallel T_2$ consisting of two threads. The memory accesses on memory locations $b$ are synchronized, whereas those on $a$ are not.

shown in Fig. 1 where memory location $b$ is accessed through acquire and release, whereas memory location $a$ is accessed through non-synchronizing loads and stores (shortly, we shall see that this leads to a data race).

Given Definition 10, we are now ready to refine our earlier conservative over-approximation of the happens-before relations (Definition 4) to get a particular form of release/acquire semantics. For this, we restrict the downward closure of programs $\mathcal{X}$ in $\mathbb{P}$, in the sense of Definition 4, by requiring all partial strings in $\mathcal{X}$ to satisfy the following partial ordering constraints:

**Definition 11 (SC-relaxed program).** *A program $\mathcal{X}$ is called **SC-relaxed** if, for all $a \in \langle ADDRESS \rangle$ and partial string $x$ in $\mathcal{X}$, the set of release events on $a$ is totally ordered by $\preceq_x$ and, for every acquire $l \in E_x$ and release $s \in E_x$ on $a$, $l \preceq_x s$ or $s \preceq_x l$.*

Henceforth, we denote loads and stores by $l, l'$ and $s, s'$, respectively. If $s$ and $s'$ are release events that modify the same memory location, either $s$ happens-before $s'$, or vice versa. If $l$ is an acquire and $s$ is a release on the same memory location, either $l$ happens-before $s$ or $s$ happens-before $l$. Importantly, however, two acquire events $l$ and $l'$ on the same memory location may still happen concurrently in the sense that neither $l$ happens-before $l'$ nor $l'$ happens-before $l$, in the same way non-synchronizing memory accesses are generally unordered.

*Example 6.* Example 4 and 5 illustrate the SC-relaxed semantics of the concurrent system in Fig. 3. In particular, the $N$-shaped partial string in Fig. 2 corresponds to a data race in $T_1 \parallel T_2$ because the non-synchronizing memory accesses on memory location $a$ happen concurrently. To see this, it may help to consider the interleaving $r_0 := [b]_{\text{acquire}}; [a]_{\text{none}} := 1; r_1 := [a]_{\text{none}}; [b]_{\text{release}} := 1$ where both memory accesses on location $a$ are unordered through the happens-before relation because there is no release instruction separating $[a]_{\text{none}} := 1$ from $r_1 := [a]_{\text{none}}$. One way of fixing this data race is by changing thread $T_1$ to **if** $[b]_{\text{acquire}} = 1$ **then** $r_1 := [a]_{\text{none}}$. Since CKA supports non-deterministic choice with the $\cup$ binary operator (recall Theorem 1), it would not be difficult to give semantics to such conditional checks, particularly if we introduce 'assume' labels into the alphabet in Definition 10.

We ultimately want to show that the conjunction of three existing weak memory axioms as studied in [17] fully characterizes our particular interpretation of relaxed sequential consistency, thereby paving the way for Theorem 4. For this, we recall the following memory axioms which can be thought of as relations on loads and stores on the same memory location:

**Definition 12 (Memory axioms).** *Let $x$ be a partial string in $\mathbb{P}_f$. The **read-from** function, denoted by $\text{rf} : E_x \to E_x$, is defined to map every load to a store on the same* memory location. A load $l$ **synchronizes-with** a store $s$ if $rf(l) = s$ implies $s \preceq_x l$. **Write-coherence** means that all stores $s, s'$ on the same memory location are totally ordered by $\preceq_x$. The **from-read axiom** holds whenever, for all loads $l$ and stores $s, s'$ on the same memory location, if $rf(l) = s$ and $s \prec_x s'$, then $l \preceq_x s'$.

By definition, the read-from function is total on all loads. The synchronizes-with axiom says that if a load reads-from a store (necessarily on the same memory location), then the store happens-before the load. This is also known as the global read-from axiom [17]. Write-coherence, in turn, ensures that all stores on the same memory location are totally ordered. This corresponds to the fact that "all writes to the same location are serialized in some order and are performed in that order with respect to any processor" [24]. Note that this is different from the modification order ('mo') on atomics in C++14 [25] because 'mo' is generally not a subset of the happens-before relation. The from-read axiom [17] requires that, for all loads $l$ and two different stores $s, s'$ on the same location, if $l$ reads-from $s$ and $s$ happens-before $s'$, then $l$ happens-before $s'$. We start by deriving from these three memory axioms the notion of SC-relaxed programs.

**Proposition 6 (SC-relaxed consistency).** *For all $\mathcal{X}$ in $\mathbb{P}$, if, for each partial string $x$ in $\mathcal{X}$, the synchronizes-with, write-coherence and from-read axioms hold on all release and acquire events in $E_x$ on the same memory location, then $\mathcal{X}$ is an SC-relaxed program.*

*Proof.* Let $a \in \langle ADDRESS \rangle$ be a memory location, $l$ be an acquire on $a$ and $s'$ be a release on $a$. By write-coherence on release/acquire events, it remains to show $l \preceq_x s'$ or $s' \preceq_x l$. Since the read-from function is total, $rf(l) = s$ for some release $s$ on $a$. By the synchronizes-with axiom, $s \preceq_x l$. We therefore assume $s \neq s'$. By write-coherence, $s \prec_x s'$ or $s' \prec_x s$. The former implies $l \preceq_x s'$ by the from-read axiom, whereas the latter implies $s' \preceq_x l$ by transitivity. This proves, by case analysis, that $\mathcal{X}$ is an SC-relaxed program.                    □

We need to prove some form of converse of the previous implication in order to characterize SC-relaxed semantics in terms of the three aforementioned weak memory axioms. For this purpose, we define the following:

**Definition 13 (Read consistency).** *Let $a \in \langle ADDRESS \rangle$ be a memory location and $x$ be a finite partial string in $P_f$. For all loads $l \in E_x$ on $a$, define the following set of store events: $\mathcal{H}_x(l) \triangleq \{s \in E_x \mid s \preceq_x l \text{ and } s \text{ is a store on } a\}$. The read-from function $rf$ is said to satisfy **weak read consistency** whenever, for all loads $l \in E_x$ and stores $s \in E_x$ on memory location $a$, the least upper bound $\bigvee \mathcal{H}_x(l)$ exists, and $rf(l) = s$ implies $\bigvee \mathcal{H}_x(l) \preceq_x s$; **strong read consistency** implies $rf(l) = s = \bigvee \mathcal{H}_x(l)$.*

By the next proposition, a natural sufficient condition for the existence of the least upper bound $\bigvee \mathcal{H}_x(l)$ is the finiteness of the partial strings in $P_f$ and the total ordering of all stores on the same memory location from which the load $l$ reads, i.e. write coherence. This could be generalized to well-ordered sets.

**Proposition 7 (Weak read consistency existence).** *For all partial strings $x$ in $P_f$, write coherence on memory location $a$ implies that $\bigvee \mathcal{H}_x(l)$ exists for all loads $l$ on $a$.*

We remark that $\bigvee \mathcal{H}_x(l) = \bot$ if $\mathcal{H}_x(l) = \varnothing$; alternatively, to avoid that $\mathcal{H}_x(l)$ is empty, we could require that programs are always constructed such that their partial strings have minimal store events that initialize all memory locations.

**Proposition 8 (Weak read consistency equivalence).** *Write coherence implies that weak read consistency is equivalent to the following: for all loads $l$ and stores $s, s'$ on memory location $a \in \langle ADDRESS \rangle$, if $\mathrm{rf}(l) = s$ and $s' \preceq_x l$, then $s' \preceq_x s$.*

*Proof.* By write coherence, $\bigvee \mathcal{H}_x(l)$ exists, and $s' \preceq_x \bigvee \mathcal{H}_x(l)$ because $s' \in \mathcal{H}_x(l)$ by assumption $s' \preceq_x l$ and Definition 13. By assumption of weak read consistency, $\bigvee \mathcal{H}_x(l) \preceq_x s$. From transitivity follows $s' \preceq_x s$.

Conversely, assume $\mathrm{rf}(l) = s$. Let $s'$ be a store on $a$ such that $s' \in \mathcal{H}_x(l)$. Thus, by hypothesis, $s' \preceq_x s$. Since $s'$ is arbitrary, $s$ is an upper bound. Since the least upper bound is well-defined by write coherence, $\bigvee \mathcal{H}_x(l) \preceq_x s$. $\qquad\square$

Weak read consistency therefore says that if a load $l$ reads from a store $s$ and another store $s'$ on the same memory location happens before $l$, then $s'$ happens before $s$. This implies the next proposition.

**Proposition 9 (From-Read Equivalence).** *For all SC-relaxed programs in $\mathbb{P}$, weak read consistency with respect to release/acquire events is equivalent to the from-read axiom with respect to release/acquire events.*

We can characterize strong read consistency as follows:

**Proposition 10 (Strong Read Consistency Equivalence).** *Strong read consistency is equivalent to weak read consistency and the synchronizes-with axiom.*

*Proof.* Let $x$ be a partial string in $\mathsf{P}_f$. Let $l$ be a load and $s$ be a store on the same memory location. The forward implication is immediate from $\bigvee \mathcal{H}_x(l) \preceq_x l$.

Conversely, assume $\mathrm{rf}(l) = s$. By synchronizes-with, $s \preceq_x l$, whence $s \in \mathcal{H}_x(l)$. By definition of least upper bound, $s \preceq_x \bigvee \mathcal{H}_x(l)$. Since $s \succeq_x \bigvee \mathcal{H}_x(l)$, by hypothesis, and $\preceq_x$ is antisymmetric, we conclude $s = \bigvee \mathcal{H}_x(l)$. $\qquad\square$

**Theorem 3 (SC-relaxed Equivalence).** *For every program $\mathcal{X}$ in $\mathbb{P}$, $\mathcal{X}$ is SC-relaxed where, for all partial strings $x$ in $\mathcal{X}$ and acquire events $l$ in $E_x$, $\mathrm{rf}(l) = \bigvee \mathcal{H}_x(l)$, if and only if the synchronizes-with, write-coherence and from-read axioms hold for all $x$ in $\mathcal{X}$ with respect to all release/acquire events in $E_x$ on the same memory location.*

*Proof.* Assume $\mathcal{X}$ is an SC-relaxed program according to Definition 11. Let $x$ be a partial string in $\mathcal{X}$ and $l$ be an acquire in the set of events $E_x$. By Proposition 7, $\bigvee \mathcal{H}_x(l)$ exists. Assume $\mathrm{rf}(l) = \bigvee \mathcal{H}_x(l)$. Since $l$ is arbitrary, this is equivalent to assuming strong read consistency. Since release events are totally ordered in $\preceq_x$, by assumption, it remains to show that the synchronizes-with and from-read axioms hold. This follows from Proposition 10 and 9, respectively.

Conversely, assume the three weak memory axioms hold on $x$ with respect to all release/acquire events in $E_x$ on the same memory location. By Proposition 6, $\mathcal{X}$ is an SC-relaxed program. Therefore, by Proposition 9 and 10, $\mathrm{rf}(l) = \bigvee \mathcal{H}_x(l)$, proving the equivalence. $\qquad\square$

While the state-of-the-art weak memory encoding is cubic in size [18], the previous theorem has as immediate consequence that there exists an asymptotically smaller weak memory encoding with only a quadratic number of partial order constraints.

**Theorem 4 (Quadratic-size Weak Memory Encoding).** *There exists a quantifier-free first-order logic formula that has a quadratic number of partial order constraints and is equisatisfiable to the cubic-size encoding given in [18].*

*Proof.* Instead of instantiating the three universally quantified events in the from-read axiom, symbolically encode the least upper bound of weak read consistency. This can be accomplished with a new symbolic variable for every acquire event. It is easy to see that this reduces the cubic number of partial order constraints to a quadratic number.                                    □

In short, the asymptotic reduction in the number of partial order constraints is due to a new symbolic encoding for how values are being overwritten in memory: the current cubic-size formula [18] encodes the from-read axiom (Definition 12), whereas the proposed quadratic-size formula encodes a certain least upper bound (Definition 13). We reemphasize that this formulation is in terms of release/acquire events rather than machine-specific accesses as in [18]. The construction of the quadratic-size encoding, therefore, is generally only applicable if we can translate the machine-specific reads and writes in a shared memory program to acquire and release events, respectively. This may require the program to be data race free, as illustrated in Example 6.

Furthermore, as mentioned in the introduction of this section, the primary application of Theorem 4 is in the context of BMC. Recall that BMC assumes that all loops in the shared memory program under scrutiny have been unrolled (the same restriction as in [18]). This makes it possible to symbolically encode branch conditions, thereby alleviating the need to explicitly enumerate each finite partial string in an elementary program.

## 5   Concluding Remarks

This paper has studied a partial order model of computation that satisfies the axioms of a unifying algebraic concurrency semantics by Hoare et al. By further restricting the partial string semantics, we obtained a relaxed sequential consistency semantics which was shown to be equivalent to the conjunction of three weak memory axioms by Alglave et al. This allowed us to prove the existence of an equisatisfiable but asymptotically smaller weak memory encoding that has only a quadratic number of partial order constraints compared to the state-of-the-art cubic-size encoding. In upcoming work, we will experimentally compare both encodings in the context of bounded model checking using SMT solvers. As future theoretical work, it would be interesting to study the relationship between categorical models of partial string theory and event structures.

**Acknowledgements..** We would like to thank Tony Hoare and Stephan van Staden for their valuable comments on an early draft of this paper, and we thank Jade Alglave, César Rodríguez, Michael Tautschnig, Peter Schrammel, Marcelo Sousa, Björn Wachter and John Wickerson for invaluable discussions.

# References

1. Hoare, C.A., Möller, B., Struth, G., Wehrman, I.: Concurrent Kleene algebra and its foundations. J. Log. Algebr. Program. 80(6), 266–296 (2011)
2. Hoare, T., van Staden, S.: The laws of programming unify process calculi. Sci. Comput. Program. 85, 102–114 (2014)
3. Hoare, T., van Staden, S.: In praise of algebra. Formal Aspects of Computing 24(4-6), 423–431 (2012)
4. Hoare, T., van Staden, S., Möller, B., Struth, G., Villard, J., Zhu, H., O'Hearn, P.: Developments in Concurrent Kleene Algebra. In: Höfner, P., Jipsen, P., Kahl, W., Müller, M.E. (eds.) RAMiCS 2014. LNCS, vol. 8428, pp. 1–18. Springer, Heidelberg (2014)
5. Pratt, V.: Modeling concurrency with partial orders. Int. J. Parallel Program. 15(1), 33–71 (1986)
6. Gischer, J.L.: The equational theory of pomsets. Theor. Comput. Sci. 61(2-3), 199–224 (1988)
7. Petri, C.A.: Communication with automata. PhD thesis, Universität Hamburg (1966)
8. Lamport, L.: Time, clocks, and the ordering of events in a distributed system. Commun. ACM 21(7), 558–565 (1978)
9. Grabowski, J.: On partial languages. Fundam. Inform. 4(2), 427–498 (1981)
10. Nielsen, M., Plotkin, G.D., Winskel, G.: Petri nets, event structures and domains, part I. Theor. Comput. Sci. 13(1), 85–108 (1981)
11. Bloom, B., Kwiatkowska, M.: Trade-offs in true concurrency: Pomsets and Mazurkiewicz traces. In: Brookes, S., Main, M., Melton, A., Mislove, M., Schmidt, D. (eds.) MFPS 1991. LNCS, vol. 598, pp. 350–375. Springer, Heidelberg (1992)
12. Feigenbaum, J., Kahn, J., Lund, C.: Complexity results for POMSET languages. SIAM J. Discret. Math. 6(3), 432–442 (1993)
13. Laurence, M.R., Struth, G.: Completeness theorems for Bi-Kleene algebras and series-parallel rational pomset languages. In: Höfner, P., Jipsen, P., Kahl, W., Müller, M.E. (eds.) RAMiCS 2014. LNCS, vol. 8428, pp. 65–82. Springer, Heidelberg (2014)
14. Sewell, P., Sarkar, S., Owens, S., Nardelli, F.Z., Myreen, M.O.: x86-TSO: A rigorous and usable programmer's model for x86 multiprocessors. Commun. ACM 53(7), 89–97 (2010)
15. Ševčík, J., Vafeiadis, V., Zappa Nardelli, F., Jagannathan, S., Sewell, P.: Relaxed-memory concurrency and verified compilation. SIGPLAN Not. 46(1), 43–54 (2011)
16. Batty, M., Owens, S., Sarkar, S., Sewell, P., Weber, T.: Mathematizing C++ concurrency. SIGPLAN Not. 46(1), 55–66 (2011)
17. Alglave, J., Maranget, L., Sarkar, S., Sewell, P.: Fences in weak memory models (extended version). FMSD 40(2), 170–205 (2012)
18. Alglave, J., Kroening, D., Tautschnig, M.: Partial orders for efficient bounded model checking of concurrent software. In: Sharygina, N., Veith, H. (eds.) CAV 2013. LNCS, vol. 8044, pp. 141–157. Springer, Heidelberg (2013)
19. Ésik, Z.: Axiomatizing the subsumption and subword preorders on finite and infinite partial words. Theor. Comput. Sci. 273(1-2), 225–248 (2002)

20. Alglave, J., Maranget, L., Sarkar, S., Sewell, P.: Litmus: Running tests against hardware. In: Abdulla, P.A., Leino, K.R.M. (eds.) TACAS 2011. LNCS, vol. 6605, pp. 41–44. Springer, Heidelberg (2011)
21. Horn, A., Alglave, J.: Concurrent Kleene algebra of partial strings. ArXiv e-prints abs/1407.0385 (July 2014)
22. de Bakker, J.W., Warmerdam, J.H.A.: Metric pomset semantics for a concurrent language with recursion. In: Guessarian, I. (ed.) LITP 1990. LNCS, vol. 469, pp. 21–49. Springer, Heidelberg (1990)
23. Lamport, L.: How to make a multiprocessor computer that correctly executes multiprocess programs. IEEE Trans. Comput. 28(9), 690–691 (1979)
24. Gharachorloo, K., Lenoski, D., Laudon, J., Gibbons, P., Gupta, A., Hennessy, J.: Memory consistency and event ordering in scalable shared-memory multiprocessors. SIGARCH Comput. Archit. News 18(2SI), 15–26 (1990)
25. ISO: International Standard ISO/IEC 14882:2014(E) Programming Language C++. International Organization for Standardization (2014) (Ratified, to appear soon)

# A Strategy for Automatic Verification of Stabilization of Distributed Algorithms

Ritwika Ghosh[(✉)] and Sayan Mitra

University of Illinois, Urbana Champaign, USA
{rghosh9,mitras}@illinois.edu

**Abstract.** Automatic verification of convergence and stabilization properties of distributed algorithms has received less attention than verification of invariance properties. We present a semi-automatic strategy for verification of stabilization properties of arbitrarily large networks under structural and fairness constraints. We introduce a sufficient condition that guarantees that every fair execution of any (arbitrarily large) instance of the system stabilizes to the target set of states. In addition to specifying the protocol executed by each agent in the network and the stabilizing set, the user also has to provide a measure function or a ranking function. With this, we show that for a restricted but useful class of distributed algorithms, the sufficient condition can be automatically checked for arbitrarily large networks, by exploiting the small model properties of these conditions. We illustrate the method by automatically verifying several well-known distributed algorithms including link-reversal, shortest path computation, distributed coloring, leader election and spanning-tree construction.

## 1 Introduction

A system is said to stabilize to a set of states $\mathcal{X}^*$ if all its executions reach some state in $\mathcal{X}^*$ [1]. This property can capture common progress requirements like absence of deadlocks and live-locks, counting to infinity, and achievement of self-stabilization in distributed systems. Stabilization is a liveness property, and like other liveness properties, it is generally impossible to verify automatically. In this paper, we present sufficient conditions which can be used to automatically prove stabilization of distributed systems with arbitrarily many participating processes.

A sufficient condition we propose is similar in spirit to Tsitsiklis' conditions given in [2] for convergence of iterative asynchronous processes. We require the user to provide a measure function, parameterized by the number of processes, such that its sub-level sets are *invariant* with respect to the transitions and there is a *progress* making action for each state.[1] Our point of departure is a

---

This work is supported in part by research grants NSF CAREER 1054247 and AFOSR YIP FA9550-12-1-0336.

[1] A sub-level set of a function comprises of all points in the domain which map to the same value or less.

© IFIP International Federation for Information Processing 2015
S. Graf and M. Viswanathan (Eds.): FORTE 2015, LNCS 9039, pp. 35–49, 2015.
DOI: 10.1007/978-3-319-19195-9_3

*non-interference* condition that turned out to be essential for handling models of distributed systems. Furthermore, in order to handle non-deterministic communication patterns, our condition allows us to encode fairness conditions and different underlying communication graphs.

Next, we show that these conditions can be transformed to a forall-exists form with a small model property. That is, there exists a cut-off number $N_0$ such that if the condition(s) is(are) valid in all models of sizes up to $N_0$, then it is valid for all models. We use the small model results from [3] to determine the cut-off parameter and apply this approach to verify several well-known distributed algorithms.

We have a Python implementation based on the sufficient conditions for stabilization we develop in Section 3. We present precondition-effect style transition systems of algorithms in Section 4 and they serve as pseudo-code for our implementation. The SMT-solver is provided with the conditions for *invariance*, *progress* and *non-interference* as assertions. We encode the distributed system models in Python and use the Z3 theorem-prover module [4] provided by Python to check the conditions for stabilization for different model sizes.

We have used this method to analyze a number of well-known distributed algorithms, including a simple distributed coloring protocol, a self-stabilizing algorithm for constructing a spanning tree of the underlying network graph, a link-reversal routing algorithm, and a binary gossip protocol. Our experiments suggest that this method is effective for constructing a formal proof of stabilization of a variety of algorithms, provided the measure function is chosen carefully. Among other things, the measure function should be *locally computable*: changes from the measure of the previous state to that of the current state only depend on the vertices involved in the transition. It is difficult to determine whether such a measure function exists for a given problem. For instance, consider Dijkstra's self-stabilizing token ring protocol [5]. The proof of correctness relies on the fact that the leading node cannot push for a value greater than its previous unique state until every other node has the same value. We were unable to capture this in a locally computable measure function because if translated directly, it involves looking at every other node in the system.

## 1.1 Related Work

The motivation for our approach is from the paper by John Tsitsiklis on convergence of asynchronous iterative processes [2], which contains conditions for convergence similar to the sufficient conditions we state for stabilization. Our use of the measure function to capture stabilization is similar to the use of Lyapunov functions to prove stability as explored in [6], [7] and [8]. In [9], Dhama and Theel present a *progress monitor* based method of designing self-stabilizing algorithms with a weakly fair scheduler, given a self-stabilizing algorithm with an arbitrary, possibly very restrictive scheduler. They also use the existence of a ranking function to prove convergence under the original scheduler. Several authors [10] employ functions to prove termination of distributed algorithms, but while they may provide an idea of what the measure function can be, in general they do not translate exactly to the measure functions that our verification strategy can employ. The notion of fairness we have is also essential in dictating what the measure function should be, while not prohibiting too many behaviors. In [7], the assumption of serial execution semantics is compatible with our notions of fair executions.

The idea central to our proof method is the small model property of the sufficient conditions for stabilization. The small model nature of certain invariance properties of distributed algorithms (eg. distributed landing protocols for small aircrafts as in [11]) has been used to verify them in [12]. In [13], Emerson and Kahlon utilize a small model argument to perform parameterized model checking of ring based message passing systems.

## 2   Preliminaries

We will represent distributed algorithms as transition systems. Stabilization is a liveness property and is closely related to *convergence* as defined in the works of Tsitsiklis [2]; it is identical to the concept of *region stability* as presented in [14]. We will use measure functions in our definition of stabilization. A *measure function* on a domain provides a mapping from that domain to a well-ordered set. A well-ordered set $W$ is one on which there is a total ordering $<$, such that there is a minimum element with respect to $<$ on every non-empty subset of $W$. Given a measure function $C : A \to B$, there is a partition of $A$ into sub level-sets. All elements of $A$ which map to the same element $b \in B$ under $C$ are in the same sub level-set $L_b$.

We are interested in verifying stabilization of distributed algorithms independent of the number of participating processes or nodes. Hence, the transition systems are parameterized by $N$—the number of nodes. Given a non-negative integer $N$, we use $[N]$ to denote a set of indices $\{1, 2, \ldots, N\}$.

**Definition 1.** *For a natural number $N$ and a set $Q$, a transition system $A(N)$ with $N$ nodes is defined as a tuple (X,A,D) where*

a) *$\mathcal{X}$ is the state space of the system. If the state space of of each node is $Q$, $\mathcal{X} = Q^N$.*
b) *$A$ is a set of actions.*
c) *$D : \mathcal{X} \times A \to \mathcal{X}$ is a transition function, that maps a system-state action pair to a system-state.*

For any $x \in \mathcal{X}$, the $i^{th}$ component of $x$ is the state of the $i^{th}$ node and we refer to it as $x[i]$. Given a transition system $\mathcal{A}(N) = (\mathcal{X}, A, D)$ we refer to the state obtained by the application of the action $a$ on a state $x \in \mathcal{X}$ i.e, $D(x, a)$, by $a(x)$.

An execution of $\mathcal{A}(N)$ records a particular run of the distributed system with $N$ nodes. Formally, an *execution* $\alpha$ of $\mathcal{A}(N)$ is a (possibly infinite) alternating sequence of states and actions $x_0, a_1, x_1, \ldots$, where each $x_i \in \mathcal{X}$ and each $a_i \in A$ such that $D(x_i, a_{i+1}) = x_{i+1}$. Given that the choice of actions is non-deterministic in the execution, it is reasonable to expect that not all executions may stabilize. For instance, an execution in which not all nodes participate, may not stabilize.

**Definition 2.** *A fairness condition $\mathcal{F}$ for $\mathcal{A}(N)$ is a finite collection of subsets of actions $\{A_i\}_{i \in I}$, where $I$ is a finite index set. An action-sequence $\sigma = a_1, a_2, \ldots$ is $\mathcal{F}$-Fair if every $A_i$ in $\mathcal{F}$ is represented in $\sigma$ infinitely often, that is,*

$$\forall A' \in \mathcal{F}, \ \forall i \in \mathbb{N}, \ \exists k > i, \ a_k \in A'.$$

For instance, if the fairness condition is the collection of all singleton subsets of $A$, then each action occurs infinitely often in an execution. This notion of fairness is similar to action based fairness constraints in temporal logic model checking [15]. The network graph itself enforces whether an action is enabled: every pair of adjacent nodes determines a continuously enabled action. An execution is strongly fair, if given a set of actions $A$ such that all actions in $A$ are infinitely often enabled; some action in $A$ occurs infinitely often in the it. An $\mathcal{F}$-fair execution is an infinite execution such that the corresponding sequence of actions is $\mathcal{F}$-fair.

**Definition 3.** *Given a system $\mathcal{A}(N)$, a fairness condition $\mathcal{F}$, and a set of states $\mathcal{X}^* \subseteq \mathcal{X}$, $\mathcal{A}(N)$ is said to $\mathcal{F}$-stabilize to $\mathcal{X}^*$ iff for any $\mathcal{F}$-fair execution $\alpha = x_0, a_1, x_1, a_2, \ldots$, there exists $k \in \mathbb{N}$ such that $x_k \in \mathcal{X}^*$. $\mathcal{X}^*$ is called a **stabilizing set** for $\mathcal{A}$ and $\mathcal{F}$.*

It is different from the definition of self-stabilization found in the literature [1], in that the stabilizing set $\mathcal{X}^*$ is not required to be an invariant of $\mathcal{A}(N)$. We view proving the invariance of $\mathcal{X}^*$ as a separate problem that can be approached using one of the available techniques for proving invariance of parametrized systems in [3], [12].

*Example 1.* (Binary Gossip) We look at binary gossip in a ring network composed of $N$ nodes. The nodes are numbered clockwise from 1, and nodes 1 and N are also neighbors. Each node has one of two states : $\{0, 1\}$. A pair of neighboring nodes communicates to exchange their values, and the new state is set to the binary Or ($\vee$) of the original values. Clearly, if all the interactions happen infinitely often, and the initial state has at least one node state 1, this transition system stabilizes to the state $x = 1^N$. The set of actions is specified by the set of edges of the ring. We first represent this protocol and its transitions using a standard precondition-effect style notation similar to one used in [16].

```
Automaton Gossip[N : N]
type indices : [N]
type   values : {0,1}
variables
          x[indices  →  values]
transitions
          step(i: indices, j: indices)
          pre True
          eff x[i] = x[j] = x[i] ∨ x[j]
measure
          func C : x ↦ Sum(x)
```

The above representation translates to the transition system $\mathcal{A}(N) = (\mathcal{X}, A, D)$ where

1. The state space of each node is $Q = \{0, 1\}$, i.e $\mathcal{X} = \{0, 1\}^N$.
2. The set of actions is $A = \{step(i, i+1) \mid 1 \leq i < N\} \cup \{(N, 1)\}$.
3. The transition function is $D(x, step(i, j)) = x'$ where $x'[i] = x'[j] = x[i] \vee x[j]$.

We define the stabilizing set to be $X^* = \{1^N\}$, and the fairness condition is $\mathcal{F} = \{\{(i, i+1) \mid 1 < i < N\} \cup \{1, N\}$, which ensures that all possible interactions take place infinitely often. In Section 3 we will discuss how this type of stabilization can be proven automatically with a user-defined measure function.

## 3   Verifying Stabilization

### 3.1   A Sufficient Condition for Stabilization

We state a sufficient condition for stabilization in terms of the existence of a *measure function*. The measure functions are similar to Lyapunov stability conditions in control theory [17] and well-founded relations used in proving termination of programs and rewriting systems [18].

**Theorem 1.** *Suppose* $\mathcal{A}(N) = \langle \mathcal{X}, A, D \rangle$ *is a transition system parameterized by* $N$, *with a fairness condition* $\mathcal{F}$, *and let* $\mathcal{X}^*$ *be a subset of* $\mathcal{X}$. *Suppose further that there exists a measure function* $C : \mathcal{X} \to W$, *with minimum element* $\perp$ *such that the following conditions hold for all states* $x \in X$:

- (invariance) $\forall\, a \in A,\ C(a(x)) \leq C(x)$,
- (progress) $\exists\, A_x \in \mathcal{F},\ \forall a \in A_x,\ C(x) \neq \perp \Rightarrow C(a(x)) < C(x)$,
- (noninterference) $\forall a, b \in A,\ C(a(x)) < C(x) \Rightarrow C(a(b(x))) < C(x)$,   *and*
- (minimality) $C(x) = \perp \Rightarrow x \in \mathcal{X}^*$.

*Then,* $\mathcal{A}[N]$ $\mathcal{F}$-*stabilizes to* $\mathcal{X}^*$.

*Proof.* Consider an $\mathcal{F}$-fair execution $\alpha = x_0 a_1 x_1 \ldots$ of $\mathcal{A}(N)$ and let $x_i$ be an arbitrary state in that execution. If $C(x_i) = \perp$, then by *minimality*, we have $x_i \in \mathcal{X}^*$. Otherwise, by the *progress* condition we know that there exists a set of actions $A_{x_i} \in \mathcal{F}$ and $k > i$, such that $a_k \in A_{x_i}$, and $C(a_k(x_i)) < C(x_i)$. We perform induction on the length of the sub-sequence $x_i a_{i+1} x_{i+1} \ldots a_k x_k$ and prove that $C(x_k) < C(x_i)$. For any sequence $\beta$ of intervening actions of length $n$,

$$C(a_k(x_i)) < C(x_i) \Rightarrow C(a_k(\beta(x_i))) < C(x_i).$$

The base case of the induction is $n = 0$, which is trivially true. By induction hypothesis we have: for any $j < n$, with length of $\beta$ equal to $j$,

$$C(a_k(\beta(x_i))) < C(x_i).$$

We have to show that for any action $b \in A$,

$$C(a_k(\beta(b(x_i)))) < C(x_i).$$

There are two cases to consider. If $C(b(x_i)) < C(x_i)$ then the result follows from the *invariance* property. Otherwise, let $x' = b(x_i)$. From the invariance of $b$ we have $C(x') = C(x_i)$. From the noninterference condition we have

$$C(a(b(x_i))) < C(x_i),$$

which implies that $C(a(x')) < C(x')$. By applying the induction hypothesis to $x'$ we have the required inequality $C(a_k(\beta(b(x_i)))) < C(x_i)$. So far we have proved that either a state $x_i$ in an execution is already in the stabilizing set, or there is a state $x_k, k > i$ such that $C(x_k) < C(x_i)$. Since $<$ is a well-ordering on $C(\mathcal{X})$, there cannot be an infinite descending chain. Thus

$$\exists j (j > i \wedge C(j) = \bot).$$

By minimality , $x_j \in X^*$. By invariance again, we have $\mathcal{F}$-stabilization to $X^*$ $\square$

We make some remarks on the conditions of Theorem 1. It requires the measure function $C$ and the transition system $\mathcal{A}(N)$ to satisfy four conditions. The *invariance* condition requires the sub-level sets of $C$ to be invariant with respect to all the transitions of $\mathcal{A}(N)$. The *progress* condition requires that for every state $x$ for which the measure function is not already $\bot$, there exists a fair set of actions $A_x$ that takes $x$ to a lower value of $C$.

The *minimality* condition asserts that $C(x)$ drops to $\bot$ only if the state is in the stabilizing set $\mathcal{X}^*$. This is a part of the specification of the stabilizing set.

The *noninterference* condition requires that if $a$ results in a decrease in the value of the measure function at state $x$, then application of $a$ to another state $x'$ that is reachable from $x$ also decreases the measure value below that of $x$. Note that it doesn't necessarily mean that $a$ decreases the measure value at $x'$, only that either $x'$ has measure value less than $x$ at the time of application of $a$ or it drops after the application. In contrast, the progress condition of Theorem 1 requires that for every sub-level set of $C$ there is a fair action that takes *all* states in the sub-level set to a smaller sub-level set.

To see the motivation for the noninterference condition, consider a sub-level set with two states $x_1$ and $x_2$ such that $b(x_1) = x_2, a(x_2) = x_1$ and there is only one action $a$ such that $C(a(x_1)) < C(x_1)$. But as long as $a$ does not occur at $x_1$, an infinite (fair) execution $x_1 b x_2 a x_1 b x_2 \ldots$ may never enter a smaller sub-level set.

In our examples, the actions change the state of a node or at most a small set of nodes while the measure functions succinctly captures global progress conditions such as the number of nodes that have different values. Thus, it is often impossible to find actions that reduce the measure function for all possible states in a level-set. In Section 4, we will show how a candidate measure function can be checked for arbitrarily large instances of a distributed algorithm, and hence, lead to a method for automatic verification of stabilization.

## 3.2    Automating Stabilization Proofs

For finite instances of a distributed algorithm, we can use formal verification tools to check the sufficient conditions in Theorem 1 to prove stabilization. For transition systems with invariance, progress and noninterference conditions that can be encoded appropriately in an SMT solver, these checks can be performed automatically. Our goal, however, is to prove stabilization of algorithms with an arbitrary or unknown number of participating nodes. We would like to define a parameterized family of measure functions and show that $\forall N \in \mathbb{N}$, $\mathcal{A}(N)$ satisfies the conditions of Theorem 1. This is a parameterized verification problem and most of the prior work on this problem has focused on verifying invariant properties (see Section 1 for related works). Our approach will be based on exploiting the small model nature of the logical formulas representing these conditions.

Suppose we want to check the validity of a logical formula of the form $\forall N \in \mathbb{N}, \phi(N)$. Of course, this formula is valid iff the negation $\exists N \in \mathbb{N}, \neg\phi(N)$ has no satisfying solution. In our context, checking if $\neg\phi(N)$ has a satisfying solution over all integers is the (large) search problem of finding a counter-example. That is, a particular instance of the distributed algorithm and specific values of the measure function for which the conditions in Theorem 1 do not hold. The formula $\neg\phi(N)$ is said to have a small model property if there exists a cut-off value $N_0$ such that if there is no counter-example found in any of the instances $\mathcal{A}(1), \mathcal{A}(2), \ldots, \mathcal{A}(N_0)$, then there are no counter-examples at all. Thus, if the conditions of Theorem 1 can be encoded in such a way that they have these small model properties then by checking them over finite instances, we can infer their validity for arbitrarily large systems.

In [3], a class of $\forall\exists$ formulas with small model properties were used to check invariants of timed distributed systems on arbitrary networks. In this paper, we will use the same class of formulas to encode the sufficient conditions for checking stabilization. We use the following small model theorem as presented in [3]:

**Theorem 2.** *Let $\Gamma(N)$ be an assertion of the form*

$$\forall i_1, \ldots, i_k \in [N] \exists j_1, \ldots, j_m \in [N], \phi(i_1, \ldots, i_k, j_1, \ldots, j_m)$$

*where $\phi$ is a quantifier-free formula involving the index variables, global and local variables in the system. Then, $\forall N \in \mathbb{N} : \Gamma(N)$ is valid iff for all $n \leq N_0 = (e+1)(k+2)$, $\Gamma(n)$ is satisfied by all models of size $n$, where $e$ is the number of index array variables in $\phi$ and $k$ is the largest subscript of the universally quantified index variables in $\Gamma(N)$.*

## 3.3    Computing the Small Model Parameter

Computing the small model parameter $N_0$ for verifying a stability property of a transition system first requires expressing all the conditions of Theorem 1 using formulas which have the structure specified by Theorem 2. There are a few important considerations while doing so.

*Translating the sufficient conditions.* In their original form, none of the conditions of Theorem 1 have the structure of $\forall\exists$-formulas as required by Theorem 2. For instance, a leading $\forall x \in \mathcal{X}$ quantification is not allowed by Theorem 2, so we transform the conditions into formulas with implicit quantification. Take for instance the invariance condition: $\forall x \in \mathcal{X}, \forall a \in A, (C(a(x)) \leq C(x))$. Checking the validity of the invariance condition is equivalent to checking the satisfiability of $\forall a \in A, (a(x) = x' \Rightarrow C(x') \leq C(x))$, where $x'$ and $x$ are free variables, which are checked over all valuations. Here we need to check that $x$ and $x'$ are actually states and they satisfy the transition function. For instance in the binary gossip example, we get

$$
\begin{aligned}
\textit{Invariance} :~ &\forall x \in \mathcal{X}, \forall a \in A,~ C(a(x)) \leq C(x) \text{ is verified as} \\
&\forall a \in A,~ x' = a(x) \Rightarrow C(x') \leq C(x). \\
\equiv~ &\forall i, j \in [N],~ x' = step(i,j)(x) \Rightarrow Sum(x') \leq Sum(x). \\
\textit{Progress} :~ &\forall x \in \mathcal{X}, \exists a \in A,~ C(x) \neq \bot \Rightarrow C(a(x)) < C(x) \\
\text{is verified as}~ &C(x) \neq 0 \\
&\Rightarrow \exists i, j \in [N], x' = step(i,j)(x) \wedge Sum(x)' < Sum(x). \\
\textit{Noninterference} :~ &\forall x \in \mathcal{X}, \forall a, b \in A,~ (C(a(x)) < C(x) \equiv C(a(b(x))) < C(x)) \\
\text{is verified as}~ &\forall i, j, k, l \in [N],~ x' = step(i,j)(x) \wedge x'' = step(k,l)(x) \\
&\wedge x''' = step(i,j)(x'') \Rightarrow (C(x') < C(x) \Rightarrow C(x''') < C(x)).
\end{aligned}
$$

*Interaction graphs.* In distributed algorithms, the underlying network topology dictates which pairs of nodes can interact, and therefore the set of actions. We need to be able to specify the available set of actions in a way that is in the format demanded by the small-model theorem. In this paper we focus on specific classes of graphs like complete graphs, star graphs, rings, $k$-regular graphs, and $k$-partite complete graphs, as we know how to capture these constraints using predicates in the requisite form. For instance, we use *edge predicates* $E(i,j)$ : $i$ and $j$ are node indices, and the predicate is true if there is an undirected edge between them in the interaction graph. For a complete graph, $E(i,j) = true$. In the Binary Gossip example, the interaction graph is a ring, and $E(i,j) = (i < N \wedge j = i+1) \vee (i > 1 \wedge j = i - 1) \vee i = 1 \wedge j = N)$. If the graph is a $d$-regular graph, we express use $d$ arrays, $reg_1, \ldots, reg_d$, where $\exists i, reg_i[k] = l$ if there is an edge between $k$ and $l$, and $i \neq j \equiv reg_i[k] \neq reg_j[k]$. This only expresses that the degree of each vertex is $d$, but there is no information about the connectivity of the graph. For that, we can have a separate index-valued array which satisfies certain constraints if the graph is connected. These constraints need to be expressed in a format satisfying the small model property as well. Other graph predicates can be introduced based on the model requirements, for instance, $Parent(i,j)$, $Child(i,j)$, $Direction(i,j)$. In our case studies we verify stabilization under the assumption that all pairs of nodes in $E$ interact infinitely often. For the progress condition, the formula simplifies to $\exists a \in A, C(x) \neq \bot \Rightarrow C(a(x)) < C(x)$. More general fairness constraints can be encoded in the same way as we encode graph constraints.

# 4    Case Studies

In this section, we will present the details of applying our strategy to various distributed algorithms. We begin by defining some predicates that are used in our case studies. Recall that we want wanted to check the conditions of Theorem 1 using the transformation outlined in Section 3.3 involving $x, x'$ etc., representing the states of a distributed system that are related by the transitions. These conditions are encoded using the following predicates, which we illustrate using the binary gossip example given in Section 2:

- $isState(x)$ returns true iff the array variable $x$ represents a state of the system. In the binary gossip example, $isState(x) = \forall i \in [N], x[i] = 0 \vee x[i] = 1$.
- $isAction(a)$ returns true iff $a$ is a valid action for the system. Again, for the binary gossip example $isAction(step(i,j)) = $ True for all $i, j \in [N]$ in the case of a complete communication graph.
- $isTransition(x, step(i,j), x')$ returns true iff the state $x$ goes to $x'$ when the transition function for action $step(i,j)$ is applied to it. In case of the binary gossip example, $isTransition(x, step(i,j), x')$ is

$$(x'[j] = x'[i] = x[i] \vee x[j]) \wedge (\forall p,\ p \notin \{i,j\} \Rightarrow x[p] = x'[p]).$$

- Combining the above predicates, we define $P(x, x', i, j)$ as

$$isState(x) \wedge isState(x') \wedge isTransition(x, step(i,j), x') \wedge isAction(step(i,j)).$$

Using these constructions, we rewrite the conditions of Theorem 1 as follows:

$$Invariance:\ \forall i, j,\ P(x, x', i, j) \Rightarrow C(x') \leq C(x). \tag{1}$$

$$Progress:\ C(x) \neq \bot \Rightarrow \exists i, j,\ P(x, x', i, j) \wedge C(x') < C(x). \tag{2}$$

$$Noninterference:\ \forall p, r, s, t,\ P(x, x', p, q) \wedge P(x, x'', s, t) \wedge P(x'', x''', p, q)$$
$$\Rightarrow (C(x') < C(x) \Rightarrow C(x''') < C(x)). \tag{3}$$

$$Minimality:\ C(x) = \bot \Rightarrow x \in X^*. \tag{4}$$

## 4.1    Graph Coloring

This algorithm colors a given graph in $d + 1$ colors, where $d$ is the maximum degree of a vertex in the graph [10]. Two nodes are said to have a conflict if they have the same color. A transition is made by choosing a single vertex, and if it has a conflict with any of its neighbors, then it sets its own state to be the least available value which is *not* the state of any of its neighbours. We want to verify that the system stabilizes to a state with no conflicts. The measure function is chosen as the set of pairs with conflicts.

```
Automaton Coloring[N : N]
type indices  :  [N]
type  values  :  {1,..., N}
variables
        x[indices ↦ values]
transitions
        internal step(i: indices)
        pre ∃j ∈ [N](E(j, i) ∧ x[j] = x[i])
        eff x[i] = min(values \{c | j ∈ [N] ∧ E(i, j) ∧ x[j] = c})
measure
        func C : x ↦ {(i, j) | E(i, j) ∧ x[i] = x[j]}
```

Here, the ordering on the image of the measure function is set inclusion.

$$Invariance : \forall i \in [N], \; P(x, x', i) \Rightarrow C(x') \subseteq C(x). \qquad \text{(From (1))}$$
$$\equiv \forall i, j, k \in [N], \; P(x, x', i) \Rightarrow ((j, k) \in C(x')$$
$$\Rightarrow (j, k) \in C(x)).$$
$$\equiv \forall i, j, k \in [N], \; P(x, x', i)$$
$$\Rightarrow (E(j, k) \wedge x[j] \neq x[k] \Rightarrow x'[j] \neq x'[k]).$$

(E is the set of edges in the underlying graph)

$$Progress : \exists m \in [N], \; C(x) \neq \emptyset \Rightarrow C(step(m)(x)) < C(x).$$
$$\equiv \forall i, j \in [N], \exists m, n \in [N], \; (E(i, j) \wedge x[i] \neq x[j]) \vee$$
$$(P(x, x', m) \wedge E(m, n) \wedge x[m] = x[n] \wedge x'[m] \neq x'[n]).$$

$$Noninterference : \forall q, r, s, t \in [N], \; (P(x, x', q) \wedge P(x, x'', s) \wedge P(x'', x''', q))$$
$$\Rightarrow (E(q, r) \wedge x[q] = x[r] \wedge x'[q] \neq x'[r] \Rightarrow E(s, t)$$
$$\wedge (x'[s] \neq x'[t] \Rightarrow x'''[s] \neq x'''[t]) \wedge x'''[r] \neq x'''[q])).$$

(from (3 and expansion of ordering)

$$Minimality : \; C(x) = \emptyset \Rightarrow x \in X^*.$$

From the above conditions, using Theorem 2 $N_0$ is calculated to be 24.

## 4.2   Leader Election

This algorithm is a modified version of the Chang-Roberts leader election algorithm [10]. We apply Theorem 1 directly by defining a straightforward measure function. The state of each node in the network consists of a) its own uid, b) the index and uid of its proposed candidate, and c) the status of the election according to the node (0 : the node itself is elected, 1 : the node is not the leader, 2 : the node is still waiting for the election to finish). A node $i$ communicates its state to its clockwise neighbor $j$ ($i + 1$ if $i < N$, 0 otherwise) and if the UID of $i$'s proposed candidate is greater than $j$, then $j$ is out of the running. The proposed candidate for each node is itself to begin with. When a node gets back its own index and uid, it sets its election status to 0. This status, and the correct leader identity propagates through the network, and we want to verify that the system stabilizes to a state where a leader is elected. The measure function is the number of nodes with state 0.

```
Automaton Leader[N : N]
type indices    : [N]
variables
          uid[indices ↦ [N]]
          candidate[indices ↦ [N]]
          leader[indices ↦ {0,1,2}]
transitions
          internal step(i: indices, j: indices)
          pre leader[i] = 1 ∧ uid[candidate[i]] > uid[candidate[j]]
          eff leader[j] = 1 ∧ candidate[j] = candidate[i]
          pre leader[j] = 2 ∧ candidate[i] = j
          eff leader[j] = 0 ∧ candidate[j] = j
          pre leader[i] = 0
          eff leader[j] = 1 ∧ candidate[j] = i
measure
          func C : x ↦ Sum(x.leader[i])
```

The function $Sum()$ represents the sum of all elements in the array, and it can be updated when a transition happens by just looking at the interacting nodes. We encode the sufficient conditions for stabilization of this algorithm using the strategy outlined in Section 3.2.

$$Invariance : \forall i, j \in [N], \ P(x, x', i, j) \Rightarrow (Sum(x'.leader) \leq Sum(x.leader)).$$

$$\equiv \forall i, j \in [N], \ (P(x, x', i, j) \Rightarrow (Sum(x.leader) - x.leader[i] - x.leader[j] + x'.leader[i] + x'.leader[j] \leq Sum(x.leader)).$$

(difference only due to interacting nodes)

$$\equiv \forall i, j \in [N], \ P(x, x', i, j)$$
$$\Rightarrow (x'.leader[i] + x'.leader[j] \leq x.leader[i] + x.leader[j])$$

$$Progress : \exists m, n \in [N], \ Sum(x.leader) \neq N - 1$$
$$\Rightarrow Sum(step(m, n)(x).leader) < Sum(x.leader)).$$

$$\equiv \forall p \in [N], x.leader[p] = 2 \Rightarrow$$
$$\exists m, n \in [N], \ (P(x, x', m, n) \wedge E(m, n) \wedge$$
$$x'.leader[m] + x'.leader[n] < x.leader[m] + x.leader[n]).$$

(one element still waiting for election to end)

$$Noninterference : \forall q, r, s, t \in [N], \ P(x, x', q, r) \wedge P(x, x'', s, t) \wedge P(x'', x''', q, r)$$
$$\Rightarrow (x'[q] + x'[r] < x[q] + x[r]$$
$$\Rightarrow (x'''[q] + x'''[r] + x'''[s] + x'''[t] < x[q] + x[r] + x[s] + x[t])).$$

(expanding out $Sum$)

$$Minimality : C(x) = N - 1 \Rightarrow x \in X^*.$$

From the above conditions, using Theorem 2, $N_0$ is calculated to be 35.

## 4.3   Shortest Path

This algorithm computes the shortest path to every node in a graph from a root node. It is a simplified version of the Chandy-Misra shortest path algorithm [10]. We are allowed to distinguish the nodes with indices 1 or $N$ in the formula structure specified by Theorem 2. The state of the node represents the distance from the root node. The root node (index 1) has state 0. Each pair of neighboring nodes communicates their states to each other, and if one of them has a lesser value $v$, then the one with the larger value updates its state to $v + 1$. This stabilizes to a state where all nodes have the shortest distance from the root stored in their state. We don't have an explicit value of $\perp$ for the measure function for this, but it can be seen that we don't need it in this case. Let the interaction graph be a $d-$regular graph. The measure function is the sum of distances.

```
Automaton Shortest[N : ℕ]
type indices : [N]
type  values : {1,...,N}
variables
        x[indices ↦ values]
transitions
        internal step(i: indices, j: indices)
        pre x[j] > x[i] + 1
        eff x[j] = x[i] + 1
        pre x[i] = 0
        eff x[j] = 1
measure
        func C : x ↦ Sum(x[i])
```

Ordering on the image of measure function is the usual one on natural numbers.

$$Invariance : \forall i, j \in [N], \ P(x, x', i, j) \Rightarrow Sum(x') \leq Sum(x).$$
$$\equiv \forall, j \in [N], \ P(x, x', i, j)$$
$$\Rightarrow Sum(x) - x[i] - x[j] + x'[i] + x'[j] \leq Sum(x).$$
$$\equiv \forall i, j \in [N], \ P(x, x', i, j) \Rightarrow x'[i] + x'[j] \leq x[i] + x[j].$$
$$Progress : \exists m, n \in [N], \ C(x) \neq \perp \Rightarrow P(x, x', m, n) \wedge Sum(x)' < Sum(x).$$
$$\equiv \forall k, l \in [N], \ (E(k, l) \Rightarrow x[k] \leq x[l] + 1)$$
$$\vee \exists m, n \in [N](P(x, x', m, n) \wedge E(m, n)$$
$$\wedge x[m] + x[n] > x'[m] + x'[n]).$$
$$(C(x) = \perp \text{ if there is no pair of neighboring}$$
$$\text{vertices more than 1 distance apart from each other })$$
$$Noninterference : \forall q, r, s, t \in [N], \ P(x, x', q, r) \wedge P(x, x'', s, t) \wedge P(x', x'', q, r)$$
$$\Rightarrow (x'[q] + x'[r] < x[q] + x[r]$$
$$\Rightarrow (x'''[q] + x'''[r] + x'''[s] + x'''[t] < x[q] + x[r] + x[s] + x[t])).$$
$$Minimality : \ C(x) \neq \perp \Rightarrow x \in X^*$$
$$\equiv \forall i, j(E(i, j) \Rightarrow x[i] - x[j] \leq 1 \Rightarrow x \in X^*) \quad \text{(definition)}$$

$N_0$ is $7(d + 1)$ where the graph is $d$-regular.

## 4.4   Link Reversal

We describe the full link reversal algorithm as presented by Gafni and Bertsekas in [19], where, given a directed graph with a distinguished sink vertex, it outputs a graph in which there is a path from every vertex to the sink. There is a distinguished sink node(index N). Any other node which detects that it has only incoming edges, reverses the direction of all its edges with its neighbours. We use the vector of reversal distances (the least number of edges required to be reversed for a node to have a path to the sink, for termination. The states store the reversal distances, and the measure function is identity.

```
Automaton Reversal[N : ℕ]
type    indices : [N]
type    values  : [N]
variables
        x[indices ↦ values]
transitions
        internal step(i: indices)
        pre  i ≠ N ∧ ∀j ∈ [N](E(i,j) ∧ (direction(i,j) = −1)
        eff  ∀j ∈ [N](E(i,j) ⇒ (Reverse(i,j)) ∧ x(i) = min(x(j)))
measure
        func C: x ↦ x
```

The ordering on the image of the measure function is component-wise comparison:

$$V_1 < V_2 \Leftrightarrow \forall i(V_1[i] < V_2[i])$$

We mentioned earlier that the image of $C$ has a well-ordering. That is a condition formulated with the idea of continuous spaces in mind. The proposed ordering for this problem works because the image of the measure function is discrete and has a lower bound (specifically, $0^N$). We elaborate a bit on $P$ here, because it needs to include the condition that the reversal distances are calculated accurately. The node $N$ has reversal distance 0. Any other node has reversal distance $rd(i) = min(rd(j_1), \ldots rd(j_m), rd(k_1) + 1, \ldots rd(k_n) + 1)$ where $j_p(p = 1 \ldots m)$ are the nodes to which it has outgoing edges, and $k_q(q = 1 \ldots n)$ are the nodes it has incoming edges from. $P$ also needs to include the condition that in a transition, reversal distances of no other nodes apart from the transitioning nodes change. The interaction graph in this example is complete.

$$Invariance: \forall i, j \in [N], \ P(x, x', i) \Rightarrow x'[j] \leq x[j] \quad \text{(ordering)}$$
$$Progress: \exists m \in [N], \ C(x) \neq \bot \Rightarrow (C(step(m)(x)) < C(x)).$$
$$\equiv \forall n \in [N], \ (x[n] = 0) \vee \exists m \in [N](P(x, x', m) \wedge x'[m] < x[m]).$$
$$Noninterference: \forall i, j \in [N], \ P(x, x', i) \wedge P(x', x'', j) \wedge P(x', x''', i)$$
$$\Rightarrow (x'[i] < x[i] \wedge x'''[i] < x[i]). \quad \text{(decreasing measure)}$$
$$Minimality: \ C(x) = 0^N \Rightarrow x \in X^*.$$

From the above conditions, using Theorem 2, $N_0$ is calculated to be 21.

## 5   Experiments and Discussion

We verified that instances of the aforementioned systems with sizes less than the small model parameter $N_0$ satisfy the four conditions(*invariance, progress, non-interference, minimality*) of Theorem 1 using the Z3 SMT-solver [4]. The models are checked by symbolic execution.

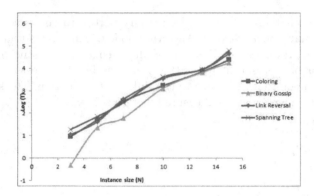

**Fig. 1.** Instance size vs $\log_{10}(T)$, where T is the running time in seconds

The interaction graphs were complete graphs in all the experiments. In Figure 5, the $x$-axis represents the problem instance sizes, and the $y$-axis is the log of the running time (in seconds) for verifying Theorem 1 for the different algorithms. [2]

We observe that the running times grow rapidly with the increase in the model sizes. For the binary gossip example, the program completes in $\sim 17$ seconds for a model size 7, which is the $N_0$ value. In case of the link reversal, for a model size 13, the program completes in $\sim 30$ mins. We have used complete graphs in all our experiments, but as we mentioned earlier in Section 3.2, we can encode more general graphs as well. This method is a general approach to automated verification of stabilization properties of distributed algorithms under specific fairness constraints, and structural constraints on graphs. The small model nature of the conditions to be verified is crucial to the success of this approach. We saw that many distributed graph algorithms, routing algorithms and symmetry-breaking algorithms can be verified using the techniques discussed in this paper. The problem of finding a suitable measure function which satisfies Theorem 2, is indeed a non-trivial one in itself, however, for the problems we study, the natural measure function of the algorithms seems to work.

# References

1. Dolev, S.: Self-stabilization. MIT Press (2000)
2. Tsitsiklis, J.N.: On the stability of asynchronous iterative processes. Mathematical Systems Theory 20(1), 137–153 (1987)
3. Johnson, T.T., Mitra, S.: A small model theorem for rectangular hybrid automata networks. In: Giese, H., Rosu, G. (eds.) FMOODS/FORTE 2012. LNCS, vol. 7273, pp. 18–34. Springer, Heidelberg (2012)
4. de Moura, L., Bjørner, N.: Z3: An efficient SMT solver. In: Ramakrishnan, C.R., Rehof, J. (eds.) TACAS 2008. LNCS, vol. 4963, pp. 337–340. Springer, Heidelberg (2008)

---

[2] The code is available at
http://web.engr.illinois.edu/rghosh9/code.

5. Dijkstra, E.W.: Self-stabilization in spite of distributed control. In: Selected Writings on Computing: A Personal Perspective, pp. 41–46. Springer (1982)
6. Theel, O.: Exploitation of ljapunov theory for verifying self-stabilizing algorithms. In: Herlihy, M. (ed.) DISC 2000. LNCS, vol. 1914, pp. 209–222. Springer, Heidelberg (2000)
7. Oehlerking, J., Dhama, A., Theel, O.: Towards automatic convergence verification of self-stabilizing algorithms. In: Tixeuil, S., Herman, T. (eds.) SSS 2005. LNCS, vol. 3764, pp. 198–213. Springer, Heidelberg (2005)
8. Theel, O.E.: A new verification technique for self-stabilizing distributed algorithms based on variable structure systems and lyapunov theory. In: HICSS (2001)
9. Dhama, A., Theel, O.: A tranformational approach for designing scheduler-oblivious self-stabilizing algorithms. In: Dolev, S., Cobb, J., Fischer, M., Yung, M. (eds.) SSS 2010. LNCS, vol. 6366, pp. 80–95. Springer, Heidelberg (2010)
10. Ghosh, S.: Distributed systems: an algorithmic approach. CRC Press (2010)
11. Umeno, S., Lynch, N.: Safety verification of an aircraft landing protocol: A refinement approach. In: Bemporad, A., Bicchi, A., Buttazzo, G. (eds.) HSCC 2007. LNCS, vol. 4416, pp. 557–572. Springer, Heidelberg (2007)
12. Johnson, T.T., Mitra, S.: Invariant synthesis for verification of parameterized cyber-physical systems with applications to aerospace systems. In: Proceedings of the AIAA Infotech at Aerospace Conference (AIAA Infotech 2013), Boston, MA. AIAA (August 2013)
13. Allen Emerson, E., Kahlon, V.: Reducing model checking of the many to the few. In: McAllester, D. (ed.) CADE-17. LNCS (LNAI), vol. 1831, pp. 236–254. Springer, Heidelberg (2000)
14. Duggirala, P.S., Mitra, S.: Abstraction refinement for stability. In: 2011 IEEE/ACM International Conference on Cyber-Physical Systems (ICCPS), pp. 22–31. IEEE (2011)
15. Huth, M., Ryan, M.: Logic in Computer Science: Modelling and reasoning about systems. Cambridge University Press (2004)
16. Mitra, S.: A verification framework for hybrid systems. PhD thesis, Massachusetts Institute of Technology (2007)
17. Khalil, H.K., Grizzle, J.W.: Nonlinear systems, vol. 3. Prentice Hall, Upper Saddle River (2002)
18. Dershowitz, N.: Termination of rewriting. Journal of Symbolic Computation 3(1), 69–115 (1987)
19. Gafni, E.M., Bertsekas, D.P.: Distributed algorithms for generating loop-free routes in networks with frequently changing topology. IEEE Transactions on Communications 29(1), 11–18 (1981)

# Faster Linearizability Checking
# via $P$-Compositionality

Alex Horn[(⊠)] and Daniel Kroening

University of Oxford, Oxford, UK
alex.horn@cs.ox.ac.uk

**Abstract.** Linearizability is a well-established consistency and correctness criterion for concurrent data types. An important feature of linearizability is Herlihy and Wing's locality principle, which says that a concurrent system is linearizable if and only if all of its constituent parts (so-called objects) are linearizable. This paper presents $P$-compositionality, which generalizes the idea behind the locality principle to operations on the same concurrent data type. We implement $P$-compositionality in a novel linearizability checker. Our experiments with over nine implementations of concurrent sets, including Intel's TBB library, show that our linearizability checker is one order of magnitude faster and/or more space efficient than the state-of-the-art algorithm.

## 1 Introduction

*Linearizability* [1] is a well-established correctness criterion for concurrent data types and it corresponds to one of the three desirable properties of a distributed system, namely *consistency* [2]. The intuition behind linearizability is that every operation on a concurrent data type is guaranteed to take effect instantaneously at some point between its call and return.

The significance of linearizability for contemporary distributed key/value stores has been highlighted recently by the *Jepsen* project, an extensive case study into the correctness of distributed systems.[1] Interestingly, Jepsen found linearizability bugs in several distributed key/value stores despite the fact that they were designed based on formally verified distributed consensus protocols. This illustrates that there is often a gap between the design and the implementation of distributed systems. This gap motivates the study in this paper into runtime verification techniques (in the form of so-called *linearizability checkers*) for finding linearizability bugs in a single run of a concurrent system.

The input to a linearizability checker consists of a sequential specification of a data type and a certain partially ordered set of operations, called a *history*. A history represents a single terminating run of a concurrent system. We assume

---

This work is funded by a gift from Intel Corporation for research on Effective Validation of Firmware and the ERC project ERC 280053.

[1] https://aphyr.com/posts/316-call-me-maybe-etcd-and-consul

that the concurrent system is deadlock-free since there already exist good deadlock detection tools. Despite the restriction to single histories, the problem of checking linearizability is NP-complete [3]. This high computational complexity means that writing an efficient linearizability checker is inherently difficult. The problem is to find ways of pruning a huge search space: in the worst case, its size is $O(N!)$ where $N$ is the length of the run of a concurrent system.

This paper presents a novel linearizability checker that efficiently prunes the search space by partitioning it into independent, faster to solve, subproblems. To achieve this, we propose *P-compositionality* (Definition 6), a *new partitioning scheme* of which Herlihy and Wing's locality principle [1] is an instance. Recall that locality says that a concurrent system $Q$ is linearizable if and only if each concurrent object in $Q$ is linearizable. The crux of *P*-compositionality is that it generalizes the idea behind the locality principle to operations on the same concurrent object. For example, the operations on a concurrent unordered set and map are linearizable if and only if the *restriction to each key* is linearizable. This is not a consequence of Herlihy and Wing's locality principle.

In this paper, we study the pragmatics of *P*-compositionality through its implementation in a novel linearizability checker and experimental evaluation. Our implementation is based on Wing and Gong's algorithm (*WG algorithm*) [4] and a recent extension by Lowe [5]. We call Lowe's extension of Wing and Gong's algorithm the *WGL algorithm*. The idea behind the WGL algorithm is to prune states that are equivalent to an already seen state. Lowe's experiments show that the WGL algorithm can solve a significantly larger number of problem instances than the WG algorithm. We therefore use the more recent WGL algorithm as our starting point.

Our linearizability checker preserves three practical properties of the algorithms in the WG-family that we deem important. Firstly, our tool is precise, i.e., it reports no false alarms. This is particularly significant for evaluating large code bases, as effectively shown by the Jepsen project. Secondly, our tool takes as input an *executable specification* of the data type to be checked. This significantly simplifies the task of expressing the expected behaviour of a data type because one merely writes code, i.e., no expertise in formal modeling is required. Finally, our tool can be easily integrated with a range of runtime monitors to generate a history from a run of a concurrent system. This is essential to make it a viable runtime verification technique.

We experimentally evaluate our linearizability checker using nine different implementations of concurrent sets, including Intel's TBB library, as exemplars of *P*-compositionality. Our experiments show that our linearizability checker is at least one order of magnitude faster and/or more space efficient than the WGL algorithm. Overall, the results of our work can therefore dramatically increase the number of runs that can be checked for linearizability bugs in a given time budget.

The rest of this paper is organized as follows. We first formalize the problem by recalling familiar concepts (§ 2). We then present *P*-compositionality (§ 3) on which our decision procedure (§ 4) is based. We implement and experimentally

$$\text{call}_1 \overset{\textit{set}.\text{insert}(1)\colon \textbf{true}}{\vdash\!\!\!-\!\!\!-\!\!\!-\!\!\!-\!\!\!-\!\!\!-\!\!\dashv} \text{ret}_1$$

$$\text{call}_3 \overset{\textit{set}.\text{contains}(1)\colon \textbf{true}}{\vdash\!\!\!-\!\!\!-\!\!\!-\!\!\!-\!\!\!-\!\!\!-\!\!\dashv} \text{ret}_3$$

$$\text{call}_2 \overset{\textit{set}.\text{remove}(1)\colon \textbf{false}}{\vdash\!\!\!-\!\!\!-\!\!\!-\!\!\!-\!\!\!-\!\!\!-\!\!\dashv} \text{ret}_2$$

**Fig. 1.** A history diagram $H_1$ for the operations on a concurrent set

evaluate our decision procedure (§ 5). Finally, we discuss related work (§ 6) and conclude the paper (§ 7).

## 2  Background

We recall familiar concepts that are fundamental to everything that follows.

**Definition 1 (History).** *Let* $E \triangleq \{\text{call}, \text{ret}\} \times \mathbb{N}$. *For all natural numbers* $n$ *in* $\mathbb{N}$, $\text{call}_n \triangleq \langle\text{call}, n\rangle$ *in* $E$ *is called a* **call** *and* $\text{ret}_n \triangleq \langle\text{ret}, n\rangle$ *in* $E$ *is called a* **return**. *The invocation of a procedure with input and output arguments is called an* **operation**. *An* **object** *comprises a finite set of such operations. For all* $e$ *in* $E$, $obj(e)$ *and* $op(e)$ *denote the object and operation of* $e$, *respectively. A* **history** *is a tuple* $\langle H, obj, op \rangle$ *where* $H$ *is a finite sequence of calls and returns, totally ordered by* $\preceq_H$. *When no ambiguity arises, we simply write* $H$ *for a history. We write* $|H|$ *for the* **length** *of* $H$.

Intuitively, a history $H$ records a particular run of a concurrent system. Using the implicitly associated functions $obj$ and $op$, a history $H$ gives relevant information on all operations performed at runtime, and the sequence of calls and returns in $H$ give the relative points in time at which an operation started and completed with respect to other operations. This can be visualized using the familiar history diagrams [1], as illustrated next.

*Example 1.*  Consider a concurrent set with the usual operations: 'insert' adds an element to a set, whereas 'remove' does the opposite, and 'contains' checks membership. The return value indicates the success of the operation. For example, '$set$.remove(1): **true**' denotes the operation that successfully removed '1' from the object '$set$', whereas '$set$.remove(1): **false**' denotes the operation that did not modify '$set$' because '1' is already not in the set. Then the history diagram in Fig. 1 can be defined by $H_1 = \langle\text{call}_1, \text{call}_2, \text{ret}_1, \text{ret}_2, \text{call}_3, \text{ret}_3\rangle$ such that, for all $1 \leq i \leq 3$, $obj(\text{call}_i) = obj(\text{ret}_i) = \text{'}set\text{'}$, and the following holds:

- $op(\text{call}_1) = op(\text{ret}_1) = \text{'insert}(1)\colon \textbf{true'}$,
- $op(\text{call}_2) = op(\text{ret}_2) = \text{'remove}(1)\colon \textbf{false'}$,
- $op(\text{call}_3) = op(\text{ret}_3) = \text{'contains}(1)\colon \textbf{true'}$.

Note that $|H_1| = 6$ and the total ordering $\preceq_{H_1}$ satisfies, among other constraints, $\text{ret}_1 \preceq_{H_1} \text{call}_3$ because $\text{ret}_1$ precedes $\text{call}_3$ in the sequence $H_1$.

Henceforth, we draw diagrams as in Fig. 1. Linearizability is ultimately defined in terms of sequential histories, in the following sense:

**Definition 2 (Complete and Sequential History).** *Let $e, e' \in E$ and $H$ be a history. If $e$ is a call and $e'$ is a return in $H$, both are **matching** whenever $e \preceq_H e'$ and their objects and operations are equal, i.e. $obj(e) = obj(e')$ and $op(e) = op(e')$. A history is called **complete** if every call has a unique matching return. A complete history is called **sequential** whenever it alternates between matching calls and returns (necessarily starting with a call).*

*Example 2.* The following history $H_2$ is sequential:

$$\underset{\vdash\!\!-\!\!-\!\!-\!\!\dashv}{\text{remove}(1): \textbf{false}} \quad \underset{\vdash\!\!-\!\!-\!\!-\!\!\dashv}{\text{insert}(1): \textbf{true}} \quad \underset{\vdash\!\!-\!\!-\!\!-\!\!\dashv}{\text{contains}(1): \textbf{true}}$$

And so is $H_3$ that we get when we swap the first two operations in $H_2$ (although the resulting sequence of operations is not what we would expect from a sequential set, as discussed next):

$$\underset{\vdash\!\!-\!\!-\!\!-\!\!\dashv}{\text{insert}(1): \textbf{true}} \quad \underset{\vdash\!\!-\!\!-\!\!-\!\!\dashv}{\text{remove}(1): \textbf{false}} \quad \underset{\vdash\!\!-\!\!-\!\!-\!\!\dashv}{\text{contains}(1): \textbf{true}}$$

$H_3$ in Example 2 illustrates that a history can be sequential even though it may not satisfy the expected sequential behaviour of the data type. This is addressed by the following definition:

**Definition 3 (Specification).** *A **specification**, denoted by $\phi$ (possibly with a subscript), is a unary predicate on sequential histories.*

*Example 3.* Define $\phi_{set}$ to be the specification of a sequential finite set. This means that, given a sequential history $S$ according to Definition 2, the predicate $\phi_{set}(S)$ holds if and only if the input and output of 'insert', 'remove' and 'contains' in $S$ are consistent with the operations on a set. For example, $\phi_{set}(H_2) = \textbf{true}$, whereas $\phi_{set}(H_3) = \textbf{false}$ for the histories from Example 2.

*Remark 1.* In the upcoming decision procedure (§ 4), every $\phi$ is an *executable specification*. Informally, this is achieved by 'replaying' all operations in a sequential history $S$ in the order in which they appear in $S$. If in any step the output deviates from the expected result, the executable specification returns false; otherwise, if it reaches the end of $S$, it returns true.

The next definition will be key to answer which calls may be reordered in a history in order to satisfy a specification.

**Definition 4 (Happens-before).** *Given a history $H$, the **happens-before** relation is defined to be a partial order $<_H$ over calls $e$ and $e'$ such that $e <_H e'$ whenever $e$'s matching return, denoted by $\text{ret}(e)$, precedes $e'$ in $H$, i.e. $\text{ret}(e) \preceq_H e'$. We say that two calls $e$ and $e'$ **happen concurrently** whenever $e \nless_H e'$ and $e' \nless_H e$.*

*Example 4.* For the history $H_1$ in Fig. 1, we get:

- $\text{call}_1 <_{H_1} \text{call}_3$ and $\text{call}_2 <_{H_1} \text{call}_3$, i.e. $\text{call}_1$ and $\text{call}_2$ happen-before $\text{call}_3$;
- $\text{call}_1 \not<_{H_1} \text{call}_2$ and $\text{call}_2 \not<_{H_1} \text{call}_1$, i.e. $\text{call}_1$ and $\text{call}_2$ happen concurrently.

Note that a history $H$ is sequential if and only if $<_H$ is a total order. More generally, $<_H$ is an interval order [6]: for every $x, y, u, v$ in $H$, if $x <_H y$ and $u <_H v$, then $x <_H v$ or $u <_H y$. Observe that a partial order $\langle P, \leq \rangle$ is an interval order if and only if no restriction of $\langle P, \leq \rangle$ is isomorphic to the following Hasse diagram [7]:

Put differently, this paper is about a decision procedure (§ 4) that concerns a certain class of partial orders. The decision problem rests on the next definition:

**Definition 5 (Linearizability).** *Let $\phi$ be a specification. A $\phi$-sequential history is a sequential history $H$ that satisfies $\phi(H)$. A history $H$ is **linearizable with respect to** $\phi$ if it can be extended to a complete history $H'$ (by appending zero or more returns) and there is a $\phi$-sequential history $S$ with the same obj and op functions as $H'$ such that*

**L1** *$H'$ and $S$ are equal when seen as two sets of calls and returns;*
**L2** *$<_H \subseteq <_S$, i.e. for all calls $e, e'$ in $H$, if $e$ happens-before $e'$, the same is true in $S$.*

Informally, extending $H$ to $H'$ means that all pending operations have completed. This paper therefore considers only complete histories. This is fully justified under our stated assumption (§ 1) that the concurrent system is deadlock-free [5]. Condition **L1** means that $H'$ and $S$ are identical if we disregard the order in which calls and returns occur in both sequences. Condition **L2** says that the happens-before relation between calls in $H$ must be preserved in $S$.

*Example 5.* Recall Example 3. Then $H_1$ in Fig. 1 is linearizable with respect to $\phi_{set}$ because $H_2$ is a witness for a $\phi_{set}$-sequential history that respects the happens-before relation $<_{H_1}$ detailed in Example 4. In particular, $\text{call}_1 <_{H_1} \text{call}_3$ and $\text{call}_2 <_{H_1} \text{call}_3$ cannot be reordered.

## 3   P-compositionality

In this section, we introduce $P$-compositionality. We illustrate our new partitioning scheme in Examples 7–9.

**Definition 6 (P-compositionality).** *Let $P$ be a function that maps a history $H$ to a non-trivial partition of $H$, i.e. $P$ satisfies $P(H) \neq \{H\}$. A specification $\phi$ is called **P-compositional** whenever any history $H$ is linearizable with respect to $\phi$ if and only if, for every history $H' \in P(H)$, $H'$ is linearizable with respect to $\phi$. When this equivalence holds we speak of **P-compositionality**.*

In the following examples, we assume that the partitions are non-trivial. The first example illustrates that the locality principle [1] is an instance of *P*-compositionality.

*Example 6.* Denote with *Obj* the set of objects. Let $\phi$ be a specification for all objects in *Obj*. Let $P_{Obj}$ be the function that maps every history $H$ to the set of histories $\mathcal{H}$ where each sub-history $H' \in \mathcal{H}$ is the restriction of $H$ to an object in *Obj*. Then $P_{Obj}(H)$ is a partition of $H$. By the locality principle [1], a history $H$ is linearizable with respect to $\phi$ if and only if, for all $H_{obj} \in P_{Obj}(H)$, $H_{obj}$ is linearizable with respect to $\phi$. Therefore $\phi$ is a $P_{Obj}$-compositional specification.

The remaining examples show that *P*-compositionality strictly generalizes the locality principle because *P*-compositionality can partition a history even if the implementation details or constituent parts (i.e. objects) of a concurrent system are unknown. For example, there are at least eight different implementations of concurrent sets (Table 2), but we do not need to know the objects (e.g. registers, buckets) of which such implementations consist in order to partition one of their histories. This is in contrast to the locality principle where such knowledge is required. Put differently, *P*-compositionality is all about the *interface* of a concurrent data type, whereas the locality principle hinges on the *implementation details* of such an interface.

*Example 7.* Reconsider $\phi_{set}$, the specification of a set from Example 3, where all operations have the form insert$(k)$, remove$(k)$ and contains$(k)$ for some $k$. Let $P_{set}$ be the function that partitions every history $H$ according to such $k$. Since the 'insert', 'remove' and 'contains' operations on a single set object are linearizable if and only if the restriction to each $k$ is linearizable, $\phi_{set}$ is a $P_{set}$-compositional specification of a set.

Similarly, there exists a $P_{map}$-compositional specification for concurrent unordered maps where every history is partitioned by each key $k$.

*Example 8.* Consider a concurrent array. As their sequential counterparts, a concurrent array can be only read or written at a particular array index. Let $P_{array}$ be the function that partitions a history based on such array indexes. This gives a $P_{array}$-compositional specification of an array.

*Example 9.* Consider a concurrent stack where each pop and push operation also returns the height of the stack before it is modified. Among other things, the return value can be used to determine whether the operation has succeeded. For example, if *stack*.pop returns zero, we know the pop operation was unsuccessful (and the popped element is undefined) because the stack was empty at the time the operation was called. We can use the returned height to partition a history such that a concurrent stack is linearizable if and only if each partition is linearizable. This way we get a $P_{stack}$-compositional specification of a stack.

Intuitively, the reason why the previous specifications are *P*-compositional is because all operations in one partition are, informally speaking, unaffected by all operations in every other partition. For example, the return value of $set.\text{insert}(k)$ is unaffected by $set.\text{insert}(k')$, $set.\text{remove}(k')$ and $set.\text{contains}(k')$ for $k \neq k'$. This clearly, however, has its limitations. For example, a 'size' operation that returns the number of elements in a concurrent collection data type cannot be generally partitioned this way.

Note that all these examples have in common that their $P$-compositional specifications can be expressed as a conjunction of specifications that each partition a history. For example, $\phi_{set} = \bigwedge_{k \in K} \phi_{set(k)}$ where $\phi_{set(k)}$ for every $k$ is a sequential specification that only concerns operations on $k$, e.g. $set.\text{insert}(k)$.

Next, we show how to leverage the concept of $P$-compositionality to more efficiently find linearizability bugs.

## 4　Decision Procedure

In this section, we explain our linearizability checking algorithm that decides whether a history is linearizable with respect to some $P$-compositional specification (Definition 6). The novelty of our decision procedure is Algorithm 3 that leverages $P$-compositionality. In the next section (§ 5), we experimentally evaluate the effectiveness of Algorithm 3.

Since we base our work on the WGL algorithm (recall § 1), we use the following data structures to represent the input to the decision procedure:

1. The specification (Definition 3) is modelled by a persistent data structure, e.g. [8]. Most standard data types in functional programming languages can be almost directly used this way. For instance, the specification of a set can be modelled through an immutable sequential set.
2. A history (Definition 1), in turn, is represented by a doubly-linked list of so-called **entries**. Consequently, each entry $e$ has a $e.\text{next}$ and $e.\text{prev}$ field that point to the next and previous entry, respectively. In addition, each entry $e$ has a match field, and we say that $e$ is a **call entry** exactly if $e.\text{match} \neq \textbf{null}$; otherwise, $e$ is called a **return entry**. Given a call entry $e$, $e.\text{match}$ corresponds to the **matching return entry** of $e$. This linked-list data structure therefore aligns directly with the usual definition of history (Definition 1).

The idea behind the WGL Algorithm 1 is threefold: it keeps track of provisionally linearized call entries in a stack; it uses the stack to backtrack if necessary, and caches already seen configurations. We briefly explain each idea in turn. Denote the stack of call entries by calls. Given a history $H$, the height of calls is at most half of $H$'s length, i.e. $|\text{calls}| \leq 0.5 \times |H| = N$. Note that there is no rounding involved because $|H|$ is always even since every call entry has a matching return entry. The height of the stack grows only if a call entry can be linearized (line 5). When the stack grows or shrinks, the history is modified (lines 13 and 23) by the LIFT and UNLIFT procedures (Algorithm 2). We remark that the workings of both procedures are illustrated by Example 10. If no further call entries can be linearized but the stack is nonempty, the algorithm backtracks and tries the next possible call entry (lines 18–24). The backtracking

---

**Algorithm 1.** WGL linearizability checker [5]

---

**Require:** head_entry is such that head_entry.next points to the beginning of history $H$.
**Require:** $N = 0.5 \times |H|$ is half of the total number of entries reachable from head_entry.
**Require:** linearized is a bitset (array of bits) such that linearized$[k] = 0$ for all $0 \leq k < N$.
**Require:** For all entries $e$ in $H$, $0 \leq entry\_id(e) < N$.
**Require:** For all entries $e$ and $e'$ in $H$, if $entry\_id(e) = entry\_id(e')$, then $e = e'$.
**Require:** cache is an empty set and calls is an empty stack.

```
 1: while head_entry.next ≠ null do
 2:     if entry.match ≠ null then                        ▷ Is call entry?
 3:         ⟨is_linearizable, s'⟩ ← apply(entry, s)       ▷ Simulate entry's operation
 4:         cache' ← cache                                ▷ Copy set
 5:         if is_linearizable then
 6:             linearized' ← linearized                  ▷ Copy bitset
 7:             linearized'[entry_id(entry)] ← 1          ▷ Insert entry_id(entry) into bitset
 8:             cache ← cache ∪ {⟨linearized', s'⟩}       ▷ Update configuration cache
 9:         if cache' ≠ cache then
10:             calls ← push(calls, ⟨entry, s⟩)  ▷ Provisionally linearize call entry and state
11:             s ← s'                                    ▷ Update state of persistent data type
12:             linearized[entry_id(entry)] ← 1           ▷ Keep track of linearized entries
13:             LIFT(entry)                    ▷ Provisionally remove the entry from the history
14:             entry ← head_entry.next                   ▷ Continue search in shortened history
15:         else                                          ▷ Cannot linearize call entry
16:             entry ← entry.next                        ▷ Continue search in unmodified history
17:     else                                              ▷ Handle "return entry"
18:         if is_empty(calls) then
19:             return false                              ▷ Cannot linearize entries in history
20:         ⟨entry, s⟩ ← top(calls)                       ▷ Revert to earlier state
21:         linearized[entry_id(entry)] ← 0
22:         calls ← pop(calls)
23:         UNLIFT(entry)                                 ▷ Undo provisional linearization
24:         entry ← entry.next
25: return true
```

---

points depend on the return value of $apply(\text{entry}, s)$ and the cache. The former (line 3) models the specification $\phi$: by Remark 1, it determines whether entry can be applied to the current state $s$ of a persistent data type. The latter (lines 4–8) is an optimization due to Lowe [5] that prunes the search space by memoizing already seen configurations which are known to be non-linearizable. More accurately, each configuration is a pair that consists of a set of unique call entry identifiers and a state of the persistent data structure. The intuition behind pruning already seen configurations is that only one of two permutations of operations on a concurrent data type need to be considered if they lead to an identical state [5]. We remark that the total correctness of the WGL algorithm follows from Wing and Gong's total correctness argument [4].

*Example 10.* We illustrate the handling of entries in the history data structure. For this, consider the two histories in Fig. 2. In Fig. 2a, the entries satisfy the following: $call_2.prev = call_1$, $call_2.next = call_3$ and $call_2.match = ret_2$ etc. Then LIFT($call_2$) (Algorithm 2) produces the history shown in Fig. 2b. Note that both $call_2$ and $ret_2$ are still valid entry pointers whose fields remain unchanged. This explains how UNLIFT($call_2$) reverts the change in constant-time.

Algorithm 3 gives our partitioning scheme. This is an iterative algorithm that, given an entry in a history $H$ and positive integer $n$, partitions $H$ starting from that entry into at most $n$ separate sub-histories. The partitioning is controlled by the function $partition: E \to \mathbb{N}$ from the set of call and return entries to the natural numbers.

*Example 11.* Consider the history in Fig. 2b. For all entries $e$ in this history, let $partition(e) = k$ where $k$ is the integer argument of the operation. For example, $partition(call_3) = partition(ret_3) = 1$ because $op(call_3) = op(ret_3) =$ 'remove(1): **false**'. Then the function PARTITION($call_1$) returns two disjoint sub-histories for the operations on '0' and '1', respectively:

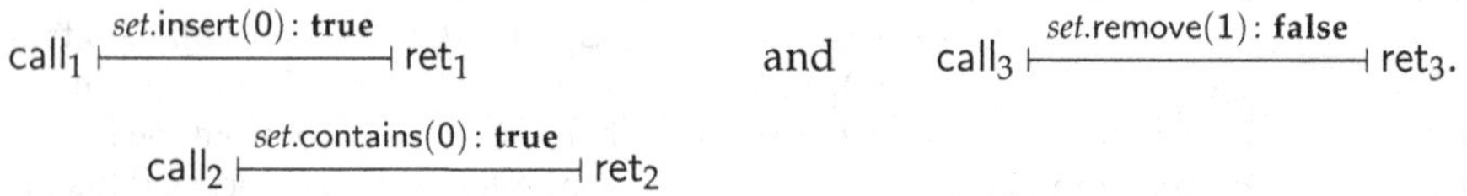

$$call_1 \underset{set.insert(0):\ \mathbf{true}}{\vdash\!\!-\!\!-\!\!-\!\!-\!\!-\!\!-\!\!\dashv} ret_1 \qquad \text{and} \qquad call_3 \underset{set.remove(1):\ \mathbf{false}}{\vdash\!\!-\!\!-\!\!-\!\!-\!\!-\!\!-\!\!\dashv} ret_3.$$

$$call_2 \underset{set.contains(0):\ \mathbf{true}}{\vdash\!\!-\!\!-\!\!-\!\!-\!\!-\!\!-\!\!\dashv} ret_2$$

Given a nonempty set of disjoint sub-histories returned by the PARTITION function (Algorithm 3), we invoke Algorithm 1 on each sub-history. It is not too difficult to implement sub-histories such that there is no sharing between them, and Algorithm 1 could be therefore run in parallel for each sub-history. Nevertheless, this addresses a challenging problem that was identified independently by Lowe [5] and Kingsbury [9].

**Theorem 1.** *Let $\phi$ be a P-compositional specification and $H$ be a history. Denote with head_entry the entry that represents the beginning of $H$. Associate with each disjoint history $H_k$ in partition $P(H)$ a unique number $0 \le k < |P(H)| = n$. If, for all $H_k \in P(H)$ and $e \in H_k$, $partition(e) = k$, then $H$ is linearizable with respect to $\phi$ if and only if Algorithm 1 returns true for every history in PARTITION(head_entry, $n$).*

We next experimentally quantify the benefits of the previous theorem.

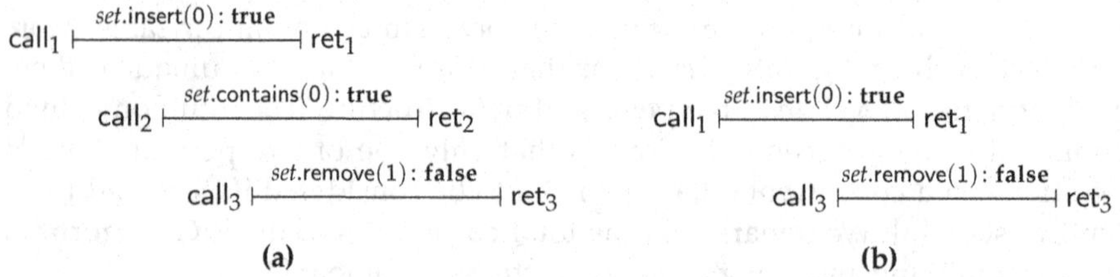

$$call_1 \underset{set.insert(0):\ \mathbf{true}}{\vdash\!\!-\!\!-\!\!-\!\!-\!\!-\!\!-\!\!\dashv} ret_1$$

$$call_2 \underset{set.contains(0):\ \mathbf{true}}{\vdash\!\!-\!\!-\!\!-\!\!-\!\!-\!\!-\!\!\dashv} ret_2 \qquad\qquad call_1 \underset{set.insert(0):\ \mathbf{true}}{\vdash\!\!-\!\!-\!\!-\!\!-\!\!-\!\!-\!\!\dashv} ret_1$$

$$call_3 \underset{set.remove(1):\ \mathbf{false}}{\vdash\!\!-\!\!-\!\!-\!\!-\!\!-\!\!-\!\!\dashv} ret_3 \qquad\qquad call_3 \underset{set.remove(1):\ \mathbf{false}}{\vdash\!\!-\!\!-\!\!-\!\!-\!\!-\!\!-\!\!\dashv} ret_3$$

**(a)**                                    **(b)**

**Fig. 2.** After calling LIFT($call_2$) in history (2a), we get the history in (2b). UNLIFT($call_2$) reverts this change in constant-time.

| **Algorithm 2.** History modifications | **Algorithm 3.** History partitioner |
|---|---|
| 1: **procedure** LIFT(entry) | **Require:** $n$ is a positive integer |
| 2:    entry.prev.next ← entry.next | **Require:** entries is an array of size $n$ |
| 3:    entry.next.prev ← entry.prev | 1: **function** PARTITION(entry, $n$) |
| 4:    match ← entry.match | 2:    **for** $0 \leq i < n$ **do** |
| 5:    match.prev.next ← match.next | 3:        entries[$i$] ← **null** |
| 6:    **if** match.next $\neq$ **null then** | 4:    **while** entry $\neq$ **null do** |
| 7:        match.next.prev ← match.prev | 5:        $i$ ← $partition$(entry) **mod** $n$ |
| 8: | 6:        **if** entries[$i$] $\neq$ **null then** |
| 9: **procedure** UNLIFT(entry) | 7:            entries[$i$].next ← entry |
| 10:    match ← entry.match | 8:        next_entry ← entry.next |
| 11:    match.prev.next ← match | 9:        entry.prev ← entries[$i$] |
| 12:    **if** match.next $\neq$ **null then** | 10:        entry.next ← **null** |
| 13:        match.next.prev ← match | 11:        entries[$i$] ← entry |
| 14:    entry.prev.next ← entry | 12:        entry ← next_entry |
| 15:    entry.next.prev ← entry | 13:    **return** entries |

## 5 Implementation and Experiments

In this section, we discuss and experimentally evaluate our implementation of the decision procedure (§ 5). As an exemplar of *P*-compositionality, our experiments use Intel's TBB library and Lowe's implementations of concurrent sets.

### 5.1 Implementation

The implementation details of an NP-complete decision procedure matter, especially for our experimental evaluation of *P*-compositionality. We particularly consider hashing and cache eviction options because these were not studied in previous implementations of the WG-based algorithms [4,5].

For experimental robustness, we implemented our linearizability checker in C++11 [10] because this language has built-in concurrency support while allowing us to rule out interference from managed runtime environments (e.g. JVM) due to garbage collection etc. The choice of language, though, meant that we had to implement persistent data structures from scratch. In doing so, we focused on optimizing equality checks for our specific purposes. This way, we managed to avoid a known performance bottleneck in Lowe's implementation of the WGL algorithm [5] where the cost of equality checks had to be compensated with an additional union-find data structure. Another optimization in our implementation is a constant-time (instead of linear-time) hash function for bitsets where we exploit the fact that the bitwise XOR operator over fixed-size bit vectors forms an abelian group. This optimization turns out to be important when histories are longer than 8 K, cf. [5]. To see this, consider the computational steps for retrieving a configuration from the cache and updating it (line 8 in Algorithm 1). For example, a history of length $2^{16}$ means that each bitset in a configuration is at least 3 KiB, and so a constant-time hash function can

**Table 1.** Experimental results for three variants of the same linearizability checker. The results for the baseline are reported in the WGL column. The rows correspond to benchmarks drawn from Intel's TBB library and Lowe's implementations of concurrent sets (see Table 2 for mnemonics).

| Benchmark | WGL | | | WGL+LRU | | | WGL+P | | |
|---|---|---|---|---|---|---|---|---|---|
| | Time | Memory | Timeout | Time | Memory | Timeout | Time | Memory | Timeout |
| TBB | 101 s | 9792 MiB | 0% | 11 s | **670 MiB** | 0% | **6 s** | 672 MiB | 0% |
| CRLSL | 20 s | 15738 MiB | 0% | 25 s | 678 MiB | 0% | **6 s** | **400 MiB** | 0% |
| CRLFSL | 14 s | 15029 MiB | 0% | 18 s | 678 MiB | 0% | **5 s** | **401 MiB** | 0% |
| FGL | 16 s | 14297 MiB | 0% | 81 s | 678 MiB | 0% | **5 s** | **401 MiB** | 0% |
| LLL | 23 s | 16494 MiB | 0% | 94 s | 678 MiB | 0% | **6 s** | **401 MiB** | 0% |
| LSL | 20 s | 15736 MiB | **0%** | 25 s | 678 MiB | 14% | **6 s** | **401 MiB** | 0% |
| LFLL | 11 s | 11847 MiB | 0% | 15 s | 678 MiB | 0% | **5 s** | 402 MiB | 0% |
| LFSL | 14 s | 14712 MiB | 0% | 18 s | 678 MiB | 0% | **5 s** | **401 MiB** | 0% |
| LFSLF0 | 14 s | 13125 MiB | 0% | 18 s | 678 MiB | 0% | **5 s** | 402 MiB | 0% |
| LFSLF1 | < 1 s | 404 MiB | 0% | < 1 s | 407 MiB | 0% | < 1 s | 402 MiB | 0% |
| OPTIMIST | 16 s | 13818 MiB | **0%** | 54 s | 678 MiB | 9% | **5 s** | **401 MiB** | **0%** |

make a measurable difference when the cache is frequently accessed. In fact, it is not uncommon for the cache to contain more than 27 K of such configurations. For this reason, we also implemented a *least recently used* (LRU) cache eviction feature that can optionally be enabled at compile-time. The effects of the LRU cache will be evaluated shortly.

Overall, our implementation and experimental setup is around 4 K lines of code, including several dozen unit tests. All the code and benchmarks are publicly available in our source code repository.[2]

## 5.2 TBB and Concurrent Set Experiments

For the experimental evaluation of our partitioning scheme, we collected over 700 histories from nine different implementations of concurrent sets by Lowe [5] and the concurrent unordered set implementation in Intel's TBB library.[3] We performed all experiments on a 64-bit machine running GNU/Linux 3.17 with 12 Intel Xeon 2.4 GHz cores and 94 GB of main memory.

Each history is generated by running 4 concurrent threads that pseudo randomly invoke operations on a single shared concurrent set. The argument of each operation is a pseudo random uniformly distributed integer between 0

---

[2] https://github.com/ahorn/linearizability-checker
[3] https://www.threadingbuildingblocks.org/

(inclusive) and 24 (exclusive). Each thread invokes 70 K such operations. Note that this is significantly more than in previous experiments where each process is limited to $2^{13} \approx 8$ K operations [5]. In total, since every call generates a pair of entries, every history $H$ in our benchmarks has length $|H| = 4 \times 2 \times 70$ K $=$ 560 K. We discuss the experimental results using Intel's TBB library and Lowe's concurrent set implementations in turn.

The experimental results are given in Table 1. Each of the three main columns corresponds to one variant of the same linearizability checker: 'WGL' is the baseline, 'WGL+LRU' is the WGL algorithm with LRU cache eviction enabled (§ 5.1), and 'WGL+P' is the WGL algorithm combined with our partitioning algorithm (Algorithm 3 in § 4). We tried to use the WG algorithm [4] without the extension by Lowe [5] but WG times out on the majority of benchmarks. We therefore do not report the results on the WG algorithm and focus on WGL, WGL+LRU and WGL+P. The meaning of the sub-columns is as follows. The 'Time' and 'Memory' columns give the average of the elapsed time and virtual memory usage, respectively. These averages exclude runs that we had to terminate after 1 hour. The percentage of such terminated runs is given in the 'Timeout' column. In each row, all variants are compared with respect to the same benchmark data. We therefore do not report confidence intervals.

The TBB benchmark corresponds to the first row in Table 1 and consists of a total of 100 histories. Table 1 clearly shows that the WGL+P algorithm is at least one order of magnitude faster compared to the baseline. We also see that enabling the LRU cache eviction decreases the memory footprint by at least one order of magnitude, approximately 10 GiB versus 700 MiB. In fact, the runtime performance of WGL+LRU is almost one order of magnitude faster than the baseline. The WGL+P algorithm is at least as fast and almost as space efficient as WGL+LRU. In the experiments with Lowe's implementations of concurrent sets (see next paragraph), we further investigate the effect of the LRU cache eviction feature and how it compares to the partitioning scheme.

We give Lowe's implementations of concurrent sets mnemonics (Table 2) that identify the remaining ten benchmarks in Table 1. Each of these ten benchmarks comprises between 50 and 100 histories with an average of 70 histories per benchmark. To avoid bias, we collected these using Lowe's tool. The significance of the experimental results in Table 1 is twofold. Firstly, they show that on average, WGL+P is three times faster than WGL, and WGL+P consumes one order of magnitude less space than WGL. Secondly, and more crucially, however, these experiments reveal that WGL+LRU is not as efficient as WGL+P, in neither time nor space. For example, for WGL+LRU the average elapsed time of the FGL and LLL benchmark is 81 s and 94 s, respectively, with an average memory usage of 678 MiB in both cases. By contrast, WGL+P achieves an average runtime of less than 7 s (and so WGL+P is one order of magnitude faster than WGL+LRU) and consumes even less memory on average (401 MiB) than WGL+LRU. The higher average runtime of WGL+LRU in the FGL benchmark is due to a single check that took several orders of magnitude longer (3068 s) than the remaining checks (20 s on average when the 3068 s outlier is excluded).

**Table 2.** Mnemonics for Lowe's implementation of concurrent sets [5]

| Benchmark name | Mnemonic | Benchmark name | Mnemonic |
|---|---|---|---|
| collision resistance lazy skip list | CRLSL | lock-free linked-list | LFLL |
| collision resistance lock-free skip list | CRLFSL | lock-free skip list | LFSL |
| fine-grained lock | FGL | lock-free skip list faulty (bad hash) | LFSLF0 |
| lazy linked-list | LLL | lock-free skip list faulty (good hash) | LFSLF1 |
| lazy skip list | LSL | optimistic lock | OPTIMIST |

In the LLL benchmark there are two such outliers (2201 s and 675 s, whereas the other checks average 27 s). The observed difference between WGL+LRU and WGL+P is even more pronounced in both the LSL and OPTIMIST benchmarks where the LRU cache eviction causes 14% and 9% of runs to timeout, whereas the WGL+P algorithm always runs to completion in less than a few seconds.

This experimentally confirms that the WGL+P is one order of magnitude faster as well as more space efficient than the baseline and WGL+P consumes even less space than our WGL+LRU implementation.

## 6   Related Work

Linearizability is related to the concept of atomicity, including weaker forms such as $k$-atomicity [11]. An important difference is that atomicity is typically not defined in terms of a sequential specification, e.g. [12]. The theoretical limitations of automatically verifying linearizability are well understood. Of course, the problem is generally undecidable [13]. In fact, even checking finite-state implementation against atomic specifications, provided the number of program threads is bounded, is EXPSPACE [14]. And the best known lower bound for this problem is PSPACE-hardness. This explains the restrictions in this paper and its focus on runtime verification instead.

The literature on machine-assisted techniques for checking linearizability can be broadly divided into simulation-based methods (e.g. [15,16]), model checking (e.g. [17,18,19,20]), static analysis (e.g. [21,22,23,24]) and fully automatic testing (e.g. [4,25,26,27,28,29,30,5]). The simulation-based methods have been used by experts to mechanically verify simple fine-grained and lock-free implementations. Model checking requires less expertise but is typically limited to very small programs and a small number of threads due to the state explosion problem. By contrast, static analysis tools aim to prove correctness with respect to an unbounded number of threads. In general, these techniques are necessarily incomplete and require the user to supply linearization points and/or invariants. Vafeiadis [24] proposes a more automatic form of static analysis that works well on simpler concurrent data types such as stacks but reportedly not so well on data types that have more complicated invariants, including the CAS-based and lazy concurrent sets extensively studied in our experiments.

Our work is most closely related to linearizability testing techniques that are precise, fully automatic and necessarily incomplete, e.g. [4,25,26,27,28,29,30,5]. We focus our discussion on tools that do not require the notion of commit points, cf. [31]. The work in [25,30] checks *k*-atomicity with a polynomial-time algorithm assuming that each write to a register assigns a distinct value. By contrast, we solve a more general NP-complete problem of which *k*-atomicity is an instance. The tool in [26] analyzes code that uses concurrent collection data types such as maps. To make the analysis scale, the authors assume that the collection data types are linearizable, whereas our tool could be used to check such an assumption. A different tool [27] requires programmers to annotate concurrent implementations with so-called state summary functions that act as a form of specification. Our approach is more modular because it strictly separates the concurrent implementation from its specification. By contrast, [28] works without the programmer having to provide a sequential specification. As a result, however, the tool can only find linearizability violations when an exception is thrown or a deadlock occurs. Subsequent work [29] circumvents this, in the context of object-oriented programs, by considering the special case of a superclass serving as an executable, possibly non-deterministic, specification for all its subclasses. The fact that the superclass can be non-deterministic may explain why even checks of two threads can take a significant amount of time (e.g. 108 min) despite the fact that each concurrent test considers only two possible linearizations [29]. By contrast, the WGL algorithm [4,5], on which our decision procedure is based (§ 4), is significantly faster but limited to deterministic specifications. Crucially, our experiments (§ 5) with *P*-compositional specifications show a significant improvement over the WGL algorithm.

## 7   Concluding Remarks

We have presented a precise, fully automatic runtime verification technique for finding linearizability bugs in implementations of concurrent data types that are expected to satisfy a *P*-compositional specification. Our experiments show that our partitioning scheme improves the WGL algorithm [4,5] by one order of magnitude, in both time and space. An additional strength of our technique is that it is applicable to any linearizability checker. For this, however, our work assumes that the specification is *P*-compositional. This is generally not always the case and it would be therefore interesting to further generalize *P*-compositionality, perhaps with a less modular partitioning scheme that can make more assumptions about the underlying decision procedure.

**Acknowledgements..** We would like to thank Gavin Lowe, Kyle Kingsbury and Alexey Gotsman for invaluable discussions.

# References

1. Herlihy, M.P., Wing, J.M.: Linearizability: A correctness condition for concurrent objects. ACM Trans. Program. Lang. Syst. 12(3), 463–492 (1990)
2. Gilbert, S., Lynch, N.: Brewer's conjecture and the feasibility of consistent, available, partition-tolerant web services. SIGACT News 33(2), 51–59 (2002)
3. Gibbons, P.B., Korach, E.: Testing shared memories. SIAM J. Comput. 26(4), 1208–1244 (1997)
4. Wing, J.M., Gong, C.: Testing and verifying concurrent objects. J. Parallel Distrib. Comput. 17(1-2), 164–182 (1993)
5. Lowe, G.: Testing for linearizability. In: PODC 2015 (2015) (Under submission), http://www.cs.ox.ac.uk/people/gavin.lowe/LinearizabiltyTesting/
6. Bouajjani, A., Emmi, M., Enea, C., Hamza, J.: Tractable refinement checking for concurrent objects. In: POPL 2015, pp. 651–662. ACM (2015)
7. Rabinovitch, I.: The dimension of semiorders. Journal of Combinatorial Theory, Series A 25(1), 50–61 (1978)
8. Okasaki, C.: Purely Functional Data Structures. Cambridge University Press (1998)
9. Kingsbury, K.: Computational techniques in Knossos (May 2014), https://aphyr.com/posts/314-computational-techniques-in-knossos
10. ISO: International Standard ISO/IEC 14882:2011(E) Programming Language C++. International Organization for Standardization (2011)
11. Aiyer, A., Alvisi, L., Bazzi, R.A.: On the availability of non-strict quorum systems. In: Fraigniaud, P. (ed.) DISC 2005. LNCS, vol. 3724, pp. 48–62. Springer, Heidelberg (2005)
12. Wang, L., Stoller, S.D.: Static analysis of atomicity for programs with non-blocking synchronization. In: PPoPP 2005, pp. 61–71. ACM (2005)
13. Bouajjani, A., Emmi, M., Enea, C., Hamza, J.: Verifying concurrent programs against sequential specifications. In: Felleisen, M., Gardner, P. (eds.) ESOP 2013. LNCS, vol. 7792, pp. 290–309. Springer, Heidelberg (2013)
14. Alur, R., McMillan, K., Peled, D.: Model-checking of correctness conditions for concurrent objects. Inf. Comput. 160(1-2), 167–188 (2000)
15. Colvin, R., Doherty, S., Groves, L.: Verifying concurrent data structures by simulation. Electron. Notes Theor. Comput. Sci. 137(2), 93–110 (2005)
16. Derrick, J., Schellhorn, G., Wehrheim, H.: Mechanically verified proof obligations for linearizability. ACM Trans. Program. Lang. Syst. 33(1), 4:1–4:43 (2011)
17. Vechev, M., Yahav, E., Yorsh, G.: Experience with model checking linearizability. In: Păsăreanu, C.S. (ed.) SPIN 2009. LNCS, vol. 5578, pp. 261–278. Springer, Heidelberg (2009)
18. Burckhardt, S., Dern, C., Musuvathi, M., Tan, R.: Line-up: A complete and automatic linearizability checker. SIGPLAN Not. 45(6), 330–340 (2010)
19. Černý, P., Radhakrishna, A., Zufferey, D., Chaudhuri, S., Alur, R.: Model checking of linearizability of concurrent list implementations. In: Touili, T., Cook, B., Jackson, P. (eds.) CAV 2010. LNCS, vol. 6174, pp. 465–479. Springer, Heidelberg (2010)
20. Liu, Y., Chen, W., Liu, Y.A., Sun, J., Zhang, S.J., Dong, J.S.: Verifying linearizability via optimized refinement checking. IEEE Trans. Softw. Eng. 39(7), 1018–1039 (2013)
21. Amit, D., Rinetzky, N., Reps, T., Sagiv, M., Yahav, E.: Comparison under abstraction for verifying linearizability. In: Damm, W., Hermanns, H. (eds.) CAV 2007. LNCS, vol. 4590, pp. 477–490. Springer, Heidelberg (2007)
22. Berdine, J., Lev-Ami, T., Manevich, R., Ramalingam, G., Sagiv, M.: Thread quantification for concurrent shape analysis. In: Gupta, A., Malik, S. (eds.) CAV 2008. LNCS, vol. 5123, pp. 399–413. Springer, Heidelberg (2008)

23. Vafeiadis, V.: Shape-value abstraction for verifying linearizability. In: Jones, N.D., Müller-Olm, M. (eds.) VMCAI 2009. LNCS, vol. 5403, pp. 335–348. Springer, Heidelberg (2009)
24. Vafeiadis, V.: Automatically proving linearizability. In: Touili, T., Cook, B., Jackson, P. (eds.) CAV 2010. LNCS, vol. 6174, pp. 450–464. Springer, Heidelberg (2010)
25. Anderson, E., Li, X., Shah, M.A., Tucek, J., Wylie, J.J.: What consistency does your key-value store actually provide? In: HotDep 2010, pp. 1–16. USENIX Association (2010)
26. Shacham, O., Bronson, N., Aiken, A., Sagiv, M., Vechev, M., Yahav, E.: Testing atomicity of composed concurrent operations. SIGPLAN Not. 46(10), 51–64 (2011)
27. Fonseca, P., Li, C., Rodrigues, R.: Finding complex concurrency bugs in large multi-threaded applications. In: EuroSys 2011, pp. 215–228. ACM (2011)
28. Pradel, M., Gross, T.R.: Fully automatic and precise detection of thread safety violations. SIGPLAN Not. 47(6), 521–530 (2012)
29. Pradel, M., Gross, T.R.: Automatic testing of sequential and concurrent substitutability. In: ICSE 2013, pp. 282–291. IEEE Press (2013)
30. Golab, W., Hurwitz, J., Li, X.S.: On the k-atomicity-verification problem. In: ICDCS 2013, pp. 591–600. IEEE Computer Society (2013)
31. Elmas, T., Tasiran, S., Qadeer, S.: VYRD: Verifying concurrent programs by runtime refinement-violation detection. SIGPLAN Not. 40(6), 27–37 (2005)

# Translation Validation for Synchronous Data-Flow Specification in the SIGNAL Compiler

Van Chan Ngo[✉], Jean-Pierre Talpin, and Thierry Gautier

INRIA, 35042 Rennes, France
{chan.ngo,jean-pierre.talpin,thierry.gautier}@inria.fr

**Abstract.** We present a method to construct a validator based on translation validation approach to prove the value-equivalence of variables in the compilation of the SIGNAL compiler. The computation of output *signals* in a SIGNAL program and their counterparts in the generated C code is represented by a *Synchronous Data-flow Value-Graph* (SDVG). Our validator proves that every output signal and its counterpart variable have the same values by transforming the SDVG graph.

**Keywords:** Value-Graph · Graph transformation · Formal verification · Translation validation · Certified compiler · Synchronous programs

## 1 Introduction

**Motivation** A compiler is a large and very complex program which often consists of hundreds of thousands, if not millions, lines of code, and is divided into multiple sub-systems and modules. In addition, each compiler implements a particular algorithm in its own way. That results in two main drawbacks regarding the formal verification of the compiler itself. First, constructing the specifications of the actual compiler implementation is a long and tedious task. Second, the correctness proof of a compiler implementation, in general, cannot be reused for another compiler.

To deal with these drawbacks of formally verifying the compiler itself, one can prove that the source program and the compiled program are semantically equivalent, which is the approach of *translation validation* [13,12,5]. The principle of translation validation is as follows: the source and the compiled programs are represented in a common semantics. Based on the representations of the input and compiled programs, the notion of *"correct transformation"* is formalized. An automated *proof method* is provided to generate the *proof scripts* in case the compiled program implements correctly the input program. Otherwise, it produces a counter-example.

In this work, to adopt the translation validation approach, we use a value-graph as a common semantics to represent the computation of variables in the source and compiled programs. The "correct transformation" is defined by the assertion that every output variable in the source program and the corresponding variable in the compiled program have the same values.

© IFIP International Federation for Information Processing 2015
S. Graf and M. Viswanathan (Eds.): FORTE 2015, LNCS 9039, pp. 66–80, 2015.
DOI: 10.1007/978-3-319-19195-9_5

**The Language.** SIGNAL [3,7] is a synchronous data-flow language that allows the specification of multi-clocked systems. SIGNAL handles unbounded sequences of *typed* values $(x(t))_{t \in \mathbb{N}}$, called *signals*, denoted by $x$. Each signal is implicitly indexed by a logical *clock* indicating the set of instants at which the signal is present, noted $C_x$. At a given instant, a signal may be present where it holds a value, or absent where it holds no value (denoted by $\perp$). Given two signals, they are *synchronous* iff they have the same clock. In SIGNAL, a process (written $P$ or $Q$) consists of the synchronous composition, noted $|$, of equations over signals $x, y, z$, written $x := y \, op \, z$ or $x := op(y, z)$, where $op$ is an operator. Naturally, equations and processes are concurrent.

**Contribution.** A SDVG symbolically represents the computation of the output signals in a SIGNAL program and their counterparts in its generated C code. The same structures are shared in the graph, meaning that they are represented by the same subgraphs. Suppose that we want to show that an output signal and its counterpart have the same values. In order to do that we simply check that they are represented by the same subgraphs, meaning they label the same node. We manage to realize this check by transforming the graph using some rewrite rules, which is called *normalizing* process.

Let $A$ and $C$ be the source program and its generated C code. $Cp$ denotes the unverified SIGNAL compiler which compiles $A$ into $C = Cp(A)$ or a compilation error. We now associate $Cp$ with a validator checking that for any output signal $x$ in $A$ and the corresponding variable $x^c$ in $C$, they have the same values (denoted by $\widetilde{x} = \widetilde{x^c}$). We denote this fact by $C \sqsubseteq_{val} A$.

```
1  if (Cp(A) is Error) return Error;
2  else {
3      if (C ⊑_val A) return C;
4      else return Error;
5  }
```

The main components of the validator are depicted in Fig. 1. It works as follows. First, a shared value-graph that represents the computation of all signals and variables in both programs is constructed. The value-graph can be considered as a generalization of symbolic evaluation. Then, the shared value-graph is transformed by applying graph rewrite rules (the normalization). The set of rewrite rules reflects the general rules of inference of operators, or the optimizations of the compiler. For instance, consider the 3-node subgraph representing the expression $(1 > 0)$, the normalization will transform that graph into a single node subgraph representing the value **true**, as it reflects the constant folding. Finally, the validator compares the values of the output signals and the corresponding variables in the C code. For every output signal and its corresponding variable, the validator checks whether they point to the same node in the graph, meaning that their computation is represented by the same subgraph. Therefore, in the best case, when semantics has been preserved, this check has constant time complexity $\mathcal{O}(1)$. In fact, it is always expected that most transformations and optimizations are semantics-preserving, thus the best-case complexity is important.

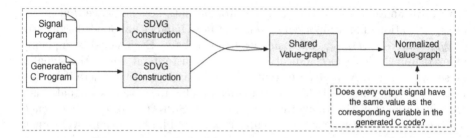

**Fig. 1.** SDVG Translation Validation Architecture

This work is a part of the whole work of the SIGNAL compiler formal verification. Our approach is that we separate the concerns and prove each analysis and transformation stage of the compiler separately with respect to ad-hoc
data-structures to carry the semantic information relevant to that phase. The
preservation of the semantics can be decomposed into the preservation of clock
semantics at the *clock calculation and Boolean abstraction* phase, the preservation of data dependencies at the *static scheduling* phase, and value-equivalence
of variables at the *code generation* phase. Fig. 2 shows the integration of this
verification framework into the compilation process of the SIGNAL compiler. For
each phase, the validator takes the source program and its compiled counterpart,
then constructs the corresponding formal models of both programs. Finally, it
checks the existence of the *refinement* relation to prove the preservation of the
considered semantics. If the result is that the relation does not exist then a
"compiler bug" message is emitted. Otherwise, the compiler continues its work.

**Outline** The remainder of this paper is organized as follows. In Section 2,
we consider the formal definition of SDVG and the representation of a SIGNAL
program and its generated C code as a shared SDVG. Section 3 addresses the
mechanism of the verification process based on the normalization of a SDVG.
Section 4 illustrates the concept of SDVG and the verification procedure. Section
5 terminates this paper with some related work, a conclusion and an outlook to
future work.

## 2    Synchronous Data-Flow Value-Graph

Let $X$ be the set of variables which are used to denote the signals, clocks and
variables in a SIGNAL program and its generated C code, and $F$ be the set of
function symbols. In our consideration, $F$ contains usual logic operators (not,
and, or), numerical comparison functions (<, >, =, <=, >=, /=), numerical
operators (+, -, *, /), and gated $\phi$-function [2]. A gated $\phi$-function such as
$x = \phi(c, x_1, x_2)$ represents a branching in a program, which means $x$ takes the
value of $x_1$ if the condition $c$ is satisfied, and the value of $x_2$ otherwise. A constant
is defined as a function symbol of arity 0.

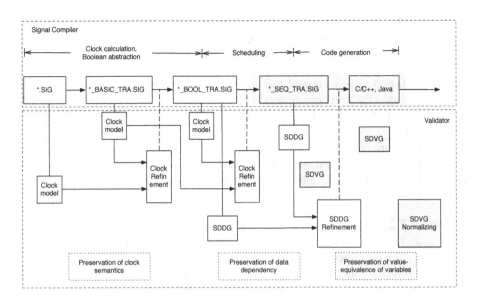

**Fig. 2.** The Translation Validation for the SIGNAL Compiler

**Definition 1.** *A* SDVG *associated with a* SIGNAL *program and its generated C code is a directed graph* $G = \langle N, E, l_N, m_N \rangle$ *where* $N$ *is a finite set of nodes that represent clocks, signals, variables, or functions.* $E \subseteq N \times N$ *is the set of edges that describe the computation relations between nodes.* $l_N : N \longrightarrow X \cup F$ *is a mapping labeling each node with an element in* $X \cup F$. $m_N : N \longrightarrow \mathcal{P}(N)$ *is a mapping labeling each node with a finite set of clocks, signals, and variables. It defines the set of equivalent clocks, signals and variables.*

A subgraph rooted at a node is used to describe the computation of the corresponding element labelled at this node. In a graph, for a node labelled by $y$, the set of clocks, signals or variables $m_N(y) = \{x_0, ..., x_n\}$ is written as a node with label $\{x_0, ..., x_n\}$ $y$.

## 2.1  SDVG of SIGNAL Program

Let $P$ be a SIGNAL program, we write $X = \{x_1, ..., x_n\}$ to denote the set of all signals in $P$ which consists of input, output, state (corresponding to delay operator) and local signals, denoted by $I, O, S$ and $L$, respectively. For each $x_i \in X$, $\mathbb{D}_{x_i}$ denotes its domain of values, and $\mathbb{D}_{x_i}^{\perp} = \mathbb{D}_{x_i} \cup \{\perp\}$ is the domain of values with the absent value. Then, the domain of values of $X$ with absent value is defined as follows: $\mathbb{D}_X^{\perp} = \bigcup_{i=1}^{n} \mathbb{D}_{x_i} \cup \{\perp\}$. For each signal $x_i$, it is associated with a Boolean variable $\widehat{x_i}$ to encode its clock at a given instant $t$ (**true**: $x_i$ is present at $t$, **false**: $x_i$ is absent at $t$), and $\widetilde{x_i}$ with the same type as $x_i$ to encode its value. Formally, the abstract values to represent the clock and value of a signal can be represented by a gated $\phi$-function, $x_i = \phi(\widehat{x_i}, \widetilde{x_i}, \perp)$.

Assume that the computation of signals in processes $P_1$ and $P_2$ is represented as shared value-graphs $G_1$ and $G_2$, respectively. Then the value-graph $G$ of the synchronous combination process $P_1|P_2$ can be defined as $G = \langle N, E, l_N, m_N \rangle$ in which for any node labelled by $x$, we replace it by the subgraph that is rooted by the node labelled by $x$ in $G_1$ and $G_2$. Every identical subgraph is reused, in other words, we maximize sharing among graph nodes in $G_1$ and $G_2$. Thus, the shared value-graph of $P$ can be constructed as a combination of the sub-value-graphs of its equations.

A SIGNAL program is built through a set of primitive operators. Therefore, to construct the SDVG of a SIGNAL program, we construct a subgraph for each primitive operator. In the following, we present the value-graph corresponding to each SIGNAL primitive operator.

**Stepwise Function.** Consider the equation using the stepwise function $y := f(x_1, ..., x_n)$, it indicates that if all signals from $x_1$ to $x_n$ are defined, then the output signal $y$ is defined by applying $f$ on the values of $x_1, ..., x_n$. Otherwise, it is assigned no value. Thus, the computation of $y$ can be represented by the following gated $\phi$-function: $y = \phi(\hat{y}, f(\widetilde{x_1}, \widetilde{x_2}, ..., \widetilde{x_n}), \bot)$, where $\hat{y} \Leftrightarrow \widehat{x_1} \Leftrightarrow \widehat{x_2} \Leftrightarrow ... \Leftrightarrow \widehat{x_n}$ (since they are *synchronous*). The graph representation of the stepwise function is depicted in Fig. 3. Note that in the graph, the node labelled by $\{\widehat{x_1}, ..., \widehat{x_n}\} \hat{y}$ means that $m_N(\hat{y}) = \{\widehat{x_1}, ..., \widehat{x_n}\}$. In other words, the subgraph representing the computation of $\hat{y}$ is also the computation of $\widehat{x_1}, ...,$ and $\widehat{x_n}$.

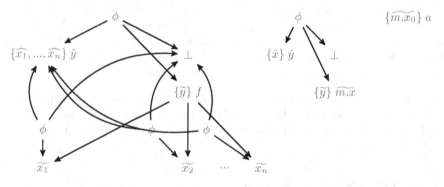

**Fig. 3.** The graphs of $y := f(x_1, ..., x_n)$ and $y := x\$1$ init $a$

**Delay.** Consider the equation using the delay operator $y := x\$1$ init $a$. The output signal $y$ is defined by the last value of the signal $x$ when the signal $x$ is present. Otherwise, it is assigned no value. The computation of $y$ can be represented by the following nodes: $y = \phi(\hat{y}, \widetilde{m.x}, \bot)$ and $\widetilde{m.x_0} = a$, where $\hat{y} \Leftrightarrow \hat{x}$. $\widetilde{m.x}$ and $\widetilde{m.x_0}$ are the last value of $x$ and the initialized value of $y$. The graph representation is depicted in Fig. 3.

**Merge.** Consider the equation which corresponds to the merge operator $y :=$ $x$ default $z$. If the signal $x$ is defined then the signal $y$ is defined and holds the value of $x$. The signal $y$ is assigned the value of $z$ when the signal $x$ is not defined and the signal $z$ is defined. When both $x$ and $z$ are not defined, $y$ holds no value. The computation of $y$ can be represented by the following node: $y = \phi(\hat{y}, \phi(\hat{x}, \widetilde{x}, \widetilde{z}), \perp)$, where $\hat{y} \Leftrightarrow (\hat{x} \vee \hat{z})$. The graph representation is depicted in Fig. 4. Note that in the graph, the clock $\hat{y}$ is represented by the subgraph of $\hat{x} \vee \hat{z}$.

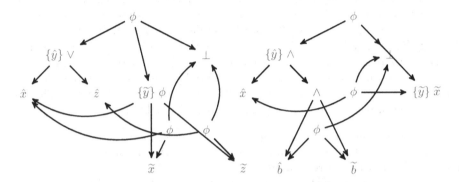

**Fig. 4.** The graphs of $y := x$ default $z$ and $y := x$ when $b$

**Sampling.** Consider the equation which corresponds to the sampling operator $y := x$ when $b$. If the signal $x, b$ are defined and $b$ holds the value `true`, then the signal $y$ is defined and holds the value of $x$. Otherwise, $y$ holds no value. The computation of $y$ can be represented by the following node: $y = \phi(\hat{y}, \widetilde{x}, \perp)$, where $\hat{y} \Leftrightarrow (\hat{x} \wedge \hat{b} \wedge \widetilde{b})$. Fig. 4 shows its graph representation.

**Restriction.** The graph representation of restriction process $P_1 \backslash x$ is the same as the graph of $P_1$.

**Clock Relations.** Given the above graph representations of the primitive operators, we can obtain the graph representations for the derived operators on clocks as the following gated $\phi$-function $z = \phi(\hat{z}, true, \perp)$, where $\hat{z}$ is computed as $\hat{z} \Leftrightarrow \hat{x}$ for $z := \hat{} x$, $\hat{z} \Leftrightarrow (\hat{x} \vee \hat{y})$ for $z := x \hat{} + y$, $\hat{z} \Leftrightarrow (\hat{x} \wedge \hat{y})$ for $z := x \hat{} * y$, $\hat{z} \Leftrightarrow (\hat{x} \wedge \neg \hat{y})$ for $z := x \hat{} - y$, and $\hat{z} \Leftrightarrow (\hat{b} \wedge \widetilde{b})$ for $z :=$ when $b$. For the clock relation $x \hat{} = y$, it is represented by a single node graph labelled by $\{\hat{x}\}\, \hat{y}$.

## 2.2   SDVG of Generated C Code

For constructing the shared value-graph, the generated C code is translated into a subgraph along with the subgraph of the SIGNAL program. Let $A$ be a SIGNAL program and $C$ its generated C code, we write $X_A = \{x_1, ..., x_n\}$ to denote the set of all signals in $A$, and $X_C = \{x_1^c, ..., x_m^c\}$ to denote the set of all variables in

$C$. We added "c" as superscript for the variables, to distinguish them from the signals in $A$.

As described in [4,8,6,1], the generated C code of $A$ consists of the following files:

- A_main.c is the implementation of the *main function*. It opens the IO communication channels by calling functions provided in A_io.c, and calls the *initialization function*. Then it calls the *step function* repeatedly in an infinite loop to interact with the environment.
- A_body.c is the implementation of the initialization function and the step function. The initialization function is called once to provide initial values to the program variables. The step function, which contains also the step initialization and finalization functions, is responsible for the calculation of the outputs to interact with the environment. This function, which is called repeatedly in an infinite loop, is the essential part of the concrete code.
- A_io.c is the implementation of the *IO communication functions*. The IO functions are called to setup communication channels with the environment.

The scheduling and the computations are done inside the step function. Therefore, it is natural to construct a graph of this function in order to prove that its variables and the corresponding signals have the same values. To construct the graph of the step function, the following considerations need to be studied. The generated C code in the step function consists of only the assignment and if-then statements. For each signal named $x$ in $A$, it has a corresponding Boolean variable named $C\_x$ in the step function. Then the computation of $x$ is implemented by a conditional if-then statement as follows:

```
1  if (C_x) {
2      computation(x);
3  }
```

If $x$ is an input signal then its computation is the reading operation which gets the value of $x$ from the environment. In case $x$ is an output signal, after computing its value, it will be written to the IO communication channel with the environment. Note that the C programs use persistent variables (e.g., variables which always have some value) to implement the SIGNAL program $A$ which uses volatile variables. As a result, there is a difference in the types of a signal in the SIGNAL program and of the corresponding variable in the C code. When a signal has the absent value, $\perp$, at a given instant, the corresponding C variable always has a value. This implies that we have to detect when a variable in the C code such that whose value is not updated. In this case, it will be assigned the absent value, $\perp$. Thus, the computation of a variable, called $x^c$, can fully be represented by a gated $\phi$-function $x^c = \phi(C\_x^c, \tilde{x}^c, \perp)$, where $\tilde{x}^c$ denotes the newly updated value of the variable.

In the generated C code, the computation of the variable whose clock is the *master clock*, which ticks every time the step function is called, and the computation of some local variables (introduced by the SIGNAL compiler) are implemented using the forms below.

It is obvious that $x$ is always updated when the step function is invoked. The computation of such variables can be represented by a single node graph labelled by $\{\widetilde{x^c}\}\ x^c$. That means the variable $x^c$ is always updated and holds the value $\widetilde{x^c}$.

```
1  if (C_x) {
2    computation(x);
3  } else computation(x);
4  // or without if-then
5  computation(x)
```

Considering the following code segment, we observe that the variable $x$ is involved in the computation of the variable $y$ before the updating of $x$.

```
1  if (C_y) {
2    y = x + 1;
3  }
4  // code segment
5  if (C_x) {
6    x = ...
7  }
```

In this situation, we refer to the value of $x$ as the previous value, denoted by $m.x^c$. It happens when a *delay* operator is applied on the signal $x$ in the SIGNAL program. The computation of $y$ is represented by the following gated $\phi$-function: $y^c = \phi(C\_y^c, m.x^c + 1, \bot)$.

## 3    Translation Validation of SDVG

In this section, we introduce the set of rewrite rules to transform the shared value-graph resulting from the previous step. This procedure is called *normalizing*. At the end of the normalization, for any output signal $x$ and its corresponding variable $x^c$ in the generated C code, we check whether $x$ and $x^c$ label the same node in the resulting graph. The normalizing procedure can be adapted with any future optimization of the compiler by updating the set of rewrite rules.

### 3.1    Normalizing

Once a shared value-graph is constructed for the SIGNAL program and its generated C code, if the values of an output signal and its corresponding variable in the C code are not already equivalent (they do not point the same node in the shared value-graph), we start to normalize the graph. Given a set of term rewrite rules, the normalizing process works as described below. The normalizing algorithm indicates that we apply the rewrite rules to each graph node individually. When there are no more rules that can be applied to the resulting graph, we maximize the shared nodes, reusing the identical subgraphs. The process terminates when there exists no more sharing or rules that can be applied.

We classify our set of rewrite rules into three basic types: *general simplification rules*, *optimization-specific rules* and *synchronous rules*. In the following, we shall present the rewrite rules of these types, and we assume that all nodes in our shared value-graph are typed. We write a rewrite rule in form of term rewrite rules, $t_l \rightarrow t_r$, meaning that the subgraph represented by $t_l$ is replaced by the subgraph represented by $t_r$ when the rule is applied. Due to the lack of space, we only present a part of these rules, the full set of rules is shown in the appendix.

```
 1  // Input: G: A shared value-graph. R: The set of
 2  // rewrite rules. S: The sharing among graph nodes.
 3  // Output: The normalized graph
 4  while (∃s ∈ S or ∃r ∈ R that can be applied on G) {
 5     while (∃r ∈ R that can be applied on G) {
 6        for (n ∈ G)
 7           if (r can be applied on n)
 8              apply the rewrite rule to n
 9     }
10     maximize sharing
11  }
12  return G
```

**General Simplification Rules.** The general simplification rules contain the rules which are related to the general rules of inference of operators, denoted by the corresponding function symbols in $F$. In our consideration, the operators used in the primitive stepwise functions and in the generated C code are usual logic operators, numerical comparison functions, and numerical operators. When applying these rules, we will replace a subgraph rooted at a node by a smaller subgraph. In consequence of this replacement, we will reduce the number of nodes by eliminating some unnecessary structures. The first set of rules simplifies numerical and Boolean comparison expressions. In these rules, the subgraph $t$ represents a structure of value computing (e.g., the computation of expression $b = x \neq$ **true**). These rules are self explanatory, for instance, with any structure represented by a subgraph $t$, the expression $t = t$ can always be replaced with a single node subgraph labelled by the value **true**.

$$= (t, t) \rightarrow \text{true}$$
$$\neq (t, t) \rightarrow \text{false}$$

The second set of general simplification rules eliminates unnecessary nodes in the graph that represent the $\phi$-functions, where $c$ is a Boolean expression. For instance, we consider the following rules.

$$\phi(\text{true}, x_1, x_2) \rightarrow x_1$$
$$\phi(c, \text{true}, \text{false}) \rightarrow c$$
$$\phi(c, \phi(c, x_1, x_2), x_3) \rightarrow \phi(c, x_1, x_3)$$

The first rule replaces a $\phi$-function with its left branch if the condition always holds the value **true**. The second rule operates on Boolean expressions represented by the branches. When the branches are Boolean constants and hold different values, the $\phi$-function can be replaced with the value of the condition

c. Consider a $\phi$-function such that one of its branches is another $\phi$-function. The third rule removes the $\phi$-function in the branches if the conditions of the $\phi$-functions are the same.

**Optimization-Specific Rules.** Based on the optimizations of the SIGNAL compiler, we have a number of optimization-specific rules in a way that reflects the effects of specific optimizations of the compiler. These rules do not always reduce the graph or make it simpler. One has to know specific optimizations of the compiler when she wants to add them to the set of rewrite rules. In our case, the set of rules for simplifying constant expressions of the SIGNAL compiler such as:

$$+(cst_1, cst_2) \rightarrow cst, \text{ where } cst = cst_1 + cst_2$$
$$\wedge(cst_1, cst_2) \rightarrow cst, \text{ where } cst = cst_1 \wedge cst_2$$
$$\Box(cst_1, cst_2) \rightarrow cst$$

where $\Box$ denotes a numerical comparison function, and the Boolean value $cst$ is the evaluation of the constant expression $\Box(cst_1, cst_2)$ which can hold either the value `false` or `true`.

We also may add a number of rewrite rules that are derived from the list of *rules of inference* for propositional logic. For example, we have a group of laws for rewriting formulas with and operator, such as:

$$\wedge(x, \text{true}) \quad \rightarrow x$$
$$\wedge(x, \Rightarrow (x, y)) \rightarrow x \wedge y$$

**Synchronous Rules.** In addition to the general and optimization-specific rules, we also have a number of rewrite rules that are derived from the semantics of the code generation mechanism of the SIGNAL compiler.

The first rule is that if a variable in the generated C code is always updated, then we require that the corresponding signal in the source program is present at every instant, meaning that the signal never holds the absent value. In consequence of this rewrite rule, the signal $x$ and its value when it is present $\tilde{x}$ (resp. the variable $x^c$ and its updated value $\widetilde{x^c}$ in the generated C code) point to the same node in the shared value-graph. Every reference to $x$ and $\tilde{x}$ (resp. $x^c$ and $\widetilde{x^c}$) point to the same node.

We consider the equation $pz := z\$1 \text{ init } 0$. We use the variable $\widetilde{m.z}$ to capture the last value of the signal $z$. In the generated C program, the last value of the variable $z^c$ is denoted by $m.z^c$. The second rule is that it is required that the last values of a signal and the corresponding variable in the generated C code are the same. That means $\widetilde{m.z} = m.z^c$.

Finally, we add rules that mirror the relation between input signals and their corresponding variables in the generated C code. First, for any input signal $x$ and the corresponding variable $x^c$ in the generated C code, if $x$ is present, then the value of $x$ which is read from the environment and the value of the variable $x^c$ after the reading statement must be equivalent. That means $\widetilde{x^c}$ and $\tilde{x}$ are represented by the same subgraph in the graph. Second, if the clock of $x$ is also read from the environment as a parameter, then the clock of the input signal $x$

is equivalent to the condition in which the variable $x^c$ is updated. It means that we represent $\hat{x}$ and $C\_x^c$ by the same subgraph. Consequently, every reference to $\hat{x}$ and $C\_x^c$ (resp. $\tilde{x}$ and $\tilde{x}^c$) points to the same node.

# 4  Illustrative Example

Let us illustrate the verification process in Fig. 1 on the program DEC in Listing 1.1 and its generated C code DEC_step() in Listing 1.2.

In the first step, we shall compute the shared value-graph for both programs to represent the computation of all signals and their corresponding variables. This graph is depicted in Fig. 5.

```
1  process DEC=
2  (? integer FB;
3   ! integer N)
4  (| FB ^= when (ZN<=1)
5   | N := FB default (ZN-1)
6   | ZN := N$1 init 1
7   |)
8  where integer ZN init 1
9  end;
```

Listing 1.1. DEC in Signal

```
1  EXTERN logical DEC_step() {
2     C_FB = N <= 1;
3     if (C_FB) {
4        if (!r_DEC_FB(&FB)) return FALSE; // read input FB
5     }
6     if (C_FB) N = FB; else N = N - 1;
7     w_DEC_N(N); // write output N
8     DEC_step_finalize();
9     return TRUE;
10 }
```

Listing 1.2. Generated C code of DEC

Note that in the C program, the variable $N^c$ ("c" is added as superscript for the C program variables, to distinguish them from the signals in the SIGNAL program) is always updated (line (6)). In lines (2) and (6), the references to the variable $N^c$ are the references to the last value of $N^c$ denoted by $m.N^c$. The variable $FB^c$ which corresponds to the input signal $FB$ is updated only when the variable $C\_FB^c$ is true.

In the second step, we shall normalize the above initial graph. Below is a potential normalization scenario, meaning that it might have more than one normalization scenario, and the validator can choose one of them. For example, given a set of rules that can be applied, the validator can apply these rules with different order. Fig. 6 depicts the intermediate resulting graph of this normalization scenario, and Fig. 7 is the final normalized graph from the initial graph when we cannot perform any more normalization.

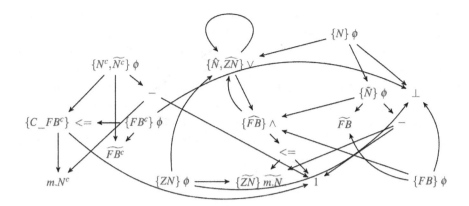

**Fig. 5.** The shared value-graph of DEC and DEC_step

1. The clock of the output signal $N$ is a master clock which is indicated in the generated C by the variable $N^c$ being always updated. The node $\{\hat{N}, \widehat{ZN}\} \vee$ is rewritten into **true**.
2. By rule $\wedge(\textbf{true}, x) \to x$, the node $\{\widehat{FB}\} \wedge$ is rewritten into $\{\widehat{FB}\}$ <=.
3. The $\phi$-function node representing the computation of $N$ is removed and $N$ points to the node $\{\tilde{N}\} \phi$.
4. The $\phi$-function node representing the computation of $ZN$ is removed and $ZN$ points to the node $\{\widetilde{ZN}\} \widetilde{m.N}$.
5. The nodes $\widetilde{FB^c}$ and $\widetilde{FB}$ are rewritten into a single node $\{\widetilde{FB}\} \widetilde{FB^c}$. All references to them are replaced by references to $\{\widetilde{FB}\} \widetilde{FB^c}$.
6. The nodes $m.N^c$ and $\widetilde{m.N}$ are rewritten into a single node $\{\widetilde{m.N}\} m.N^c$. All references to them are replaced by references to $\{\widetilde{m.N}\} m.N^c$.

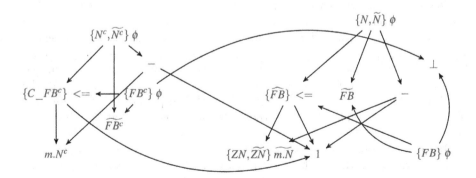

**Fig. 6.** The resulting value-graph of DEC and DEC_step

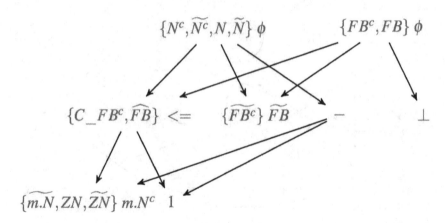

**Fig. 7.** The final normalized graph of DEC and DEC_step

In the final step, we check that the value of the output signal and its corresponding variable in the generated code merge into a single node. In this example, we can safely conclude that the output signal $N$ and its corresponding variable $N^c$ are equivalent since they point to the same node in the final normalized graph.

## 5   Related Work and Conclusion

There is a wide range of works for value-graph representations of expression evaluations in a program. For example, in [16], Weise et al. present a nice summary of the various types of value-graph. In our context, the value-graph is used to represent the computation of variables in both source program and its generated C code in which the identical structures are shared. We believe that this representation will reduce the required storage and make the normalizing process more efficient than two separated graphs. Another remark is that the calculation of clocks as well as the special value, the absent value, are also represented in the shared graph.

Another related work which adopts the translation validation approach in verification of optimizations, Tristan et al. [15], recently proposed a framework for translation validation of LLVM optimizer. For a function and its optimized counterpart, they construct a shared value-graph. The graph is *normalized* (the graph is reduced). After the normalization, if the outputs of two functions are represented by the same sub-graph, they can safely conclude that both functions are equivalent.

On the other hand, Tate et al. [14] proposed a framework for translation validation. Given a function in the input program and the corresponding optimized version of the function in the output program, they compute two value-graphs to represent the computations of the variables. Then they transform the graph by adding equivalent terms through a process called *equality saturation*. After the saturation, if both value-graphs are the same, they can conclude that the return value of two given functions are the same. However, for translation validation purposes, our normalization process is more efficient and scalable since we can add rewrite rules into the validator that reflect what a typical compiler intends to do (e.g., a compiler will do the constant folding optimization, then we can add the rewrite rule for constant expressions such as three nodes subgraph $(1 + 2)$ is replaced by a single node 3).

The present paper provides a verification framework to prove the value-equivalence of variables and applies this approach to the synchronous data-flow compiler SIGNAL. With the simplicity of the graph normalization, we believe that translation validation of synchronous data-flow value-graph for the industrial compiler SIGNAL is feasible and efficient. Moreover, the normalization process can always be extended by adding new rewrite rules. That makes the translation validation of SDVG scalable and flexible.

We have considered sequential code generation. A possibility is to extend this framework to use with other code generation schemes including cluster code with static and dynamic scheduling, modular code, and distributed code. One path forward is the combination of this work and the work on data dependency graph in [10,11,9]. That means that we use synchronous data-flow dependency graphs and synchronous data-flow value-graphs as a common semantic framework to represent the semantics of the generated code. The formalization of the notion of "correct transformation" is defined as the refinements between two synchronous data-flow dependency graphs and in a shared value-graph as described above.

Another possibility is that we use an SMT solver to reason on the rewriting rules. For example, we recall the following rules:

$$\phi(c_1, \phi(c_2, x_1, x_2), x_3) \rightarrow \phi(c_1, x_1, x_3) \text{ if } c_1 \Rightarrow c_2$$
$$\phi(c_1, \phi(c_2, x_1, x_2), x_3) \rightarrow \phi(c_1, x_2, x_3) \text{ if } c_1 \Rightarrow \neg c_2$$

To apply these rules on a shared value-graph to reduce the nested $\phi$-functions (e.g., from $\phi(c_1, \phi(c_2, x_1, x_2), x_3)$ to $\phi(c_1, x_1, x_3)$), we have to check the validity of first-order logic formulas, for instance, we check that $\models (c_1 \Rightarrow c_2)$ and $\models c_1 \Rightarrow \neg c_2$. We consider the use of SMT to solve the validity of the conditions as in the above rewrite rules to normalize value-graphs.

# References

1. Aubry, P., Guernic, P.L., Machard, S.: Synchronous distribution of signal programs. In: Proceedings of the 29th Hawaii International Conference on System Sciences, vol. 1, pp. 656–665. IEEE Computer Society Press (1996)
2. Ballance, R., Maccabe, A., Ottenstei, K.: The program dependence web: A representation supporting control, data, and demand driven interpretation of imperative languages. In: Proc. of the SIGPLAN 1990 Conference on Programming Language Design and Implementation, pp. 257–271 (1990)
3. Benveniste, A., Guernic, P.L.: Hybrid dynamical systems theory and the signal language. IEEE Transactions on Automatic Control 35(5), 535–546 (1990)

4. Besnard, L., Gautier, T., Guernic, P.L., Talpin, J.-P.: Compilation of polychronous data-flow equations. In: Synthesis of Embedded Software, pp. 01–40. Springer (2010)
5. Blazy, S.: Which c semantics to embed in the front-end of a formally verified compiler? In: Tools and Techniques for Verification of System Infrastructure, TTVSI (2008)
6. Gautier, T., Guernic, P.L.: Code generation in the sacres project. In: Towards System Safety, Proceedings of the Safety-critical Systems Symposium, pp. 127–149 (1999)
7. Gautier, T., Guernic, P.L., Besnard, L.: SIGNAL: A declarative language for synchronous programming of real-time systems. In: Kahn, G. (ed.) FPCA 1987. LNCS, vol. 274, pp. 257–277. Springer, Heidelberg (1987)
8. Maffeis, O., Guernic, P.L.: Distributed implementation of SIGNAL: Scheduling & graph clustering. In: Langmaack, H., de Roever, W.-P., Vytopil, J. (eds.) FTRTFT 1994 and ProCoS 1994. LNCS, vol. 863, pp. 547–566. Springer, Heidelberg (1994)
9. Ngo, V.C.: Formal verification of a synchronous data-flow compiler: from signal to c. Ph.D Thesis (2014), http://tel.archives-ouvertes.fr/tel-01058041
10. Ngo, V.C., Talpin, J.-P., Gautier, T., Guernic, P.L., Besnard, L.: Formal verification of compiler transformations on polychronous equations. In: Derrick, J., Gnesi, S., Latella, D., Treharne, H. (eds.) IFM 2012. LNCS, vol. 7321, pp. 113–127. Springer, Heidelberg (2012)
11. Ngo, V.C., Talpin, J.-P., Gautier, T., Guernic, P.L., Besnard, L.: Formal verification of synchronous data-flow program transformations toward certified compilers. Frontiers of Computer Science, Special Issue on Synchronous Programming 7(5), 598–616 (2013)
12. Pnueli, A., Shtrichman, O., Siegel, M.: Translation validation: From SIGNAL to C. In: Olderog, E.-R., Steffen, B. (eds.) Correct System Design. LNCS, vol. 1710, pp. 231–255. Springer, Heidelberg (1999)
13. Pnueli, A., Siegel, M., Singerman, E.: Translation validation. In: Steffen, B. (ed.) TACAS 1998. LNCS, vol. 1384, pp. 151–166. Springer, Heidelberg (1998)
14. Tate, R., Stepp, M., Tatlock, Z., Lerner, S.: Equility saturation: A new approach to optimization. In: 36th Principles of Programming Languages, pp. 264–276 (2009)
15. Tristan, J.-B., Govereau, P., Morrisett, G.: Evaluating value-graph translation validation for llvm. In: ACM SIGPLAN Conference on Programming and Language Design Implementation (2011)
16. Weise, D., Crew, R., Ernst, M., Steensgaard, B.: Value dependence graphs: Representation without taxation. In: 21st Principles of Programming Languages, pp. 297–310 (1994)

# Formal Models of Concurrent
# and Distributed Systems

# Dynamic Causality in Event Structures

Youssef Arbach, David Karcher, Kirstin Peters, and Uwe Nestmann$^{(\boxtimes)}$

Technische Universität Berlin, Berlin, Germany
{youssef.arbach,david.s.karcher,kirstin.peters,uwe.nestmann}@tu-berlin.de

**Abstract** Event Structures (ESs) address the representation of direct relationships between individual events, usually capturing the notions of causality and conflict. Up to now, such relationships have been static, i.e. they cannot change during a system run. Thus the common ESs only model a static view on systems. We dynamize causality such that causal dependencies between some events can be changed by occurrences of other events. We first model and study the case in which events may entail the *removal* of causal dependencies, then we consider the *addition* of causal dependencies, and finally we combine both approaches in the so-called *Dynamic Causality ESs*. For all three newly defined types of ESs, we study their expressive power in comparison to the well-known *Prime* ESs, *Dual* ESs, *Extended Bundle* ESs, and ESs for *Resolvable Conflicts*. Interestingly Dynamic Causality ESs subsume Extended Bundle ESs and Dual ESs but are incomparable with ESs for Resolvable Conflicts.

## 1 Introduction

*Concurrency Model.* Event Structures (ESs) usually address statically defined relationships that constrain the possible occurrences of events, typically represented as *causality* (for precedence) and *conflict* (for choice). An event is a single occurrence of an action; it cannot be repeated. ESs were first used to give semantics to Petri nets [14], then to process calculi [4,8], and recently to model quantum strategies and games [16]. The semantics of an ES itself is usually provided by the sets of traces compatible with the constraints, or by configuration-based sets of events, possibly in their partially-ordered variant (*posets*).

*Motivation.* Modern process-aware systems emphasize the need for flexibility into their design to adapt to changes in their environment [13]. One form of flexibility is the ability to change the work-flow during the runtime of the system deviating from the default path, due to changes in regulations or to exceptions. Such changes could be ad hoc or captured at the build time of the system [10]. For instance—as taken from [13]—*during the treatment process, and for a particular patient, a planned computer tomography must not be performed due to the fact that she has a cardiac pacemaker. Instead, an X-ray activity shall be performed.* In this paper, we provide a formal model that can be used for such scenarios, showing what is the *regular* execution path and what is the *exceptional*

Supported by the DFG Research Training Group SOAMED.

© IFIP International Federation for Information Processing 2015
S. Graf and M. Viswanathan (Eds.): FORTE 2015, LNCS 9039, pp. 83–97, 2015.
DOI: 10.1007/978-3-319-19195-9_6

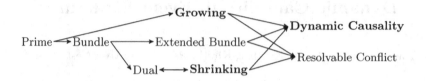

**Fig. 1.** Landscape of Event Structures (new ESs are bold)

one [10]. In the conclusion, we highlight the advantages of our model over other static-causality models w.r.t. such scenarios.

*Overview.*

We study the idea—motivated by application scenarios—of events changing the causal dependencies of other events. In order to deal with dynamicity in causality usually duplications of events are used (see e.g. [5], where copies of the same event have the same label, but different dependencies). In this paper we want to express dynamic changes of causality more directly without duplications. We allow dependencies to change during a system run, by modifying the causality itself. In this way we avoid duplications of events, and keep the model simple and more intuitive. We separate the idea of dropping (shrinking) causality from adding (growing) causality and study each one separately first, and then combine them. In § 3 we define *Shrinking Causality Event Structures* (SESs), and compare their expressive power with other types of ESs. In § 4 we do the same for *Growing Causality Event Structures* (GESs). In § 5 we combine both concepts within the *Dynamic Causality Event Structures* (DCESs) and show that they are strictly more expressive than Extended Bundle Event Structures (EBESs) [8], which are incomparable to SESs and GESs. Although *Event Structures for Resolvable conflicts* (RCESs) [12] are shown to be more expressive than GESs and SESs, they are incomparable with DCESs. The relations among the various classes of ESs are summarised in Fig. 1, where an arrow from one class to another means that the first is less expressive than the second. In § 6 we summarize the contributions and show the limitations of other static-causality models w.r.t. our example, and conclude by future work.

*Related Work.* Kuske and Morin in [7] worked on local independence, using local traces. There actions can be independent from each other after a given history. Comparing to our work we provide a mechanism for independence of events, through the growing and shrinking causality, while this related work abstracts from the way actions become independent. In [12], van Glabbeek and Plotkin introduced RCESs, where conflicts can be resolved or created by the occurrence of other events. This dynamicity of conflicts is complementary to our approach. As visualized in Fig. 1 DCESs and RCESs are incomparable but—similarly to RCESs—DCESs are more expressive than many other types of ESs.

# 2   Technical Preliminaries

We investigate the idea of dynamically evolving dependency between events. Therefore we want to allow that the occurrence of events creates new causal dependencies between events or removes such dependencies. We base our extension on prime event structures, because they provide a very simple causality model. In the following we shortly revisit the main definitions of the types of ESs from literature we compare with. We omit the labels of events since our results are not influenced by their presence.

## 2.1   Prime Event Structures

A prime event structure (PES) [15] consists of a set of events and two relations describing conflicts and causal dependencies. To cover the intuition, that events causally depending on an infinite number of other events can never occur, [15] requires PESs to satisfy the *axiom of finite causes*. Additionally the enabling relation is assumed to be a partial order, i.e. is transitive and reflexive. Furthermore the concept of *conflict heredity* is required; saying that an event conflicting with another event conflicts with all its causal successors.

If we allow to add or drop causal dependencies, it is hard to maintain the conflict heredity and the transitivity and reflexivity of enabling. Because of that we do not consider the partial order property nor the axiom of conflict heredity in our definition of PESs. The same applies for the finite causes property which will be covered through finite configurations, like Def. 13 later on. Note however that the following version of PESs has the same expressive power as PESs in [15] w.r.t. to finite configurations.

**Definition 1.** *A* Prime Event Structure (PES) *is a triple* $\pi = (E, \#, \rightarrow)$, *where* $E$ *is a set of* events, $\# \subseteq E^2$ *is an irreflexive symmetric relation (the* conflict *relation), and* $\rightarrow \subseteq E^2$ *is the* enabling *relation.*

The computation state of a process that is modeled as a PES is represented by the set of events that have occurred. Given a PES $\pi = (E, \#, \rightarrow)$ we call such sets $C \subseteq E$ that respect $\#$ and $\rightarrow$ as configurations of $\pi$.

**Definition 2.** *Let* $\pi = (E, \#, \rightarrow)$ *be a PES. A set of events* $C \subseteq E$ *is a con-figuration of* $\pi$ *if it is* conflict-free, *i.e.* $\forall e, e' \in C . \neg (e \# e')$, downward-closed, *i.e.* $\forall e, e' \in E . e \rightarrow e' \wedge e' \in C \implies e \in C$, *and the transitive closure of the enabling relation is* acyclic, *i.e.* $\rightarrow^* \cap C^2$ *is free of cycles. We denote the set of configurations of* $\pi$ *by* $\mathrm{C}(\pi)$.

An event $e$ is called *impossible* in a PES if it does not occur in any of its configurations. Events can be impossible because of enabling cycles, or an over-lapping between the enabling and the conflict relation, or because of impossible predecessors.

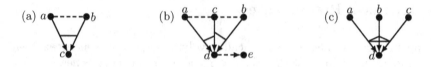

**Fig. 2.** A Bundle ES, an Extended Bundle ES, and a Dual ES

## 2.2   Bundle, Extended Bundle and Dual Event Structures

PESs are simple but also limited. They do not allow to describe optional or conditional enabling of events. Bundle event structures (BESs)—among others—were designed to overcome these limitations [8]. Enabling of events is based on bundles which are pairs $(X, e)$, denoted as $X \mapsto e$, where $X$ is a set of events and $e$ is the event pointed by that bundle. A bundle is satisfied when one event of $X$ occurs. An event is enabled when all bundles pointing to it are satisfied. This disjunctive causality allows for optionality in enabling events.

**Definition 3.** *A* Bundle Event Structure (BES) *is a triple* $\beta = (E, \#, \mapsto)$, *where $E$ is a set of* events, *$\# \subseteq E^2$ is an irreflexive symmetric relation (the* conflict *relation), and $\mapsto \subseteq \mathcal{P}(E) \times E$ is the* enabling *relation, such that for all $X \subseteq E$ and $e \in E$ the bundle $X \mapsto e$ implies that for all $e_1, e_2 \in X$ with $e_1 \neq e_2$ it holds $e_1 \# e_2$ (Stability).*

Figure 2 (a) shows an example of a BES. The solid arrows denote causality, i.e. reflect the enabling relation, where the bar between the arrows indicates a bundle, and the dashed line denotes a mutual conflict.

A configuration of a BES is again a conflict-free set of events that is downward-closed. Therefore the stability condition avoids causal ambiguity [9]. To exclude sets of events that result from enabling cycles we use traces. For a sequence $t = e_1 \cdots e_n$ of events let $\overline{t} = \{e_1, \ldots, e_n\}$ and $t_i = e_1 \cdots e_i$. Let $\epsilon$ denote the empty sequence.

**Definition 4.** *Let $\beta = (E, \#, \mapsto)$ be a BES. A* trace *is a sequence of distinct events $t = e_1 \cdots e_n$ with $\overline{t} \subseteq E$ such that $\forall 1 \leq i, j \leq n \,.\, \neg (e_i \# e_j)$ and such that $\forall 1 \leq i \leq n \,.\, \forall X \subseteq E \,.\, X \mapsto e_i \implies \overline{t_{i-1}} \cap X \neq \emptyset$.*

A set of events $C \subseteq E$ is a *configuration* of $\beta$ if there is a trace $t$ such that $C = \overline{t}$. This trace-based definition of a configuration will be the same for Extended Bundle and Dual ESs. Let $\mathrm{T}(\beta)$ denote the set of traces and $\mathrm{C}(\beta)$ the set of configurations of $\beta$.

Partially ordered sets, abbreviated as posets, are used as a semantic model for different kinds of ESs and other concurrency models (see e.g. [11]). In contrast to configurations, a poset does not only record the set of events that happened, but also captures the precedence relations between the events. Formally a poset is a pair $(A, \leq)$, where $A$ is a finite set of *events* and $\leq$ is a *partial order* over $A$.

A poset represents a set of system runs, differing for permutation of independent events. To describe the semantics of the entire ES, families of posets [11]

with a prefix relation are used. According to Rensink in [11], families of posets form a convenient underlying model for models of concurrency, and are more expressive than families of configurations.

To obtain the posets of a BES, wndow each of its configurations with a partial order. Let $\beta = (E, \#, \mapsto)$ be a BES and $C \in C(\beta)$, and $e, e' \in C$. Then $e \prec_C e'$ if $\exists X \subseteq E . e \in X \wedge X \mapsto e'$. Let $\leq_C$ be the reflexive and transitive closure of $\prec_C$. It is proved in [8] that $\leq_C$ is a partial order over $C$. Let $P(\beta)$ denote the set of posets of $\beta$.

Let $x$ and $y$ be two ESs of arbitrary kind on which posets are defined. We denote that $x$ and $y$ have the same set of posets by $x \simeq_p y$. Note that for BESs, EBES, and DESs families of posets are the most discriminating semantics studied in the literature. So, in these cases, we consider two ESs as behaviorally equivalent if they have the same set of posets.

The first extension of BESs we consider are *Extended Bundle Event Structures* (EBESs) from [8]. The conflict relation $\#$ is replaced by a *disabling* relation. An event $e_1$ disables another event $e_2$, means once $e_1$ occurs $e_2$ cannot occur anymore. The symmetric conflict $\#$ can be modeled through mutual disabling. Therefore EBESs are a generalization of BESs, and thus are more expressive [8].

**Definition 5.** *An* Extended Bundle Event Structure (EBES) *is a triple* $\xi = (E, \rightsquigarrow, \mapsto)$, *where* $E$ *is a set of* events, $\rightsquigarrow \subseteq E^2$ *is the irreflexive disabling relation, and* $\mapsto \subseteq \mathcal{P}(E) \times E$ *is the enabling relation, such that for all* $X \subseteq E$ *and* $e \in E$ *the bundle* $X \mapsto e$ *implies that for all* $e_1, e_2 \in X$ *with* $e_1 \neq e_2$ *it holds* $e_1 \rightsquigarrow e_2$ *(Stability).*

Stability ensures that two distinct events of a bundle set are in mutual disabling. Figure 2 (b) shows an EBES with the two bundles $\{a, c\} \mapsto d$ and $\{b, c\} \mapsto d$. The dashed lines denote again mutual disabling as required by stability. A disabling $d \rightsquigarrow e$, to be read '$e$ disables $d$', is represented by a dashed arrow.

**Definition 6.** *Let* $\xi = (E, \rightsquigarrow, \mapsto)$ *be an EBES. A trace is a sequence of distinct events* $t = e_1 \cdots e_n$ *with* $\overline{t} \subseteq E$ *such that* $\forall 1 \leq i, j \leq n . e_i \rightsquigarrow e_j \implies i < j$ *and* $\forall 1 \leq i \leq n . \forall X \subseteq E . X \mapsto e_i \implies \overline{t_{i-1}} \cap X \neq \emptyset$.

We adapt the definitions of configurations and traces of BESs accordingly. For $C \in C(\xi)$ and $e, e' \in C$, let $e \prec_C e'$ if $\exists X \subseteq E . e \in C \wedge X \mapsto e'$ or if $e \rightsquigarrow e'$. Again $\leq_C$ denotes the reflexive and transitive closure of $\prec_C$, and $P(\xi)$ denotes the set of posets of $\xi$.

*Dual Event Structures* (DESs) are the second extension of BES examined here. They are obtained by dropping the stability condition. This leads to causal ambiguity, i.e. given a trace and one of its events, it is not always possible to determine what caused this event. The definition of DESs varies between [6] (based on EBESs) and [9] (based on BESs). Here we rely on the version of [9].

**Definition 7.** *A* Dual Event Structure (DES) *is a triple* $\delta = (E, \#, \mapsto)$, *where* $E$ *is a set of* events, $\# \subseteq E^2$ *is an irreflexive symmetric relation (the conflict relation), and* $\mapsto \subseteq \mathcal{P}(E) \times E$ *is the enabling relation.*

Figure 2 (c) shows a DES with one bundle, namely $\{a, b, c\} \mapsto d$, and without conflicts. Again the definitions of configurations and traces are exactly the same as in BESs (cf. Def. 4), therefore we omit them here.

Because of the causal ambiguity, the definition of $\leq_C$ is difficult and the behavior of a DES w.r.t. a configuration cannot be described by a single poset anymore. [9] illustrates that there are different possible interpretations of causality. The authors defined five different intentional posets: liberal, bundle satisfaction, minimal, early and late posets. They show the equivalence of the behavioral semantics, and that the early causality and trace equivalence coincide. Thus we concentrate on early causality. The remaining intentional partial order semantics are discussed in [1]. To capture causal ambiguity we have to consider all traces of a configuration to obtain its posets. Below $U_1$ is earlier than $U_2$ if the largest index in $U_1 \setminus U_2$ is smaller than the largest index in $U_2 \setminus U_1$ [9].

**Definition 8.** *Let* $\delta = (E, \#, \mapsto)$ *be a DES,* $t = e_1 \cdots e_n$ *one of its traces,* $1 \leq i \leq n$, *and* $X_1 \mapsto e_i, \ldots, X_m \mapsto e_i$ *all bundles pointing to* $e_i$. *A set* $U$ *is a cause of* $e_i$ *in* $t$ *if* $\forall e \in U . \exists 1 \leq j < i . e = e_j$, $\forall 1 \leq k \leq m . X_k \cap U \neq \emptyset$, *and* $U$ *is the earliest set satisfying the previous two conditions. Let* $P_d(t)$ *be the set of posets obtained this way for* $t$.

## 2.3  Event Structures for Resolvable Conflicts

Event Structures for Resolvable Conflicts (RCES) were introduced in [12] to generalize former types of ESs and to give semantics to general Petri Nets. They allow to model the case where $a$ and $c$ cannot occur together until $b$ takes place, i.e. initially $a$ and $c$ are in a conflict until the occurrence of $b$ resolves this conflict. An RCES consists of a set of events and an enabling relation between sets of events. Here the enabling relation also models conflicts between events. The behavior is defined by a transition relation between sets of events that is derived from the enabling relation $\vdash$.

**Definition 9.** *An* Event Structure for Resolvable Conflicts (RCES) *is a pair* $\rho = (E, \vdash)$, *where* $E$ *is a set of* events *and* $\vdash \subseteq \mathcal{P}(E)^2$ *is the* enabling relation.

In [12] several versions of configurations are defined. Here we consider only configurations which are both reachable and finite.

**Definition 10.** *Let* $\rho = (E, \vdash)$ *be an RCES and* $X, Y \subseteq E$. *Then* $X \rightarrow_{rc} Y$ *if* $(X \subseteq Y \wedge \forall Z \subseteq Y . \exists W \subseteq X . W \vdash Z)$. *The set of* configurations of $\rho$ *is defined as* $C(\rho) = \{X \subseteq E \mid \emptyset \rightarrow_{rc}^* X \wedge X \text{ is finite }\}$, *where* $\rightarrow_{rc}^*$ *is the reflexive and transitive closure of* $\rightarrow_{rc}$.

As an example consider the RCES $\rho = (E, \vdash)$, where $E = \{a, b, c\}$, $\{b\} \vdash \{a, c\}$, and $\emptyset \vdash X$ iff $X \subseteq E$ and $X \neq \{a, c\}$. It models the above described initial conflict between $a$ and $c$ that can be resolved by $b$. In Fig. 3 $(\rho)$ the respective transition graph is shown, i.e. the nodes are all reachable configurations of $\rho$ and the directed edges represent $\rightarrow_{rc}$. Note, because of $\{a, c\} \subset \{a, b, c\}$ and $\emptyset \nvdash \{a, c\}$, there is no transition from $\emptyset$ to $\{a, b, c\}$.

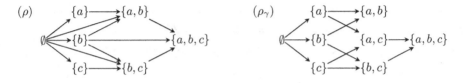

**Fig. 3.** Transition graphs of RCESs with resolvable conflict ($\rho$) and disabling ($\rho_\gamma$)

We consider two RCESs as equivalent if they have the same transition graphs. Note that, since we consider only reachable configurations, the transition equivalence defined below is denoted as reachable transition equivalence in [12].

**Definition 11.** *Two RCESs* $\rho = (E, \to_{\mathrm{rc}})$ *and* $\rho' = (E', \to'_{\mathrm{rc}})$ *are* transition equivalent, *denoted by* $\rho \simeq_t \rho'$, *if* $E = E'$ *and* $\to_{\mathrm{rc}} \cap (\mathrm{C}(\rho))^2 = \to'_{\mathrm{rc}} \cap (\mathrm{C}(\rho'))^2$.

Again we adapt the notion of transition equivalence to arbitrary types of ESs with a transition relation. Let $x$ and $y$ be two arbitrary types of ESs on that a transition relation is defined. We denote the fact that $x$ and $y$ have the same transition graphs by $x \simeq_t y$. Note that for RCESs, transition equivalence is the most discriminating semantics studied in the literature. So we consider two RCESs as behavioral equivalent if they have the same transition graphs.

## 3  Shrinking Causality

Now we add a new relation which represents the removal of causal dependencies as a ternary relation between events $\rhd \subseteq E^3$. For instance $(a, c, b) \in \rhd$, denoted as $[a \to b] \rhd c$, models that $a$ is dropped from the set of causal predecessors of $b$ by the occurrence of $c$. The dropping is visualized in Fig. 4(a) by a dashed arrow with empty head from the initial cause $a \to b$ to its dropper $c$. We add this relation to PESs and denote the result as shrinking causality event structures.

**Definition 12.** *A Shrinking Causality Event Structure (SES) is a pair* $\sigma = (\pi, \rhd)$, *where* $\pi = (E, \#, \to)$ *is a PES and* $\rhd \subseteq E^3$ *is the* shrinking causality relation *such that* $[e \to e''] \rhd e'$ *implies* $e \to e''$ *for all* $e, e', e'' \in E$.

Sometimes we expand $(\pi, \rhd)$ and write $(E, \#, \to, \rhd)$. For $[c \to t] \rhd m$ we call $m$ the modifier, $t$ the target, and $c$ the contribution. We denote the set of all modifiers dropping $c \to t$ by $[c \to t] \rhd$. We refer to the set of dropped causes of an event w.r.t. a specific history by the function $\mathrm{dc} : \mathcal{P}(E) \times E \to \mathcal{P}(E)$ defined as: $\mathrm{dc}(H, e) = \{e' \mid \exists d \in H \,.\, [e' \to e] \rhd d\}$. We refer to the initial causes of an event by the function $\mathrm{ic} : E \to \mathcal{P}(E)$ such that: $\mathrm{ic}(e) = \{e' \mid e' \to e\}$. The semantics of a SES can be defined based on posets similar to BESs, EBESs, and DESs, or based on a transition relation similar to RCESs. We consider both.

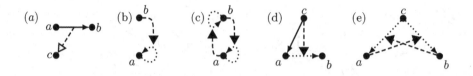

**Fig. 4.** A SES and GESs modeling disabling, conflict, temporary disabling, and resolvable conflicts

**Definition 13.** *Let $\sigma = (E, \#, \rightarrow, \rhd)$ be a SES.*

- *A trace of $\sigma$ is a sequence of distinct events $t = e_1 \cdots e_n$ with $\bar{t} \subseteq E$ such that $\forall 1 \leq i, j \leq n . \neg (e_i \# e_j)$ and $\forall 1 \leq i \leq n . \left( \mathrm{ic}(e_i) \setminus \mathrm{dc}(\overline{t_{i-1}}, e_i) \right) \subseteq \overline{t_{i-1}}.$ $C \subseteq E$ is a traced-based configuration of $\sigma$ if there is $t$ such that $C = \bar{t}$. Let $\mathrm{C}_{Tr}(\sigma)$ be the set of traced-based configurations, $\mathrm{T}(\sigma)$ the set of traces of $\sigma$.*
- *Let $t = e_1 \cdots e_n \in \mathrm{T}(\sigma)$ and $1 \leq i \leq n$. A set $U$ is a cause of $e_i$ in $t$ if $\forall e \in U . \exists 1 \leq j < i . e = e_j$, $(\mathrm{ic}(e_i) \setminus \mathrm{dc}(U, e_i)) \subseteq U$, and $U$ is the earliest set satisfying the previous two conditions. Let $\mathrm{P}_{\mathrm{s}}(t)$ be the set of posets obtained this way for $t$.*
- *Let $X, Y \subseteq E$. Then $X \rightarrow_{\mathrm{s}} Y$ if $X \subseteq Y$, $\forall e, e' \in Y . \neg (e \# e')$, and $\forall e \in Y \setminus X .$ $(\mathrm{ic}(e) \setminus \mathrm{dc}(X, e)) \subseteq X$.*
- *The set of all configurations of $\sigma$ is $\mathrm{C}(\sigma) = \{X \subseteq E \mid \emptyset \rightarrow_{\mathrm{s}}^* X \wedge X$ is finite $\}$, where $\rightarrow_{\mathrm{s}}^*$ is the reflexive and transitive closure of $\rightarrow_{\mathrm{s}}$.*

The combination of initial and dropped causes ensures that for each $e_i \in \bar{t}$, all its initial causes are either preceding $e_i$ or dropped by other events preceding $e_i$. Note that as for DESs we concentrate on early causality. We consider the reachable and finite configurations w.r.t. to $\rightarrow_{\mathrm{s}}$ as well as configurations based on the traces. Note that both definitions coincide.

To show that $\simeq_{\mathrm{p}}$ and $\simeq_{\mathrm{t}}$ coincide on SESs we make use of the result that $\simeq_{\mathrm{p}}$ and trace equivalence coincide on DES (compare to [9]) and show that SESs are as expressive as DESs. Consider the shrinking-causality $[c \rightarrow t] \rhd d$. It models the case that initially $t$ causally depends on $c$ which can be dropped by the occurrence of $d$. Thus for $t$ to be enabled either $c$ occurs or $d$ does. This is a disjunctive causality as modeled by DESs. In fact $[c \rightarrow t] \rhd d$ corresponds to the bundle $\{c, d\} \mapsto t$. We prove that we can map each SES into a DES with the same behavior and vice versa. To translate a SES into a DES we create a bundle for each initial causal dependence and add all its droppers to the bundle set.

In the opposite direction we map each DES into a set of similar SESs such that each SES in this set has the same behavior as the DES. Intuitively we have to choose an initial dependency for each bundle from its set, and to translate the rest of the bundle set into droppers for that dependency. Unfortunately the bundles that point to the same event are not necessarily disjoint. Consider for example $\{a, b\} \mapsto e$ and $\{b, c\} \mapsto e$. If we choose $b \rightarrow e$ as initial dependency for both bundles to be dropped as $[b \rightarrow e] \rhd a$ and $[b \rightarrow e] \rhd c$, then $\{a, e\}$ is a configuration of the resulting SES but not of the original DES. So we have to ensure that we choose distinct events as initial causes for all bundles pointing to the same event. Thus for each bundle we choose a fresh event as initial cause, make it impossible by a self-loop, and add all events of the bundle as droppers. Note that to translate a DES into a SES we have to introduce additional events, i.e. it is not always possible to translate a DES into a SES without additional impossible events. All proofs can be found in [1].

**Theorem 1.** *SESs are as expressive as DESs.*

In [1] we show that each SES and its translation as well as each DES and its translation have the same set of posets considering not only early but also liberal, minimal, and late causality. Thus the concepts of SESs and DESs are not only behaviorally equivalent but—except for the additional impossible events—also structurally closely related.

Note that $\simeq_p$, $\simeq_t$, and trace-equivalence coincide on SES.

**Theorem 2.** *Let $\sigma, \sigma'$ be two SESs. Then $\sigma \simeq_p \sigma'$ iff $\sigma \simeq_t \sigma'$ iff $\mathrm{T}(\sigma) = \mathrm{T}(\sigma')$.*

As shown above SESs allow to model disjunctive causality. As an example consider the dropping of a causality as in Fig. 4(a). Such a disjunctive causality is not possible in EBESs. On the other hand the asymmetric conflict of an EBES cannot be modeled with a SES. As an example consider Fig. 2 (b),where $e$ cannot precede $d$.

**Theorem 3.** *SESs and EBESs are incomparable.*

SESs are strictly less expressive than RCESs, because each SES can be translated into a transition-equivalent RCES, and on the other hand there are RCESs that cannot be translated into a transition-equivalent SES. As a counterexample we use the RCES $\rho_\sigma = (\{e, f\}, \{\emptyset \vdash \emptyset, \emptyset \vdash \{e\}, \emptyset \vdash \{f\}, \{e\} \vdash \{e, f\}\})$ that captures disabling in an EBES.

**Theorem 4.** *SESs are strictly less expressive than RCESs.*

## 4   Growing Causality

As in SESs we base our extension for growing causality on PESs. We add the new relation $\blacktriangleright \subseteq E^3$, where $(a, c, b) \in \blacktriangleright$, denoted as $c \blacktriangleright [a \to b]$, models that $c$ adds $a$ as a cause for $b$. Thus $c$ is a condition for the causal dependency $a \to b$.

The adding is visualized in Fig. 4(d) by a dashed line with a filled head from the modifier $c$ to the added dependency $a \to b$, which is dotted denoting that this dependency does not exist initially (In this example there is an additional causality $c \to a$).

**Definition 14.** *A Growing Causality Event Structure (GES) is a pair $\gamma = (\pi, \blacktriangleright)$, where $\pi = (E, \#, \to)$ is a PES and $\blacktriangleright \subseteq E^3$ is the growing causality relation such that $\forall e, e', e'' \in E . e' \blacktriangleright [e \to e''] \implies \neg(e \to e'')$.*

We refer to the causes added to an event w.r.t. a specific history by the function $\mathrm{ac} : \mathcal{P}(E) \times E \to \mathcal{P}(E)$, defined as $\mathrm{ac}(H, e) = \{e' \mid \exists a \in H . a \blacktriangleright [e' \to e]\}$, and to the initial causality by the function ic as defined in § 3. Similar to the RCESs the behavior of a GES can be defined by a transition relation. Thus we consider two GESs as equally expressive if they are transition-equivalent.

**Definition 15.** *Let $\gamma = (E, \#, \rightarrow, \blacktriangleright)$ be a GES.*

- *A trace of $\gamma$ is a sequence of distinct events $t = e_1 \cdots e_n$ with $\bar{t} \subseteq E$ such that $\forall 1 \leq i, j \leq n . \neg (e_i \# e_j)$ and $\big(\mathrm{ic}(e_i) \cup \mathrm{ac}(\overline{t_{i-1}}, e_i)\big) \subseteq \overline{t_{i-1}}$ for all $i \leq n$. Then $C \subseteq E$ is a trace-based configuration of $\gamma$ if there is a trace $t$ such that $C = \bar{t}$. The set of traces of $\gamma$ is denoted by $\mathrm{T}(\gamma)$ and the set of its trace-based configurations is denoted by $\mathrm{C}_{Tr}(\gamma)$.*

- *Let $X, Y \subseteq E$. Then $X \rightarrow_g Y$ if $X \subseteq Y$, $\forall e, e' \in Y . \neg (e \# e')$, $\forall e \in Y \setminus X$. $(\mathrm{ic}(e) \cup \mathrm{ac}(X, e)) \subseteq X$, and $\forall t, m \in Y \setminus X . \forall c \in E . m \blacktriangleright [c \rightarrow t] \implies (c \in X \vee m \in \{c, t\})$.*

- *The set of all configurations of $\gamma$ is $\mathrm{C}(\gamma) = \big\{ X \subseteq E \mid \emptyset \rightarrow_g^* X \wedge X \text{ is finite} \big\}$, where $\rightarrow_g^*$ is the reflexive and transitive closure of $\rightarrow_g$.*

The last condition in the transition definition prevents the concurrent occurrence of a target and its modifier since they are not independent. One exception is when the contribution has already occurred; in that case, the modifier does not change the target's predecessors. It also captures the trivial case of self adding, i.e. when a target adds a contribution to itself or a modifier adds itself to a target. Again we consider the reachable and finite configurations, and show in [1] that the definitions of reachable and trace-based configurations coincide.

Disabling as defined in EBESs or the asymmetric event structure of [3] can be modeled by $\blacktriangleright$. For example $b \rightsquigarrow a$ can be modeled by $b \blacktriangleright [a \rightarrow a]$ as depicted in Fig. 4 (b). Conflicts can be modeled by $\blacktriangleright$ through mutual disabling, as depicted in Fig. 4 (c), and thus the conflict relation can be omitted in this ES model.

In inhibitor event structures [2] there is a kind of disabling, where an event $e$ can be disabled by another event $d$ until an event out of a set $X$ occurs. This kind of temporary disabling provides disjunction in the re-enabling that cannot be modeled in GESs but in DCESs (cf. the next section). However temporary disabling without a disjunctive re-enabling can be modeled by a GES as in Fig. 4 (d).

Also resolvable conflicts can be modeled by a GES. For example the GES in Fig. 4 (e) with $a \blacktriangleright [c \rightarrow b]$ and $b \blacktriangleright [c \rightarrow a]$ models a conflict between $a$ and $b$ that can be resolved by $c$. Note that this example depends on the idea that a modifier and its target cannot occur concurrently (cf. Def. 15). Note also that resolvable conflicts are a reason why families of configurations cannot be used to define the semantics of GESs or RCESs.

As shown in Fig. 4 (b) GESs can model disabling. Nevertheless EBESs and GESs are incomparable, because GESs cannot model the disjunction in the enabling relation that EBESs inherit from BESs. On the other hand EBESs cannot model conditional causal dependencies. Thus GESs are incomparable to BESs as well as EBESs.

**Theorem 5.** *GESs are incomparable to BESs and EBESs.*

GESs are also incomparable to SESs, because the adding of causes cannot be modeled by SESs. As a counterexample we use the GES of Fig. 4 (c). Then since BESs are incomparable to GESs, BESs are less expressive than DESs, and DESs are as expressive as SESs, we conclude that GESs and SESs are incomparable.

**Theorem 6.** *GESs and SESs are incomparable.*

As illustrated in Fig. 4 (d) GESs can model resolvable conflicts. Nevertheless they are strictly less expressive than RCESs, because each GES can be translated into a transition equivalent RCES and on the other hand there exists no transition equivalent GES for the RCES $\rho_\gamma = (\{a, b, c\}, \vdash)$ that is given by the second transition graph in Fig. 3. It models the case, where after $a$ and $b$ the event $c$ becomes impossible, i.e. it models disabling by a set instead of a single event.

**Theorem 7.** *GESs are strictly less expressive than RCESs.*

## 5  Dynamic Causality

Up to now we have investigated shrinking, and growing causality separately. In this section we combine them and examine the resulting expressiveness.

**Definition 16.** *A* Dynamic Causality Event Structure (DCES) *is a triple* $\Delta = (\pi, \rhd, \blacktriangleright)$—*expanded* $(E, \#, \rightarrow, \rhd, \blacktriangleright)$—*, where* $\pi = (E, \#, \rightarrow)$ *is a PES,* $\rhd \subseteq E^3$ *is the shrinking causality relation, and* $\blacktriangleright \subseteq E^3$ *is the growing causality relation such that for all* $e, e', e'' \in E$: *1.* $[e \rightarrow e''] \rhd e' \wedge \nexists m \in E \,.\, m \blacktriangleright [e \rightarrow e''] \Longrightarrow e \rightarrow e''$ *2.* $e' \blacktriangleright [e \rightarrow e''] \wedge \nexists m \in E \,.\, [e \rightarrow e''] \rhd m \Longrightarrow \neg(e \rightarrow e'')$ *3.* $e' \blacktriangleright [e \rightarrow e''] \Longrightarrow \neg([e \rightarrow e''] \rhd e')$.

Conditions 1 and 2 are just a generalization of the conditions in Defs. 12 and 14 respectively. If there are droppers and adders for the same causal dependency we do not specify whether this dependency is contained in $\rightarrow$, because the semantics depends on the order in which the droppers and adders occur. Condition 3 prevents that a modifier adds and drops the same cause for the same target.

The order of occurrence of droppers and adders determines the causes of an event. For example assume $a \blacktriangleright [c \rightarrow t]$ and $[c \rightarrow t] \rhd d$, then after $ad$, $t$ does not depend on $c$, whereas after $da$, $t$ depends on $c$. Thus configurations like $\{a, d\}$ are not expressive enough to represent the state of such a system (cf. Lem. 1).

Therefore in a DCES a state is a pair of a configuration $C$ and a causal state function cs, which computes the causal predecessors of an event, that are still needed.

**Definition 17.** *Let* $\Delta = (E, \#, \rightarrow, \rhd, \blacktriangleright)$ *be a DCES. The function* mc $: \mathcal{P}(E) \times E \rightarrow \mathcal{P}(E)$ *denotes the* maximal causality *that an event can have after some history* $C \subseteq E$, *and is defined as* $\mathrm{mc}(C, e) = \{e' \in E \setminus C \mid e' \rightarrow e \vee \exists a \in C \,.\, a \blacktriangleright [e' \rightarrow e]\}$. *A* state *of* $\Delta$ *is a pair* $(C, \mathrm{cs})$ *where* cs $: E \setminus C \rightarrow \mathcal{P}(E \setminus C)$ *such that* $C \subseteq E$ *and* $\mathrm{cs}(e) \subseteq \mathrm{mc}(C, e)$. *We denote* cs *as* causality state function, *which shows for an event* $e$ *that did not occur, which events are still missing such that* $e$ *is enabled. An* initial state *of* $\Delta$ *is* $S_0 = (\emptyset, \mathrm{cs_i})$, *where* $\mathrm{cs_i}(e) = \{e' \in E \mid e' \rightarrow e\}$.

Note that $S_0$ is the only state with an empty set of events; for other sets of events there can be multiple states. The behavior of a DCES is defined by the transition relation on its reachable states with finite configurations.

**Definition 18.** *Let $\Delta = (E, \#, \rightarrow, \rhd, \blacktriangleright)$ be a DCES and $C, C' \subseteq E$. Then $(C, cs) \rightarrow_d (C', cs')$ if:*

1. $C \subseteq C'$     2. $\forall e, e' \in C'. \neg(e \# e')$     3. $\forall e \in C' \setminus C. cs(e) = \emptyset$
4. $\forall e, e' \in E \setminus C'. e' \in cs(e) \setminus cs'(e) \implies [e' \rightarrow e] \rhd \cap (C' \setminus C) \neq \emptyset$
5. $\forall e, e' \in E \setminus C'. [e' \rightarrow e] \rhd \cap (C' \setminus C) \neq \emptyset \implies e' \notin cs'(e)$
6. $\forall e \in E \setminus C'. e' \in cs'(e) \setminus cs(e) \implies \blacktriangleright [e' \rightarrow e] \cap (C' \setminus C) \neq \emptyset$
7. $\forall e, e' \in E \setminus C'. \blacktriangleright [e' \rightarrow e] \cap (C' \setminus C) \neq \emptyset \implies e' \in cs'(e)$
8. $\forall e, e' \in E \setminus C. [e' \rightarrow e] \rhd \cap (C' \setminus C) = \emptyset \vee \blacktriangleright [e' \rightarrow e] \cap (C' \setminus C) = \emptyset$
9. $\forall t, m \in C' \setminus C. \forall c \in E. m \blacktriangleright [c \rightarrow t] \implies (c \in C \vee m \in \{c, t\})$.

Condition 1 ensures the accumulation of events. Condition 2 ensures conflict freeness. Condition 3 ensures that only events which are enabled after $C$ can take place in $C'$. Condition 4 ensures that, if a cause disappears, there has to be a dropper of it. The same is ensured by Condition 6 for appearing causes. Condition 5 ensures that if there are adders, the cause has to appear in the new causal state, unless it occurred. Similarly, Condition 7 ensures, that causes disappear, when there are droppers. To keep the theory simple, Condition 8 avoids race conditions; it forbids the occurrence of an adder and a dropper of the same causal dependency within one transition. Condition 9 ensures that DCESs coincide with GESs.

**Definition 19.** *Let $\Delta$ be a DCES. The set of (reachable) states of $\Delta$ is defined as $S(\Delta) = \{(X, cs_X) \mid S_0 \rightarrow_d^* (X, cs_X) \wedge X$ is finite $\}$, where $\rightarrow_d^*$ is the reflexive and transitive closure of $\rightarrow_d$.*

*Two DCESs $\Delta = (E, \#, \rightarrow, \rhd, \blacktriangleright)$ and $\Delta' = (E', \#', \rightarrow', \rhd', \blacktriangleright')$ are state transition equivalent, denoted by $\Delta \simeq_s \Delta'$, if $E = E'$ and $\rightarrow_d \cap (S(\Delta))^2 = \rightarrow_d' \cap (S(\Delta'))^2$.*

**Lemma 1.** *There are DCESs that are transition equivalent but not state transition equivalent.*

Because of the previous Lemma, we consider the more discriminating equivalence $\simeq_s$—instead of $\simeq_t$—to compare DCESs and to compare with DCESs. To compare with RCESs, we use the counterexample $\rho_\gamma$ of Fig. 3 to show that not for every RCES there is a transition-equivalent DCES. Moreover RCESs cannot distinguish between different causality states of one configuration (cf. Lem. 1). Consequently DCESs and RCESs are incomparable.

**Theorem 8.** *DCESs and RCESs are incomparable.*

By construction, DCESs are at least as expressive as GESs and SESs. To embed a SES (or GES) into a DCES it suffice to choose $\blacktriangleright = \emptyset$ (or $\rhd = \emptyset$). Furthermore are DCESs incomparable to RCESs which are strictly more expressive than GESs and SESs. Thus DCESs are strictly more expressive then GESs and SESs.

**Theorem 9.** *DCESs are strictly more expressive than GESs and SESs.*

To compare with EBESs, we use the disabling of GESs, and the disjunctive causality of SESs. The translation of an EBES into a DCES is formally defined in

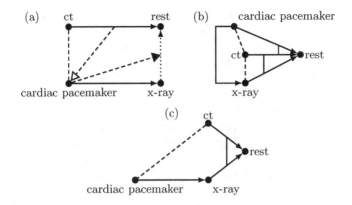

**Fig. 5.** A DCES, a BES, and a DES modeling the medical example

[1], where disabling uses self-loops of target events, while droppers use auxiliary impossible events, not to intervene with the disabling. Besides we construct posets for the configurations of the translation, and compare them with those of the original EBES. In this way we prove that DCESs are at least as expressive as EBESs. But since EBESs cannot model the disjunctive causality—without a conflict—of SESs which are included in DCESs, the following result holds.

**Theorem 10.** *DCESs are strictly more expressive than EBESs.*

## 6  Conclusions

We study the idea that causality may change during system runs in event structures. For this, we enhance a simple type of ESs—the PES—by means of additional relations capturing the changes in events' dependencies, driven by the occurrence of other events.

First, in § 3, we limit our concern to the case where dependencies can only be dropped. We call the new resulting event structure Shrinking Causality ES (SES). In that section, we show that the exhibited dynamic causality can be expressed through a completely static perspective, by proving equivalence between SESs and DESs. By such a proof, we do not only show the expressive power of our new ES, but also the big enhancement in expressive power (w.r.t. PESs) gained by adding only this one relation.

Later on, in § 4, we study the complementary style where dependencies can be added to events, resulting in Growing Causality ES (GES). We show that the growing causality can model both permanent and temporary disabling. Besides, it can be used to resolve conflicts and, furthermore, to force conflicts. Unlike the SESs, the GESs are not directly comparable to other types of ESs from the literature, except for PESs; one reason is that they provide a conjunctive style of causality, another is their ability to express conditioning in causality.

Finally, in § 5, we combine both approaches of dynamicity with a new type of event structures, which we called the Dynamic Causality ES (DCES). Therein a dependency can be both added and dropped. For this new type of ESs the following two—possibly surprising—facts can be observed: (1) There are types of ESs that are incomparable to both SESs and GESs, but that are comparable to (here: strictly less expressive than) DCESs, i.e. the combination of SESs and GESs; one such type is EBESs. (2) Though SESs and GESs are strictly less expressive than RCESs, their combination—the newly defined DCESs—is incomparable to RCESs, or any other type of ESs with a static causality.

To highlight the pragmatic advantages of dynamic-causality ESs over their equivalent and non-equivalent competitor ESs, we go back to our example mentioned in the motivation. Reichert et al. in [10] emphasize that the model of such processes should distinguish between the regular execution path and the exceptional one. Accordingly, they define two labels, *REGULAR* and *EXCEPTIONAL*, to be assigned to tasks. Fig. 5 (a) shows a DCES model of our example, where *rest* represents the rest of the treatment process, and *ct* represents the computer tomography. The initial causality in a DCES e.g. $ct \rightarrow rest$ corresponds to the regular path of a process, while the changes carried by modifiers e.g. *cardiac pacemaker* correspond to exceptional one. Other static-causality ESs like a BES and a DES can model the fact that either the computer tomography XOR the X-ray is needed, as shown in Fig. 5(b) and 5(c). The same can be done by an equivalent RCES. However, we argue that none of these models can distinguish between regular and exceptional paths.

Thus our main contributions are: 1. We provide a formal model that allows us to express dynamicity in causality. Using this model, we enhance the PESs yielding SESs, GESs and DCESs. 2. We show the equivalence of SESs and DESs. 3. We show the incomparability of GESs to many other types of ESs. 4. We show that DCESs are strictly more expressive than EBESs and thus strictly more expressive than many other existing types of ESs. 5. We show that DCESs are incomparable to RCESs. 6. The new model succinctly supports modern workflow management systems.

In [5] Crafa et al. defined an Event Structure semantics for the $\pi$-calculus based on Prime ESs. Since the latter do not allow for disjunctive causality which they needed, and in order to avoid duplications of events, they extended Prime ESs with a set of bound names, and altered the configuration definition to allow for such disjunction. With Shrinking-Causality ESs—that can express disjunctive causality—this problem could possibly be addressed more naturally without copying events. Here higher-order dynamicity, i.e. to allow for adding and dropping of adders and droppers, might help to deal with the instantiation of variables caused by communications involving bound names.

Up to now, we limit the execution of a DCESs such that an interleaving between adders and droppers of the same causal dependency is forced. As a future work, we want to study the case where modifiers of the same dependency can occur concurrently—read: at the very same instant of time—in DCESs. Similarly, we want to investigate the situation of concurrent occurrence of an adder and its target in GESs. Furthermore, we want to study the ideas of adding and dropping by sets of events or even higher-order dynamics, i.e. events that may change the role of events to adders, dropper or back to normal events. Additionally, the set of possible changes in our newly defined ESs must still be declared statically. We will also investigate the idea that ESs can evolve, by supporting ad hoc changes, such that new dependencies as well as events can be added to a structure.

# References

1. Arbach, Y., Karcher, D., Peters, K., Nestmann, U.: Dynamic Causality in Event Structures (Technical Report). TU Berlin (2015), http://arxiv.org/
2. Baldan, P., Busi, N., Corradini, A., Pinna, G.M.: Domain and event structure semantics for Petri nets with read and inhibitor arcs. Theoretical Computer Science 323(1-3), 129–189 (2004)
3. Baldan, P., Corradini, A., Montanari, U.: Contextual Petri Nets, Asymmetric Event Structures, and Processes. Information and Computation 171(1), 1–49 (2001)
4. Boudol, G., Castellani, I.: Flow Models of Distributed Computations: Three Equivalent Semantics for CCS. Information and Computation 114(2), 247–314 (1994)
5. Crafa, S., Varacca, D., Yoshida, N.: Event structure semantics of parallel extrusion in the pi-calculus. In: Birkedal, L. (ed.) FOSSACS 2012. LNCS, vol. 7213, pp. 225–239. Springer, Heidelberg (2012)
6. Katoen, J.P.: Quantitative and Qualitative Extensions of Event Structures. PhD thesis, Twente (1996)
7. Kuske, D., Morin, R.: Pomsets for Local Trace Languages - Recognizability, Logic & Petri Nets. In: Palamidessi, C. (ed.) CONCUR 2000. LNCS, vol. 1877, pp. 426–441. Springer, Heidelberg (2000)
8. Langerak, R.: Transformations and Semantics for LOTOS. PhD thesis, Twente (1992)
9. Langerak, R., Brinksma, E., Katoen, J.P.: Causal Ambiguity and Partial Orders in Event Structures. In: Mazurkiewicz, A., Winkowski, J. (eds.) CONCUR 1997. LNCS, vol. 1243, pp. 317–331. Springer, Heidelberg (1997)
10. Reichert, M., Dadam, P., Bauer, T.: Dealing with forward and backward jumps in workflow management systems. Software and Systems Modeling 2(1), 37–58 (2003)
11. Rensink, A.: Posets for Configurations! In: Cleaveland, W.R. (ed.) CONCUR 1992. LNCS, vol. 630, pp. 269–285. Springer, Heidelberg (1992)
12. van Glabbeek, R., Plotkin, G.: Event Structures for Resolvable Conflict. In: Fiala, J., Koubek, V., Kratochvíl, J. (eds.) MFCS 2004. LNCS, vol. 3153, pp. 550–561. Springer, Heidelberg (2004)
13. Weber, B., Reichert, M., Rinderle-Ma, S.: Change patterns and change support features - enhancing flexibility in process-aware information systems. Data & Knowledge Engineering 66(3), 438–466 (2008)
14. Winskel, G.: Events in Computation. PhD thesis, Edinburgh (1980)
15. Winskel, G.: An introduction to event structures. In: de Bakker, J.W., de Roever, W.-P., Rozenberg, G. (eds.) Linear Time, Branching Time and Partial Order in Logics and Models for Concurrency. LNCS, vol. 354, pp. 364–397. Springer, Heidelberg (1989)
16. Winskel, G.: Distributed Probabilistic and Quantum Strategies. In: Proceedings of MFPS. ENTCS, vol. 298, pp. 403–425. Elsevier (2013)

# Loop Freedom in AODVv2

Kedar S. Namjoshi[1]  and Richard J. Trefler[2(✉)]

[1]  Bell Laboratories, Alcatel-Lucent, Newyork, USA
kedar@research.bell-labs.com
[2]  University of Waterloo, Waterloo, Canada
trefler@cs.waterloo.ca

**Abstract.** The AODV protocol is used to establish routes in a mobile, ad-hoc network (MANET). The protocol must operate in an adversarial environment where network connections and nodes can be added or removed at any point. While the ability to establish routes is best-effort under these conditions, the protocol is required to ensure that no routing loops are ever formed. AODVv2 is currently under development at the IETF, we focus attention on version 04. We detail two scenarios that show how routing loops may form in AODVv2 routing tables. The second scenario demonstrates a problem with the route table update performed on a **Broken** route entry. Our solution to this problem has been incorporated by the protocol designers into AODVv2, version 05. With the fix in place, we present an inductive and compositional proof showing that the corrected core protocol is loop-free for all valid configurations.

## 1 Introduction

The AODV ("Ad-Hoc On-Demand Distance Vector") protocol family is under development by the IETF MANET (Mobile, Ad-Hoc Networking) group. Its current form is AODVv2[1], which has evolved from the earlier DYMO[2] and AODV[3] protocols. As stated in the protocol description, AODVv2 "*is intended for use by mobile routers in wireless, multihop networks. AODVv2 determines unicast routes among AODVv2 routers within the network in an on-demand fashion, offering rapid convergence in dynamic topologies.*" AODVv2 is still evolving; our work focuses on the recent version 04 (which we refer to as AODVv2-04), published in July 2014. Subsequently, AODVv2-05 was issued in October of 2014, and AODVv2-06 in December 2014.

K.S. Namjoshi – Supported, in part, by DARPA under agreement number FA8750-12-C-0166. The U.S. Government is authorized to reproduce and distribute reprints for Governmental purposes notwithstanding any copyright notation thereon. The views and conclusions contained herein are those of the authors and should not be interpreted as necessarily representing the official policies or endorsements, either expressed or implied, of DARPA or the U.S. Government.

R.J. Trefler – Supported in part by Natural Sciences and Engineering Research Council of Canada Discovery and Collaborative Research and Development Grants.

[1] http://datatracker.ietf.org/doc/draft-ietf-manet-aodvv2/
[2] http://datatracker.ietf.org/doc/draft-ietf-manet-dymo/
[3] http://datatracker.ietf.org/doc/rfc3561/

© IFIP International Federation for Information Processing 2015
S. Graf and M. Viswanathan (Eds.): FORTE 2015, LNCS 9039, pp. 98–112, 2015.
DOI: 10.1007/978-3-319-19195-9_7

The environment in which AODVv2 operates is challenging, as network connections and nodes may be added or removed at any point. In such a setting, routes are established in a best-effort mode. However, the protocol is required to enforce a key safety property, that there are no routing loops in any reachable global state. A routing loop is formed when the next-hop entries in routing tables are connected in a cyclic manner (E.g., node A has next-hop B; node B has next-hop C; and node C has next-hop A).

We construct a formal, inductive proof that an *abstract model* of the protocol has no routing loops. Such a proof has utility, even though AODVv2 is still not finalized. A proof elucidates broad conditions under which loop-freedom can be guaranteed; those conditions can then be taken into account as the protocol is refined, and any fixes necessary can be incorporated quickly and with relatively little cost. Indeed, in the course of our analysis, we found that AODVv2-04 allows routing loops to form under certain sequences of actions, we discuss those scenarios in Section 1.2. The first example illustrates that if instance-specific timing constants are not set correctly, then routing loops may form. The second example is more serious since it can occur even if the protocol parameters are set correctly. This problem was quickly acknowledged by the protocol designers and corrected, based on our input, for version 05 of AODVv2 (cf. [14], `Appendix C: Changes since revision ...-04.txt`).

Our model aims to capture the core of the AODVv2 protocol by abstracting away some detail and by leaving out optional features. The main abstraction is that timer-driven actions are replaced either with non-determinism or with global predicate guards. For instance, our model allows a route entry to be invalidated at any point, while the protocol permits this only after timer expiration. In another instance, routes marked as `Expired` are expunged (i.e., removed completely) only after there is no activity for at least `MAX_SEQNUM_LIFETIME` seconds. Note that `MAX_SEQNUM_LIFETIME` is one of several instance specific constants in the protocol. Our model abstracts away from such constants by replacing the time-based preconditions with global network predicates. The predicates abstract nicely from the specifics of network structure, delays and processing power, which must go into determining a correct setting for these symbolic constants.

The full AODVv2 protocol has mechanisms that allow a wide variety of metrics to determine the cost of a route. Our model considers only the hopcount metric, i.e. the metric that counts the number of network edge hops between the origin node of a route and the target node of a route. Hop count is an important metric used in practice, and AODVv2 correctness requires at a minimum that the protocol behave correctly with the hop count metric. Our proof can be adapted to other cost metrics, where the cost of a link is greater than 0, and cost along a path is additive. Within these limits, the model exhibits all of the actual protocol computations, and more: hence, any proof that the model is correct shows also that the protocol, under the stated restrictions, is correct.

To summarize, our work makes two contributions: (1) we exhibit scenarios where AODVv2-04 allows routing loops to form, and suggest a protocol fix, which has been adopted by the designers, and (2) we construct a formal model of the protocol and an inductive proof showing that the corrected core protocol ensures loop freedom. This proof is interesting in its treatment of adversarial actions and its use of compositional reasoning.

## 1.1  Protocol Sketch

We informally sketch the main features of the protocol before proceeding to the proof. The model we use is given in Section 3. The model fixes an origin node, $O$, and a target node, $T$. The protocol establishes a route from $O$ to $T$ in two phases. The first phase is initiated by $O$, and consists of flooding a RREQ (route request) message through the network[4]. Every node receiving this RREQ message maintains an "origin route", next-hop entry which points to the neighboring node from which it has received the best route so far from $O$, i.e., (roughly) the (first) path with the least cost. Note that a node may receive multiple copies of the RREQ message sent from $O$, through different paths. Whenever the target node $T$ receives a better RREQ route from $O$, it responds with an RREP (route reply) message. This message is not flooded: it follows (backwards) the path to $O$ that has been established by the origin route entries. With fixed network connectivity and no message losses, this procedure converges (under mild conditions) to a least cost path from $O$ to $T$. Under the network disruptions that are expected in the MANET model, though, there is no guarantee of convergence. Under adversarial control of the network and message transmission, the only property that is *required* of the protocol is that it should never form a global state which has a routing loop: i.e., a state where the set of origin route entries form a cycle, such as where node $A$ has next-hop $B$, $B$ has next-hop $C$, and $C$ has next-hop $A$.

The tricky part of the analysis has to do with the case of "broken" route entries, which are created when links in the network fail. If $A$ has next-hop $B$ and the $A - B$ link fails, then the entry at $A$ is marked as `Broken`. However, new copies of the RREQ message from $O$ may arrive at $A$ after the breakage. *When should a route from one of those messages be accepted at $A$?* Accepting any route at all – which makes sense in a way: an unbroken route, however bad, is surely preferable to a broken one – may lead to a routing loop, as shown in the second scenario below. This scenario was possible in version 04 of the protocol, and it

---

[4] A data structure, the `RREQ Table`, is used in AODVv2-04 to control the flooding. Appendices A.1 and A.2.2 of AODVv2-04 describe precisely how the table is used: an incoming `RREQ` message is used to update a route entry, then the message is checked against the table to determine if it should be regenerated and sent to neighboring nodes. (We have confirmed this order of actions with the protocol authors, to resolve a slight ambiguity in the main text.) Hence, the table does not influence route updates; it may only stop the regeneration of `RREQ`s, which is already included in our model as message loss. Therefore, we do not model the table.

was discovered by us in the attempt to construct a proof of loop-freedom[5]. The partial proof pointed to the condition "accept any route that is not worse than the current broken route" as a possible resolution. We confirm that this is indeed a correct resolution through the formal proof given next. That resolution has also been accepted by the authors of AODVv2 and included starting with revision 05 of AODVv2 (cf. [14], `Appendix C: Changes since revision ...-04.txt`).

## 1.2    Loop Formation Scenarios

The first scenario creates a loop when the timer `MAX_SEQNUM_LIFETIME` is not set to a large enough value. The second creates a loop when any route is accepted in place of a broken one. Reading through the scenarios helps build intuition about how the protocol operates, which is helpful in understanding the proofs.

*Poor choice of timer values.* The AODVv2 protocol has several actions that are triggers by symbolic time constants. A protocol implementer has to give concrete values to these constants, a very difficult decision, as the correct values depend on the topology of the network, processing speeds, and transmission delays. As shown in the scenario below, a routing loop may result if the constants are inadvertently not set properly. The loop prevents RREP messages that are sent back from $T$, the target node, from reaching $O$, the originating node. As a result, no messages can be transferred from $O$ to $T$.

We should note that this is *not* an error in the protocol – with a correct choice of constants, the loop will not occur. We model the time-based actions as guarded commands with an untimed guard over the network state. The proof shows that the model is loop-free. The modeling, therefore, helps to narrow down the choice of time constants: the values chosen for a network instance should be such that the guard condition is guaranteed to hold when the timers expire.

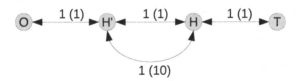

**Fig. 1.** Network: Early Expunge Scenario. Number by edge indicates hop-count, number in brackets indicates transmission delay in time units.

---

[5]  From Section 6.3 of AODVv2-04, one case of the condition for acceptance of a new route is "`((Route.State == Broken) && LoopFree(RteMsg, Route))`". The predicate `LoopFree` is defined in Section 5.6 as "`LoopFree (R1, R2) is TRUE when Cost(R2) <= (Cost(R1) + 1)`". Thus, `LoopFree(RteMsg,Route)` is true iff `Cost(Route) <= (Cost(RteMsg) + 1)`. This allows the cost of the route in the incoming message, `RteMsg`, to be arbitrarily larger than the cost of the stored route, `Route`, if the stored route is in a `Broken` state.

The network is fixed as shown in Figure 1. The scenario is as follows:

1. An RREQ message created by $O$ travels along the path O; H'; H; T. As a result, the origin route entries at these nodes have hop counts O=0, H'=1, H=2, T=3. A copy of the RREQ message remains undelivered on the link $H - H'$.

2. The route entry at H' is expired and then expunged.
   This is the critical step. In AODVv2-04, timer conditions say when a route *must* be expunged. For non-timed routes, this happens (ref. Section 6.3) when (`Current_Time - Route.LastUsed`)>= `MAX_SEQNUM_LIFETIME`. However, the protocol (ref. Section 6.3) also allows routes to be expunged without reference to `MAX_SEQNUM_LIFETIME`: an Expired route *may* be expunged at any time (least recently used first). If this constant is set to too low a value, there will be messages within the network which are still undelivered. In the network of Figure 1, if `MAX_SEQNUM_LIFETIME` is set to 4 units, and the $H - H'$ path (a single link is shown but it could be a path through intermediate nodes) has the delay shown in the figure, the protocol will force the routing entry at $H$ to be expunged while there is an undelivered RREQ. The correct value depends on many factors, including the size of the network, the length of paths in the network, and processing speeds and buffering at the nodes. In the model, we abstract this to a global predicate which must be met before the expunge action can occur.

3. The undelivered RREQ from H now reaches H'. Since H' has no entry, it accepts this route; its next-hop is now H.

4. H' sends a RREQ to H with hopcount 3. Since H already has an entry with a better hopcount, it rejects this message. At this point, there are no undelivered RREQ messages. The H'-H entries form a routing loop.

*Broken Routes.* A route entry at a node is marked as `Broken` if the node is made aware of a break in connectivity. The following scenario shows that a loop may form if a *broken* route is replaced by any *valid* route (as may seem reasonable, even if the new route has a higher cost).

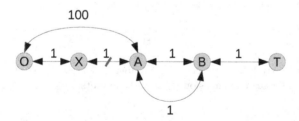

**Fig. 2.** Network: Broken Route Scenario. Number over edge indicates hop-count (cost); red (slanted) line indicates break.

1. A RREQ message generated at O sets up the route O(0);X(1);A(2);B(3);T(4). The numbers in () are the hopcounts for the origin route entries at each node. A RREQ message remains undelivered on the lower A-B link.

2. The link X-A breaks, causing the route at A to be marked as Broken. After the link breaks, both X and A are required to send out RERR messages to their neighbors. We assume that those messages are lost and therefore neither O nor B is notified of the break.

3. A now receives a long route from O, with cost 100. This is the critical point. In version 04 of AODVv2, any valid route is acceptable in place of a broken one (see footnote 5 for details on why this is permitted), so this route will be accepted. The route entry at A is now valid and has hopcount 100.

4. A now has a non-broken route. It receives the previously undelivered RREQ from B, which has cost 4. As this cost is less than that of its current route cost (i.e., 100), A switches its next-hop to B. Node A then sends an RREQ to B, but that has higher cost than B's current route, and is rejected. No further RREQ messages remain in the network, so the A-B loop is stable.

## 2    Proof of Loop Freedom

The proof method is standard: we identify a suitable assertion and prove that it is an inductive invariant by showing that it is preserved by every action. However, the proof structure is more interesting: (1) we explicitly model network disruptions as adversarial actions and (2) the induction proof is localized to the neighborhood of an arbitrarily chosen network edge; thus, it implicitly uses symmetry and is compositional in nature. Some aspects of the model are especially important for the proof (see Section 3 for more details of the model):

1. There is an underlying connectivity graph of nodes. We assume that the graph is finite but of arbitrary size. Nodes and links may fail, and new links can be formed at any point. A node can also be restarted after failure.

2. Any link change and the reaction to it happens atomically with respect to the actions of the protocol.

3. We fix an arbitrary origin node, $O$, and an arbitrary target node, $T$, such that $T$ differs from $O$. Protocol analysis is then based on the discovery and maintenance of bidirectional routes from $O$ to $T$.

4. A route entry has a sequence number, a hop-count, and a state[6]. We say that an entry $x$ is "better" than an entry $y$ if $(seq_x, -hop_x)$ is lexicographically strictly greater than $(seq_y, -hop_y)$. I.e., if $seq_x > seq_y$ or if $seq_x = seq_y$ and $hop_x < hop_y$. In this situation, we also say that $y$ is "worse" than $x$. We write this relationship as $y \prec x$. We treat sequence numbers as natural numbers; i.e., we do not model wrap-around effects. In AODV-v04, a node has its own sequence number generator, with the range $[0 \ldots 65535]$. A new sequence number is assigned for a fresh route request/response. As the numbers are assigned per node and the protocol separates routing entries by (origin, target), the AODVv2 drafts implicitly assume that comparison of a route with a wrap-around successor route is very unlikely.

---

[6] In AODVv2-04, an entry is also labeled with an (origin, target) pair. As the model fixes the origin and target nodes, we omit this label.

## 2.1   Proof Summary

We consider first the origin route established through RREQ messages, and show that it cannot have a routing loop. To avoid case-splitting, we suppose that there is a dummy route to $O$ at $O$, given by hopcount 0 and the sequence number of $O$. The proof hinges on showing the following lemma, which gives the desired theorem below.

**Lemma 1.** *The following is an inductive invariant: for any node $H$, and for any node $G$: if $H$ has a route entry to $O$ with next hop $G$, then $G$ has a route entry to $O$ that is **better than** the entry at $H$.*

**Theorem 1.** *The protocol never reaches a state with a routing loop formed from origin route entries.*

**Proof:** The proof is by contradiction. Suppose that there is a reachable protocol state with a routing loop induced by the entries for origin routes. Pick a node, say $H$, on the loop other than $O$ (there must be one such) and go around the loop from $H$ in the next-hop direction. By Lemma 1, the route entries along this circuit improve strictly at each hop. By the transitivity of $\prec$, the route entry at $H$ is strictly worse than the route entry at $H$, a contradiction. **EndProof.**

## 2.2   The Main Proof

The bulk of the proof lies in establishing the invariance condition in Lemma 1. We do so by induction: i.e., we show that the statement holds in the initial protocol configuration, and that it is preserved by protocol actions and by dynamic network changes. For brevity, we use "route" in place of "route entry" throughout; it should be understood that route does not refer to a path connecting several nodes together. We require an auxiliary lemma, given below. It states that routes in RREQ/RREP messages on outgoing channels adjacent to a node are no better than the corresponding route at that node.

**Lemma 2.** *The following is an inductive invariant:*

(a) *For any node $H$, the route to $O$ in any RREQ message for $(O,T)$ on any outgoing link from $H$ is not better than the route for $O$ at $H$.*
(b) *For any node $H$, the route to $T$ in any RREP message for $(O,T)$ on the link from $H$ to its next-hop on the route to $O$ is not better than the route for $T$ at $H$.*

*Proof of Lemma 2(a):* The claim holds trivially at the initial state, as all connection links are empty.

Consider a transition from global state $s$ to global state $t$, and suppose that the claim holds at $s$. To show that it holds for $t$, consider a node $H$ (other than $O$) in $t$. The proof is by case analysis on the transition which takes the system from $s$ to $t$.

Consider first the normal operations. Most cases are straightforward. If the transition is for a node other than $H$, it only affects the neighborhood of $H$ if a message is removed from an outgoing link of $H$; in this case, the invariant is trivially preserved. Changes to the route state of $H$ (idle-route or expire-route) do not change any routes. Expunging the route (expunge-route) preserves the invariant as its guard requires all outgoing channels from $H$ to be empty. The generation of a RREQ (rreq-gen) can only be done by $H$ if it is $O$: in that case the route generated is equal to the (dummy) route for $O$ at $O$.

The interesting case is where the route at $H$ is updated through a RREQ or RREP message (rreq-recv, rrep-recv). Let $x$ be the route at $H$ to $O$ in $s$ and let $y$ be its route in $t$. Then either $y \succ x$ (in the normal case) or $y \succeq x$ (if $x$ is Broken). Now for every route $r$ in a RREQ message on the link in $s$, the inductive hypotheses requires that $x \succeq r$, so that $y \succeq r$ by transitivity. Every new RREQ message generated by $H$ through rreq-recv carries the route $y$. This re-establishes the invariant. Processing an RERR message may only invalidate but not change the origin route.

We now consider the dynamic changes. Dropping a message, and removing a node or a link trivially preserves the invariant as no routes are changed. The addition of a link to $H$ establishes the invariant for that link, as the link is empty. The interesting case is if $H$ is a recovered node (recover-node). By the pre-condition for recovery (see the model detailed in the next sections), all of $H$'s outgoing channels are empty, so the invariant holds. **EndProof.**

The proof for part (b) is essentially identical, as the processing of RREQ messages in rreq-recv and RREP messages in rrep-recv is nearly symmetric.

*Proof of Lemma 1:* The claim holds trivially at the initial state, as all routes are undefined. Consider a transition from global state $s$ to global state $t$, and suppose that the claim holds at $s$. We show that it holds at $t$ by case analysis on the transition.

We first consider the normal protocol actions. In state $t$, consider node $H$, and a node $G$ such that the route to $O$ from $H$ has next-hop $G$. We have to show that $G$ has a route better than the route at $H$. Consider the possible actions.

(1) The action does not involve either $H$ or $G$. So there is no change in the routes at the two nodes. By assumption, the claim holds for $(G, H)$ in $s$, so it continues to hold in $t$.

(2) The action is one of $G$. Modifications to route state (idle-route, expire-route) do not affect routes, so the claim continues to hold from the assumption for $s$. The action cannot be an expunge, as its guard is not met in $s$, as the entry for $H$ in $s$ has next-hop $G$. Processing of RERR messages does not change the route at $G$ (although its state may change). The interesting case is where $G$ updates its route to $O$ from $r_G$ in $s$ to $r'_G$ in $t$ by processing an RREQ or an RREP message. By the protocol, $r'_G \succeq r_G$. Since $r'_H = r_H$, and $r_G \succ r_H$ by assumption for $s$, we get that $r'_G \succ r'_H$ in $t$.

(3) The action is one of $H$. Modifications to route state (idle-route, expire-route) do not affect routes, so the invariant is preserved from $s$. The action cannot be an expunge, as $H$ has an entry in $t$. The interesting case is if $H$

updates its route to $O$ through a rreq-recv for $(O, T)$ or through a rrep-recv for $(X, O)$, where $X$ is some node. Since $H$ points to $G$ in $t$, the updating message must be from $G$. Say this message carries a route $r$, and let $r_G$ be the route to $O$ at $G$ in $s$. By Lemma 2, regardless of the message type (RREQ or RREP), at state $s$, $r_G \succeq r$. The new route at $H$ is obtained from $r$ by incrementing its hopcount, so it is worse than $r$ (i.e., $r'_H \prec r$). The route in $G$ is unchanged in the transition (i.e., $r'_G = r_G$). Hence, we have $r'_G = r_G \succeq r \succ r'_H$. By transitivity, $r'_G \succ r'_H$, as is desired. (Note the crucial role played by the hopcount increment at $H$.) Actions which process RERR messages do not change the route at $H$, so they preserve the invariant.

We now consider dynamic changes which affect $H$ and $G$.

(4) Dropping a message from a link, and removing a link trivially preserves the invariant as no routes are changed. (Note that the link between $H$ and $G$ may be broken by the transition, yet $H$'s route entry still points to $G$ in $t$.)

(5) The action cannot be the addition or restart of $H$, as the newly added $H$ would not have an origin route in $t$. The action may not add $G$ as a fresh node either, as the next-hop entry for $G$ exists for $H$ in $s$.

(6) The action cannot be the restart of $G$, as its precondition requires there to be no entries which have $G$ as a next-hop, and $H$ has such an entry in $s$.

(7) The action cannot be the removal of nodes $G$ or $H$, as we are only stating the claim where both nodes exist in the network at $t$. (In $t$, there may be a node $H'$ which has a next-hop entry for $G'$, but $G'$ is no longer in the network at $t$. Such a $(G', H')$ pair is not part of the invariant claim.) **EndProof.**

**RREP Invariants.** RREP (route response) messages are generated whenever a new RREQ message reaches its target. They follow *a single* path from target to source which is set up by the origin route entries. I.e., unlike RREQs, the RREP messages do not flood the network. The RREP messages create "target route" entries at each node, which determine a path from that node to the target, $T$. However, the origin route path at the point an RREP message is created may change as the protocol progresses and intermediate nodes receive better routes. It may also change as the result of network disruptions and rearrangements. Hence, it is not obvious that RREP messages do not induce a routing loop in the target route entries. The proof that the target routes created by RREP messages is loop-free is similar in structure to the RREP loop-freedom proof. This is possible as the protocol is nearly symmetric in its handling of RREQ and RREP messages. We therefore omit this proof.

## 3   AODVv2 Model

We describe the protocol model from the viewpoint of a node with name $H$.

*Data Structures.* A node maintains a route table route, indexed by nodes. The route to a node may be undefined, which we denote by $\perp$. If defined, a route to a node is a pair: $(n, e)$, where $n$ is the next-hop node and $e$ is its route entry.

An entry is of the form $(s, h, x)$, where $s$ is a sequence number, $h$ is the hopcount (or, more generally, the cost), and $x$ is the state of the route (one of Active, Idle, Expired, or Broken). It is assumed that $s$ and $h$ are non-negative numbers. In addition, a node maintains its own sequence number, referred to as seq. We use standard notation to refer to these components, for instance, $n.\text{route}[O].e.h$ refers to the hopcount of the route entry to node $O$ at node $n$.

*Messages.* The protocol has three types of messages: $RREQ$ (route request), $RREP$ (route reply) and $RERR$ (route error). Each message has the following components: $h$ (a hopcount), $tlv = (sO, sT)$ (sequence numbers for origin and target, possibly undefined), and $(O, T)$ – the origin and target pair. We write a message as, for example, $RREQ(h, (sO, sT), (O, T))$.

*Initial State.* In its initial state, a node has undefined origin and target routes, and sequence number 0.

*Protocol Actions.* Here, we list the actions taken during normal operation. The actions are atomic but may occur at any time. In the protocol, actions such as expire-route are based on timers, to ensure that they do not happen too often. Since we are concerned with correctness, not performance, we replace such uses of timing by non-determinism. There are some parts of the protocol where timed actions are used as a proxy for global conditions. In the model, we replace such timers with global guards.

In the description below, we have also made certain actions (e.g., processing of RERRs) have more effect, or be more often enabled, than the actual protocol recommends. This can only result in the model having more executions than the actual protocol, so any invariants shown for the model also hold for the protocol.

The notation $y >> x$ expresses that the route in the route message $y$ is preferable to the route table entry $x$. From the AODVv2 protocol description, this is true if (1) $y.s > x.s$, or if (2) $y.s = x.s$, and either (a) $y.h + 1 < x.h$, or (b) $x$ is in the Broken state and $y.h + 1 \leq x.h$. (Term (b) is the correction introduced in AODVv2-05 based on the second loop-formation scenario from Section 1.2.)

We introduce the global predicate AllClear, which replaces the time-driven actions based on MAX_SEQNUM_LIFETIME. The predicate AllClear($H$) holds iff (1) there are no messages in any channel of the network with origin or target being $H$, and (2) all outgoing channels from $H$ are empty, and (3) no other node has an Active route entry with next-hop $H$. This global condition is not present in the actual protocol, as it cannot be checked locally. The protocol instead defines a symbolic time constant, MAX_SEQNUM_LIFETIME – a node waits until that much time has expired before expunging an entry. The protocol description does not specify how this value is to be chosen for a network instance: the value should, clearly, depend on factors such as the size of the network, the link delays, and the processing power of a node. The global condition defined here abstracts from these considerations: the time value should be set so that the global condition is guaranteed to be true after that much time has elapsed.

**skip** do nothing

**expunge-route** remove route if its state is Expired, and AllClear($H$) holds.

**idle-route** change route state to Idle if Active.

**expire-route** change route state to Expired if Idle.

**rreq-gen(T)** This generates an RREQ (request) message to node $T$.

```
true ==>
    let msg = RREQ(h=0, (s0=H.seq+1, sT=H.route[T].e.s), (H,T)) in
    H.seq := H.seq+1;
    multicast(msg)
```

**rreq-recv(RREQ(m),K)** This action processes an RREQ message $m = (h, (sO, sT), (O, T))$ from neighbor $K$. It is guarded by the condition that the route in $m$ is better than the origin route at node $H$.

```
(m.s0,m.h,Active) >> H.route[0].e ==> // m has a better route to the origin
    // update the origin route
    H.route[0] := (K,(m.s0,m.h+1),Active);

    // propagate or reply as appropriate
    if (H=T) then // H is the target node: reply with RREP
        let reply = RREP(h=0,(s0=m.s0,sT=H.seq+1), (O,T)) in
        H.seq := H.seq+1; // update local sequence number
        unicast(reply, K) // send only to K
    else // H is an intermediate node: propagate
        let msg = RREQ(m.h+1, m.tlv,(O,T)) in
        multicast(msg)  // send to all neighbors
    endif
```

**rrep-recv(RREP(m),K)** This action processes a reply (RREP) message $m = (h, (sO, sT), (O, T))$ from neighbor K if it contains a better target route.

```
(m.sT,m.h,Active) >> H.route[T].e ==>  // m has better route to the target
    // update the target route
    H.route[T] := (K,(m.sT,m.h+1),Active);

    // propagate as appropriate
    if (H = O) then // H is the origin node: do nothing
        skip
    else // H is an intermediate node
        if (H.route[0] is defined) then // propagate RREP
            let replymsg = RREP(m.h+1, m.tlv, (O,T)) in
            unicast(replymsg, H.route[0].n)
        else // generate error RERR
            let errormsg = RERR(h=0,tlv=(_,_)) in
            unicast(errormsg,K)
    endif
```

**rerr-recv(RERR(m),K)** This action processes an error (RERR) message from neighbor K. Mark any routes passing through K as broken, and propagate the error. This is more permissive than the protocol in marking routes as Broken: in the protocol, there are other fields in the RERR message which $H$ can use to distinguish whether the error message from $K$ pertains to an origin or a target route.

```
true ==>
    for all nodes w:
        if (H.route[w].n = K) then
```

```
        H.route[w].e.x := Broken; // mark route as broken.
        multicast(RERR(m))    // propagate RERR to all neighbors
    endif
```

*Dynamic Actions.* We now describe protocol actions taken in response to dynamic changes. In our model the adversary may add, recover, or delete nodes, and may add or delete edges. Edges may be deleted by the adversary at any point during protocol execution. However, the adversary may delete a node only if the node is not linked to any edge. Below we give the detailed response that the protocol takes to adversarial actions.

**remove-node(H)** Do nothing.

**new-node(H)** If $H$ is a new node, it starts at its initial state, and all outgoing channels are empty.

**recover-node(H)** $H$ is a recovered node. It does not re-join the protocol until the condition AllClear($H$) holds. This is the same global guard as that for expunge-route. That is not a coincidence, the two conditions should be the same, as shown by the first loop-formation scenario from Section 1.2. The actual AODVv2-04 protocol says that a node can re-join the protocol once MAX_SEQNUM_LIFETIME seconds have elapsed.

**remove-link(H,K)** Mark any routes through K as being broken, and send RERR messages accordingly

```
    true ==>
        for all nodes w:
            if (H.route[w].n = K) then
                H.route[w].e.x := Broken; // mark route as broken.
                multicast(RERR(m))    // propagate RERR to all neighbors
            endif
```

**add-link(H,K)** new link from H to K established. Do nothing.

## 4    Related Work and Conclusions

There is a long history of research on inductive and compositional analysis applied to network protocols: the work in [13,15,3,16,4] is representative. The contribution of this work is to apply these ideas to the verification of a protocol operating under dynamic, adversarial network changes. Our proof technique is standard (cf.[4]): we postulate an assertion and show that it is inductive by proving that it is preserved by every action. However, there are interesting aspects to the structure of the proof. Most importantly, our proof technique is 'local', that is, it is applied to a generic protocol node (or edge), and considers interference from only the nodes in the neighborhood of that node (or edge) during protocol execution. Hence, the method is compositional. It relies on symmetry in the sense that the generic node analyzed represents any of the nodes that may arise during the execution of the actual protocol. In addition, the possibility of adversarial network change is taken care of by modeling the changes as non-deterministic actions, which are always enabled, and may take effect at any point. In [12] a simpler model of AODVv2 was analyzed. In particular, the AODVv2 model in that earlier work did not incorporate node restarts or the expunging of Expired route table entries. This meant that the earlier model did not need to consider the AllClear global guard. We note that consideration of Expired routes leads to the first example of a routing loop in Section 1.2.

The formation of routing loops has been studied for earlier forms of the AODVv2 protocol (AODV and DYMO) in [1,5,17,11] and [18]. Although it operates in the same environment and has the same goals, the version of AODVv2 under development differs significantly, in part due to efforts made to ensure that routing loop scenarios discovered for earlier forms are avoided. For instance, the use of sequence numbers in AODVv2 is completely different from that in AODV and DYMO. The version of AODVv2 (DYMO) analyzed in [9] by model checking fixed configurations allows intermediate, non-target nodes to generate RREQs, this is not possible in AODVv2-04. Nonetheless, some key features have been retained across the protocol versions. An important one is the use of (sequence number, hopcount) as a metric to ensure loop freedom. That is to be expected, as the intuition given in all of the protocol descriptions is that the sequence number represents the "freshness" of a route, while hopcount represents its "cost". Our work shows that this intuition is valid; but it also shows (from the loop formation scenarios) that care must be taken when considering disruptive network changes. We have found it surprisingly easy to construct the proof, and we suspect that this is so because of a focus, through compositional reasoning, on 'local' state rather than 'global' state, and the many simplifications introduced by the designers.

The AODVv2 model verified here represents a possible abstract protocol implementation. However, several features or options of the full protocol are either not modeled or are not modeled in their full generality. For instance, in our version each addressable entity in the network is, if present, identified with a single node in any network topology. In contrast, in the full AODVv2 protocol, entities may be 'multi-homed', and therefore messages sent to the entity may be sent to multiple destinations.

Another significant difference is that in the model, we assume that the metric used by all nodes to determine the 'least cost route' to a destination is based on hop count. That is, the distance between any two neighboring nodes is 1, and the cost of a path from node $O$ to node $T$ is the number of nodes in the path minus 1. The protocol actually allows protocol implementers to choose a different metric, which changes the 'least cost route'. In practice, such metrics may include information relating to bandwidth of individual edges connecting neighboring nodes, or the implementation of individual edge connections (wireless, wired, etc.), to name just a few possible metrics.

In addition, we note that the full AODVv2 protocol allows great scope for implementation decisions in the following form. Many per-node protocol decisions are described as 'must' but some are described as 'may.' For instance, if the route from node $H$ to node $T$ is marked as 'expired' in the route table of $H$ then $H$ *must* not advertise this route to its neighbors. However, if $H$ receives an RREQ for $T$ from a neighbor $G$ then $H$ *may* choose to add this route to $O$ to $H$'s routing table and advertise the RREQ message to $H$'s neighbors. In our analysis, we model these decisions as *must* instructions. Hence, any RREQ message received at a node $H$ will be processed at $H$ and forwarded to $H$'s neighbors. We note that, the models described in our work represent models allowed by the AODVv2 protocol and therefore any errors or discrepancies found in the modelled protocol would represent discrepancies in the full AODVv2 protocol.

There are several other approaches to the analysis of dynamic and ad-hoc networks. The work in [2] shows that Hoare triples for restricted logics are decidable. Work in [8,6] applies well-quasi-ordering (wqo) theory to ad-hoc networks, while the algorithm of [7] relies on symbolic forward exploration, as does (in a different way) the method of [17]. It would be interesting to see how well these algorithmic and semi-algorithmic methods apply to the AODVv2 model. Our own recent work [12] shows that the loose coupling forced by dynamic network changes contributes to the effectiveness of compositional reasoning and local symmetry reduction.

### 4.1   Conclusion and Future Work

We describe a formal proof of loop-freedom for a model of the AODVv2 protocol. In the course of doing so, we discovered a mistake in version 04 of the protocol, which has been acknowledged and corrected by the designers. The straightforward nature of the proof strengthens the conjecture which originally inspired this work: that dynamic network protocols must be loosely coupled and, hence, especially amenable to inductive compositional analysis.

There are several open questions that remain. For instance, we are interested in techniques for the automatic generation of induction compositional assertions for use in the analysis of loosely coupled dynamic systems. Other questions surround the analysis of AODVv2 itself. One is to check whether the chosen values for timing constants are correct for a given configuration of the protocol; the work in [10] can be a good starting point. Another is to generalize this proof to apply to a richer class of distance metrics, as well as to network features such as multi-homing. A particularly important question is to find a good strategy for constructing proofs for the various combinations of "may" options which are permitted by the protocol, while avoiding a combinatorial explosion of protocol variants. As nearly all network protocols include a number of may options, this is a broadly applicable question, and especially relevant in practice.

**Acknowledgments.** We would like to thank the authors of the AODVv2-04 protocol, in particular Charles Perkins, for helpful comments on the loop-formation scenarios and the proof.

# References

1. Bhargavan, K., Obradovic, D., Gunter, C.A.: Formal verification of standards for distance vector routing protocols. J. ACM 49(4), 538–576 (2002)
2. Bouajjani, A., Jurski, Y., Sighireanu, M.: A generic framework for reasoning about dynamic networks of infinite-state processes. In: Grumberg, O., Huth, M. (eds.) TACAS 2007. LNCS, vol. 4424, pp. 690–705. Springer, Heidelberg (2007)
3. Chandy, K., Misra, J.: Proofs of networks of processes. IEEE Transactions on Software Engineering 7(4) (1981)
4. Chandy, K.M., Misra, J.: Parallel Program Design: A Foundation. Addison-Wesley (1988)
5. Das, S., Dill, D.L.: Counter-example based predicate discovery in predicate abstraction. In: Aagaard, M.D., O'Leary, J.W. (eds.) FMCAD 2002. LNCS, vol. 2517, pp. 19–32. Springer, Heidelberg (2002)
6. Delzanno, G., Sangnier, A., Traverso, R., Zavattaro, G.: On the complexity of parameterized reachability in reconfigurable broadcast networks. In: FSTTCS. LIPIcs, vol. 18, pp. 289–300. Schloss Dagstuhl - Leibniz-Zentrum fuer Informatik (2012)
7. Delzanno, G., Sangnier, A., Zavattaro, G.: Parameterized verification of safety properties in ad hoc network protocols. In: PACO. EPTCS, vol. 60, pp. 56–65 (2011)
8. Delzanno, G., Sangnier, A., Zavattaro, G.: Verification of ad hoc networks with node and communication failures. In: Giese, H., Rosu, G. (eds.) FMOODS/FORTE 2012. LNCS, vol. 7273, pp. 235–250. Springer, Heidelberg (2012)
9. Edenhofer, S., Höfner, P.: Towards a rigorous analysis of AODVv2 (DYMO). In: 20th IEEE International Conference on Network Protocols, ICNP 2012, Austin, TX, USA, October 30-November 2, pp. 1–6. IEEE (2012)
10. Fehnker, A., van Glabbeek, R., Höfner, P., McIver, A., Portmann, M., Tan, W.L.: Automated analysis of AODV using UPPAAL. In: Flanagan, C., König, B. (eds.) TACAS 2012. LNCS, vol. 7214, pp. 173–187. Springer, Heidelberg (2012)
11. Höfner, P., van Glabbeek, R.J., Tan, W.L., Portmann, M., McIver, A., Fehnker, A.: A rigorous analysis of AODV and its variants. In: MSWiM, pp. 203–212. ACM (2012)
12. Namjoshi, K.S., Trefler, R.J.: Analysis of dynamic process networks. In: Baier, C., Tinelli, C. (eds.) TACAS 2015. LNCS, vol. 9035, pp. 164–178. Springer, Heidelberg (2015)
13. Owicki, S.S., Gries, D.: Verifying properties of parallel programs: An axiomatic approach. Commun. ACM 19(5), 279–285 (1976)
14. Perkins, C., Ratliff, S., Dowdell, J.: IETF MANET WG Internet Draft (December 2014), http://datatracker.ietf.org/doc/draft-ietf-manet-aodvv2, current revision 06
15. Pnueli, A.: The temporal logic of programs. In: FOCS (1977)
16. Pnueli, A.: In transition from global to modular reasoning about programs. In: Logics and Models of Concurrent Systems. NATO ASI Series (1985)
17. Saksena, M., Wibling, O., Jonsson, B.: Graph grammar modeling and verification of ad hoc routing protocols. In: Ramakrishnan, C.R., Rehof, J. (eds.) TACAS 2008. LNCS, vol. 4963, pp. 18–32. Springer, Heidelberg (2008)
18. van Glabbeek, R.J., Höfner, P., Tan, W.L., Portmann, M.: Sequence numbers do not guarantee loop freedom – AODV can yield routing loops –. In: MSWiM, 10 pages. ACM (2013)

# Code Mobility Meets Self-organisation: A Higher-Order Calculus of Computational Fields

Ferruccio Damiani[1]([⊠]), Mirko Viroli[2], Danilo Pianini[2], and Jacob Beal[3]

[1] University of Torino, Torino, Italy
ferruccio.damiani@unito.it
[2] University of Bologna, Bologna, Italy
{mirko.viroli,danilo.pianini}@unibo.it
[3] Raytheon BBN Technologies, Cambridge, USA
jakebeal@bbn.com

**Abstract.** Self-organisation mechanisms, in which simple local interactions result in robust collective behaviors, are a useful approach to managing the coordination of large-scale adaptive systems. Emerging pervasive application scenarios, however, pose an openness challenge for this approach, as they often require flexible and dynamic deployment of new code to the pertinent devices in the network, and safe and predictable integration of that new code into the existing system of distributed self-organisation mechanisms. We approach this problem of combining self-organisation and code mobility by extending "computational field calculus", a universal calculus for specification of self-organising systems, with a semantics for distributed first-class functions. Practically, this allows self-organisation code to be naturally handled like any other data, e.g., dynamically constructed, compared, spread across devices, and executed in safely encapsulated distributed scopes. Programmers may thus be provided with the novel first-class abstraction of a "distributed function field", a dynamically evolving map from a network of devices to a set of executing distributed processes.

## 1 Introduction

In many different ways, our environment is becoming ever more saturated with computing devices. Programming and managing such complex distributed systems is

This work has been partially supported by HyVar (*www.hyvar-project.eu*, this project has received funding from the European Unions Horizon 2020 research and innovation programme under grant agreement No 644298 - Damiani), by EU FP7 project SAPERE (*www.sapere-project.eu*, under contract No 256873 - Viroli), by ICT COST Action IC1402 ARVI (*www.cost-arvi.eu* - Damiani), by ICT COST Action IC1201 BETTY (*www.behavioural-types.eu* - Damiani), by the Italian PRIN 2010/2011 project CINA (*sysma.imtlucca.it/cina* - Damiani & Viroli), by Ateneo/CSP project SALT (*salt.di.unito.it* - Damiani), and by the United States Air Force and the Defense Advanced Research Projects Agency under Contract No. FA8750-10-C-0242 (Beal). The U.S. Government is authorized to reproduce and distribute reprints for Governmental purposes notwithstanding any copyright notation thereon. The views, opinions, and/or findings contained in this article are those of the author(s)/presenter(s) and should not be interpreted as representing the official views or policies of the Department of Defense or the U.S. Government. Approved for public release; distribution is unlimited.

© IFIP International Federation for Information Processing 2015
S. Graf and M. Viswanathan (Eds.): FORTE 2015, LNCS 9039, pp. 113–128, 2015.
DOI: 10.1007/978-3-319-19195-9_8

a difficult challenge and the subject of much ongoing investigation in contexts such as cyber-physical systems, pervasive computing, robotic systems, and large-scale wireless sensor networks. A common theme in these investigations is *aggregate programming*, which aims to take advantage of the fact that the goal of many such systems are best described in terms of the aggregate operations and behaviours, e.g., "distribute the new version of the application to all subscribers", or "gather profile information from everybody in the festival area", or "switch on safety lights on fast and safe paths towards the emergency exit". Aggregate programming languages provide mechanisms for building systems in terms of such aggregate-level operations and behaviours, and a global-to-local mapping that translates such specifications into an implementation in terms of the actions and interactions of individual devices. In this mapping, self-organisation techniques provide an effective source of building blocks for making such systems robust to device faults, network topology changes, and other contingencies. A wide range of such aggregate programming approaches have been proposed [3]: most of them share the same core idea of viewing the aggregate in terms of dynamically evolving *fields*, where a field is a function that maps each device in some domain to a computational value. Fields then become first-class elements of computation, used for tasks such as modelling input from sensors, output to actuators, program state, and the (evolving) results of computation.

Many emerging pervasive application scenarios, however, pose a challenge to these approaches due to their openness. In these scenarios, there is need to flexibly and dynamically deploy new or revised code to pertinent devices in the network, to adaptively shift which devices are running such code, and to safely and predictably integrate it into the existing system of distributed processes. Prior aggregate programming approaches, however, have either assumed that no such dynamic changes of code exist (e.g., [2,21]), or else provide no safety guarantees ensuring that dynamically composed code will execute as designed (e.g., [15,22]). Accordingly, our goal in this paper is develop a foundational model that supports both code mobility and the predictable composition of self-organisation mechanisms. Moreover, we aim to support this combination such that these same self-organisation mechanisms can also be applied to manage and direct the deployment of mobile code.

To address the problem in a general and tractable way, we start from the *field calculus* [21], a recently developed minimal and universal [5] computational model that provides a formal mathematical grounding for the many languages for aggregate programming. In field calculus, all values are fields, so a natural approach to code mobility is to support fields of first-class functions, just as with first-class functions in most modern programming languages and in common software design patterns such as MapReduce [10]. By this mechanism, functions (and hence, code) can be dynamically consumed as input, passed around by device-to-device communication, and operated upon just like any other type of program value. Formally, expressions of the field calculus are enriched with function names, anonymous functions, and application of function-valued expressions to arguments, and the operational semantics properly accommodates them with the same core field calculus mechanisms of neighbourhood filtering and alignment [21]. This produces a unified model supporting both code mobility and self-organisation, greatly improving over the independent and generally incompatible mechanisms which have typically been employed in previous aggregate programming approaches. Programmers are thus provided with a new first-class abstraction of a "distributed function field": a dynamically evolving map from the network to a set of executing distributed processes.

Section 2 introduces the concepts of higher-order field calculus; Section 3 formalises their semantics; Section 4 illustrates the approach with an example; and Section 5 concludes with a discussion of related and future work.

## 2    Fields and First-Class Functions

The defining property of fields is that they allow us to see computation from two different viewpoints. On the one hand, by the standard "local" viewpoint, computation is seen as occurring in a single device, and it hence manipulates data values (e.g., numbers) and communicates such data values with other devices to enable coordination. On the other hand, by the "aggregate" (or "global") viewpoint [21], computation is seen as occurring on the overall network of interconnected devices: the data abstraction manipulated is hence a whole distributed *field*, a dynamically evolving data structure having extent over a subset of the network. This latter viewpoint is very useful when reasoning about aggregates of devices, and will be used throughout this document. Put more precisely, a field value $\phi$ may be viewed as a function $\phi : D \to \mathscr{L}$ that maps each device $\delta$ in the domain $D$ to an associated data value $\ell$ in range $\mathscr{L}$. Field computations then take fields as input (e.g., from sensors) and produce new fields as outputs, whose values may change over time (e.g., as inputs change or the computation progresses). For example, the input of a computation might be a field of temperatures, as perceived by sensors at each device in the network, and its output might be a Boolean field that maps to $\mathtt{true}$ where temperature is greater than 25°C, and to $\mathtt{false}$ elsewhere.

**Field Calculus.** The *field calculus* [21] is a tiny functional calculus capturing the essential elements of field computations, much as $\lambda$-calculus [7] captures the essence of functional computation and FJ [12] the essence of object-oriented programming. The primitive expressions of field calculus are data values denoted $\ell$ (Boolean, numbers, and pairs), representing constant fields holding the value $\ell$ everywhere, and variables x, which are either function parameters or state variables (see the rep construct below). These are composed into programs using a Lisp-like syntax with five constructs:

(1) *Built-in function call* ($\mathtt{o}$ $\mathtt{e}_1 \cdots \mathtt{e}_n$): A built-in operator $\mathtt{o}$ is a means to uniformly model a variety of "point-wise" operations, i.e. involving neither state nor communication. Examples include simple mathematical functions (e.g., addition, comparison, sine) and context-dependent operators whose result depends on the environment (e.g., the 0-ary operator $\mathtt{uid}$ returns the unique numerical identifier $\delta$ of the device, and the 0-ary $\mathtt{nbr-range}$ operator yields a field where each device maps to a subfield mapping its neighbours to estimates of their current distance from the device). The expression ($\mathtt{o}$ $\mathtt{e}_1 \cdots \mathtt{e}_n$) thus produces a field mapping each device identifier $\delta$ to the result of applying $\mathtt{o}$ to the values at $\delta$ of its $n \geq 0$ arguments $\mathtt{e}_1, \ldots, \mathtt{e}_n$.

(2) *Function call* ($\mathtt{f}$ $\mathtt{e}_1 \ldots \mathtt{e}_n$): Abstraction and recursion are supported by function definition: functions are declared as ($\mathtt{def}$ $\mathtt{f}(\mathtt{x}_1 \ldots \mathtt{x}_n)$ $\mathtt{e}$) (where elements $\mathtt{x}_i$ are formal

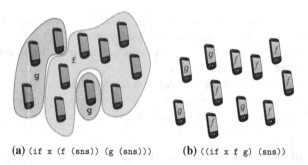

**(a)** `(if x (f (sns)) (g (sns)))`    **(b)** `((if x f g) (sns))`

**Fig. 1.** Field calculus functions are evaluated over a domain of devices. E.g., in (a) the `if` operation partitions the network into two subdomains, evaluating `f` where field `x` is true and `g` where it is false (both applied to the output of sensor `sns`). With first-class functions, however, domains must be constructed dynamically based on the identity of the functions stored in the field, as in (b), which implements an equivalent computation.

parameters and e is the body), and expressions of the form (`f` $e_1$ ... $e_n$) are the way of calling function `f` passing $n$ arguments.

(3) *Time evolution* (`rep x` $e_0$ `e`): The "repeat" construct supports dynamically evolving fields, assuming that each device computes its program repeatedly in asynchronous rounds. It initialises state variable `x` to the result of initialisation expression $e_0$ (a value or a variable), then updates it at each step by computing `e` against the prior value of `x`. For instance, (`rep x 0 (+ x 1)`) is the (evolving) field counting in each device how many rounds that device has computed.

(4) *Neighbourhood field construction* (`nbr e`): Device-to-device interaction is encapsulated in `nbr`, which returns a field $\phi$ mapping each neighbouring device to its most recent available value of `e` (i.e., the information available if devices broadcast the value of `e` to their neighbours upon computing it). Such "neighbouring" fields can then be manipulated and summarised with built-in operators, e.g., (`min-hood (nbr e)`) outputs a field mapping each device to the minimum value of `e` amongst its neighbours.

(5) *Domain restriction* (`if` $e_0$ $e_1$ $e_2$): Branching is implemented by this construct, which computes $e_1$ in the restricted domain where $e_0$ is true, and $e_2$ in the restricted domain where $e_0$ is false.

Any field calculus computation may be thus be viewed as a function $f$ taking zero or more input fields and returning one output field, i.e., having the signature $f : (D \rightarrow \mathscr{L})^k \rightarrow (D \rightarrow \mathscr{L})$. Figure 1a illustrates this concept, showing an example with complementary domains on which two functions are evaluated. This aggregate-level model of computation over fields can then be "compiled" into an equivalent system of local operations and message passing actually implementing the field calculus program on a distributed system [21].

**Higher-order Field Calculus.** The *higher-order field calculus (HFC)* is an extension of the field calculus with embedded first-class functions, with the primary goal of allowing it to handle functions just like any other value, so that code can be dynamically injected, moved, and executed in network (sub)domains. If functions are "first class" in

| | |
|---|---|
| e ::= x \| v \| (e ē) \| (rep x w e) \| (nbr e) \| (if e e e) | expression |
| v ::= ℓ \| φ | value |
| ℓ ::= b \| n \| ⟨ℓ,ℓ⟩ \| o \| f \| (fun (x̄) e) | local value |
| w ::= x \| ℓ | variable or local value |
| F ::= (def f(x̄) e) | user-defined function |
| P ::= F̄ e | program |

**Fig. 2.** Syntax of HFC (differences from field calculus are highlighted in grey)

the language, then: *(i)* functions can take functions as arguments and return a function as result (higher-order functions); *(ii)* functions can be created "on the fly" (anonymous functions); *(iii)* functions can be moved between devices (via the nbr construct); and *(iv)* the function one executes can change over time (via rep construct).

The syntax of the calculus is reported in Fig. 2. Values in the calculus include fields φ, which are produced at run-time and may not occur in source programs; also, local values may be smoothly extended by adding other ground values (e.g., characters) and structured values (e.g., lists). Borrowing syntax from [12], the overbar notation denotes metavariables over sequences and the empty sequence is denoted by •. E.g., for expressions, we let ē range over sequences of expressions, written $e_1, e_2, \ldots e_n$ ($n \geq 0$). The differences from the field calculus are as follows: function application expressions (e ē) can take an arbitrary expression e instead of just an operator o or a user-defined function name f; anonymous functions can be defined (by syntax (fun (x̄) e)); and built-in operators, user-defined function names, and anonymous functions are values. This implies that the range of a field can be a function as well. To apply the functions mapped to by such a field, we have to be able to transform the field back into a single aggregate-level function. Figure 1b illustrates this issue, with a simple example of a function call expression applied to a function-valued field with two different values.

How can we evaluate a function call with such a heterogeneous field of functions? It would seem excessive to run a separate copy of function $f$ for every device that has $f$ as its value in the field. At the opposite extreme, running $f$ over the whole domain is problematic for implementation, because it would require devices that may not have a copy of $f$ to help in evaluating $f$. Instead, we will take a more elegant approach, in which making a function call acts as a branch, with each function in the range applied only on the subspace of devices that hold that function. Formally, this may be expressed as transforming a function-valued field φ into a function $f_\phi$ that is defined as:

$$f_\phi(\psi_1, \psi_2, \ldots) = \bigcup_{f \in \phi(D)} f(\psi_1|_{\phi^{-1}(f)}, \psi_2|_{\phi^{-1}(f)}, \ldots) \qquad (1)$$

where $\psi_i$ are the input fields, $\phi(D)$ is set of all functions held as data values by some devices in the domain $D$ of φ, and $\psi_i|_{\phi^{-1}(f)}$ is the restriction of $\psi_i$ to the subspace of only those devices that φ maps to function $f$. In fact, when the field of functions is constant, this reduces to be precisely equivalent to a standard function call. This means that we can view ordinary evaluation of function $f$ as equivalent to creating a function-valued field with a constant value $f$, then making a function call applying that field to its argument fields. This elegant transformation is the key insight of this paper, enabling first-class functions to be implemented with a minimal change to the existing semantics while also ensuring compatibility with the prior semantics as well, thus also inheriting its previously established desirable properties.

## 3  The Higher-order Field Calculus: Dynamic and Static Semantics

**Dynamic Semantics (Big-Step Operational Semantics).** As for the field calculus [21], devices undergo computation in rounds. In each round, a device sleeps for some time, wakes up, gathers information about messages received from neighbours while sleeping, performs an evaluation of the program, and finally emits a message to all neighbours with information about the outcome of computation before going back to sleep. The scheduling of such rounds across the network is fair and non-synchronous. This section presents a formal semantics of device computation, which is aimed to represent a specification for any HFC-like programming language implementation.

The syntax of the HFC calculus has been introduced in Section 2 (Fig. 2). In the following, we let meta-variable $\delta$ range over the denumerable set $\mathbf{D}$ of *device identifiers* (which are numbers). To simplify the notation, we shall assume a fixed program P. We say that "device $\delta$ *fires*", to mean that the main expression of P is evaluated on $\delta$.

We model device computation by a big-step operational semantics where the result of evaluation is a *value-tree* $\theta$, which is an ordered tree of values, tracking the result of any evaluated subexpression. Intuitively, the evaluation of an expression at a given time in a device $\delta$ is performed against the recently-received value-trees of neighbours, namely, its outcome depends on those value-trees. The result is a new value-tree that is conversely made available to $\delta$'s neighbours (through a broadcast) for their firing; this includes $\delta$ itself, so as to support a form of state across computation rounds (note that any implementation might massively compress the value-tree, storing only enough information for expressions to be aligned). A *value-tree environment* $\Theta$ is a map from device identifiers to value-trees, collecting the outcome of the last evaluation on the neighbours. This is written $\overline{\delta} \mapsto \overline{\theta}$ as short for $\delta_1 \mapsto \theta_1, \ldots, \delta_n \mapsto \theta_n$.

The syntax of field values, value-trees and value-tree environments is given in Fig. 3 (top). Figure 3 (middle) defines: the auxiliary functions $\rho$ and $\pi$ for extracting the root value and a subtree of a value-tree, respectively (further explanations about function $\pi$ will be given later); the extension of functions $\rho$ and $\pi$ to value-tree environments; and the auxiliary functions *args* and *body* for extracting the formal parameters and the body of a (user-defined or anonymous) function, respectively. The computation that takes place on a single device is formalised by the big-step operational semantics rules given in Fig. 3 (bottom). The derived judgements are of the form $\delta; \Theta \vdash e \Downarrow \theta$, to be read "expression e evaluates to value-tree $\theta$ on device $\delta$ with respect to the value-tree environment $\Theta$", where: *(i)* $\delta$ is the identifier of the current device; *(ii)* $\Theta$ is the field of the value-trees produced by the most recent evaluation of (an expression corresponding to) e on $\delta$'s neighbours; *(iii)* e is a run-time expression (i.e., an expression that may contain field values); *(iv)* the value-tree $\theta$ represents the values computed for all the expressions encountered during the evaluation of e—in particular $\rho(\theta)$ is the resulting value of expression e. The first firing of a device $\delta$ after activation or reset is performed with respect to the empty tree environment, while any other firing must consider the outcome of the most recent firing of $\delta$ (i.e., whenever $\Theta$ is not empty, it includes the

---

**Field values, value-trees, and value-tree environments:**

$$\phi ::= \overline{\delta \mapsto \ell} \qquad\qquad\qquad\qquad \text{field value}$$
$$\theta ::= \mathbf{v}(\overline{\theta}) \qquad\qquad\qquad\qquad\quad \text{value-tree}$$
$$\Theta ::= \overline{\delta \mapsto \theta} \qquad\qquad\qquad \text{value-tree environment}$$

---

**Auxiliary functions:**

$$\rho(\mathbf{v}(\overline{\theta})) = \mathbf{v}$$
$$\pi_i(\mathbf{v}(\theta_1,\ldots,\theta_n)) = \theta_i \quad \text{if } 1 \le i \le n \qquad\qquad \pi^{\ell,n}(\mathbf{v}(\theta_1,\ldots,\theta_{n+2})) = \theta_{n+2} \quad \text{if } \rho(\theta_{n+1}) = \ell$$
$$\pi_i(\theta) = \bullet \quad \text{otherwise} \qquad\qquad\qquad\qquad \pi^{\ell,n}(\theta) = \bullet \quad \text{otherwise}$$

$$\text{For } aux \in \rho, \pi_i, \pi^{\ell,n} : \begin{cases} aux(\delta \mapsto \theta) = aux(\theta) & \text{if } aux(\theta) \ne \bullet \\ aux(\delta \mapsto \theta) = \bullet & \text{if } aux(\theta) = \bullet \\ aux(\Theta, \Theta') = aux(\Theta), aux(\Theta') \end{cases}$$

$$args(\mathbf{f}) = \overline{\mathbf{x}} \quad \text{if } (\mathtt{def\ f}(\overline{\mathbf{x}})\,\mathbf{e}) \qquad\qquad body(\mathbf{f}) = \mathbf{e} \quad \text{if } (\mathtt{def\ f}(\overline{\mathbf{x}})\,\mathbf{e})$$
$$args((\mathtt{fun}\ (\overline{\mathbf{x}})\ \mathbf{e})) = \overline{\mathbf{x}} \qquad\qquad\qquad body((\mathtt{fun}\ (\overline{\mathbf{x}})\ \mathbf{e})) = \mathbf{e}$$

---

**Rules for expression evaluation:** $\qquad\qquad\qquad\qquad\qquad\qquad\qquad \boxed{\delta; \Theta \vdash \mathbf{e} \Downarrow \theta}$

[E-LOC]
$$\frac{}{\delta; \Theta \vdash \ell \Downarrow \ell()}$$

[E-FLD]
$$\frac{\phi' = \phi|_{\mathbf{dom}(\Theta) \cup \{\delta\}}}{\delta; \Theta \vdash \phi \Downarrow \phi'()}$$

[E-B-APP]
$$\frac{\delta; \pi_{n+1}(\Theta) \vdash \mathbf{e}_{n+1} \Downarrow \theta_{n+1} \qquad \rho(\theta_{n+1}) = \mathbf{o} \qquad\qquad\qquad\qquad}{\delta; \pi_1(\Theta) \vdash \mathbf{e}_1 \Downarrow \theta_1 \quad \cdots \quad \delta; \pi_n(\Theta) \vdash \mathbf{e}_n \Downarrow \theta_n \qquad \mathbf{v} = \varepsilon^{\mathbf{o}}_{\delta;\Theta}(\rho(\theta_1),\ldots,\rho(\theta_n))}$$
$$\frac{}{\delta; \Theta \vdash \mathbf{e}_{n+1}(\mathbf{e}_1,\ldots,\mathbf{e}_n) \Downarrow \mathbf{v}(\theta_1,\ldots,\theta_{n+1})}$$

[E-D-APP]
$$\frac{\delta; \pi_{n+1}(\Theta) \vdash \mathbf{e}_{n+1} \Downarrow \theta_{n+1} \qquad \rho(\theta_{n+1}) = \ell \qquad args(\ell) = \mathbf{x}_1,\ldots,\mathbf{x}_n}{\delta; \pi_1(\Theta) \vdash \mathbf{e}_1 \Downarrow \theta_1 \quad \cdots \quad \delta; \pi_n(\Theta) \vdash \mathbf{e}_n \Downarrow \theta_n \qquad body(\ell) = \mathbf{e}}$$
$$\frac{\delta; \pi^{\ell,n}(\Theta) \vdash \mathbf{e}[\mathbf{x}_1 := \rho(\theta_1) \quad \ldots \quad \mathbf{x}_n := \rho(\theta_n)] \Downarrow \theta_{n+2} \qquad \mathbf{v} = \rho(\theta_{n+2})}{\delta; \Theta \vdash \mathbf{e}_{n+1}(\mathbf{e}_1,\ldots,\mathbf{e}_n) \Downarrow \mathbf{v}(\theta_1,\ldots,\theta_{n+2})}$$

[E-REP]
$$\frac{\ell_0 = \begin{cases} \rho(\Theta(\delta)) & \text{if } \Theta \ne \emptyset \\ \ell & \text{otherwise} \end{cases} \qquad \delta; \pi_1(\Theta) \vdash \mathbf{e}[\mathbf{x} := \ell_0] \Downarrow \theta_1 \qquad \ell_1 = \rho(\theta_1)}{\delta; \Theta \vdash (\mathtt{rep}\ \mathbf{x}\ \ell\ \mathbf{e}) \Downarrow \ell_1(\theta_1)}$$

[E-NBR]
$$\frac{\Theta_1 = \pi_1(\Theta) \qquad \delta; \Theta_1 \vdash \mathbf{e} \Downarrow \theta_1 \qquad \phi = \rho(\Theta_1)[\delta \mapsto \rho(\theta_1)]}{\delta; \Theta \vdash (\mathtt{nbr}\ \mathbf{e}) \Downarrow \phi(\theta_1)}$$

[E-THEN]
$$\frac{\delta; \pi_1(\Theta) \vdash \mathbf{e} \Downarrow \theta_1 \qquad \rho(\theta_1) = \mathtt{true} \qquad \delta; \pi^{\mathtt{true},0}\Theta \vdash \mathbf{e}' \Downarrow \theta_2 \qquad \ell = \rho(\theta_2)}{\delta; \Theta \vdash (\mathtt{if}\ \mathbf{e}\ \mathbf{e}'\ \mathbf{e}'') \Downarrow \ell(\theta_1, \theta_2)}$$

[E-ELSE]
$$\frac{\delta; \pi_1(\Theta) \vdash \mathbf{e} \Downarrow \theta_1 \qquad \rho(\theta_1) = \mathtt{false} \qquad \delta; \pi^{\mathtt{false},0}\Theta \vdash \mathbf{e}'' \Downarrow \theta_2 \qquad \ell = \rho(\theta_2)}{\delta; \Theta \vdash (\mathtt{if}\ \mathbf{e}\ \mathbf{e}'\ \mathbf{e}'') \Downarrow \ell(\theta_1, \theta_2)}$$

**Fig. 3.** Big-step operational semantics for expression evaluation

value of the most recent evaluation of e on $\delta$)—this is needed to support the stateful semantics of the rep construct.

The operational semantics rules are based on rather standard rules for functional languages, extended so as to be able to evaluate a subexpression e' of e with respect to the value-tree environment $\Theta'$ obtained from $\Theta$ by extracting the corresponding subtree (when present) in the value-trees in the range of $\Theta$. This process, called *alignment*, is modelled by the auxiliary function $\pi$, defined in Fig. 3 (middle). The function $\pi$ has two different behaviours (specified by its subscript or superscript): $\pi_i(\theta)$ extracts the $i$-th subtree of $\theta$, if it is present; and $\pi^{\ell,n}(\theta)$ extracts the $(n+2)$-th subtree of $\theta$, if it is present and the root of the $(n+1)$-th subtree of $\theta$ is equal to the local value $\ell$.

Rules [E-LOC] and [E-FLD] model the evaluation of expressions that are either a local value or a field value, respectively. For instance, evaluating the expression 1 produces (by rule [E-LOC]) the value-tree $1()$, while evaluating the expression $+$ produces the value-tree $+()$. Note that, in order to ensure that domain restriction is obeyed (cf. Section 2), rule [E-FLD] restricts the domain of the value field $\phi$ to the domain of $\Theta$ augmented by $\delta$.

Rule [E-B-APP] models the application of built-in functions. It is used to evaluate expressions of the form $(e_{n+1}e_1\cdots e_n)$ such that the evaluation of $e_{n+1}$ produces a value-tree $\theta_{n+1}$ whose root $\rho(\theta_{n+1})$ is a built-in function o. It produces the value-tree $v(\theta_1,\ldots,\theta_n,\theta_{n+1})$, where $\theta_1,\ldots,\theta_n$ are the value-trees produced by the evaluation of the actual parameters $e_1,\ldots,e_n$ ($n \geq 0$) and v is the value returned by the function. Rule [E-B-APP] exploits the special auxiliary function $\varepsilon$, whose actual definition is abstracted away. This is such that $\varepsilon^o_{\delta;\Theta}(\overline{v})$ computes the result of applying built-in function o to values $\overline{v}$ in the current environment of the device $\delta$. In particular, we assume that the built-in 0-ary function uid gets evaluated to the current device identifier (i.e., $\varepsilon^{uid}_{\delta;\Theta}() = \delta$), and that mathematical operators have their standard meaning, which is independent from $\delta$ and $\Theta$ (e.g., $\varepsilon^+_{\delta;\Theta}(1,2) = 3$). The $\varepsilon$ function also encapsulates measurement variables such as nbr-range and interactions with the external world via sensors and actuators. In order to ensure that domain restriction is obeyed, for each built-in function o we assume that: $\varepsilon^o_{\delta;\Theta}(v_1,\cdots,v_n)$ is defined only if all the field values in $v_1,\ldots,v_n$ have domain $\mathbf{dom}(\Theta) \cup \{\delta\}$; and if $\varepsilon^o_{\delta;\Theta}(v_1,\cdots,v_n)$ returns a field value $\phi$, then $\mathbf{dom}(\phi) = \mathbf{dom}(\Theta) \cup \{\delta\}$. For instance, evaluating the expression $(+\ 1\ 2)$ produces the value-tree $3(1(),2(),+())$. The value of the whole expression, 3, has been computed by using rule [E-B-APP] to evaluate the application of the sum operator $+$ (the root of the third subtree of the value-tree) to the values 1 (the root of the first subtree of the value-tree) and 2 (the root of the second subtree of the value-tree). In the following, for sake of readability, we sometimes write the value v as short for the value-tree $v()$. Following this convention, the value-tree $3(1(),2(),+())$ is shortened to $3(1,2,+)$.

Rule [E-D-APP] models the application of user-defined or anonymous functions, i.e., it is used to evaluate expressions of the form $(e_{n+1}\ e_1\cdots e_n)$ such that the evaluation of $e_{n+1}$ produces a value-tree $\theta_{n+1}$ whose root $\ell = \rho(\theta_{n+1})$ is a user-defined function name or an anonymous function. It is similar to rule [E-B-APP], however it produces a value-tree which has one more subtree, $\theta_{n+2}$, which is produced by evaluating the body of the function $\ell$ with respect to the value-tree environment $\pi^{\ell,n}(\Theta)$ containing only the value-trees associated to the evaluation of the body of the same function $\ell$.

To illustrate rule [E-REP] (rep construct), as well as computational rounds, we consider program (rep x 0 (+ x 1)) (cf. Section 2). The first firing of a device $\delta$ after activation or reset is performed againstthe empty tree environment. Therefore, according to rule [E-REP], to evaluate (rep x 0 (+ x 1)) means to evaluate the subexpression (+ 0 1), obtained from (+ x 1) by replacing x with 0. This produces the value-tree $\theta_1 = 1(1(0,1,+))$, where root 1 is the overall result as usual, while its sub-tree is the result of evaluating the third argument. Any subsequent firing of the device $\delta$ is performed with respect to a tree environment $\Theta$ that associates to $\delta$ the outcome of the most recent firing of $\delta$. Therefore, evaluating (rep x 0 (+ x 1)) at the second firing means to evaluate the subexpression (+ 1 1), obtained from (+ x 1) by replacing x with 1, which is the root of $\theta_1$. Hence the results of computation are 1, 2, 3, and so on.

Value-trees also support modelling information exchange through the nbr construct, as of rule [E-NBR]. Consider the program $e' = (\texttt{min-hood}\,(\texttt{nbr}\,(\texttt{sns-num})))$, where the 1-ary built-in function min-hood returns the lower limit of values in the range of its field argument, and the 0-ary built-in function sns-num returns the numeric value measured by a sensor. Suppose that the program runs on a network of three fully connected devices $\delta_A$, $\delta_B$, and $\delta_C$ where sns-num returns 1 on $\delta_A$, 2 on $\delta_B$, and 3 on $\delta_C$. Considering an initial empty tree-environment $\emptyset$ on all devices, we have the following: the evaluation of $(\texttt{sns-num})$ on $\delta_A$ yields $1\,(\texttt{sns-num})$ (by rules [E-LOC] and [E-B-APP], since $\varepsilon_{\delta_A;\emptyset}^{\texttt{sns-num}}() = 1$); the evaluation of $(\texttt{nbr}\,(\texttt{sns-num}))$ on $\delta_A$ yields $(\delta_A \mapsto 1)\,(1\,(\texttt{sns-num}))$ (by rule [E-NBR]); and the evaluation of $e'$ on $\delta_A$ yields

$$\theta_A = 1((\delta_A \mapsto 1)\,(1\,(\texttt{sns-num})),\texttt{min-hood})$$

(by rule [E-B-APP], since $\varepsilon_{\delta_A;\emptyset}^{\texttt{min-hood}}((\delta_A \mapsto 1)) = 1$). Therefore, after its first firing, device $\delta_A$ produces the value-tree $\theta_A$. Similarly, after their first firing, devices $\delta_B$ and $\delta_C$ produce the value-trees

$$\theta_B = 2((\delta_B \mapsto 2)\,(2\,(\texttt{sns-num})),\texttt{min-hood})$$
$$\theta_C = 3((\delta_C \mapsto 3)\,(3\,(\texttt{sns-num})),\texttt{min-hood})$$

respectively. Suppose that device $\delta_B$ is the first device that fires a second time. Then the evaluation of $e'$ on $\delta_B$ is now performed with respect to the value tree environment $\Theta_B = (\delta_A \mapsto \theta_A,\ \delta_B \mapsto \theta_B,\ \delta_C \mapsto \theta_C)$ and the evaluation of its subexpressions $(\texttt{nbr}(\texttt{sns-num}))$ and $(\texttt{sns-num})$ is performed, respectively, with respect to the following value-tree environments obtained from $\Theta_B$ by alignment:

$$\Theta_B' = \pi_1(\Theta_B) = (\delta_A \mapsto (\delta_A \mapsto 1)\,(1\,(\texttt{sns-num})),\ \delta_B \mapsto \cdots,\ \delta_C \mapsto \cdots)$$
$$\Theta_B'' = \pi_1(\Theta_B') = (\delta_A \mapsto 1\,(\texttt{sns-num}),\ \delta_B \mapsto 2\,(\texttt{sns-num}),\ \delta_C \mapsto 3\,(\texttt{sns-num}))$$

We have that $\varepsilon_{\delta_B;\Theta_B''}^{\texttt{sns-num}}() = 2$; the evaluation of $(\texttt{nbr}\,(\texttt{sns-num}))$ on $\delta_B$ with respect to $\Theta_B'$ yields $\phi\,(2\,(\texttt{sns-num}))$ where $\phi = (\delta_A \mapsto 1, \delta_B \mapsto 2, \delta_C \mapsto 3)$; and $\varepsilon_{\delta_B;\Theta_B}^{\texttt{min-hood}}(\phi) = 1$. Therefore the evaluation of $e'$ on $\delta_B$ produces the value-tree $1\,(\phi\,(2\,(\texttt{sns-num})),\texttt{min-hood})$. Namely, the computation at device $\delta_B$ after the first round yields 1, which is the minimum of sns-num across neighbours—and similarly for $\delta_A$ and $\delta_C$.

We now present an example illustrating first-class functions. Consider the program $((\texttt{pick-hood}\,(\texttt{nbr}\,(\texttt{sns-fun}))))$, where the 1-ary built-in function pick-hood returns at random a value in the range of its field argument, and the 0-ary built-in function sns-fun returns a 0-ary function returning a value of type num. Suppose that the program runs again on a network of three fully connected devices $\delta_A$, $\delta_B$, and $\delta_C$ where sns-fun returns $\ell_0 = (\texttt{fun}\,()\,0)$ on $\delta_A$ and $\delta_B$, and returns $\ell_1 = (\texttt{fun}\,()\,e')$ on $\delta_C$, where $e' = (\texttt{min-hood}\,(\texttt{nbr}\,(\texttt{sns-num})))$ is the program illustrated in the previous example. Assume that sns-num returns 1 on $\delta_A$, 2 on $\delta_B$, and 3 on $\delta_C$. Then after its first firing, device $\delta_A$ produces the value-tree

$$\theta_A' = 0(\ell_0((\delta_A \mapsto \ell_0)\,(\ell_0\,(\texttt{sns-fun})),\texttt{pick-hood}),0)$$

where the root of the first subtree of $\theta'_A$ is the anonymous function $\ell_0$ (defined above), and the second subtree of $\theta'_A$, 0, has been produced by the evaluation of the body 0 of $\ell_0$. After their first firing, devices $\delta_B$ and $\delta_C$ produce the value-trees

$$\theta'_B = 0\,(\ell_0\,((\delta_B \mapsto \ell_0)\,(\ell_0\,(\text{sns-fun}),\text{pick-hood}),0)$$
$$\theta'_C = 3\,(\ell_1\,((\delta_C \mapsto \ell_1)\,(\ell_1\,(\text{sns-fun}),\text{pick-hood}),\theta_C)$$

respectively, where $\theta_C$ is the value-tree for e given in the previous example.

Suppose that device $\delta_A$ is the first device that fires a second time. The computation is performed with respect to the value tree environment $\Theta'_A = (\delta_A \mapsto \theta'_A,\ \delta_B \mapsto \theta'_B,\ \delta_C \mapsto \theta'_C)$ and produces the value-tree $1\,(\ell_1\,(\phi'\,(\ell_1\,(\text{sns-fun}),\text{pick-hood},\theta''_A)$, where

$$\phi' = (\delta_A \mapsto \ell_1, \delta_C \mapsto \ell_1) \quad \text{and} \quad \theta''_A = 1\,((\delta_A \mapsto 1, \delta_C \mapsto 3)\,(1\,(\text{sns-num})),\text{min-hood}),$$

since, according to rule [E-D-APP], the evaluation of the body $e'$ of $\ell_1$ (which produces the value-tree $\theta''_A$) is performed with respect to the value-tree environment $\pi^{\ell_1,0}(\Theta'_A) = (\delta_C \mapsto \theta_C)$. Namely, device $\delta_A$ executed the anonymous function $\ell_1$ received from $\delta_C$, and this was able to correctly align with execution of $\ell_1$ at $\delta_C$, gathering values perceived by sns-num of 1 at $\delta_A$ and 3 at $\delta_C$.

**Static Semantics (Type-Inference System).**  We have developed a variant of the Hindley-Milner type system [9] for the HFC calculus. This type system has two kinds of types, *local types* (the types for local values) and *field types* (the types for field values), and is aimed to guarantee the following two properties:

**Type Preservation.** If a well-typed expression e has type T and e evaluates to a value tree $\theta$, then $\rho(\theta)$ also has type T.
**Domain Alignment.** The domain of every field value arising during the evaluation of a well-typed expression on a device $\delta$ consists of $\delta$ and of the aligned neighbours.

Alignment is key to guarantee that the semantics correctly relates the behaviour of if, nbr, rep and function application—namely, two fields with different domain are never allowed to be combined. Besides performing standard checks (i.e., in a function application expression $(e_{n+1}\,e_1 \cdots e_n)$ the arguments $e_1,\dots e_n$ have the expected type; in an if-expression (if $e_0\,e_1\,e_2$) the condition $e_0$ has type bool and the branches $e_1$ and $e_2$ have the same type; etc.) the type system perform additional checks in order to ensure domain alignment. In particular, the type rules check that:

- In an anonymous function $(\text{fun}\,(\bar{x})\,e)$ the free variables $\bar{y}$ of e that are not in $\bar{x}$ have local type. This prevents a device $\delta$ from creating a closure $e' = (\text{fun}\,(\bar{x})\,e)[\bar{y} := \bar{\phi}]$ containing field values $\bar{\phi}$ (whose domain is by construction equal to the subset of the aligned neighbours of $\delta$). The closure $e'$ may lead to a domain alignment error since it may be shifted (via the nbr construct) to another device $\delta'$ that may use it (i.e., apply $e'$ to some arguments); and the evaluation of the body of $e'$ may involve use of a field value $\phi$ in $\bar{\phi}$ such that the set of aligned neighbours of $\delta'$ is different from the domain of $\phi$.
- In a rep-expression (rep x w e) it holds that x, w and e have (the same) local type. This prevents a device $\delta$ from storing in x a field value $\phi$ that may be reused in the next computation round of $\delta$, when the set of the set of aligned neighbours may be different from the domain of $\phi$.

- In a nbr-expression (nbr e) the expression e has local type. This prevents the attempt to create a "field of fields" (i.e., a field that maps device identifiers to field values)—which is pragmatically often overly costly to maintain and communicate.
- In an if-expression (if $e_0$ $e_1$ $e_2$) the branches $e_1$ and $e_2$ have (the same) local type. This prevents the if-expression from evaluating to a field value whose domain is different from the subset of the aligned neighbours of $\delta$.

# 4    A Pervasive Computing Example

We now illustrate the application of first-class functions using a pervasive computing example. In this scenario, people wandering a large environment (like an outdoor festival, an airport, or a museum) each carry a personal device with short-range point-to-point ad-hoc capabilities (e.g. a smartphone sending messages to others nearby via Bluetooth or Wi-Fi). All devices run a minimal "virtual machine" that allows runtime injection of new programs: any device can initiate a new distributed process (in the form of a 0-ary anonymous function), which the virtual machine spreads to all other devices within a specified range (e.g., 30 meters). For example, a person might inject a process that estimates crowd density by counting the number of nearby devices or a process that helps people to rendezvous with their friends, with such processes likely implemented via various self-organisation mechanisms. The virtual machine then executes these using the first-class function semantics above, providing predictable deployment and execution of an open class of runtime-determined processes.

**Virtual Machine Implementation.** The complete code for our example is listed in Figure 4, with syntax coloring to increase readability: grey for comments, red for field calculus keywords, blue for user-defined functions, and green for built-in operators. In this code, we use the following naming conventions for built-ins: functions sns-* embed sensors that return a value perceived from the environment (e.g., sns-injection-point returns a Boolean indicating whether a device's user wants to inject a function); functions *-hood yield a local value $\ell$ obtained by aggregating over the field value $\phi$ in input (e.g., sum-hood sums all values in each neighbourhood); functions *-hood+ behave the same but exclude the value associated with the current device; and built-in functions pair, fst, and snd respectively create a pair of locals and access a pair's first and second component. Additionally, given a built-in o that takes $n \geq 1$ locals an returns a local, the built-ins o[*,...,*] are variants of o where one or more inputs are fields (as indicated in the bracket, 1 for local or f for field), and the return value is a field, obtained by applying operator o in a point-wise manner. For instance, as = compares two locals returning a Boolean, =[f,f] is the operator taking two field inputs and returns a Boolean field where each element is the comparison of the corresponding elements in the inputs, and similarly =[f,1] takes a field and a local and returns a Boolean field where each element is the comparison of the corresponding element of the field in input with the local.

The first two functions in Figure 4 implement frequently used self-organisation mechanisms. Function distance-to, also known as *gradient* [8,14], computes a field of minimal distances from each device to the nearest "source" device (those mapping to

```
;; Computes a field of minimum distance from 'source' devices
(def distance-to (source)     ;; has type: (bool) → num
  (rep d infinity (mux source 0 (min-hood+ (+[f,f] (nbr d) (nbr-range))))))

;; Computes a field of pairs of distance to nearest 'source' device, and the most recent value of 'v' there
(def gradcast (source v)      ;; has type: ∀β.(bool, β) → β
  (snd ((fun (x)
            (rep t x (mux source (pair 0 v)
                    (min-hood+
                        (pair[f,f] (+[f,f] (nbr-range) (nbr (fst t)))
                                   (nbr (snd t))))))
        (pair infinity v))))

;; Evaluate a function field, running 'f' from 'source' within 'range' meters, and 'no-op' elsewhere
(def deploy (range source g no-op)     ;; has type: ∀β. (num, bool, () → β, () → β) → β
  ((if (< (distance-to source) range) (gradcast source g) no-op)))

;; The entry-point function executed to run the virtual machine on each device
(def virtual-machine ()    ;; has type: () → num
  (deploy (sns-range) (sns-injection-point) (sns-injected-fun) (fun () 0)))
```

```
;; Sums values of 'summand' into a minimum of 'potential', by descent
(def converge-sum (potential summand)     ;; has type: (num, num) → num
  (rep v summand (+ summand
                    (sum-hood+ (mux[f,f,l] (=[f,l] (nbr (parent potential)) (uid))
                                           (nbr v) 0)))))

;; Maps each device to the uid of the neighbour with minimum value of 'potential'
(def parent (potential)     ;; has type: (num) → num
  (snd (min-hood (pair[l,f] potential
                            (mux[f,f,l] (<[f,l] (nbr potential) potential)
                                        (nbr (uid)) NaN)))))

;; Simple low-pass filter for smoothing noisy signal 'value' with rate constant 'alpha'
(def low-pass (alpha value)     ;; has type: (num, num) → num
  (rep filtered value (+ (* value alpha) (* filtered (- 1 alpha)))))
```

**Fig. 4.** Virtual machine code (top) and application-specific code (bottom)

*true* in the Boolean input field). This is computed by repeated application of the triangle inequality (via **rep**): at every round, source devices take distance zero, while all others update their distance estimates d to the minimum distance estimate through their neighbours (min-hood+ of each neighbour's distance estimate (nbr d) plus the distance to that neighbour nbr-range); source and non-source are discriminated by mux, a built-in "multiplexer" that operates like an **if** but differently from it always evaluates both branches on every device. Repeated application of this update procedure self-stabilises into the desired field of distances, regardless of any transient perturbations or faults [13]. The second self-organisation mechanism, gradcast, is a directed broadcast, achieved by a computation identical to that of distance-to, except that the values are pairs (note that pair[f,f] produces a field of pairs, not a pair of fields), with the second element set to the value of v at the source: min-hood operates on pairs by applying lexicographic ordering, so the second value of the pair is automatically carried along shortest paths from the source. The result is a field of pairs of distance and most recent value of v at the nearest source, of which only the value is returned.

The latter two functions in Figure 4 use these self-organisation methods to implement our simple virtual machine. Code mobility is implemented by function `deploy`, which spreads a 0-ary function `g` via `gradcast`, keeping it bounded within distance `range` from sources, and holding 0-ary function `no-op` elsewhere. The corresponding field of functions is then executed (note the double parenthesis). The `virtual-machine` then simply calls `deploy`, linking its arguments to sensors configuring deployment range and detecting who wants to inject which functions (and using (**fun** () 0) as `no-op` function).

In essence, this virtual machine implements a code-injection model much like those used in a number of other pervasive computing approaches (e.g., [15,11,6])—though of course it has much more limited features, since it is only an illustrative example. With these previous approaches, however, code shares lexical scope and cannot have its network domain externally controlled. Thus, injected code may spread through the network unpredictably and may interact unpredictably with other injected code that it encounters. The extended field calculus semantics that we have presented, however, ensures that injected code moves only within the range specified to the virtual machine and remains lexically isolated from different injected code, so that no variable can be unexpectedly affected by interactions with neighbours.

**Simulated Example Application.** We further illustrate the application of first-class functions with an example in a simulated scenario. Consider a museum, whose docents monitor their efficacy in part by tracking the number of patrons nearby while they are working. To monitor the number of nearby patrons, each docent's device injects the following anonymous function (of type: () → num):

```
(fun () (low-pass 0.5 (converge-sum (distance-to (sns-injection-point))
                                     (sns-patron))))
```

This counts patrons using the function `converge-sum` defined in Figure 4(bottom), a simple version of another standard self-organisation mechanism [4] which operates like an inverse broadcast, summing the values sensed by `sns-patron` (1 for a patron, 0 for a docent) down the distance gradient back to its source—in this case the docent at the injection point. In particular, each device's local value is summed with those identifying it as their parent (their closest neighbour to the source, breaking ties with device unique identifiers from built-in function `uid`), resulting in a relatively balanced spanning tree of summations with the source at its root. This very simple version of summation is somewhat noisy on a moving network of devices, so its output is passed through a simple low-pass filter, the function `low-pass`, also defined in Figure 4(bottom), in order to smooth its output and improve the quality of estimate.

Figure 5a shows a simulation of a docent and 250 patrons in a large 100x30 meter museum gallery. Of the patrons, 100 are a large group of school-children moving together past the stationary docent from one side of the gallery to the other, while the rest are wandering randomly. In this simulation, people move at an average 1 m/s, the docent and all patrons carry personal devices running the virtual machine, executing asynchronously at 10Hz, and communicating via low-power Bluetooth to a range of 10 meters. The simulation was implemented using the ALCHEMIST [18] simulation frame-

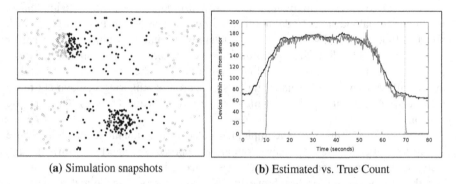

(a) Simulation snapshots          (b) Estimated vs. True Count

**Fig. 5.** (a) Two snapshots of museum simulation: patrons (grey) are counted (black) within 25 meters of the docent (green). (b) Estimated number of nearby patrons (grey) vs. actual number (black) in the simulation.

work and the Protelis [17] incarnation of field calculus, updated to the extended version of the calculus presented in this paper.

In this simulation, at time 10 seconds, the docent injects the patron-counting function with a range of 25 meters, and at time 70 seconds removes it. Figure 5a shows two snapshots of the simulation, at times 11 (top) and 35 (bottom) seconds, while Figure 5b compares the estimated value returned by the injected process with the true value. Note that upon injection, the process rapidly disseminates and begins producing good estimates of the number of nearby patrons, then cleanly terminates upon removal.

## 5    Conclusion, Related and Future Work

Conceiving emerging distributed systems in terms of computations involving aggregates of devices, and hence adopting higher-level abstractions for system development, is a thread that has recently received a good deal of attention. A wide range of aggregate programming approaches have been proposed, including Proto [2], TOTA [15], the (bio)chemical tuple-space model [19], Regiment [16], the $\sigma\tau$-Linda model [22], Paintable Computing [6], and many others included in the extensive survey of aggregate programming languages given in [3]. Those that best support self-organisation approaches to robust and environment-independent computations have generally lacked well-engineered mechanisms to support openness and code mobility (injection, update, etc.). Our contribution has been to develop a core calculus, building on the work presented in [21], that smoothly combines for the first time self-organisation and code mobility, by means of the abstraction of "distributed function field". This combination of first-class functions with the domain-restriction mechanisms of field calculus allows the predictable and safe composition of distributed self-organisation mechanisms at runtime, thereby enabling robust operation of open pervasive systems. Furthermore, the simplicity of the calculus enables it to easily serve as both an analytical framework and a programming framework, and we have already incorporated this into Protelis [17], thereby allowing these mechanisms to be deployed both in simulation and in actual distributed systems.

Future plans include consolidation of this work, by extending the calculus and its conceptual framework, to support an analytical methodology and a practical toolchain for system development, as outlined in [4]. First, we aim to apply our approach to support various application needs for dynamic management of distributed processes [1], which may also impact the methods of alignment for anonymous functions. Second, we plan to isolate fragments of the calculus that satisfy behavioural properties such as self-stabilisation, quasi-stabilisation to a dynamically evolving field, or density independence, following the approach of [20]. Finally, these foundations can be applied in developing APIs enabling the simple construction of complex distributed applications, building on the work in [4] to define a layered library of self-organisation patterns, and applying these APIs to support a wide range of practical distributed applications.

# References

1. Beal, J.: Dynamically defined processes for spatial computers. In: Spatial Computing Workshop, New York, pp. 206–211. IEEE (September 2009)
2. Beal, J., Bachrach, J.: Infrastructure for engineered emergence in sensor/actuator networks. IEEE Intelligent Systems 21, 10–19 (2006)
3. Beal, J., Dulman, S., Usbeck, K., Viroli, M., Correll, N.: Organizing the aggregate: Languages for spatial computing. In: Mernik, M. (ed.) Formal and Practical Aspects of Domain-Specific Languages: Recent Developments, ch. 16, pp. 436–501. IGI Global (2013), A longer version available at http://arxiv.org/abs/1202.5509
4. Beal, J., Viroli, M.: Building blocks for aggregate programming of self-organising applications. In: 2nd FoCAS Workshop on Fundamentals of Collective Systems, pp. 1–6. IEEE CS (2014) (to appear)
5. Beal, J., Viroli, M., Damiani, F.: Towards a unified model of spatial computing. In: 7th Spatial Computing Workshop (SCW 2014), AAMAS 2014, Paris, France (May 2014)
6. Butera, W.: Programming a Paintable Computer. PhD thesis, MIT, Cambridge, USA (2002)
7. Church, A.: A set of postulates for the foundation of logic. Annals of Mathematics 33(2), 346–366 (1932)
8. Clement, L., Nagpal, R.: Self-assembly and self-repairing topologies. In: Workshop on Adaptability in Multi-Agent Systems, RoboCup Australian Open (2003)
9. Damas, L., Milner, R.: Principal type-schemes for functional programs. In: Symposium on Principles of Programming Languages, POPL 1982, pp. 207–212. ACM (1982)
10. Dean, J., Ghemawat, S.: Mapreduce: simplified data processing on large clusters. Communications of the ACM 51(1), 107–113 (2008)
11. Gelernter, D.: Generative communication in linda. ACM Trans. Program. Lang. Syst. 7(1), 80–112 (1985)
12. Igarashi, A., Pierce, B.C., Wadler, P.: Featherweight Java: A minimal core calculus for Java and GJ. ACM Transactions on Programming Languages and Systems 23(3) (2001)
13. Kutten, S., Patt-Shamir, B.: Time-adaptive self stabilization. In: Proceedings of ACM Symposium on Principles of Distributed Computing, pp. 149–158. ACM (1997)
14. Lin, F.C.H., Keller, R.M.: The gradient model load balancing method. IEEE Trans. Softw. Eng. 13(1), 32–38 (1987)
15. Mamei, M., Zambonelli, F.: Programming pervasive and mobile computing applications: The tota approach. ACM Trans. on Software Engineering Methodologies 18(4), 1–56 (2009)

16. Newton, R., Welsh, M.: Region streams: Functional macroprogramming for sensor networks. In: Workshop on Data Management for Sensor Networks, pp. 78–87 (August 2004)

17. Pianini, D., Beal, J., Viroli, M.: Practical aggregate programming with PROTELIS. In: ACM Symposium on Applied Computing (SAC 2015) (to appear, 2015)

18. Pianini, D., Montagna, S., Viroli, M.: Chemical-oriented simulation of computational systems with Alchemist. Journal of Simulation 7, 202–215 (2013)

19. Viroli, M., Casadei, M., Montagna, S., Zambonelli, F.: Spatial coordination of pervasive services through chemical-inspired tuple spaces. ACM Transactions on Autonomous and Adaptive Systems 6(2), 14:1–14:24 (2011)

20. Viroli, M., Damiani, F.: A calculus of self-stabilising computational fields. In: Kühn, E., Pugliese, R. (eds.) COORDINATION 2014. LNCS, vol. 8459, pp. 163–178. Springer, Heidelberg (2014)

21. Viroli, M., Damiani, F., Beal, J.: A calculus of computational fields. In: Canal, C., Villari, M. (eds.) ESOCC 2013. CCIS, vol. 393, pp. 114–128. Springer, Heidelberg (2013)

22. Viroli, M., Pianini, D., Beal, J.: Linda in space-time: An adaptive coordination model for mobile ad-hoc environments. In: Sirjani, M. (ed.) COORDINATION 2012. LNCS, vol. 7274, pp. 212–229. Springer, Heidelberg (2012)

# Real Time Systems

# Timely Dataflow: A Model

Martín Abadi[1,2] and Michael Isard[3]

[1] Google, Mountain View, CA, USA
[2] University of California, Santa Cruz, CA, USA
[3] Microsoft Research, Mountain View, CA, USA

**Abstract.** This paper studies timely dataflow, a model for data-parallel computing in which each communication event is associated with a virtual time. It defines and investigates the could-result-in relation which is central to this model, then the semantics of timely dataflow graphs.

## 1 Introduction

Timely dataflow is a model of data-parallel computation that extends traditional dataflow (e.g., [10]) by associating each communication event with a virtual time [12]. Virtual times need not be linearly ordered, nor correspond to the order in which events are processed. As in the Time Warp mechanism [7], virtual times serve to differentiate between data in different phases or aspects of a computation, for example data associated with different batches of inputs and different loop iterations. Thus, an implementation may overlap, but still distinguish, work that corresponds to multiple logical parts of a computation.

In this model, each node in a dataflow graph can request to be notified when it has received all messages for a given virtual time. The facilities for asynchronous processing and completion notifications imply that, even within a single program, some components can function in batch mode (queuing inputs and delaying processing until an appropriate notification) and others in streaming mode (processing inputs as they arrive). For example, an application may process a stream of GPS readings; as these readings arrive, the application may update a map and, after each batch of readings, recompute shortest paths between landmarks.

The Naiad system [12] is the origin and an embodiment of timely dataflow. Naiad aspires to serve as a coherent platform for data-parallel applications, offering both high throughput and low latency. Timely dataflow is crucial to this goal. Naiad contrasts with other systems that focus on narrower domains (e.g., graph problems) or on particular classes of programs (e.g., without loops).

The development and presentation of timely dataflow in the context of Naiad was fairly precise but informal. Only one of its critical components (a distributed algorithm that keeps track of virtual times for which there may remain work) was rigorously specified and verified [4]. Moreover, in the context of Naiad, definitions focus on particular structures of dataflow graphs and particular types of nodes. Specifically, Naiad supports iterative computations, with loops that

---

Most of this work was done at Microsoft Research.

S. Graf and M. Viswanathan (Eds.): FORTE 2015, LNCS 9039, pp. 131–145, 2015.
DOI: 10.1007/978-3-319-19195-9_9

include special nodes for ingress, feedback, and egress, and with a set of virtual times that includes coordinates for input epochs and loop counters.

The goal of this paper is to provide a general, rigorous definition of timely dataflow. We allow arbitrary graph structures, partial orders of virtual times, and stateful local computations at each of the nodes. The local computations are deterministic (only for simplicity); non-determinism is introduced by the ordering of events. We specify the semantics of timely dataflow graphs using a linear-time temporal logic. In this setting, we explore some of the fundamental concepts and properties of the model. In particular, we study the could-result-in relation, which drives completion notifications; for instance, we investigate how it applies to recursive dataflow computations, which are beyond Naiad's present scope. The semantics serves as the basis for rigorous proofs, as we demonstrate with an example application. We are finding the semantics valuable in other, more substantial applications. Specifically, the results of this paper have already been useful to us in our work on information-flow security properties [1] and on fault-tolerance [2]. Our rather elementary formulation of the semantics amply suffices for these present purposes; we leave algebraic or categorical presentations (see, e.g., [6]) for further work.

The next section defines dataflow graphs and other basic notions. Section 3 concerns the could-result-in relation. Section 4 describes the semantics of graphs, and Section 5 applies it. Section 6 concludes. Because of space constraints, proofs are omitted.

## 2    Dataflow Graphs, Messages, and Times

As is typical in dataflow models, we specify computations as directed graphs, with distinguished input and output edges. The graphs may contain cycles. During execution, stateful nodes send and receive timestamped messages, and in addition may request and receive notifications that they have received all messages with a certain timestamp. This section defines the graphs and the behavior of individual nodes; later sections cover more global aspects of the semantics.

We write $\emptyset$ both for the empty sequence and for the empty set. We write $\langle\!\langle m_0, m_1, \ldots \rangle\!\rangle$ for the sequence (finite or infinite) that consists of $m_0, m_1, \ldots$. We use "$\cdot$" for sequence concatenation and also for appending elements to sequences, for example writing $m \cdot u$ instead of $\langle\!\langle m \rangle\!\rangle \cdot u$, where $u$ is a sequence and $m$ an element. A mapping $f$ on elements is extended to a mapping on sequences by letting $f(\langle\!\langle m_0, m_1, m_2, \ldots \rangle\!\rangle) = \langle\!\langle f(m_0), f(m_1), \ldots \rangle\!\rangle$, and to a mapping on sets by letting $f(S) = \{f(s) : s \in S\}$. When $A$ is a set, we write $\mathcal{P}(A)$ for its powerset, and $A^*$ and $A^\omega$, respectively, for the sets of finite and infinite sequences of elements of $A$. When $f$ is a function with a domain that includes $A$, we write $f{\upharpoonright}A$ for the restriction of $f$ to $A$. When $B$ is also a set, we write $\Pi_{x \in A}.B$ for the set of functions that map each $x \in A$ to an element of $B$; if $A$ is a finite set $\{a_1, \ldots, a_k\}$ and $b_1, \ldots, b_k$ are elements of $B$, we write such a function $\langle a_1 \mapsto b_1, \ldots, a_k \mapsto b_k \rangle$.

## 2.1    Basics of Graphs, Messages, and Times

We assume a set of *messages* $M$, a partial order of *times* $(T, \leq)$, and a time $time(m) \in T$ for each $m \in M$. We also assume a finite set of *nodes (processors)* $P$, and a set of *local states* $\Sigma_{\mathrm{Loc}}$ for them. Finally, we assume a set of *edges (channels)*, partitioned into *input* edges $I$, *internal* edges $E$, and *output* edges $O$. Edges have *sources* and *destinations* (not always both): for each $i \in I$, $dst(i) \in P$, and $src(i)$ is undefined; for each $e \in E$, $src(e), dst(e) \in P$, and we require that they are distinct; for each $o \in O$, $src(o) \in P$, and $dst(o)$ is undefined.

Input edges are not essential for computations getting started, because nodes can initially create data in response to notifications. We include input edges as a convenience, and because they can serve for connecting graphs.

We allow (but do not require) the set of times to be the disjoint union of multiple "time domains". For example, a node may receive inputs tagged with GMT times, and produce outputs tagged with GMT times, PST times, or perhaps with sequence numbers, and may even send outputs in different time domains along different edges. In Naiad, the nodes for loop ingress and egress, respectively, add and remove time coordinates that represent loop counters. Accordingly, we do not assume, for example, that it is always immediately meaningful to compare the times of inputs and outputs.

## 2.2    Processor Behavior

Timely dataflow supports stateful computations in which each node maintains local state. For each node $p$, a subset $Initial(p)$ of $\Sigma_{\mathrm{Loc}} \times \mathcal{P}(T)$ describes the possible initial states and initial notification requests for $p$. A *local history* for $p$ is a finite sequence of the form $\langle\!\langle (s, N), x_1, \ldots, x_n \rangle\!\rangle$ where $(s, N) \in Initial(p)$, $n \geq 0$, and each $x_i$ is either a pair $(d, m)$ where $m \in M$ and $d \in I \cup E$ with $dst(d) = p$, or a time $t \in T$. In this context, we call a pair $(d, m)$ or a time $t$ an *event*. Thus, a local history records the order in which a node consumes events; it also determines what the node does in response to these events, via the function $g_1$ introduced below. We write $Histories(p)$ for the set of local histories of node $p$.

For each node $p$, the function $g_1(p)$ maps $\Sigma_{\mathrm{Loc}} \times (T \cup (\{d \in I \cup E \mid dst(d) = p\} \times M))$ to $\Sigma_{\mathrm{Loc}} \times \mathcal{P}(T) \times (\Pi_{\{d \in E \cup O \mid src(d) = p\}}.M^*)$. Intuitively $g_1$ describes one step of computation by one node:

- $g_1(p)(s, t) = (s', \{t_1, \ldots, t_n\}, \langle e_1 \mapsto \mu_1, \ldots, e_k \mapsto \mu_k \rangle)$ means that, in response to a notification for time $t$ and at a state $s$, the node $p$ can move to state $s'$, request notifications for times $t_1, \ldots, t_n$, and add message sequences $\mu_1, \ldots, \mu_k$ on outgoing edges $e_1, \ldots, e_k$, respectively.
- $g_1(p)(s, (d, m)) = (s', \{t_1, \ldots, t_n\}, \langle e_1 \mapsto \mu_1, \ldots, e_k \mapsto \mu_k \rangle)$ means that, in response to a message $m$ on incoming edge $d$ and at a state $s$, the node $p$ can move to state $s'$, request notifications for times $t_1, \ldots, t_n$, and add message sequences $\mu_1, \ldots, \mu_k$ on outgoing edges $e_1, \ldots, e_k$, respectively.

We could easily restrict these definitions so that a message for time $t$ cannot appear in a history to the right of a notification for time $t$, and so that notifications appear only in response to notification requests. However, such restrictions do not seem necessary; each node can enforce them.

We extend the function $g_1$ to a function $g$ that applies to local histories. For each node $p$, $g(p)$ maps $Histories(p)$ to $\Sigma_{\text{Loc}} \times \mathcal{P}(T) \times (\Pi_{\{d \in E \cup O \mid src(d) = p\}} \cdot M^*)$, and is defined inductively by:

- $g(p)(\langle\!\langle\!\langle(s, N)\rangle\!\rangle\!\rangle) = (s, N, \langle e_1 \mapsto \emptyset, \ldots, e_k \mapsto \emptyset\rangle)$
- If $g(p)(h) = (s', N, \langle e_1 \mapsto \mu_1, \ldots, e_k \mapsto \mu_k\rangle)$, $h' = h \cdot t$, and $g_1(p)(s', t) = (s", N', \langle e_1 \mapsto \mu'_1, \ldots, e_k \mapsto \mu'_k\rangle)$, then

$$g(p)(h') = (s", N - \{t\} \cup N', \langle e_1 \mapsto \mu_1 \cdot \mu'_1, \ldots, e_k \mapsto \mu_k \cdot \mu'_k\rangle)$$

- If $g(p)(h) = (s', N, \langle e_1 \mapsto \mu_1, \ldots, e_k \mapsto \mu_k\rangle)$, $h' = h \cdot (d, m)$, and $g_1(p)(s', (d, m)) = (s", N', \langle e_1 \mapsto \mu'_1, \ldots, e_k \mapsto \mu'_k\rangle)$, then

$$g(p)(h') = (s", N \cup N', \langle e_1 \mapsto \mu_1 \cdot \mu'_1, \ldots, e_k \mapsto \mu_k \cdot \mu'_k\rangle)$$

Given a triple $(s, N, \langle e_1 \mapsto \mu_1, \ldots, e_k \mapsto \mu_k\rangle)$, perhaps obtained via one of these functions, we write: $\Pi_{\text{Loc}}(s, N, \langle e_1 \mapsto \mu_1, \ldots, e_k \mapsto \mu_k\rangle)$ for $s$, $\Pi_{\text{NR}}(s, N, \langle e_1 \mapsto \mu_1, \ldots, e_k \mapsto \mu_k\rangle)$ for $N$, and $\Pi_{e_i}(s, N, \langle e_1 \mapsto \mu_1, \ldots, e_k \mapsto \mu_k\rangle)$ for $\mu_i$.

In this model, each node can consume and produce multiple events in one atomic action. For example, a node may simultaneously dequeue an input message and produce two output messages on each of two distinct edges. Alternative models could be more asynchronous; in our example, the node would first dequeue the input message, and after some delay produce the two output messages one after the other. Fortunately, such an asynchronous model can be seen as a special case of ours: in our model, asynchronous behavior can be produced by buffering (see, e.g., [14]). We say that $p \in P$ is a buffer node if there exist exactly one $e_1 \in I \cup E$ such that $dst(e_1) = p$ and exactly one $e_2 \in E \cup O$ such that $src(e_2) = p$, and $g_1(p)(s, t) = (s, \emptyset, \langle e_2 \mapsto \emptyset\rangle)$ and $g_1(p)(s, (e_1, m)) = (s, \emptyset, \langle e_2 \mapsto \langle\!\langle m\rangle\!\rangle\rangle)$. Such a node $p$ is simply a relay between queues. (The term "buffer" comes from the literature.) In order to simulate a more asynchronous semantics, we could require that every non-buffer node has its output edges going into buffer nodes. However, we do not need to impose this constraint.

## 3    Pointstamps and the Could-result-in Relation

As indicated in the Introduction, each node can request to be notified when it has received all messages for a given virtual time. Furthermore, "under the covers", an implementation may benefit from knowing that a virtual time is complete in order to reclaim associated resources. Thus, the notion of completion of virtual times is central to timely dataflow and to its practical realization. Reasoning about completion is based on the *could-result-in* relation on *pointstamps*. In this section we define this relation and establish some of its properties.

### 3.1   Defining Could-result-in

A pointstamp is a pair $(x, t)$ of a location $x$ (node or edge) in a graph and a time $t$. Thus, the set of pointstamps is $((I \cup E \cup O) \cup P) \times T$. We say that pointstamp $(x, t)$ could-result-in pointstamp $(x', t')$, and write $(x, t) \rightsquigarrow (x', t')$, if a message or notification at location $x$ and time $t$ may lead to a message or notification at location $x'$ and time $t'$. We define $\rightsquigarrow$ via an auxiliary relation $\rightsquigarrow^1$ that reflects one step of computation.

**Definition 1.** $(p, t) \rightsquigarrow^1 (d, t')$ *if and only if* $src(d) = p$ *and there exist a history* $h$ *for* $p$ *and a state* $s$ *such that*

$$g(p)(h) = (s, \ldots)$$

*and an event* $x$ *such that either* $x = t$ *or* $x = (e, m)$ *for some* $e$ *and* $m$ *such that* $t = time(m)$, *and*

$$g_1(p)(s, x) = (\ldots, \langle \ldots d \mapsto \mu \ldots \rangle)$$

*where some element of* $\mu$ *has time* $t'$.

**Definition 2.** $(x, t) \rightsquigarrow (x', t')$ *if and only if*

- $x = x'$ *and* $t \leq t'$, *or*
- *there exist* $k > 1$, *distinct* $x_i$ *for* $i = 1 \ldots k$, *and (not necessarily distinct)* $t_i$ *for* $i = 1 \ldots k$, *such that* $x = x_1$, $x' = x_k$, $t \leq t_1$, *and* $t_k \leq t'$, *and for all* $i = 1 \ldots k - 1$:
  - $x_i \in I \cup E$, $x_{i+1} \in P$, $dst(x_i) = x_{i+1}$, *and* $t_i = t_{i+1}$, *or*
  - $x_i \in P$, $x_{i+1} \in E \cup O$, $src(x_{i+1}) = x_i$, *and there exist* $t'_i \geq t_i$ *and* $t''_i \leq t_{i+1}$ *such that* $(x_i, t'_i) \rightsquigarrow^1 (x_{i+1}, t''_i)$.

In the first case, we say that the proof of $(x, t) \rightsquigarrow (x', t')$ has length 1; in the second, that it has length $k$. (These lengths are helpful in inductive arguments. Different proofs of $(x, t) \rightsquigarrow (x', t')$ may in general have different lengths.)

This definition captures the semantics of an arbitrary node $p$, via the functions $g_1$ and $g$. The function $g$ is applied to a local history to generate a state $s$, then $g_1$ is applied at $s$. Thus, the definition restricts attention to states $s$ that can arise in some execution with $p$. However, we do not attempt to guarantee that this execution is one of those that can occur in the context of the other nodes in the graph of interest, in order to avoid a circularity: this latter set of executions is itself defined in terms of the relation $\rightsquigarrow$ (in Section 4.2).

An implementation, such as Naiad's, may soundly use simple, conservative approximations to the relation $\rightsquigarrow$ as we define it here. In Naiad, for most nodes $p$, it is assumed that $(p, t) \rightsquigarrow^1 (e, t)$ for all $t$ and each outgoing edge $e$; certain nodes (loop ingress, feedback, and egress) receive special treatment.

The definition implies that $\rightsquigarrow$ is reflexive. The following proposition asserts a few of the additional properties of $\rightsquigarrow$ that we have found useful.

**Proposition 1.**

1. *If $(p, t_1) \rightsquigarrow (e, t_2)$ then there are $e' \in E \cup O$ and $t' \in T$ such that $src(e') = p$,*
   *$(p, t_1) \rightsquigarrow (e', t')$ and $(e', t') \rightsquigarrow (e, t_2)$, with the proof of $(e', t') \rightsquigarrow (e, t_2)$ strictly*
   *shorter than that of $(p, t_1) \rightsquigarrow (e, t_2)$.*
2. *If $(x, t_1) \rightsquigarrow (x, t_2)$ then $t_1 \leq t_2$.*
3. *If $(x_1, t_1) \rightsquigarrow (x_2, t_2)$, $t'_1 \leq t_1$, and $t_2 \leq t'_2$, then $(x_1, t'_1) \rightsquigarrow (x_2, t'_2)$.*

The definition is designed to be convenient in proofs and to reflect important aspects of implementations (and of Naiad's specifically). In particular, the distinctness requirement ("there exist $k > 1$, distinct $x_i$ for $i = 1 \ldots k$") means that proofs and implementations do not need to chase around cycles.

On the other hand, because of the distinctness requirement, the definition does not immediately yield that $\rightsquigarrow$ is transitive, as one might expect, and as one might often want in proofs. More broadly, the definition of $\rightsquigarrow$ may not correspond to the intuitive understanding of could-result-in without some additional assumptions, which we address next.

## 3.2   On Sending Notification Requests and Messages into the Past

In timely dataflow, and in Naiad in particular, it is generally expected that events do not give rise to other events at earlier times. When those other events are notification requests, the required condition is easy to state. When they are messages, it is not, because we do not wish to compare times across time domains. In this section we formulate and study these two conditions.

The first considers the generation of notification requests, which the definition of $\rightsquigarrow$ ignores. We formulate it via an additional relation $\rightsquigarrow_N$, a local variant of the could-result-in relation that focuses on the generation of notification requests. (This relation is not intended to be reflexive or transitive.)

**Definition 3.** *$(p, t) \rightsquigarrow_N (p, t')$ if and only if there exist a history $h$ for $p$ and a state $s$ such that*

$$g(p)(h) = (s, N_1, \ldots)$$

*and an event $x$ such that either $x = \hat{t}''$ for some $t''$ such that $t \leq t''$, or $x = (e, m)$ for some $e$ and $m$ such that $t \leq time(m)$, and*

$$g_1(p)(s, x) = (\ldots, N, \ldots)$$

*where some element of $N - N_1$ is $\leq t'$.*

Using this relation, we can express that an event at time $t$ can trigger notification requests only at greater times $t'$:

**Condition 1.** *If $(p, t) \rightsquigarrow_N (p, t')$ then $t \leq t'$.*

The question of the transitivity of $\rightsquigarrow$ is closely related to the expectation that nodes should not be allowed to send messages into the past. Indeed, a sufficient condition for transitivity is that, for all pointstamps $(x, t)$ and $(x', t')$, if $(x,t) \rightsquigarrow (x',t')$ then $t \le t'$ (as implied by Theorem 1, below). However, the converse does not hold, for trivial reasons. For example, in a graph with a single node, the relation $\rightsquigarrow$ will always be transitive but we may not have that $(x,t) \rightsquigarrow (x',t')$ implies $t \le t'$. Still, we can compare times at a node and at its incoming edges, and fortunately such comparisons suffice, as the following theorem demonstrates.

**Condition 2.** *For all $p \in P$, $e \in E$ with $dst(e) = p$, and $t,t' \in T$, if $(p,t) \rightsquigarrow (e,t')$ then $t \le t'$.*

**Theorem 1.** *The relation $\rightsquigarrow$ is transitive if and only if Condition 2 holds.*

Conditions 1 and 2 both depend on the semantics of individual nodes; Condition 2 also depends on the topology of the graph. Although we assume them in some of our results, we do not discuss how they can be enforced. In practice, Naiad simply assumes analogous properties, but type systems and other static analyses may well help in checking them.

The following proposition offers another way of thinking about transitivity by comparing times at different nodes and edges, via an embedding of these times into an additional partial order $(T', \preceq)$. One may view $(T', \preceq)$ as a set of times normalized into a coherent universal time—the "GMT" of timely dataflow. (This proposition is fairly straightforward, and we do not need it below.)

**Proposition 2.** *The relation $\rightsquigarrow$ is transitive if and only if there exist a partial order $(T', \preceq)$ and a mapping $\mathcal{E}$ from the set of pointstamps $((I \cup E \cup O) \cup P) \times T$ to $T'$ such that, for all $(x,t)$ and $(x',t')$, $(x,t) \rightsquigarrow (x',t')$ if and only if $\mathcal{E}(x,t) \preceq \mathcal{E}(x',t')$.*

## 3.3   Closure

We say that a set $S$ of pointstamps is *upward closed* if and only if, for all pointstamps $(x,t)$ and $(x',t')$, $(x,t) \in S$ and $(x,t) \rightsquigarrow (x',t')$ imply $(x',t') \in S$. For any set $S$ of pointstamps, $Close_\uparrow(S)$ is the least upward closed set that contains $S$. Assuming that $\rightsquigarrow$ is transitive, the following proposition provides a simpler formulation for $Close_\uparrow$.

**Proposition 3.** *Assume that Condition 2 holds. Then $Close_\uparrow(S) = \{(x',t') \mid \exists(x,t) \in S.(x,t) \rightsquigarrow (x',t')\}$.*

## 3.4   Recursion

Naiad focuses on iterative computation, and the could-result-in relation for the nodes that support iteration (loop ingress, feedback, and egress) has been discussed informally [12]. We could revisit iteration using our definitions. However, the definitions are much more general. We demonstrate the value of this generality by outlining how they apply to recursive dataflow computation (e.g., [5]).

Let us consider a dataflow graph that includes a distinguished input node **in** with no incoming edges, a distinguished output node **out** with no outgoing edges, some ordinary nodes for operations on data, and other nodes that represent recursive calls to the entire computation. For simplicity, we let $I = O = \emptyset$, and do not consider multiple mutually recursive graphs and other variants. We assume that every node is reachable from **in**, **out** is reachable from every node, and there is a path from **in** to **out** that does not go through any call nodes. In order to make the recursion explicit, we modify the dataflow graph by splitting each call node c into a call part **call-c** and a return part **ret-c**, where the former is the source of a back edge to **in** and the latter is the destination of a back edge from **out**.

A stack $\int$ is a finite sequence of call nodes. We let $\rightsquigarrow$ be the least reflexive, transitive relation on pairs $(p, \int)$ such that

1. $(\texttt{call-c}, \int) \rightsquigarrow (\texttt{in}, \int \cdot \texttt{c})$;
2. symmetrically, $(\texttt{out}, \int \cdot \texttt{c}) \rightsquigarrow (\texttt{ret-c}, \int)$; and
3. if $p$ is not $\texttt{call-c}$ and $p'$ is not $\texttt{ret-c}$ for any c, and there is an edge from $p$ to $p'$, then $(p, \int) \rightsquigarrow (p', \int)$.

We will have that $\rightsquigarrow$ is a conservative approximation of $\rightsquigarrow$.

At each node $p$, we define a pre-order on stacks: $\int \preceq_p \int'$ if and only if $(p, \int) \rightsquigarrow (p, \int')$. We write $(T_p, \leq_p)$ for the partial order induced by $\preceq_p$ (so, $T_p$ identifies $\int$ and $\int'$ when both $\int \preceq_p \int'$ and $\int' \preceq_p \int$). The partial order is thus different at each node. The partial order of virtual times $(T, \leq)$ is the disjoint ("tagged") union of the partial orders $(T_p, \leq_p)$ for all the nodes. We write $[\int]_p$ for the element of $T$ obtained by tagging the equivalence class of $\int$ at $p$.

We assume that each node $p$ uses the appropriate tags for its outgoing messages and notification requests, and ignores inputs and notifications not tagged with $p$, and also that the behavior of $p$, as reflected in the relation $\rightsquigarrow^1$, conforms to what the relation $\rightsquigarrow$ expresses:

If $(p, [\int]_q) \rightsquigarrow^1 (d, [\int']_{p'})$ then $q = p$, $p' = dst(d)$, and $(p, \int) \rightsquigarrow (p', \int')$.

We obtain:

**Proposition 4.** *If* $(p, [\int]_p) \rightsquigarrow (p', [\int']_{p'})$ *then* $(p, \int) \rightsquigarrow (p', \int')$.

**Proposition 5.** *If* $(p, [\int]_q) \rightsquigarrow (p', [\int']_{q'})$ *and* $p \neq p'$, *then* $q = p$ *and* $q' = p'$.

Applying Theorem 1, we also obtain:

**Proposition 6.** *The relation* $\rightsquigarrow$ *is transitive.*

Furthermore, the relation $\rightsquigarrow$ can be decided quite simply by finding the first call in which two stacks differ and performing an easy check based on that difference. This check relies on an alternative modified graph, in which we split each call node c into a call part **call-c** and a return part **ret-c**, but add a direct forward edge from the former to the latter (rather than back edges). Suppose (without loss of generality) that $f$ is of the form $f_1 \cdot f_2$ and $f'$ is of the form $f_1 \cdot f_2'$, where $f_2$ and $f_2'$ start with c and c' respectively if they are not empty. We assume that c and c' are distinct if $f_2$ and $f_2'$ are both non-empty (so, $f_1$ is maximal). Let $l$ be ret-c if $f_2$ is non-empty, and be $p$ if it is empty; let $l'$ be call-c' if $f_2'$ is non-empty, and be $p'$ if it is empty. Then we can prove that $(p, f) \rightsquigarrow (p', f')$ if and only if there is a path from $l$ to $l'$ in the alternative modified graph.

Special cases (in particular, special graph topologies) may allow further simplifications which could be helpful in implementations.

## 4   Semantics

We describe the semantics of timely dataflow graphs in a state-based framework [3,11]. In this section, we first review this framework, then specify the semantics. Finally, we discuss matters of compositionality.

### 4.1   The Framework (Review)

The sequence $\langle\!\langle s_0, s_1, s_2, \ldots \rangle\!\rangle$ is said to be *stutter-free* if, for each $i$, either $s_i \neq s_{i+1}$ or the sequence is infinite and $s_i = s_j$ for all $j \geq i$. We let $\natural\sigma$ be the stutter-free sequence obtained from $\sigma$ by replacing every maximal finite subsequence $s_i, s_{i+1}, \ldots, s_j$ of identical elements with the single element $s_i$. A set of sequences $S$ is *closed under stuttering* when $\sigma \in S$ if and only if $\natural\sigma \in S$.

A *state space* $\Sigma$ is a subset of $\Sigma_E \times \Sigma_I$ for some sets $\Sigma_E$ of externally visible states and $\Sigma_I$ of internal states. If $\Sigma$ is a state space, then a $\Sigma$-*behavior* is an element of $\Sigma^\omega$. A $\Sigma_E$-behavior is called an *externally visible behavior*. A $\Sigma$-*property* $P$ is a set of $\Sigma$-behaviors that is closed under stuttering. When $\Sigma$ is clear from context or is irrelevant, we may leave it implicit. We sometimes apply the adjective "complete", as in "complete behavior", in order to distinguish behaviors and properties from externally visible behaviors and properties.

A *state machine* is a triple $(\Sigma, F, N)$ where $\Sigma$ is a state space; $F$, the set of *initial* states, is a subset of $\Sigma$; and $N$, the *next-state relation*, is a subset of $\Sigma \times \Sigma$. The *complete property generated by* a state machine $(\Sigma, F, N)$ consists of all infinite sequences $\langle\!\langle s_0, s_1, \ldots \rangle\!\rangle$ such that $s_0 \in F$ and, for all $i \geq 0$, either $\langle s_i, s_{i+1} \rangle \in N$ or $s_i = s_{i+1}$. The *externally visible property generated by* a state machine is the externally visible property obtained from its complete property by projection onto $\Sigma_E$ and closure under stuttering. For brevity, we do not consider fairness conditions or other liveness properties that can be added to state machines; their treatment is largely orthogonal to our present goals.

Although we are not fully formal in the use of TLA [11], we generally follow its approach to writing specifications. Specifically, we express state machines by formulas of the form:

$$\exists y_1, \ldots, y_n. \ F \wedge \Box [N]_{v_1, \ldots, v_k}$$

where:

- state functions that we write as variables represent the state;
- we distinguish external variables and internal variables, and the internal variables (in this case, $y_1, \ldots, y_n$) are existentially quantified;
- $F$ is a formula that may refer to the variables;
- $\Box$ is the temporal-logic operator "always";
- $N$ is a formula that may refer to the variables and also to primed versions of the variables (thus denoting the values of those variables in the next state);
- $[N]_{v_1,\ldots,v_k}$ abbreviates $N \vee ((v_1' = v_1) \wedge \ldots \wedge (v_k' = v_k))$.

## 4.2   Semantics Specification

In our semantics, the externally visible states map each $e \in I \cup O$ to a value $Q(e)$ in $M^*$. In other words, we observe only the state of input and output edges. The internally visible states map each $e \in E$ to a value $Q(e)$ in $M^*$, and each $p \in P$ to a local state $LocState(p) \in \Sigma_{\text{Loc}}$ and to a set of pending notification requests $NotRequests(p) \in \mathcal{P}(T)$.

An auxiliary state function $Clock$ (whose name comes from Naiad, and is unrelated to "clocks" elsewhere) tracks pointstamps for which work may remain:

$$Clock \triangleq Close_\uparrow \left( \begin{array}{c} \{(e, time(m)) \mid e \in I \cup E \cup O, m \in Q(e)\} \\ \cup \\ \{(p, t) \mid p \in P, t \in NotRequests(p)\} \end{array} \right)$$

We define an initial condition, the actions that constitute a next-state relation, and finally the specification.

*Initial condition:*

$$InitProp \triangleq \left( \begin{array}{l} \forall e \in E \cup O.Q(e) = \emptyset \wedge \forall i \in I.Q(i) \in M^* \\ \wedge \\ \forall p \in P.(LocState(p), NotRequests(p)) \in Initial(p) \end{array} \right)$$

*Actions:*

1. Receiving a message:

$$Mess \triangleq \exists p \in P.Mess1(p)$$

$$Mess1(p) \triangleq \left( \begin{array}{l} \exists m \in M.\exists e \in I \cup E \text{ such that } p = dst(e). \\ Q(e) = m \cdot Q'(e) \wedge Mess2(p, e, m) \end{array} \right)$$

$$Mess2(p, e, m) \triangleq \begin{pmatrix} let \\ \{e_1, \ldots, e_k\} = \{d \in E \cup O \mid src(d) = p\}, \\ s = LocState(p), \\ (s', N, \langle e_1 \mapsto \mu_1, \ldots, e_k \mapsto \mu_k \rangle) = g_1(p)(s, (e, m)) \\ in \\ LocState'(p) = s' \\ \wedge \\ NotRequests'(p) = NotRequests(p) \cup N \\ \wedge \\ Q'(e_1) = Q(e_1) \cdot \mu_1 \ldots Q'(e_k) = Q(e_k) \cdot \mu_k \\ \wedge \\ \forall q \in P \neq p.LocState'(q) = LocState(q) \\ \wedge \\ \forall q \in P \neq p.NotRequests'(q) = NotRequests(q) \\ \wedge \\ \forall d \in I \cup E \cup O - \{e, e_1, \ldots, e_k\}.Q'(d) = Q(d) \end{pmatrix}$$

These formulas describe how a node $p$ dequeues a message $m$ and reacts to it, producing messages and notification requests.

2. Receiving a notification:

$$Not \triangleq \exists p \in P.Not1(p)$$

$$Not1(p) \triangleq \begin{pmatrix} \exists t \in NotRequests(p). \\ \forall e \in I \cup E \text{ such that } dst(e) = p.(e, t) \notin Clock \\ \wedge \\ Not2(p, t) \end{pmatrix}$$

$$Not2(p, t) \triangleq \begin{pmatrix} let \\ \{e_1, \ldots, e_k\} = \{d \in E \cup O \mid src(d) = p\}, \\ s = LocState(p), \\ (s', N, \langle e_1 \mapsto \mu_1, \ldots, e_k \mapsto \mu_k \rangle) = g_1(p)(s, t) \\ in \\ LocState'(p) = s' \\ \wedge \\ NotRequests'(p) = NotRequests(p) - \{t\} \cup N \\ \wedge \\ Q'(e_1) = Q(e_1) \cdot \mu_1 \ldots Q'(e_k) = Q(e_k) \cdot \mu_k \\ \wedge \\ \forall q \in P \neq p.LocState'(q) = LocState(q) \\ \wedge \\ \forall q \in P \neq p.NotRequests'(q) = NotRequests(q) \\ \wedge \\ \forall d \in I \cup E \cup O - \{e_1, \ldots, e_k\}.Q'(d) = Q(d) \end{pmatrix}$$

These formulas describe how a node $p$ consumes a notification $t$ for which it has an outstanding notification request, and how it reacts to the notification, producing messages and notification requests.

3. External input and output changes:

$$Inp \triangleq \begin{pmatrix} \forall i \in I.Q(i) \text{ is a subsequence of } Q'(i) \\ \wedge \\ \forall p \in P.LocState'(p) = LocState(p) \\ \wedge \\ \forall p \in P.NotRequests'(p) = NotRequests(p) \\ \wedge \\ \forall d \in E \cup O.Q'(d) = Q(d) \end{pmatrix}$$

$$Outp \triangleq \begin{pmatrix} \forall o \in O.Q'(o) \text{ is a subsequence of } Q(o) \\ \wedge \\ \forall p \in P.LocState'(p) = LocState(p) \\ \wedge \\ \forall p \in P.NotRequests'(p) = NotRequests(p) \\ \wedge \\ \forall d \in I \cup E.Q'(d) = Q(d) \end{pmatrix}$$

External input changes allow the contents of input edges to be extended rather arbitrarily. We do not assume that such extensions are harmonious with notifications and the use of $Clock$; from this perspective, it would be reasonable and straightforward to add the constraint $Clock' \subseteq Clock$ to $Inp$. Similarly, external output changes allow the contents of output edges to be removed, not necessarily in order. We ask that $Q(i)$ be a subsequence of $Q'(i)$ and that $Q'(o)$ be a subsequence of $Q(o)$, so that it is easy to attribute state transitions. While variants on these two actions are viable, allowing some degree of external change to input and output edges seems attractive for composability (see Section 4.3).

*The high-level specification:*

$$ISpec \triangleq InitProp \wedge \square [Mess \vee Not \vee Inp \vee Outp]_{LocState, NotRequests, Q}$$

$$Spec \triangleq \exists LocState, NotRequests, Q \restriction E.ISpec$$

*ISpec* describes a complete property and *Spec* an externally visible property.

This specification is the most basic of several that we have studied. For instance, another one allows certain message reorderings, replacing *Mess1* $(p)$ with

$\exists m \in M.\exists e \in I \cup E$ such that $p = dst(e).\exists u, v \in M^*.$
$Q(e) = u \cdot m \cdot v \wedge Q'(e) = u \cdot v \wedge \forall n \in u.time(n) \not\leq time(m) \wedge Mess2(p, e, m)$

Given a queue of messages $Q(e)$, $p$ is allowed to process any message $m$ such that there is no message $n$ ahead of $m$ with $time(n) \leq time(m)$. Mathematically, we may think of $Q(e)$ as a partially ordered multiset (pomset) [13]; with that view, $m$ is a minimal element of $Q(e)$. This relaxation is useful, for example, for enabling optimizations in which several messages for the same time are processed together, even if they are not all at the head of a queue.

### 4.3  Composing Graphs

We briefly discuss how to compose graphs, without however fully developing the corresponding definitions and theory (in part, simply, because we have not needed them in our applications of the semantics to date).

We can regard the specifications of this paper as being parameterized by a *Clock* variable, rather than as being specifically for *Clock* as defined in Section 4.2. Once we regard *Clock* as a parameter, the specifications that correspond to multiple dataflow graphs can be composed meaningfully, and along standard lines [9]. Suppose that we are given graphs $G_1$ and $G_2$, with nodes $P_1$ and $P_2$, input edges $I_1$ and $I_2$, internal edges $E_1$ and $E_2$, and output edges $O_1$ and $O_2$, and specifications $Spec_1$ and $Spec_2$. We assume that $P_1$ and $P_2$, $I_1$ and $I_2$, $E_1$ and $E_2$, and $O_1$ and $O_2$ are pairwise disjoint. We also assume that $I_1$, $I_2$, $O_1$, and $O_2$ are disjoint from $E_1$ and $E_2$. We write $X_{12} = I_2 \cap O_1$ and $X_{21} = I_1 \cap O_2$. The edges in $X_{12}$ and $X_{21}$ will connect the two graphs. We define a specification for the composite system with nodes $P = P_1 \cup P_2$, input edges $I = I_1 \cup I_2 - X_{12} - X_{21}$, internal edges $E = E_1 \cup E_2 \cup X_{12} \cup X_{21}$, and output edges $O = O_1 \cup O_2 - X_{12} - X_{21}$, by

$$Spec_{12} = \exists Q \upharpoonright (X_{12} \cup X_{21}).Spec_1 \wedge Spec_2 \wedge \Box[\neg(Acts_1 \wedge Acts_2)]$$

where, for $j = 1, 2$,

$$Acts_j = \begin{bmatrix} \exists i \in I_j.Q'(i) \text{ is a proper subsequence of } Q(i) \\ \vee \\ \exists o \in O_j.Q(o) \text{ is a proper subsequence of } Q'(o) \end{bmatrix}$$

The formula $\Box[\neg(Acts_1 \wedge Acts_2)]$ ensures that the actions of the two subsystems that are visible on their input and output edges are not simultaneous. It does not say anything about internal edges, nor does it address notification requests.

It remains to study how $Spec_{12}$ relates to the non-compositional specification of the same system. Going further, the definition of a global *Clock* might be obtained compositionally from multiple, more local could-result-in relations. Finally, one might address questions of full abstraction. Although we rely on a state-based formalism, results such as Jonsson's [9] (which are cast in terms of I/O automata) should translate. However, a fully abstract treatment of timely dataflow would have interesting specificities, such as the handling of completion notifications and the possible restrictions on contexts (in particular contexts constrained not to send messages into the past).

## 5  An Application

In order to leverage the definitions and to test them, we state and prove a basic but important property for timely dataflow. Specifically, we argue that, once a pointstamp $(e, t)$ is not in *Clock*, messages on $e$ will never have times $\leq t$. For this property to hold, however, we require a hypothesis on inputs; we simply assume that, for all input edges $i$, $Q(i)$ never grows, though it may contain some messages initially. (Alternatively, we could add the constraint $Clock' \subseteq Clock$ to $Inp$, as suggested in Section 4.2.)

First, we establish some auxiliary propositions:

**Proposition 7.** *ISpec implies that always, for all $p \in P$, there exists a local history $H(p)$ for $p$ such that $LocState(p) = \Pi_{\text{Loc}}g(H(p))$ and $NotRequests(p) = \Pi_{\text{NR}}g(H(p))$.*

**Proposition 8.** *Assume that Conditions 1 and 2 hold. Then ISpec implies*

$$\Box[(\forall i \in I.Q'(i) \text{ is a subsequence of } Q(i)) \Rightarrow (Clock' \subseteq Clock)]$$

**Proposition 9.**

$$\Box[(\forall i \in I.Q'(i) \text{ is a subsequence of } Q(i)) \Rightarrow (Clock' \subseteq Clock)]$$
$$\wedge$$
$$\Box[\forall i \in I.Q'(i) \text{ is a subsequence of } Q(i)]$$
$$\Rightarrow$$
$$\Box\forall e \in I \cup E \cup O, t \in T. \begin{bmatrix} (e,t) \notin Clock \\ \Rightarrow \\ \Box(e,t) \notin Clock \end{bmatrix}$$

We obtain:

**Theorem 2.** *Assume that Conditions 1 and 2 hold. Then ISpec and*

$$\Box[\forall i \in I.Q'(i) \text{ is a subsequence of } Q(i)]$$

*imply*

$$\Box\forall e \in I \cup E \cup O, t \in T, m \in M. \begin{bmatrix} (e,t) \notin Clock \\ \Rightarrow \\ \Box(m \in Q(e) \Rightarrow time(m) \not\leq t) \end{bmatrix}$$

Previous work [4] studies a distributed algorithm for tracking the progress of a computation, and arrives at a somewhat analogous result. This previous work assumes a notion of virtual time but defines neither a dataflow model nor a corresponding could-result-in relation (so, in particular, it does not treat analogues of Conditions 1 and 2). In the distributed algorithm, information at each processor serves for constructing a conservative approximation of the pending work in a system. Naiad relies on such an approximation for implementing its clock, which the state function $Clock$ represents in our model.

## 6   Conclusion

This paper aims to develop a rigorous foundation for timely dataflow, a model for data-parallel computing. Some of the ingredients in timely dataflow, as defined in this paper, have a well-understood place in the literature on semantics and programming languages. For instance, many programming languages support messages and message streams. On the other hand, despite similarities to extant concepts, other ingredients are more original, so giving them self-contained semantics can be both interesting and valuable for applications. In particular, virtual times and completion notifications may be reminiscent of the notion of priorities [15,8], but a straightforward reduction seems impossible. More broadly, there should be worthwhile opportunities for further foundational and formal contributions to research on data-parallel software, currently a lively area of experimental work in which several computational abstractions and models are being revisited, adapted, or invented.

**Acknowledgments.** We are grateful to our coauthors on work on Naiad for discussions that led to this paper. In addition, conversations with Nikhil Swamy and Dimitrios Vytiniotis motivated our study of recursion.

# References

1. Abadi, M., Isard, M.: On the flow of data, information, and time. In: Focardi, R., Myers, A. (eds.) POST 2015. LNCS, vol. 9036, pp. 73–92. Springer, Heidelberg (2015)
2. Abadi, M., Isard, M.: Timely rollback: Specification and verification. In: Havelund, K., Holzmann, G., Joshi, R. (eds.) NFM 2015. LNCS, vol. 9058, pp. 19–34. Springer, Heidelberg (2015)
3. Abadi, M., Lamport, L.: The existence of refinement mappings. Theoretical Computer Science 82(2), 253–284 (1991)
4. Abadi, M., McSherry, F., Murray, D.G., Rodeheffer, T.L.: Formal analysis of a distributed algorithm for tracking progress. In: Beyer, D., Boreale, M. (eds.) FMOODS/FORTE 2013. LNCS, vol. 7892, pp. 5–19. Springer, Heidelberg (2013)
5. Blelloch, G.E.: Programming parallel algorithms. Communications of the ACM 39(3), 85–97 (1996)
6. Hildebrandt, T.T., Panangaden, P., Winskel, G.: A relational model of nondeterministic dataflow. Mathematical Structures in Computer Science 14(5), 613–649 (2004)
7. Jefferson, D.R.: Virtual time. ACM Transactions on Programming Languages and Systems 7(3), 404–425 (1985)
8. John, M., Lhoussaine, C., Niehren, J., Uhrmacher, A.M.: The attributed pi-calculus with priorities. In: Priami, C., Breitling, R., Gilbert, D., Heiner, M., Uhrmacher, A.M. (eds.) Transactions on Computational Systems Biology XII. LNCS (LNBI), vol. 5945, pp. 13–76. Springer, Heidelberg (2010)
9. Jonsson, B.: A fully abstract trace model for dataflow and asynchronous networks. Distributed Computing 7(4), 197–212 (1994)
10. Kahn, G.: The semantics of a simple language for parallel programming. In: IFIP Congress, pp. 471–475 (1974)
11. Lamport, L.: Specifying Systems, The TLA+ Language and Tools for Hardware and Software Engineers. Addison-Wesley (2002)
12. Murray, D.G., McSherry, F., Isaacs, R., Isard, M., Barham, P., Abadi, M.: Naiad: a timely dataflow system. In: ACM SIGOPS 24th Symposium on Operating Systems Principles, pp. 439–455 (2013)
13. Pratt, V.: Modeling concurrency with partial orders. International Journal of Parallel Programming 15(1), 33–71 (1986)
14. Selinger, P.: First-order axioms for asynchrony. In: Mazurkiewicz, A., Winkowski, J. (eds.) CONCUR 1997. LNCS, vol. 1243, pp. 376–390. Springer, Heidelberg (1997)
15. Versari, C., Busi, N., Gorrieri, R.: An expressiveness study of priority in process calculi. Mathematical Structures in Computer Science 19(6), 1161–1189 (2009)

# Difference Bound Constraint Abstraction for Timed Automata Reachability Checking

Weifeng Wang[1,2] and Li Jiao[1(✉)]

[1] State Key Laboratory of Computer Science, Institute of Software,
Chinese Academy of Sciences, Beijing 100190, China
{wangwf,ljiao}@ios.ac.cn
[2] University of Chinese Academy of Sciences, Beijing 100049, China

**Abstract.** We consider the reachability problem for timed automata. One of the most well-known solutions for this problem is the zone-based search method. Max bound abstraction and LU-bound abstraction on zones have been proposed to reduce the state space for zone based search. These abstractions use bounds collected from the timed automata structure to compute an abstract state space. In this paper we propose a difference bound constraint abstraction for zones. In this abstraction, sets of difference bound constraints collected from the symbolic run are used to compute the abstract states. Based on this new abstraction scheme, we propose an algorithm for the reachability checking of timed automata. Experiment results are reported on several timed automata benchmarks.

## 1 Introduction

Model checking of timed automata has been studied for a long time since it was proposed [2]. One of the most interesting properties to be verified for timed automata is the reachability property. In this paper, we will focus on the reachability problem of timed automata.

It is known that the reachability problem for timed automata is PSPACE-complete [3]. Initially region-based method [2] was used to discretize the state space, and convert the timed automata model to finite automata. However, the resulting finite automata are so large that it is not practical to perform model checking on them. BDD-based [4,8] and SAT-based [17] symbolic model checking can be used to fight the state explosion.

Zone-based method is an important approach to the reachability problem of timed automata. In zone-based method, a group of difference bound inequalities is used to symbolically represent a convex set of clock valuations (which is called a "zone"), and exhaustive search is performed on the symbolic state space [7]. Abstraction techniques for zones are used to reduce the symbolic state space, and ensure the reduced symbolic state space to be finite. In max-bound abstraction (a.k.a. k-approximation), the maximum constants appearing in the guards of the timed automata are collected, and used to compute abstractions for zones. LU-abstraction [6] improves by classifying the constants into two categories: those appearing in lower bound guards and those appearing in upper bound guards.

© IFIP International Federation for Information Processing 2015
S. Graf and M. Viswanathan (Eds.): FORTE 2015, LNCS 9039, pp. 146–160, 2015.
DOI: 10.1007/978-3-319-19195-9_10

Behrmann et al. [5] used static analysis on the structure of timed automata to obtain smaller bounds, which lead to coarser abstractions. Herbreteau et al [12] proposed to calculate the bounds on-the-fly, and used a non-convex abstraction based on LU-bounds. All the above mentioned techniques are based on bounds that are collected from the timed automata, which just capture limited amount of information about the system.

In this paper, we explore the possibility to use difference bound constraints as abstractions for zones. In our abstraction scheme, a set of difference bound constraints is used as the abstraction of the zone. In fact, the conjunction of these difference bound constraints is a zone that is larger than the original zone. This abstraction is, to some extent, similar to the predicate abstraction in the program verification field.

A lazy search algorithm similar to that in [13] is used to gradually refine the abstraction. Each node is a tuple $(l, Z, C)$, where $(l, Z)$ is the symbolic state, and $C$ is a set of difference bound constraints, which serves as the abstraction. Initially, the difference bound constraint set of each node is $\emptyset$, which means there is no difference bound constraint in the abstraction, i.e., the abstracted zone is the set of all clock valuations. If a transition $t$ is disabled from a node $(l, Z, C)$, we extract a set of difference bound constraints $C_t$ from $Z$ such that $Post_t([\![C_t]\!]) = \emptyset$, $C_t$ is sufficient to prove that the transition $t$ from the configuration $(l, Z)$ is disabled. The difference bound constraints in $C_t$ are added to $C$, after which the change in $C$ is propagated backward according to certain rules. The addition of difference bound constraints into the abstraction is in fact a refinement operation.

The key problem here is how to compute and propagate the set of difference bound constraints. We propose a method to propagate difference bound constraints, which makes use of structural information of the timed automata to identify "important" difference bound constraints in the zones from those that are "irrelevant".

Unfortunately, the lazy search algorithm using only difference bound constraint abstraction does not necessarily terminate. The LU-abstraction $Extra_{LU}^{+}$ [6] is used in our algorithm to ensure termination. The resulting algorithm can be seen as a state space reduction using difference bound constraint abstraction on top of $Extra_{LU}^{+}$-based symbolic search.

We performed experiments to compare our method with zone-based search and the lazy abstraction method proposed in [13]. Results show that in general our method behaves similarly to that in [13], while in some cases our method can achieve better reduction of the state spaces.

**Related Work.** Abstraction refinement techniques [9] have attracted much attention in recent years. This kind of techniques check the property of the system by iteratively checking and refining abstract models which tend to be smaller than the original model. Efforts have been devoted on adapting abstraction refinement techniques for the verification of timed automata [16,10].

Lazy abstraction [11] is an important abstraction refinement technique. In the lazy abstraction procedure, an abstract reachability tree is built on-the-fly, along with the refinement procedure, and predicate formulas are used to represent the abstract symbolic states. Difference bound constraint abstraction is similar to predicate abstraction, and the constraint propagation resembles interpolation [15]. In our method, abstractions only take the form of conjunctions of difference bound constraints, which is more efficient than general-purpose first order formulas. Herbreteau et al. [13] proposed a lazy search scheme to dynamically compute the LU-bounds during state space exploration, which results in smaller LU-bounds and coarser abstractions. We use a similar lazy search scheme.

**Organization of the Paper.** In Section 2 we have a simple review of basic concepts related to timed automata. We present the difference bound constraint abstraction, and the model checking algorithm based on this abstraction in Section 3. An example is given in Section 4 to illustrate how our method achieves state space reduction. Experiment results are reported in Section 5, and conclusions are given in Section 6.

## 2   Preliminaries

### 2.1   Timed Automata and the Reachability Property

A set of *clock variables* $X$ is a set of non-negative real-valued variables. A *clock constraint* is a conjunction of constraints of the form $x \sim c$, where $x, y \in X$, $c \in \mathbb{N}$, and $\sim \in \{<, \leq, >, \geq\}$. A *difference bound constraint* on $X$ is a constraint of the form $x - y \prec c$, where $x, y \in X \cup \{0\}$, $c \in \mathbb{N}$, and $\prec \in \{<, \leq\}$. Obviously a clock constraint can be re-written as conjunctions of difference bound constraints. A *clock valuation* is a function $\nu : X \mapsto \mathbb{R}_{\geq 0}$, which assigns to each clock variable a nonnegative real value. We denote $\mathbf{0}$ the special clock valuation that assigns 0 to every clock variable. For a formula $\varphi$ on $X$, we write $\nu \models \varphi$, if $\varphi$ is satisfied by the valuation $\nu$. Furthermore, we denote by $[\![\varphi]\!]$ the set of all clock valuations satisfying $\varphi$, i.e., $[\![\varphi]\!] = \{\nu | \nu \models \varphi\}$.

**Definition 1 (Timed Automata).** *A timed automaton is a tuple* $\langle L, l_{init}, X, T \rangle$, *where $L$ is a finite set of locations, $l_{init}$ is the initial location, $X$ is a finite set of clocks, and $T$ is a finite set of transitions of the form $l \xrightarrow{a,g,r} l'$, where $a$ is an action label, $g$ is a clock constraint, which we call* guard, *and $r \subseteq X$ is the set of clocks to be reset.*

For a transition $t = l \xrightarrow{a,g,r} l' \in T$, we use $t.a$, $t.g$, $t.r$ to denote the corresponding action, guard, and set of clocks to be reset.

**Definition 2 (Semantics of Timed Automata).** *A* configuration *of a timed automaton $\mathcal{A} = \langle L, l_{init}, X, T \rangle$ is a pair $(l, \nu)$ where $l \in L$ is a location, and $\nu$ is a clock valuation. The initial configuration is $(l_{init}, \mathbf{0})$. There are two kinds of transitions*

- **Action.** *For each pair of states $(l, \nu)$ and $(l', \nu')$, $(l, \nu) \rightarrow_t (l', \nu')$ iff there is a transition $t = l \xrightarrow{a,g,r} l' \in T$, and*

- $\nu \models g$, and
- $\nu'(x) = \nu(x)$ for each $x \notin r$, and
- $\nu'(x) = 0$ for each $x \in r$.

- **Delay.** For each pair of configurations $(l, \nu)$ and $(l', \nu')$, and an arbitrary $\delta \in \mathbb{R}_{\geq 0}$, $(l, \nu) \to_\delta (l', \nu')$, iff $l = l'$ and $\nu'(x) = \nu(x) + \delta$ for each clock $x \in X$.

A run of a timed automaton is a (possibly infinite) sequence of configurations $\rho = (l_0, \nu_0)(l_1, \nu_1) \cdots$, where $(l_0, \nu_0) = (l_{init}, \mathbf{0})$, and for each $i \geq 0$, either $(l_i, \nu_i) \to_t (l_{i+1}, \nu_{i+1})$ for some $t \in T$, or $(l_i, \nu_i) \to_\delta (l_{i+1}, \nu_{i+1})$ for some $\delta \in \mathbb{R}_{\geq 0}$.

The definition of timed automata is always extended to networks of timed automata, which is a parallel composition of timed automata. The parallel composition can be obtained by the product of these components. Usually this product is not computed directly, but on-the fly during the verification. In this paper we will describe our method based on timed automata, while it could be naturally extended on networks of timed automata.

In this paper we will consider the *reachability* problem. Basically, a location of a timed automaton is reachable iff there is a run of the timed automaton that reaches the location.

**Definition 3 (Reachability).** *A location $l_{acc}$ of a timed automaton $\mathcal{A}$ is reachable iff there is a finite run $\rho = (l_0, \nu_0)(l_1, \nu_1) \cdots (l_k, \nu_k)$, where $l_k = l_{acc}$.*

### 2.2   Zone Based Symbolic Semantics

The symbolic semantics of timed automata has been proposed to fight state explosion. Basically, the idea is to represent a set of clock valuations using clock constraints. Zones are used in timed automata model checking to symbolically represent the sets of clock valuations. A *zone* is a convex set of clock valuations that can be represented by a set of difference bound constraints.

For a zone $Z$ and a clock constraint $g$, we define $Z \wedge g$ as $\{\nu | \nu \in Z \wedge \nu \models g\}$, $Z[r := 0]$ as $\{\nu | \exists \nu' \in Z \cdot \forall x \in r(\nu(x) = 0) \wedge \forall x \notin r(\nu(x) = \nu'(x))\}$, and $Z \uparrow$ as $\{\nu | \exists \nu' \in Z, \delta \in \mathbb{R}_{\geq 0} \cdot \nu = \nu' + \delta\}$. Zones are closed under these operations [7].

**Definition 4 (Symbolic Semantics of Timed Automata).** *The symbolic semantics of a timed automaton $\mathcal{A} = \langle L, l_{init}, X, T \rangle$ is a labeled transition system $(S, \Rightarrow, s_0)$. Each state $s \in S$ is a symbolic configuration $(l, Z)$, where $l$ is a location, and $Z$ is a zone. The initial state is $s_0 = (l_{init}, [\![0 \leq x_1 = x_2 = \cdots = x_n]\!])$. For each pair of states $s = (l, Z)$ and $s' = (l', Z')$, $s \Rightarrow_t s'$ iff there exists a transition $t = l \xrightarrow{a,g,r} l' \in T$ such that $Z' = (Z \wedge g)[r := 0] \uparrow$. A symbolic run is a sequence $(l_0, Z_0)(l_1, Z_1) \cdots$, where $(l_0, Z_0) = (l_{init}, [\![0 \leq x_1 = x_2 = \cdots = x_n]\!])$, and for each $i \geq 0$, $(l_i, Z_i) \Rightarrow_t (l_{i+1}, Z_{i+1})$ for some $t \in T$.*

In addition, we define the *Post* operator $Post_t(Z) \overset{\text{def}}{=} (Z \wedge t.g)[t.r := 0] \uparrow$. A transition $t = l \xrightarrow{a,g,r} l' \in T$ is *disabled* at $(l, Z)$, if $Post_t(Z) = \emptyset$.

Symbolic semantics is sound and complete with respect to the reachability property [7]. A given location $l_{acc}$ is reachable iff there is a symbolic run ending with a configuration $(l_{acc}, Z)$ where $Z \neq \emptyset$.

Zones can be represented as Difference Bound Matrices (DBMs), and efficient algorithms for manipulating DBMs have already been proposed [7]. The DBM representation of a zone on the clock set $X$ is a $(|X| + 1) \times (|X| + 1)$ matrix, each element of which is a tuple $(\prec, c)$, where $\prec \in \{<, \leq\}$ and $c \in \mathbb{N}$. In a DBM $D$, $D_{0x} = (\prec, c)$ means $0 - x \prec c$, i.e. $x \succ -c$, $D_{x0} = (\prec, c)$ means $x - 0 \prec c$, i.e. $x \prec c$, for $x, y \neq 0$, $D_{ij} = (\prec, c)$ represents the constraint $x_i - x_j \prec c$. Two different DBMs might correspond to the same zone. In order to tackle this problem, the *canonical forms* of DBMs can be computed by the Floyd-Warshall algorithm [7].

The zone-based semantics described in the above is not necessarily finite. Max-bound abstraction and LU-bound abstraction are proposed to reduce the state space to finite, and the former can be seen as a special case of the latter. Basically, these abstraction techniques remove from the zone those constraints that exceed certain bounds, resulting in an abstracted zone that is larger than the original one. Coarser abstractions lead to smaller symbolic state space. As far as we know, $Extra_{LU}^+$ [6] is the coarsest convex-preserving abstraction based on LU-bounds.

An LU-bound is a pair of functions $LU$, where $L : X \to \mathbb{N} \cup \{-\infty\}$ is called a lower bound function and $U : X \to \mathbb{N} \cup \{-\infty\}$ an upper bound function.

**Definition 5 (LU-extrapolation [6]).** *Let $Z$ be a zone whose canonical DBM is $\langle c_{i,j}, \prec_{i,j} \rangle_{i,j=0,1,\dots,|X|}$. Given an LU-bound LU , the LU-extrapolation $Extra_{LU}^+(Z)$ of $Z$ is a zone $Z'$ which can be represented by a DBM $\langle c'_{i,j}, \prec'_{i,j} \rangle_{i,j=0,1,\dots,|X|}$, where*

$$\langle c'_{i,j}, \prec'_{i,j} \rangle = \begin{cases} \infty & \text{if } c_{i,j} > L(x_i) \\ \infty & \text{if } -c_{0,i} > L(x_i) \\ \infty & \text{if } -c_{0,j} > U(x_j), i \neq 0 \\ (-U(x_j), <) & \text{if } -c_{0,j} > U(x_j), i = 0 \\ (c_{i,j}, \prec_{i,j}) & \text{otherwise} \end{cases}$$

We denote by $\Rightarrow^E$ the symbolic semantics of timed automata augmented with $Extra_{LU}^+$: for two symbolic configurations $(l, Z)$ and $(l', Z')$, $(l, Z) \Rightarrow^E (l', Z')$ iff there is a zone $Z''$ such that $(l, Z) \Rightarrow (l', Z'')$ and $Z' = Extra_{LU}^+(Z'')$. We can choose the LU-bound $L(x)$ and $U(x)$ as follows: for each clock $x$, $L(x)(U(x))$ is the largest constant $c$ such that $x > c(x < c)$ or $x \geq c(x \leq c)$ appears in the guard of some transition. Intuitively, $L(x)$ $(U(x))$ collects the maximum constant appearing in the lower-bound (upper-bound) guard of $x$. It can be proved that $\Rightarrow^E$ preserves reachability [6].

# 3    Difference Bound Constraint Abstraction Based Reachability Checking

## 3.1    Difference Bound Constraint Abstraction and Adaptive Simulation Graph

For a zone $Z$ and a difference bound constraint $\mathfrak{c}$ we denote $Z \models \mathfrak{c}$ as $\forall \nu \in Z \cdot \nu \models \mathfrak{c}$. For a set $C$ of difference bound constraints we denote $[\![C]\!]$ to be the set of valuations that satisfy all the constraints in $C$, i.e., $[\![C]\!] = \{\nu | \forall \mathfrak{c} \in C \cdot \nu \models \mathfrak{c}\}$. Intuitively, a set $C$ of difference bound constraints is interpreted as a conjunction of the constraints from $C$. In fact, $[\![C]\!]$ is also a zone, although it will not be stored as a canonical DBM in our algorithm. In the sequel, we might mix the use of set-theoretic notations (e.g. intersection) and logic notations (e.g. conjunction) on zones and constraints.

**Definition 6 (Difference Bound Constraint Abstraction).** *A difference bound constraint abstraction $C$ for a zone $Z$ is a set of difference bound constraints such that $Z \subseteq [\![C]\!]$.*

This definition resembles the concept of predicate abstraction in program verification. Each difference bound constraint in $C$ can be seen as a predicate. In our algorithm, only those difference bound constraints that are useful for the reachability problem are kept, while the irrelevant constraints are ignored. The difference bound constraint abstraction of a zone is still a zone, but we store it as a set of constraints rather than a canonical DBM. Based on this abstraction, we define an Adaptive Simulation Graph (ASG) similar to that in [13].

**Definition 7 (Adaptive Simulation Graph).** *Given a timed automaton $\mathcal{A}$, the adaptive simulation graph $ASG_{\mathcal{A}}$ of $\mathcal{A}$ is a graph with nodes of the form $(l, Z, C)$, where $l$ is a location, $Z$ is a zone, and $C$ is a set of difference bound constraints such that $Z \subseteq [\![C]\!]$. A node could be marked* tentative *(which roughly means it is covered by another node). Three constraints should be satisfied:*
*G1 For the initial state $l_0$ and initial zone $Z_0$, there is a node $(l_0, Z_0, C_0)$ in the graph for some $C_0$.*
*G2 If a node $(l, Z, C)$ is not tentative, then for every transition $(l, Z) \Rightarrow_t (l', Z')$ s.t. $Z' \neq \emptyset$, there is a successor $(l', Z', C')$ for this node.*
*G3 If a node $(l, Z, C)$ is tentative, there is a non-tentative node $(l, Z', C')$ covering it, i.e., $Z \subseteq [\![C]\!] \subseteq [\![C']\!]$.*
*In addition, two invariants are required.*
*I1 If a transition $t$ is disabled from $(l, Z)$, and $(l, Z, C)$ is a non-tentative node, then $t$ should also be disabled from $(l, [\![C]\!])$.*
*I2 For every edge $(l, Z, C) \Rightarrow_t (l', Z', C')$ in the ASG: $Post_t([\![C]\!]) \subseteq [\![C']\!]$.*

For a node $v = (l, Z, C)$, we use $v.l$, $v.Z$, and $v.C$ to denote the three components. We say that a node $(l, Z, C)$ is *covered* by a node $(l, Z', C')$, if $Z \subseteq [\![C']\!]$.

The following theorem states that, the adaptive simulation graph preserves reachability of the corresponding timed automaton.

**Theorem 1.** *A location $l_{acc}$ in the timed automaton $\mathcal{A}$ is reachable, iff there is a node $(l_{acc}, Z, C)$ such that $Z \neq \emptyset$ in $ASG_{\mathcal{A}}$.*

The right-to-left direction of this theorem is obviously true: by the definition of ASG, each path in $ASG_{\mathcal{A}}$ corresponds to a symbolic run in $\mathcal{A}$. In order to prove the other direction of Theorem 1, we prove a slightly stronger lemma.

**Lemma 1.** *If there is a symbolic run $(l_0, Z_0) \cdots (l, Z)$ in $\mathcal{A}$ with $Z \neq \emptyset$, then there must be a non-tentative node $(l, Z_1, C_1)$ in $ASG_{\mathcal{A}}$ such that $Z \subseteq [\![C_1]\!]$.*

*Proof.* We prove this lemma by induction on the length of the run. For the 0-length run and $(l_0, Z_0)$, the lemma is trivially true. Assume the lemma is true for a run $(l_0, Z_0) \cdots (l, Z)$, now we prove that the lemma holds for every successor $(l', Z')$ of $(l, Z)$ with $(l, Z) \Rightarrow_t (l', Z')$ and $Z' \neq \emptyset$.

We need to prove that there is a node in $ASG_{\mathcal{A}}$ corresponding to $(l', Z')$ as described in the lemma. By induction hypothesis, there is a non-tentative node $v$ such that $Z \subseteq [\![v.C]\!]$. We now assert that $Post_t(v.Z) \neq \emptyset$. Because, otherwise, by **I1** of Definition 7 we will have $Post_t([\![v.C]\!]) = \emptyset$, and consequently $Post_t(Z) \subseteq Post_t([\![v.C]\!]) = \emptyset$, which contradicts the assumption $Z' \neq \emptyset$. From **G2** we know that there is a successor $v'$ of $v$ such that $(v.l, v.Z) \Rightarrow_t (v'.l, v'.Z)$. By **I2** we have $Post_t([\![v.C]\!]) \subseteq [\![v'.C']\!]$, so $Z' = Post_t(Z) \subseteq Post_t([\![v.C]\!]) \subseteq [\![v'.C]\!]$, If $v'$ is non-tentative, then it is a node that we want to find, and the lemma is proved. Otherwise, there is a non-tentative node $v''$ covering $v'$. From **G3** we know that $[\![v'.C]\!] \subseteq [\![v''.C]\!]$, so $Z' \subseteq [\![v''.C]\!]$, and $v''$ is the qualifying node.

According to Theorem 1, the reachability problem could be solved by exploring the ASG. The algorithm for constructing the ASG will be described in the next subsection.

### 3.2 The ASG-Constructing Algorithm

The algorithm for constructing the ASG is shown in Algorithm 1. The main procedure repeatedly calls EXPLORE to explore the nodes until an accepting node is found (lines 10-11), or the worklist is empty (line 8).

The function EXPLORE proceeds as follows. For a node $v$ to be explored, first it checks whether $v$ is an accepting node. If so, the algorithm exits with the result "reachable", otherwise it checks whether there is a non-tentative node $v''$ covering $v$. If so, $v$ is marked tentative with respect to $v''$ (line 13), and the set of difference bound constraints of $v''$ is copied to $v$ to maintain **G3** of Definition 7 (line 14). There is no need to generate successor nodes for a tentative node. Otherwise, the difference bound constraint set of $v$ is computed using the transitions disabled at $v$ to maintain **I1** (line 17), after which successor nodes of $v$ are generated (maintaining **G2**) and put into the worklist for exploration (lines 19-21).

Whenever the difference bound constraint set of a node $v'$ is changed, PROPAGATE will be called (lines 15, 18, 38) to propagate the newly-added constraints backward to its parent $v$ (to maintain **I2**) (lines 29-31), and further to the nodes

**Algorithm 1.** The ASG-constructing algorithm

```
 1: function MAIN                          20:          create the successor v' =
 2:    let v_root = (l_0, Z_0, ∅)                           (l', Z', ∅) of v
 3:    add v_root to the worklist          21:             add v' to worklist
 4:    while worklist not empty do         22: function RESOLVE
 5:       remove v from the worklist       23:    for all v tentative w.r.t. v' do
 6:       EXPLORE(v)                        24:       if v.Z ⊈ [[v'.C]] then
 7:       RESOLVE                           25:          mark v non-tentative
 8:    return "not reachable"              26:          set v.C ← ∅
 9: function EXPLORE(v)                     27:          add v to worklist
10:    if v.l is accepting then            28: function PROPAGATE(v', C')
11:       exit "reachable"                 29:    let v = parent(v')
12:    else if ∃v'' non-tentative s.t. v.l =  30:   C ← BACKPROP(v, v', C')
          v''.q ∧ v.Z ⊆ [[v''.C]] then     31:    C_1 ← UPDATE(v, C)
13:       mark v tentative w.r.t. v''      32:    if C_1 ≠ ∅ then
14:       v.C ← v''.C                       33:       for all v_t tentative w.r.t. v do
15:       PROPAGATE(v, v.C)                 34:          if v_t.Z ⊆ [[v.C]] then
16:    else                                35:             C_t ← UPDATE(v_t, C_1)
17:       v.C ← DISABLED(v.l, v.Z)          36:             PROPAGATE(v_t, C_t)
18:       PROPAGATE(v, v.C)                 37:       if v ≠ v_root then
19:       for all (l', Z') s.t. (v.l, v.Z) ⇒  38:          PROPAGATE(v, C_1)
          (l', Z') and Z' ≠ ∅ do
```

tentative with respect to $v$ (to maintain **G3**) (line 36). If a tentative node $v_t$ is no longer covered by $v$, the function RESOLVE will eventually be called (line 7) to mark it non-tentative, remove all constraints from its difference bound constraint set, and put it into the worklist for exploration (lines 25-27).

For each node $v$, the difference bound constraint abstraction $v.C$ is stored as a set of difference bound constraints, rather than a canonical DBM. Checking whether $Z \subseteq [[C]]$ for a zone $Z$ and a difference bound constraint set $C$ can be accomplished by checking whether $Z \models \mathfrak{c}$ for all $\mathfrak{c} \in C$. When adding constraints to a difference bound constraint abstraction, only the strongest constraints are kept, which is handled by the function UPDATE, whose code is omitted here.

### 3.3   Computing the Difference Bound Constraint Sets

The algorithm for building the ASG relies on two functions DISABLED, and BACKPROP to extract the "important" difference bound constraints from zones. In this subsection we describe an implementation of the two functions. Before doing that we introduce the arithmetic on $\{<, \leq\} \times \mathbb{N}$. For two arbitrary pairs $(\prec_1, c_1), (\prec_2, c_2) \in \{<, \leq\} \times (\mathbb{N} \cup \{+\infty\})$, $(\prec_1, c_1) + (\prec_2, c_2) = (\prec_3, c_3)$, where $c_3 = c_1 + c_2$, and $\prec_3 = <$ iff $\prec_1 = <$ or $\prec_2 = <$. The order "$<$" is defined as: $(\prec_1, c_1) < (\prec_2, c_2)$ iff $c_1 < c_2$ or $c_1 = c_2 \wedge \prec_1 = < \wedge \prec_2 = \leq$.

**DISABLED.** In order to maintain the invariant **I1**, the result $C$ computed by DISABLED($l$, $Z$) should satisfy: i) $Z \subseteq \llbracket C \rrbracket$, and ii) $Post_t(\llbracket C \rrbracket) = \emptyset$ for each $t$ disabled at $(l, Z)$.

By Definition 4 we know that $Post_t(Z) = \emptyset$ iff $Z \wedge t.g = \emptyset$. Thus the problem is reduced to: given a zone $Z$, and a formula $\varphi$ which is conjunctions of difference bound constraints, such that $Z \wedge \varphi = \emptyset$, find a set $C$ of difference bound constraints such that $Z \subseteq \llbracket C \rrbracket$ and $\llbracket C \rrbracket \wedge \varphi = \emptyset$. Since $Z \wedge \varphi = \emptyset$, there must be a sequence of difference bound constraints $x_0 - x_1 \prec_0 c_0, x_1 - x_2 \prec_1 c_1, \ldots x_{m-1} - x_m \prec_{m-1} c_{m-1}, x_m - x_0 \prec_m c_m$ such that

- **C1** Each of them appears either in $\varphi$, or in the canonical DBM of $Z$.
- **C2** $x_i \neq x_j$ for $i, j \in \{0, 1, \ldots, m\}$ and $i \neq j$
- **C3** $(\prec_0, c_0) + \cdots + (\prec_m, c_m) < (<, 0)$, i.e., this sequence of difference bound constraints forms a contradiction.

We take $C$ to be $\{\mathfrak{c} = x_i - x_{(i+1) \mod (m+1)} \prec_i c_i | \mathfrak{c}$ is from $Z\}$. Obviously, the $C$ obtained above satisfies i) and ii).

As shown in [7], a conjunction of difference bound constraints can be seen as a directed weighted graph, where each clock variable corresponds to a node, and each constraint corresponds to a weighted edge, whose weight is a pair in $\{<, \leq\} \times (\mathbb{N} \cup \{+\infty\})$. Figure 1 illustrates the directed weighted graph for the zone $x \geq 0 \wedge y - x = 10$. There is a contradiction in the conjunction iff there is a negative cycle in the graph, i.e., the sum of weights in the cycle is less than $(\leq, 0)$.

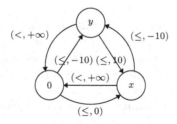

**Fig. 1.** Directed weighted graph of zone $x \geq 0 \wedge y - x = 10$

The difference bound constraints in $C$ correspond to the edges in the graph of $Z$ that form a negative cycle with the edges from the graph of $\varphi$. So the problem is reduced to finding a negative cycle in the merged graph of $Z$ and $\varphi$, and picking the edges in the cycle that belong to $Z$. This task is accomplished by the function FINDCONTRA in Algorithm 2, where Floyd-Warshall algorithm is used to find a negative cycle. Function DISABLED in Algorithm 2 calls FINDCONTRA for every disabled transition, and collects all the constraints obtained.

**BACKPROP.** In order to maintain the invariant **I2**, the result $C$ computed by BACKPROP($v$, $v'$, $C'$) (where $(v.l, v.Z) \Rightarrow_t (v'.l, v'.Z)$) should satisfy: i) $Post_t(\llbracket C \rrbracket) \subseteq \llbracket C' \rrbracket$ and ii) $v.Z \subseteq \llbracket C \rrbracket$.

If there is a set $C_{c'}$ of difference bound constraints for each $c' \in C'$, such that $v.Z \subseteq [\![C_{c'}]\!]$ and $Post_t([\![C_{c'}]\!]) \models c'$, then we can choose $C$ as $\bigcup_{c' \in C'} C_{c'}$. One can easily check that such a $C$ satisfies the above two conditions. We only need to consider the propagation of each difference bound constraint in $C'$ one by one.

For simplicity, we break up each transition into three steps: guard, reset, and time delay, and explain the propagation for each step. The overall description of BACKPROP is shown in Algorithm 2.

We assume two zones $Z_1, Z_2$ and a difference bound constraint $c_2$ which corresponds to $Z_2$ (i.e. $Z_2 \models c_2$).

*Delay.* Now we have $Z_1 \uparrow = Z_2$, we want to find a $C_{c_2}$ such that $Z_1 \subseteq [\![C_{c_2}]\!]$ and $[\![C_{c_2}]\!] \uparrow \models c_2$. Observe that $c_2$ must be in one of the three cases: $x - 0 \prec c$, $0 - x \prec c$, and $x - y \prec c$, where $x, y \in X$ and $c \in \mathbb{N}$. Since $Z_1 \uparrow = Z_2$, $c_2$ can not be of the form $x - 0 \prec c$, and for the other two cases we have $Z_1 \models c_2$ and $[\![\{c_2\}]\!] \uparrow \models c_2$. So we can just choose $C_{c_2}$ to be $\{c_2\}$. Intuitively, for time delay, we just copy $c_2$ from the successor to the predecessor.

*Reset.* For a set $r$ of clocks such that $Z_1[r] = Z_2$, we want to find a $C_{c_2}$ such that $Z_1 \subseteq [\![C_{c_2}]\!]$ and $[\![C_{c_2}]\!][r] \models c_2$. Let $c_2$ be $x - y \prec c$, where $x \in X \cup \{0\}$, $y \in X$ and $c \in \mathbb{N}$, we choose $C_{c_2}$ as $\{c_1\}$, where:

$$
c_1 = \begin{cases} x - y \prec c, & \text{if } x, y \notin r \\ 0 - y \prec c, & \text{if } x \in r, y \notin r \\ x - 0 \prec c, & \text{if } x \notin r, y \in r \\ 0 - 0 \prec c, & \text{if } x, y \in r \end{cases} \tag{1}
$$

The first and the last cases are trivial. Let's look at the second case. Since $x \in r$, according to the definition of reset operation, it must be the case that $Z_2 \models x = 0$. According to the assumption, $Z_2 \models c_2$. Note that $c_2$ is $x - y \prec c$. Combining the above two results we have $Z_2 \models 0 - y \prec c$. Since $y \notin r$, the value of $y$ has not changed during the reset operation, thus we have $Z_1 \models 0 - y \prec c$. Conversely, we can check that $[\![\{0 - y \prec c\}]\!][r] \models x - y \prec c$. Thus $\{c_1\}$ is a qualified candidate for $C_{c_2}$. It is similar for the third case.

Here we ignore the case when $c_2$ is $x - 0 \prec c$ because, according to the time delay operation (which always follows the reset operation in the timed automata run), this is impossible.

*Guard.* For a guard $g$ such that $Z_1 \wedge g = Z_2$, we want to find a $C_{c_2}$ such that $Z_1 \subseteq [\![C_{c_2}]\!]$ and $[\![C_{c_2}]\!] \wedge g \models c_2$. Notice that $Z_1 \wedge g \models c_2$ iff $Z_1 \wedge (g \wedge \neg c_2) = \emptyset$, similarly, $[\![C_{c_2}]\!] \wedge g \models c_2$ iff $[\![C_{c_2}]\!] \wedge (g \wedge \neg c_2) = \emptyset$. Like $c_2$, its negation $\neg c_2$ is also a difference bound constraint, so $g \wedge \neg c_2$ is a conjunction of difference bound constraints, and we can use FINDCONTRA to compute the set $C_{c_2}$.

## Algorithm 2

```
1: function FINDCONTRA(Z, φ)
2:     Find a negative cycle using Floyd-
           Warshall algorithm on the
           merged graph of Z and φ
3:     Take the sequence of constraints
           corresponding to the negative
           cycle in Z ∧ φ: c₀, c₁, ... cₘ₋₁.
4:     return {cᵢ|cᵢ is from Z}
5: function DISABLED(l, Z)
6:     C ← ∅
7:     for all t disabled at (l, Z) do
8:         C ← C ∪ FINDCONTRA(Z, t.g)
9:     return C
10: function BACKPROP(v, v', C')
11:     Given v ⇒ₜ v'
12:     C ← ∅
13:     for all c₂ ∈ C' do
14:         Compute c₁ according to (1)
15:         C ← C∪ FINDCONTRA(v.Z, g ∧
               ¬c₂)
16:     return C
```

### 3.4   Termination of the ASG-Constructing Algorithm

In order to ensure that the ASG-constructing algorithm terminates, we make slight modifications on Definition 7 and on Algorithm 1. The condition **G2** of Definition 7 is modified to:

**G2'** If a node $(l, Z, C)$ is not tentative, then for every transition $(l, Z) \Rightarrow_t^E$ $(l', Z')$ s.t. $Z' \neq \emptyset$, there is a successor $(l', Z', C')$ for this node.

The symbolic transition relation $\Rightarrow$ is replaced with $\Rightarrow^E$, which means that the operator $Extra_{LU}^+$ is used when computing the successor nodes. Accordingly, in Line 19 of Algorithm 1, $(v.l, v.Z) \Rightarrow (v'.q, v'.Z)$ should be changed to $(v.l, v.Z) \Rightarrow^E (v'.q, v'.Z)$.

Now our algorithm can be seen as a further reduction made on top of $Extra_{LU}^+$-based search.

**Theorem 2.** *For an arbitrary timed automaton $\mathcal{A}$, the modified version of Algorithm 1 as described above will terminate.*

*Proof.* Assume, to the contrary, that the algorithm does not terminate. There must be an infinite sequence of explored nodes $v_1, v_2, \ldots$ (listed in the order of exploration) such that $v_1.l = v_2.l = \cdots$. Since the symbolic state space with $Extra_{LU}^+$ abstraction is finite, there must be two nodes $v_i, v_j$ (with $i < j$) in the sequence such that $v_i.Z = v_j.Z$. From Definition 6 we know that $v_j.Z = v_i.Z \subseteq \llbracket v_i.C \rrbracket$, so $v_j$ will never be explored, which contradicts the assumption.

## 4   An Example

Here we illustrate how our method works on the example timed automaton $\mathcal{A}_1$ shown in Figure 2a, where $q_4$ is the accepting location. Following [5], instead of considering one global LU-bound, we associate a local LU-bound to each location using static guard analysis. The LU-bound at each location is given in Figure 2c.

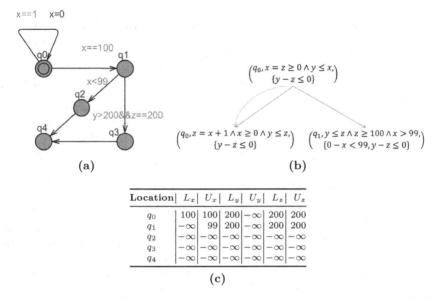

**Fig. 2.** (2a): a timed automaton $\mathcal{A}_1$, (2b): the ASG of $\mathcal{A}_1$. Solid arrows represent the transition relation, while doted arrows represent the cover relation. (2c): the LU-bounds of $\mathcal{A}_1$

Using zone-based search, the following symbolic configurations will be generated: $(q_0, x = z \geq 0 \wedge y \leq z), (q_0, z = x + 1 \wedge y \leq z \wedge x \geq 0), (q_0, z = x + 2 \wedge y \leq z \wedge x \geq 0), \ldots, (q_0, z = x + 100 \wedge y \leq z \wedge x \geq 0), \ldots$, which is more than 100 nodes. When using our method, the resulting ASG has only 3 nodes, as shown in Figure 2b. In this example our method successfully ignores many of the constraints that are irrelevant to the reachability problem, achieving a huge reduction.

The algorithm in [13] can not avoid generating too many nodes either. The reason is that, LU-bound based abstractions can not find that the difference bound constraints on $z - x$ and $y - x$ are irrelevant. In our abstraction scheme, we consider more information than just LU-bounds, so our method can identify these constraints to be irrelevant.

## 5   Experiments

We have implemented UPPAAL's search algorithm, the algorithm in [13], and our algorithm. Similar to [14], an improvement is made on Algorithm 1 in the implementation: for each node $v$, if there is a node $v'$ such that $v.l = v'.l$ and $v.Z \subseteq v'.Z$, then $v$ will be deleted, parents of $v$ will be inherited by $v'$, and the difference bound constraints in $v'.C$ will be propagated to the parents of $v$, and nodes that are covered by $v$ (if there is any) will be marked non-tentative.

We performed experiments on several benchmarks. The results are shown in Table 1 and Table 2, which are the results for breadth-first search (bfs) and

**Table 1.** Experiment results of the three methods using bfs search. "**Search-Extra$_{LU}^+$**" stands for $Extra_{LU}^+$-based search similar to UPPAAL. "$\mathfrak{a}_{\preceq LU}$, **disabled**" is the algorithm in [13]. "**DBCA-Extra$_{LU}^+$**" is difference bound constraint abstraction combined with $Extra_{LU}^+$. "tnds" is the total number of nodes generated, "fnds" is the number of nodes finally left, and "tm(s)" is the running time (in seconds). "to" stands for time-out(200s).

| Model | Search-Extra$_{LU}^+$ | | | $\mathfrak{a}_{\preceq LU}$, disabled | | | DBCA-Extra$_{LU}^+$ | | |
|---|---|---|---|---|---|---|---|---|---|
| | tnds | fnds | tm(s) | tnds | fnds | tm(s) | tnds | fnds | tm(s) |
| $\mathcal{A}_1$ | 405 | 204 | 0.03 | 405 | 203 | 0.14 | 3 | 3 | 0.00 |
| $D_7''$ | 12869 | 12869 | 6.77 | 113 | 113 | 0.00 | 113 | 113 | 0.01 |
| $D_8''$ | 48619 | 48619 | 100.08 | 145 | 145 | 0.01 | 145 | 145 | 0.01 |
| $D_{70}''$ | | | to | 9941 | 9941 | 4.35 | 9941 | 9941 | 90.19 |
| CSMA/CD 9 | 99288 | 45836 | 3.13 | 78552 | 35084 | 7.33 | 78552 | 35084 | 4.38 |
| CSMA/CD 10 | 258249 | 120845 | 8.44 | 200649 | 90125 | 12.15 | 200649 | 90125 | 14.91 |
| CSMA/CD 11 | 656312 | 311310 | 25.30 | 501432 | 226830 | 65.16 | 501432 | 226830 | 38.27 |
| CSMA/CD 12 | 1636261 | 786447 | 68.81 | 1230757 | 561167 | 118.12 | 1230757 | 561167 | 98.58 |
| FDDI 12 | 52555 | 727 | 13.72 | 422 | 341 | 0.56 | 176 | 154 | 0.13 |
| FDDI 30 | | | to | 2923 | 2227 | 26.84 | 464 | 406 | 2.29 |
| Fischer 8 | 132593 | 25080 | 2.61 | 132593 | 25080 | 8.44 | 132593 | 25080 | 7.55 |
| Fischer 9 | 487459 | 81035 | 11.24 | 487459 | 81035 | 30.82 | 487459 | 81035 | 22.35 |
| Critical 4 | 434421 | 53937 | 6.83 | 499441 | 53697 | 31.58 | 548781 | 54180 | 23.59 |
| Lynch 4 | 46432 | 12700 | 1.19 | 46432 | 12700 | 1.26 | 46432 | 12700 | 1.05 |

**Table 2.** Experiment results of the three methods using dfs search. All settings are the same as in Table 1, except that dfs search is performed here

| Model | Search-Extra$_{LU}^+$ | | | $\mathfrak{a}_{\preceq LU}$, disabled | | | DBCA-Extra$_{LU}^+$ | | |
|---|---|---|---|---|---|---|---|---|---|
| | tnds | fnds | tm(s) | tnds | fnds | tm(s) | tnds | fnds | tm(s) |
| $\mathcal{A}_1$ | 405 | 204 | 0.02 | 405 | 203 | 0.23 | 3 | 3 | 0.00 |
| $D_7''$ | 12869 | 12869 | 6.61 | 113 | 113 | 0.01 | 113 | 113 | 0.01 |
| $D_8''$ | 48619 | 48619 | 110.15 | 145 | 145 | 0.01 | 145 | 145 | 0.01 |
| $D_{70}''$ | | | to | 9941 | 9941 | 4.68 | 9941 | 9941 | 55.30 |
| CSMA/CD 9 | 246072 | 45836 | 9.43 | 136813 | 36901 | 18.63 | 129718 | 35415 | 11.58 |
| CSMA/CD 10 | 822699 | 120845 | 37.98 | 452788 | 98731 | 96.94 | 362407 | 90769 | 35.57 |
| CSMA/CD 11 | 2758945 | 311310 | 150.23 | | | to | 997243 | 228054 | 120.85 |
| FDDI 12 | 1016 | 727 | 0.27 | 96 | 96 | 0.02 | 96 | 96 | 0.03 |
| FDDI 30 | 6308 | 4507 | 5.73 | 240 | 240 | 0.26 | 240 | 240 | 0.41 |
| FDDI 50 | 17508 | 12507 | 53.21 | 400 | 400 | 0.72 | 400 | 400 | 1.35 |
| Fischer 8 | 218017 | 25080 | 4.37 | 196738 | 25080 | 14.00 | 156634 | 25080 | 7.84 |
| Fischer 9 | 1058685 | 81035 | 25.80 | 906766 | 81035 | 86.21 | 642739 | 81035 | 44.13 |
| Critical 4 | 1067979 | 54469 | 15.19 | 1025269 | 53731 | 66.45 | 1009995 | 54488 | 38.25 |
| Lynch 4 | 84421 | 12700 | 1.21 | 83171 | 12700 | 3.81 | 83967 | 12700 | 3.25 |

depth-first search (dfs), respectively. $D''$ is from [13], Fischer comes from the demos in the UPPAAL tool. The other models are from [1]. In our experiment settings, no location is set to be accepting, thus forcing the algorithms to perform exhaustive state space exploration. The programs are run on a VMware virtual machine with Ubuntu 10.04 operating system, which is allocated 2GB of memory. The underlying PC has an Intel Core i7 CPU of 2.93GHz and 3GB of RAM.

The results on the model $\mathcal{A}_1$ show the advantage of our method over LU-bound based abstractions. This is the case when LU-bound information is not sufficient to identify irrelevant constraints. On the other models, our method behaves similarly as $\mathfrak{a}_{\preceq LU}$, **disabled**. This is quite reasonable, since we use the same lazy search framework.

In many cases **DBCA-Extra**$^+_{LU}$ generates less nodes, but costs more time than **Search-Extra**$^+_{LU}$. This is due to the overhead of the effort to maintain the invariants of ASGs The situation is similar for $\mathfrak{a}_{\preceq LU}$, **disabled**. However, for some of the models we can see that the state space reduction of our method over **Search-Extra**$^+_{LU}$ is large enough to cover the overhead.

## 6   Conclusion

In this paper we proposed a difference bound constraint abstraction on zones for timed automata reachability checking. Difference bound constraint sets are used as abstractions in a lazy search algorithm, and $Extra^+_{LU}$ is used to ensure termination. Experiments show that in some of the cases the new abstraction scheme reduces the state spaces. A future work would be to perform experiments on other models to further investigate the performance.

Our abstraction is not necessarily coarser than [13], because non-convex abstractions [12] are used in [13], while difference bound constraint abstraction is in fact conjunctions of constraints, which is convex. However, our abstraction scheme makes it possible to make use of more information than just LU-bounds, achieving state space reduction in some cases.

The difference bound constraint abstraction is used in a forward lazy search scheme, and $Extra^+_{LU}$ is used to ensure termination. In fact, backward zone-based search is also possible [18], and does not need Max-bound abstraction or LU-abstraction to ensure termination. A possible future work is to explore the possibility to perform lazy search using difference bound constraint abstraction in a backward manner.

**Acknowledgements.** We thank the anonymous reviewers for their helpful comments on the earlier version of this paper.

## References

1. Benchmarks of Timed Automata,
   http://www.comp.nus.edu.sg/~pat/bddlib/timedexp.html
2. Alur, R., Dill, D.: Automata for modeling real-time systems. In: Paterson, M. (ed.) ICALP 1990. LNCS, vol. 443, pp. 322–335. Springer, Heidelberg (1990)

3. Alur, R., Dill, D.L.: A theory of timed automata. Theor. Comput. Sci. 126(2), 183–235 (1994)
4. Asarin, E., Bozga, M., Kerbrat, A., Maler, O., Pnueli, A., Rasse, A.: Data-structures for the verification of timed automata. In: Maler, O. (ed.) HART 1997. LNCS, vol. 1201, pp. 346–360. Springer, Heidelberg (1997)
5. Behrmann, G., Bouyer, P., Fleury, E., Larsen, K.G.: Static guard analysis in timed automata verification. In: Garavel, H., Hatcliff, J. (eds.) TACAS 2003. LNCS, vol. 2619, pp. 254–270. Springer, Heidelberg (2003)
6. Behrmann, G., Bouyer, P., Larsen, K.G., Pelánek, R.: Lower and upper bounds in zone based abstractions of timed automata. In: Jensen, K., Podelski, A. (eds.) TACAS 2004. LNCS, vol. 2988, pp. 312–326. Springer, Heidelberg (2004)
7. Bengtsson, J., Yi, W.: Timed automata: Semantics, algorithms and tools. In: Desel, J., Reisig, W., Rozenberg, G. (eds.) ACPN 2003. LNCS, vol. 3098, pp. 87–124. Springer, Heidelberg (2004)
8. Beyer, D.: Improvements in BDD-based reachability analysis of timed automata. In: Oliveira, J.N., Zave, P. (eds.) FME 2001. LNCS, vol. 2021, pp. 318–343. Springer, Heidelberg (2001)
9. Clarke, E., Grumberg, O., Jha, S., Lu, Y., Veith, H.: Counterexample-guided abstraction refinement. In: Emerson, E.A., Sistla, A.P. (eds.) CAV 2000. LNCS, vol. 1855, pp. 154–169. Springer, Heidelberg (2000)
10. Dierks, H., Kupferschmid, S., Larsen, K.G.: Automatic abstraction refinement for timed automata. In: Raskin, J.-F., Thiagarajan, P.S. (eds.) FORMATS 2007. LNCS, vol. 4763, pp. 114–129. Springer, Heidelberg (2007)
11. Henzinger, T.A., Jhala, R., Majumdar, R., Sutre, G.: Lazy abstraction. In: POPL, pp. 58–70. ACM (2002)
12. Herbreteau, F., Kini, D., Srivathsan, B., Walukiewicz, I.: Using non-convex approximations for efficient analysis of timed automata. In: FSTTCS 2011, pp. 78–89 (2011)
13. Herbreteau, F., Srivathsan, B., Walukiewicz, I.: Lazy abstractions for timed automata. In: Sharygina, N., Veith, H. (eds.) CAV 2013. LNCS, vol. 8044, pp. 990–1005. Springer, Heidelberg (2013)
14. Herbreteau, F., Srivathsan, B., Walukiewicz, I.: Lazy abstractions for timed automata. CoRR abs/1301.3127 (2013)
15. McMillan, K.L.: Lazy abstraction with interpolants. In: Ball, T., Jones, R.B. (eds.) CAV 2006. LNCS, vol. 4144, pp. 123–136. Springer, Heidelberg (2006)
16. Sorea, M.: Lazy approximation for dense real-time systems. In: Lakhnech, Y., Yovine, S. (eds.) FORMATS/FTRTFT 2004. LNCS, vol. 3253, pp. 363–378. Springer, Heidelberg (2004)
17. Wozna, B., Zbrzezny, A., Penczek, W.: Checking reachability properties for timed automata via sat. Fundam. Inf. 55(2), 223–241 (2003)
18. Yovine, S.: Model checking timed automata. In: Rozenberg, G., Vaandrager, F.W. (eds.) Lectures on Embedded Systems. LNCS, vol. 1494, pp. 114–152. Springer, Heidelberg (1998)

# Compliance and Subtyping
# in Timed Session Types

Massimo Bartoletti[✉], Tiziana Cimoli, Maurizio Murgia,
Alessandro Sebastian Podda, and Livio Pompianu

Università degli Studi di Cagliari, Cagliari, Italy
bart@unica.it

**Abstract.** We propose an extension of binary session types, to formalise timed communication protocols between two participants at the endpoints of a session. We introduce a decidable compliance relation, which generalises to the timed setting the usual progress-based notion of compliance between untimed session types. We then show a sound and complete technique to decide when a timed session type admits a compliant one, and if so, to construct the least session type compliant with a given one, according to the subtyping preorder induced by compliance. Decidability of subtyping follows from these results. We exploit our theory to design and implement a message-oriented middleware, where distributed modules with compliant protocols can be dynamically composed, and their communications monitored, so to guarantee safe interactions.

## 1 Introduction

Session types are formal descriptions of interaction protocols involving two or more participants over a network [18,23]. They can be used to specify the behavioural interface of a service or a component, and to statically check through a (session-)type system that this conforms to its implementation, so enabling compositional verification of distributed applications. Session types support formal definitions of compatibility or *compliance* (when two or more session types, composed together, behave correctly), and of substitutability or *subtyping* (when a service can be safely replaced by another one, while preserving the interaction capabilities with the context). Since these notions are often decidable and computationally tractable (for synchronous session types), or safely approximable (for asynchronous ones), session typing is becoming a particularly attractive approach to the problem of correctly designing distributed applications. This is witnessed by a steady flow of foundational studies [16,10,15] and of tools [12,24] based on them in the last few years.

In the simplest setting, session types are terms of a process algebra featuring a selection construct (an *internal choice* among a set of branches), a branching construct (an *external choice* offered to the environment), and recursion. In this basic form, session types cannot faithfully capture a natural and relevant aspect of interaction protocols, i.e., the timing constraints among the communication actions. While formal methods for time have been studied for at least a couple

© IFIP International Federation for Information Processing 2015
S. Graf and M. Viswanathan (Eds.): FORTE 2015, LNCS 9039, pp. 161–177, 2015.
DOI: 10.1007/978-3-319-19195-9_11

of decades, they have approached the realm of session types very recently [9,22]. However, these approaches introduce time into an already sophisticated framework, featuring multiparty session types with asynchronous communication (via unbounded buffers). While on the one hand this has the advantage of extending to the timed setting type techniques which enable compositional verification [19], on the other hand it seems that some of the key notions of the untimed setting (e.g., compliance, duality) have not been explored yet in the timed case.

We think that studying timed session types in a basic setting (synchronous communication between two endpoints, as in the seminal untimed version) is worthy of attention. From a theoretical point of view, the objective is to lift to the timed case some decidability results, like those of compliance and subtyping. Some intriguing problems arise: unlike in the untimed case, a timed session type not always admits a compliant; hence, besides deciding if two session types *are* *compliant*, it becomes a relevant problem whether a session type *has a compli-* *ant*. From a more practical perspective, decision procedures for timed session types, like those for compliance and for dynamic verification, enable the implementation of programming tools and infrastructures for the development of safe communication-oriented distributed applications.

*Contributions.* In this paper we introduce a theory of binary timed session types (TSTs), and we explore its viability as a foundation for programming tools to leverage the complexity of developing distributed applications.

We start in Section 2 by giving the syntax and semantics of TSTs. E.g., we describe as the following TST the contract of a service taking as input a zip code, and then either providing as output the current weather, or aborting:

$$p = \text{?zip}\{x\}. (\text{!weather}\{5 < x < 10\} \oplus \text{!abort}\{x < 1\})$$

The prefix $\text{?zip}\{x\}$ states that the service can receive a zip code, and then reset a clock $x$. The continuation is an *internal choice* between two outputs: either the service sends weather in a time window of $(5, 10)$ time units, or it will abort the protocol within 1 time unit.

The semantics of TSTs is a conservative extension of the synchronous semantics of untimed session types [4], adding *clock valuations* to associate each clock with a positive real. We also extend to the timed setting the standard semantic notion of *compliance*, which relates two session types whenever they enjoy progress until reaching success. For instance, $p$ above is *not* compliant with:

$$q = \text{!zip}\{y\}. (\text{?weather}\{y < 7\} + \text{?abort}\{y < 5\})$$

because $q$ is available to receive weather until 7 time units since it has sent the zip code, while $p$ can choose to send weather until 10 time units (note that $p$ and $q$, cleaned from all time annotations, are compliant in the untimed setting). Despite the semantics of TSTs being infinite-state (while it is finite-state in the untimed case), we develop a sound and complete decision procedure for verifying compliance (Theorem 1). To do that, we reduce this problem to that of model-checking deadlock freedom in timed automata [2], which is decidable, and we implement our technique using the Uppaal model checker [7].

Another difference from the untimed case is that not every TST admits a compliant (while in the untimed case, a session type is always compliant to its syntactic dual). For instance, consider the client contract:

$$q' = \text{!zip}\{y < 10\}.(\text{?weather}\{y < 7\} + \text{?abort}\{y < 5\})$$

No service can be compliant with $q'$, because if $q'$ sends the zip code, e.g., at time 8, one cannot send weather or abort in the given time constraints. We develop a procedure to detect whether a TST admits a compliant. This takes the form of a kind system which associates, to each $p$, a set of clock valuations under which $p$ admits a compliant. The kind system is sound and complete (Theorems 4 and 5), and kind inference is decidable (Theorem 3), so summing up we have a (sound and complete) decision procedure for the existence of compliant. When $p$ admits a compliant, by exploiting the kind system we can construct the *greatest* TST compliant with $p$ (Theorem 7), according to the semantic subtyping relation [4]. Decidability of subtyping follows from that of compliance and kind inference. This provides us with an effective way of checking whether a service with type $p$ can be replaced by one with a subtype $p'$ of $p$, guaranteeing that all the services which interacted correctly with the old one will do the same with the new one.

In Section 4 we address the problem of dynamically monitoring interactions regulated by TSTs. To do that, we will provide TSTs with a *monitoring semantics*, which detects when a participant is not respecting its TST. This semantics enjoys some desirable properties: it is deterministic, and it guarantees that in each state of an interaction, either we have reached success, or someone is in charge of a move, or not respecting its TST. We then exploit all the theoretical results discussed above, to discuss the design and implementation of a message-oriented middleware which uses TSTs to enable and regulate the interaction of distributed services. This infrastructure pursues the bottom-up approach to service composition: it allows services to advertise contracts (in the form of TSTs); all the advertised TSTs are collected by a *broker*, which finds pairs of compliant TSTs, and creates *sessions* between the respective services. These can then start interacting, by doing the actions prescribed by their TSTs (or even by choosing not to do so). In a system of honest services, compliance between TSTs ensures progress of the whole system; in any case, dynamic verification of all the exchanged messages guarantees safe executions.

Due to space constraints, the proofs of our statements, additional examples, as well as some tools related to the middleware, are available in [5].

## 2   Timed Session Types

We introduce binary timed session types (TSTs), by giving their syntax and semantics, and by defining a compliance relation between them. The main result of this section is Theorem 1, which states that compliance is decidable.

*Syntax.* Let A be a set of *actions*, ranged over by a, b, . . .. We denote with $A^!$ the set $\{!a \mid a \in A\}$ of *output actions*, with $A^?$ the set $\{?a \mid a \in A\}$ of *input actions*, and with $L = A^! \cup A^?$ the set of *branch labels*, ranged over by $\ell, \ell', \ldots$.

We use $\delta, \delta', \ldots$ to range over the set $\mathbb{R}_{\geq 0}$ of positive real numbers including zero, and $d, d', \ldots$ to range over $\mathbb{N}$. Let $\mathbb{C}$ be a set of *clocks*, namely variables in $\mathbb{R}_{\geq 0}$, ranged over by $t, t', \ldots$. We use $R, T, \ldots \subseteq \mathbb{C}$ to range over sets of clocks.

**Definition 1 (Guards).** *The set $\mathcal{G}_{\mathbb{C}}$ of guards over clocks $\mathbb{C}$ is defined as:*

$$g ::= \texttt{true} \mid \neg g \mid g \wedge g \mid t \circ d \mid t - t' \circ d \quad (\text{where } \circ \in \{<, \leq, =, \geq, >\})$$

Definition 2 below introduces the syntax of TSTs. A TST $p$ models the behaviour of a single participant involved in an interaction. TSTs are terms of a process algebra featuring the *success* state 1, *internal choice* $\bigoplus_{i \in I} !a_i\{g_i, R_i\} . p_i$, *external choice* $\sum_{i \in I} ?a_i\{g_i, R_i\} . p_i$, and recursion $\text{rec } X . p$.

To give some intuition, we consider two participants, Alice (A) and Bob (B), which want to interact. Alice advertises an internal choice $\bigoplus_i !a_i\{g_i, R_i\} . p_i$ when she wants to do one of the outputs $!a_i$ in a time window where $g_i$ is true; further, the clocks in $R_i$ will be reset after the output is performed. The meaning of an external choice $\sum_i ?a_i\{g_i, R_i\} . q_i$ (advertised, say, by B) is somehow dual: B is saying that he is available to receive each message $a_i$ in *any instant* within the time window defined by $g_i$ (and the clocks in $R_i$ will be reset after the input).

**Definition 2 (Timed session types).** Timed session types $p, q, \ldots$ *are terms of the following grammar:*

$$p ::= 1 \mid \bigoplus_{i \in I} !a_i\{g_i, R_i\} . p_i \mid \sum_{i \in I} ?a_i\{g_i, R_i\} . p_i \mid \text{rec } X . p \mid X$$

*where (i) the set $I$ is finite and non-empty, (ii) the actions in internal/external choices are pairwise distinct, (iii) recursion is guarded. Unless stated otherwise, we consider TSTs up-to unfolding of recursion. A TST is closed when it has no recursion variables. If $q = \bigoplus_{i \in I} !a_i\{g_i, R_i\} . p_i$ and $0 \notin I$, we write $!a_0.p_0 \oplus q$ for $\bigoplus_{i \in I \cup \{0\}} !a_i\{g_i, R_i\} . p_i$ (the same for external choices). True guards, empty resets, and trailing occurrences of the success state can be omitted.*

*Example 1.* Along the lines of PayPal User Agreement [1], we specify the protection policy for buyers of a simple on-line payment platform, called PayNow (see [5] for the full version). PayNow helps customers in on-line purchasing, providing protection against misbehaviours. In case a buyer has not received what he has paid for, he can open a dispute within 180 days from the date the buyer made the payment. After opening of the dispute, the buyer and the seller may try to come to an agreement. If this is not the case, within 20 days, the buyer can escalate the dispute to a claim. However, the buyer must wait at least 7 days from the date of payment to escalate a dispute. Upon not reaching an agreement, if still the buyer does not escalate the dispute to a claim within 20 days, the dispute is considered aborted. During a claim procedure, PayNow will ask the buyer to provide documentation to certify the payment, within 3 days of the date the dispute was escalated to a claim. After that, the payment will be refunded within 7 days. The contract of PayNow is described by the following TST $p$:

$$p = \text{?pay}\{t_{pay}\}.(\text{?ok} + \text{?dispute}\{t_{pay} < 180, t_d\}.p') \qquad \text{where}$$
$$p' = \text{?ok}\{t_d < 20\} +$$
$$\text{?claim}\{t_d < 20 \wedge t_{pay} > 7, t_c\}.\text{?rcpt}\{t_c < 3, t_c\}.\text{!refund}\{t_c < 7\} +$$
$$\text{?abort}$$

*Semantics.* To define the behaviour of TSTs we use *clock valuations*, which associate each clock with its value. The state of the interaction between two TSTs is described by a *configuration* $(p, \nu) \mid (q, \eta)$, where the clock valuations $\nu$ and $\eta$ record (keeping the same pace) the time of the clocks in $p$ and $q$, respectively. The dynamics of the interaction is formalised as a transition relation between configurations (Definition 5). This relation describes all and only the *correct* interactions: for instance, we do not allow time passing to make unsatisfiable all the guards in an internal choice, since doing so would prevent a participant from respecting her protocol. In Section 4 we will study another semantics of TSTs, which can also describe the behaviour of dishonest participants who do not respect their protocols.

We denote with $\mathbb{V} = \mathbb{C} \rightarrow \mathbb{R}_{\geq 0}$ the set of clock valuations (ranged over by $\nu, \eta, \ldots$), and with $\nu_0$ the valuation mapping each clock to zero. We write $\nu + \delta$ for the valuation which increases $\nu$ by $\delta$, i.e., $(\nu + \delta)(t) = \nu(t) + \delta$ for all $t \in \mathbb{C}$. For a set $R \subseteq \mathbb{C}$, we write $\nu[R]$ for the *reset* of the clocks in $R$, i.e., $\nu[R](t) = 0$ if $t \in R$, and $\nu[R](t) = \nu(t)$ otherwise.

**Definition 3 (Semantics of guards).** *For all guards $g$, we define the set of clock valuations $[\![g]\!]$ inductively as follows, where $\circ \in \{<, \leq, =, \geq, >\}$:*

$$[\![\text{true}]\!] = \mathbb{V} \qquad\qquad [\![\neg g]\!] = \mathbb{V} \setminus [\![g]\!] \qquad\qquad [\![g_1 \wedge g_2]\!] = [\![g_1]\!] \cap [\![g_2]\!]$$
$$[\![t \circ d]\!] = \{\nu \mid \nu(t) \circ d\} \qquad\qquad [\![t - t' \circ d]\!] = \{\nu \mid \nu(t) - \nu(t') \circ d\}$$

Before defining the semantics of TSTs, we recall from [8] some basic operations on *sets* of clock valuations (ranged over by $\mathcal{K}, \mathcal{K}', \ldots \subseteq \mathbb{V}$).

**Definition 4 (Past and inverse reset).** *For all sets $\mathcal{K}$ of clock valuations, the set of clock valuations $\downarrow \mathcal{K}$ (the past of $\mathcal{K}$) and $\mathcal{K}[T]^{-1}$ (the inverse reset of $\mathcal{K}$) are defined as: $\downarrow \mathcal{K} = \{\nu \mid \exists \delta \geq 0 : \nu + \delta \in \mathcal{K}\}$, $\mathcal{K}[T]^{-1} = \{\nu \mid \nu[T] \in \mathcal{K}\}$.*

**Definition 5 (Semantics of TSTs).** *A configuration is a term of the form $(p, \nu) \mid (q, \eta)$, where $p, q$ are TSTs extended with* committed choices $[!\text{a}\{g, R\}]\, p$. *The semantics of TSTs is defined as a labelled relation $\rightarrow$ over configurations, whose labels are either silent actions $\tau$, delays $\delta$, or branch labels.*

We now comment the rules in Figure 1. The first four rules are auxiliary, as they describe the behaviour of a TST in isolation. Rule $[\oplus]$ allows a TST to commit to the branch !a of her internal choice, provided that the corresponding guard is satisfied in the clock valuation $\nu$. This results in the term $[!\text{a}\{g, R\}]\, p$, which represents the fact that the endpoint has committed to branch !a in a specific time instant: actually, it can only fire !a through rule $[!]$ (which also

$$(!\mathtt{a}\{g, R\}.p \oplus p', \ \nu) \xrightarrow{\tau} ([!\mathtt{a}\{g, R\}]\,p, \ \nu) \qquad \text{if } \nu \in [\![g]\!] \qquad\qquad [\oplus]$$

$$([!\mathtt{a}\{g, R\}]\,p, \ \nu) \xrightarrow{!\mathtt{a}} (p, \ \nu[R]) \qquad\qquad\qquad\qquad [!]$$

$$(?\mathtt{a}\{g, R\}.p + p', \ \nu) \xrightarrow{?\mathtt{a}} (p, \ \nu[R]) \qquad \text{if } \nu \in [\![g]\!] \qquad\qquad [?]$$

$$(p, \ \nu) \xrightarrow{\delta} (p, \ \nu + \delta) \qquad\qquad\qquad \text{if } \delta > 0 \ \wedge \ \nu + \delta \in \mathbf{rdy}(p) \quad [\text{DEL}]$$

$$\frac{(p, \nu) \xrightarrow{\tau} (p', \nu')}{(p, \nu) \mid (q, \eta) \xrightarrow{\tau} (p', \nu') \mid (q, \eta)} \ [\text{S-}\oplus] \qquad \frac{(p, \nu) \xrightarrow{\delta} (p', \nu') \quad (q, \eta) \xrightarrow{\delta} (q, \eta')}{(p, \nu) \mid (q, \eta) \xrightarrow{\delta} (p', \nu') \mid (q, \eta')} \ [\text{S-DEL}]$$

$$\frac{(p, \nu) \xrightarrow{!\mathtt{a}} (p', \nu') \quad (q, \eta) \xrightarrow{?\mathtt{a}} (q', \eta')}{(p, \nu) \mid (q, \eta) \xrightarrow{\tau} (p', \nu') \mid (q', \eta')} \ [\text{S-}\tau]$$

$$\mathbf{rdy}\Big(\bigoplus !\mathtt{a}_i\{g_i, R_i\}.p_i\Big) = \ \downarrow \bigcup [\![g_i]\!] \quad \mathbf{rdy}\big(\textstyle\sum \cdots\big) = \mathbf{rdy}(1) = \mathbb{V} \quad \mathbf{rdy}([!\mathtt{a}\{g, R\}]\,p) = \emptyset$$

**Fig. 1.** Semantics of timed session types (symmetric rules omitted)

resets the clocks in $R$), while time cannot pass. Rule [?] allows an external choice to fire any of its input actions whose guard is satisfied. Rule [DEL] allows time to pass; this is always possible for external choices and success term, while for an internal choice we require that at least one of the guards remains satisfiable; this is obtained through the function $\mathbf{rdy}$ in Figure 1. The last three rules deal with configurations of two TSTs. Rule [S-$\oplus$] allows a TSTs to commit in an internal choice. Rule [S-$\tau$] is the standard synchronisation rule à la CCS; note that B is assumed to read a message as soon as it is sent, so A never blocks on internal choices. Rule [S-DEL] allows time to pass, equally for both endpoints.

*Example 2.* Let $p = \ !\mathtt{a} \oplus !\mathtt{b}\{t > 2\}$, let $q = ?\mathtt{b}\{t > 5\}$, and consider the following computations:

$$(p, \nu_0) \mid (q, \eta_0) \xrightarrow{7} \xrightarrow{\tau} ([!\mathtt{b}\{t > 2\}], \nu_0 + 7) \mid (q, \eta_0 + 7)$$
$$\xrightarrow{\tau} (1, \nu_0 + 7) \mid (1, \eta_0 + 7) \tag{1}$$

$$(p, \nu_0) \mid (q, \eta_0) \xrightarrow{\delta} \xrightarrow{\tau} ([!\mathtt{a}], \nu_0 + \delta) \mid (q, \eta_0 + \delta) \tag{2}$$

$$(p, \nu_0) \mid (q, \eta_0) \xrightarrow{3} \xrightarrow{\tau} ([!\mathtt{b}\{t > 2\}], \nu_0 + 3) \mid (q, \eta_0 + 3) \tag{3}$$

The computation in (1) reaches success, while the other two computations reach the deadlock state. In (2), $p$ commits to the choice $!\mathtt{a}$ after some delay $\delta$; at this point, time cannot pass (because the leftmost endpoint is a committed choice), and no synchronisation is possible (because the other endpoint is not offering $?\mathtt{a}$). In (3), $p$ commits to $!\mathtt{b}$ after 3 time units; here, the rightmost endpoint would offer $?\mathtt{b}$, — but not in the time chosen by the leftmost endpoint. Note that, were we allowing time to pass in committed choices, then we would have obtained e.g. that $(!b\{t > 2\}, \nu_0) \mid (q, \eta_0)$ never reaches deadlock — contradicting our intuition that these endpoints should not be considered compliant.

*Compliance.* We now extend to the timed setting the standard progress-based compliance between (untimed) session types [21,11,4]. If $p$ is compliant with $q$, then whenever an interaction between $p$ and $q$ becomes stuck, it means that both participants have reached the success state. Intuitively, when two TSTs are compliant and participants behave honestly (according to their TSTs), then the interaction will progress, until both of them reach the success state.

**Definition 6 (Compliance).** *We say that* $(p, \nu) \mid (q, \eta)$ *is deadlock whenever (i) it is not the case that both* $p$ *and* $q$ *are 1, and (ii) there is no* $\delta$ *such that* $(p, \nu + \delta) \mid (q, \eta + \delta) \xrightarrow{\tau}$. *We then write* $(p, \nu) \bowtie (q, \eta)$ *whenever:*

$$(p, \nu) \mid (q, \eta) \to^* (p', \nu') \mid (q', \eta') \quad implies \quad (p', \nu') \mid (q', \eta') \ not \ deadlock$$

*We say that* $p$ *and* $q$ *are* compliant *whenever* $(p, \nu_0) \bowtie (q, \eta_0)$ *(in short,* $p \bowtie q$*).*

*Example 3.* Let $p = {?}a\{t < 5\}.!b\{t < 3\}$. We have that $p$ is compliant with $q = {!}a\{t < 2\}.{?}b\{t < 3\}$, but it is not compliant with $q' = {!}a\{t < 5\}.{?}b\{t < 3\}$.

*Example 4.* Consider a customer of PayNow (see Example 1) who is willing to wait 10 days to receive the item she has paid for, but after that she will open a claim. Further, she will instantly provide PayNow with any documentation required. The customer contract is described by the following TST, which is compliant with PayNow's contract $p$ in Example 1:

!pay$\{t_{pay}\}.(!$ok$\{t_{pay} < 10\} \oplus$
    !dispute$\{t_{pay} = 10\}.!$claim$\{t_{pay} = 10\}.!$rcpt$\{t_{pay} = 10\}.?$refund$)$

Compliance between TSTs is somehow more liberal than the untimed notion, as it can relate terms which, when cleaned from all the time annotations, would not be compliant in the untimed case. The following example shows e.g., that a recursive internal choice can be compliant with a non-recursive external choice — which can never happen in untimed session types.

*Example 5.* Consider the TSTs $p = \text{rec} X.\big(!a \oplus !b\{x \leq 1\}.?c. X\big)$, and $q = {?}a + {?}b\{y \leq 1\}.!c\{y > 1\}.?a$. We have that $p \bowtie q$. Indeed, if $p$ chooses the output $!a$, then $q$ has the corresponding input, and they both succeed; instead, if $p$ chooses $!b$, then it will read $?c$ when $x > 1$, and so at the next loop it is forced to choose $!a$, since the guard of $!b$ has become unsatisfiable.

Definition 7 and Lemma 1 below coinductively characterise compliance between TSTs, by extending to the timed setting the coinductive compliance for untimed session types in [3]. Intuitively, an internal choice $p$ is compliant with $q$ when (i) $q$ is an external choice, (ii) for each output $!a$ that $p$ can fire after $\delta$ time units, there exists a corresponding input $?a$ that $q$ can fire after $\delta$ time units, and (iii) their continuations are coinductively compliant. The case where $p$ is an external choice is symmetric.

**Definition 7.** *We say* $\mathcal{R}$ *is a* coinductive compliance *iff* $(p, \nu)\,\mathcal{R}\,(q, \eta)$ *implies:*

1. $p = 1 \iff q = 1$
2. $p = \bigoplus_{i \in I} !a_i\{g_i, R_i\} . p_i \implies \nu \in \mathbf{rdy}(p) \wedge q = \sum_{j \in J} ?a_j\{g_j, R_j\} . q_j \wedge$
   $\forall \delta, i : \nu + \delta \in [\![g_i]\!] \implies \exists j : a_i = a_j \wedge \eta + \delta \in [\![g_j]\!] \wedge (p_i, \nu + \delta[R_i])\,\mathcal{R}\,(q_j, \eta + \delta[R_j])$
3. $p = \sum_{j \in J} ?a_j\{g_j, R_j\} . p_j \implies \eta \in \mathbf{rdy}(q) \wedge q = \bigoplus_{i \in I} !a_i\{g_i, R_i\} . q_i \wedge$
   $\forall \delta, i : \eta + \delta \in [\![g_i]\!] \implies \exists j : a_i = a_j \wedge \nu + \delta \in [\![g_j]\!] \wedge (p_j, \nu + \delta[R_j])\,\mathcal{R}\,(q_i, \eta + \delta[R_i])$

**Lemma 1.** $p \bowtie q \iff \exists \mathcal{R}$ *coinductive compliance* : $(p, \nu_0)\,\mathcal{R}\,(q, \eta_0)$

The following theorem establishes decidability of compliance. To prove it, we reduce the problem of checking $p \bowtie q$ to that of model-checking deadlock freedom in a network of timed automata constructed from $p$ and $q$ (see [5] for details).

**Theorem 1.** *Compliance between TSTs is decidable.*

## 3   On Duality and Subtyping

The dual of an untimed session type is computed by simply swapping internal choices with external ones (and inputs with outputs) [10]. A naïve attempt to extend this construction to TSTs can be to swap internal with external choices, as in the untimed case, and leave guards and resets unchanged. This construction does not work as expected, as shown by the following example.

*Example 6.* Consider the following TSTs:

$$p_1 = !a\{x \le 2\} . !b\{x \le 1\} \qquad p_2 = !a\{x \le 2\} \oplus !b\{x \le 1\} . ?a\{x \le 0\}$$
$$p_3 = \mathrm{rec}\, X . ?a\{x \le 1 \wedge y \le 1\} . !a\{x \le 1, \{x\}\} . X$$

The TST $p_1$ is not compliant with its naïve dual $q_1 = ?a\{x \le 2\} . ?b\{x \le 1\}$: even though $q_1$ can do the input $?a$ in the required time window, $p_1$ cannot perform $!b$ if $!a$ is performed after 1 time unit. For this very reason, no TST is compliant with $p_1$. Note instead that $q_1 \bowtie !a\{x \le 1\} . !b\{x \le 1\}$, which is not its naïve dual. In $p_2$, a similar deadlock situation occurs if the $!b$ branch is chosen, and so also $p_2$ does not admit a compliant. The reason why $p_3$ does not admit a compliant is more subtle: actually, $p_3$ can loop until the clock $y$ reaches the value 1; after this point, the guard $y \le 1$ can no longer be satisfied, and then $p_3$ reaches a deadlock.

As suggested in the above example, the dual construction makes sense only for those TSTs for which a compliant exists. To this purpose, we define a procedure (more precisely, a kind system) which computes the set of clock valuations $\mathcal{K}$ (called *kinds*) such that $p$ admits a compliant TST in all $\nu \in \mathcal{K}$. We then provide a constructive proof of its soundness, by showing a TST $q$ compliant with $p$, which we call the dual of $p$.

We now define our kind system for TSTs.

$$\Gamma \vdash 1 : \mathbb{V} \quad \text{[T-1]} \qquad \frac{\Gamma \vdash p_i : \mathcal{K}_i \qquad \text{for } i \in I}{\Gamma \vdash \sum_{i \in I} ?a_i\{g_i, T_i\} . p_i : \bigcup_{i \in I} \downarrow (\llbracket g_i \rrbracket \cap \mathcal{K}_i[T_i]^{-1})} \quad \text{[T-+]}$$

$$\frac{\Gamma \vdash p_i : \mathcal{K}_i \qquad \text{for } i \in I}{\Gamma \vdash \bigoplus_{i \in I} !a_i\{g_i, T_i\} . p_i : \left(\bigcup_{i \in I} \downarrow \llbracket g_i \rrbracket\right) \setminus \left(\bigcup_{i \in I} \downarrow (\llbracket g_i \rrbracket \setminus \mathcal{K}_i[T_i]^{-1})\right)} \quad \text{[T-⊕]}$$

$$\Gamma, X : \mathcal{K} \vdash X : \mathcal{K} \quad \text{[T-VAR]} \qquad \frac{\exists \mathcal{K}, \mathcal{K}' : \Gamma\{\mathcal{K}/x\} \vdash p : \mathcal{K}'}{\Gamma \vdash \text{rec } X . p : \bigcup\{\mathcal{K} \mid \Gamma\{\mathcal{K}/x\} \vdash p : \mathcal{K}' \wedge \mathcal{K} \subseteq \mathcal{K}'\}} \quad \text{[T-REC]}$$

**Fig. 2.** Kind system for TSTs

**Definition 8 (Kind system).** *Kind judgements* $\Gamma \vdash p : \mathcal{K}$ *are defined in Figure 2. where* $\Gamma$ *is a partial function which associates kinds to recursion variables.*

Rule [T-1] says that the success TST 1 admits compliant in every $\nu$: indeed, 1 is compliant with itself. The kind of an exernal choice is the union of the kinds of its branches (rule [T-+]), where the kind of a branch is the past of those clock valuations which satisfy both the guard and, after the reset, the kind of their continuation. Internal choices are dealt with by rule [T-⊕], which computes the difference between the union of the past of the guards and a set of error clock valuations. The error clock valuations are those which can satisfy a guard but not the kind of its continuation. Rule [T-VAR] is standard. Rule [T-REC] looks for a kind which is preserved by unfolding of recursion (hence a fixed point). In order to obtain completeness of the kind system we need the greatest fixed point.

*Example 7.* Recall $p_2$ from Example 6. We have the following kind derivation:

$$\frac{\vdash 1 : \mathbb{V} \qquad \dfrac{\vdash 1 : \mathbb{V}}{\vdash !a\{x \leq 0\} : \downarrow \llbracket x \leq 0 \rrbracket \cap \mathbb{V} = \llbracket x \leq 0 \rrbracket} \; \text{[T-+]}}{\vdash p_2 : \left(\downarrow \llbracket x \leq 2 \rrbracket \cup \downarrow \llbracket x \leq 1 \rrbracket\right) \setminus \left(\downarrow \llbracket x \leq 2 \rrbracket \setminus \mathbb{V}\right) \cup \downarrow \llbracket x \leq 1 \rrbracket \setminus \llbracket x \leq 0 \rrbracket\right) = \mathcal{K}} \; \text{[T-⊕]}$$

where $\mathcal{K} = \llbracket (x > 1) \wedge (x \leq 2) \rrbracket$. As noted in Example 6, intuitively $p_2$ has no compliant; this will be asserted by Theorem 5 below, as a consequence of the fact that $\nu_0 \notin \mathcal{K}$. However, since $\mathcal{K}$ is non-empty, Theorem 4 guarantees that there exist $q$ and $\eta$ such that $(p_2, \nu) \bowtie (q, \eta)$, for all clock valuations $\nu \in \mathcal{K}$.

The following theorem states that every TST is kindable. We stress the fact that being kindable does not imply admitting a compliant. This holds if and only if $\nu_0$ belongs to the kind (see Theorems 4 and 5).

**Theorem 2.** *For all closed* $p$, *there exists some* $\mathcal{K}$ *such that* $\vdash p : \mathcal{K}$.

The following theorem states that the problem of determining the kind of a TST is decidable. This might seem surprising, as the cardinality of kinds is $2^{2^{\aleph_0}}$. However, the kinds constructed by our inference rules can always be represented syntactically by guards (as in Definition 1) [17].

**Theorem 3.** *Kind inference is decidable.*

$$\mathsf{co}_\Gamma(1) = 1$$
$$\mathsf{co}_\Gamma\left(\sum_{i\in I} ?\mathsf{a}_i\{g_i, T_i\}.p_i\right) = \bigoplus_{i\in I} !\mathsf{a}_i\{g_i \wedge \mathcal{K}_i[T_i]^{-1}, T_i\}.\mathsf{co}_\Gamma(p_i) \quad \text{if } \Gamma \vdash p_i : \mathcal{K}_i$$
$$\mathsf{co}_\Gamma\left(\bigoplus_{i\in I} !\mathsf{a}_i\{g_i, T_i\}.p_i\right) = \sum_{i\in I} ?\mathsf{a}_i\{g_i, T_i\}.\mathsf{co}_\Gamma(p_i)$$
$$\mathsf{co}_\Gamma(X) = X \qquad\qquad\qquad\qquad\qquad \text{if } \Gamma(X) \text{ defined}$$
$$\mathsf{co}_\Gamma(\mathrm{rec}\,X.p) = \mathrm{rec}\,X.\mathsf{co}_{\Gamma\{\kappa/X\}}(p) \qquad\qquad \text{if } \Gamma \vdash \mathrm{rec}\,X.p : \mathcal{K}$$

**Fig. 3.** Dual of a TST

We now define the *canonical compliant* of kindable TSTs. Roughly, we turn internal choices into external ones (without changing guards nor resets), and external into internal, changing the guards so that the kind of continuations is preserved. Decidability of this construction follows from that of kind inference.

**Definition 9 (Dual).** *For all kindable $p$ and kinding environments $\Gamma$, we define the TST $\mathsf{co}_\Gamma(p)$ (in short, $\mathsf{co}(p)$ when $\Gamma = \emptyset$) in Figure 3.*

The following theorem states the soundness of the kind system: is particular, if the clock valuation $\nu_0$ belongs to the kind of $p$, then $p$ admits a compliant.

**Theorem 4 (Soundness).** *If $\vdash p : \mathcal{K}$ and $\nu \in \mathcal{K}$, then $(p, \nu) \bowtie (\mathsf{co}(p), \nu)$.*

*Example 8.* Recall the TST $q_1 = ?\mathsf{a}\{x \le 2\}.?\mathsf{b}\{x \le 1\}$ in Example 6. We have:

$$\mathsf{co}(q_1) = !\mathsf{a}\{x \le 1\}.!\mathsf{b}\{x \le 1\}$$

Since $\vdash q_1 : \mathcal{K} = [\![x \le 1]\!]$ and $\nu_0 \in \mathcal{K}$, by Theorem 4 we have that $q_1 \bowtie \mathsf{co}(q_1)$, as anticipated in Example 6.

The following theorem states the kind system is also complete: in particular, if $p$ admits a compliant, then the clock valuation $\nu_0$ belongs to the kind of $p$.

**Theorem 5 (Completeness).** *If $\vdash p : \mathcal{K}$ and $\exists q, \eta. (p, \nu) \bowtie (q, \eta)$, then $\nu \in \mathcal{K}$.*

Compliance is not transitive, in general (see [5]); however, the following Theorem 6 states that transitivity holds when passing through duals.

**Theorem 6.** *If $p \bowtie p'$ and $\mathsf{co}(p') \bowtie q$, then $p \bowtie q$.*

We now show that the dual is maximal w.r.t. the subtyping relation, like the dual in the untimed setting. We start by defining the semantic subyting preorder, which is a sound and complete model of the Gay and Hole subtyping relation (in reverse order) for untimed session types [4]. Intuitively, $p$ is subtype of $q$ if every $q'$ compliant with $q$ is compliant with $p$, too.

**Definition 10 (Semantic subtyping).** *For all TSTs $p$, we define the set $p^{\bowtie}$ as $\{q \mid p \bowtie q\}$. Then, we define the relation $p \sqsubseteq q$ whenever $p^{\bowtie} \supseteq q^{\bowtie}$.*

The following theorem states that $\mathsf{co}(p)$ is the maximum (i.e., the most "precise") in the set of the compliants of $p$, if not empty.

**Theorem 7.** $q \bowtie p \implies q \sqsubseteq \mathrm{co}(p)$

The following theorem reduces the problem of deciding $p \sqsubseteq q$ to that of checking compliance between $p$ and $\mathrm{co}(q)$. Since both compliance and the dual construction are decidable, this implies decidability of subtyping.

**Theorem 8.** *If $q$ admits a compliant, then:* $p \sqsubseteq q \iff p \bowtie \mathrm{co}(q)$.

## 4   Runtime Monitoring

In this section we study runtime monitoring based on TSTs. The setting is the following: two participants A and B want to interact according to two (compliant) TSTs $p_A$ and $p_B$, respectively. This interaction happens through a server, which monitors all the messages exchanged between A and B, while keeping track of the passing of time. If a participant (say, A) sends a message not expected by her TST, then the monitor classifies A as *culpable* of a violation. There are other two circumstances where A is culpable: (i) $p_A$ is an internal choice, but A loses time until all the branches become unfeasible, or (ii) $p_A$ is an external choice, but A does not readily receive an incoming message sent by B.

Note that the semantics in Figure 1 cannot be directly exploited to define such a runtime monitor, for two reasons. First, the synchronisation rule is purely symmetric, while the monitor outlined above assumes an asymmetry between internal and external choices. Second, the semantics in Figure 1 does not have transitions (either messages or delays) which are not allowed by the TSTs: for instance, $(!a\{t \leq 1\}, \nu)$ cannot take any transitions (neither $!a$ nor $\delta$) if $\nu(t) > 1$. In a runtime monitor we want to avoid such kind of situations, where no actions are possible, and the time is frozen. More specifically, our desideratum is that the runtime monitor acts as a *deterministic* automaton, which reads a *timed trace* (a sequence of actions and time delays) and it reaches a unique state $\gamma$, which can be inspected to find which of the two participants (if any) is culpable.

To reach this goal, we define the semantics of the runtime monitor on two levels. The first level, specified by the relation $\twoheadrightarrow$, deals with the case of honest participants; however, differently from the semantics in Section 2, here we decouple the action of sending from that of receiving. More precisely, if A has an internal choice and B has an external choice, then we postulate that A must move first, by doing one of the outputs in her choice, and then B must be ready to do the corresponding input. The second level, called *monitoring semantics* and specified by the relation $\twoheadrightarrow_M$, builds upon the first one. Each move accepted by the first level is also accepted by the monitor. Additionally, the monitoring semantics defines transitions for actions not accepted by the first level, for instance unexpected input/output actions, and improper time delays. In these cases, the monitoring semantics signals which of the two participants is culpable.

**Definition 11 (Monitoring semantics of TSTs).** Monitoring configurations $\gamma, \gamma', \dots$ are terms of the form $P \| Q$, $P$ and $Q$ are triples $(p, c, \nu)$, where

$$(!\mathtt{a}\{g,R\}.p \oplus p', [], \nu) \parallel (q, [], \eta) \xrightarrow{\text{A}:!\mathtt{a}} (p, [!\mathtt{a}], \nu[R]) \parallel (q, [], \eta) \quad \text{if } \nu \in [\![g]\!] \quad \text{[M-}\oplus\text{]}$$

$$(p, [!\mathtt{a}], \nu) \parallel (?\mathtt{a}\{g,R\}.q + q', [], \eta) \xrightarrow{\text{B}:?\mathtt{a}} (p, [], \nu) \parallel (q, [], \eta[R]) \quad \text{if } \nu \in [\![g]\!] \quad \text{[M-+]}$$

$$\frac{\nu + \delta \in \mathbf{rdy}(p) \qquad \eta + \delta \in \mathbf{rdy}(q)}{(p, [], \nu) \parallel (q, [], \eta) \xrightarrow{\delta} (p, [], \nu + \delta) \parallel (q, [], \eta + \delta)} \quad \text{[M-Del]}$$

$$\frac{(p, c, \nu) \parallel (q, d, \eta) \xrightarrow{\lambda} (p', c', \nu') \parallel (q', d', \eta')}{(p, c, \nu) \parallel (q, d, \eta) \xrightarrow{\lambda}_M (p', c', \nu') \parallel (q', d', \eta')} \quad \text{[M-Ok]}$$

$$\frac{(p, c, \nu) \parallel (q, d, \eta) \xrightarrow{\text{A}:\ell} \hspace{-1.3em}/\hspace{0.8em}}{(p, c, \nu) \parallel (q, d, \eta) \xrightarrow{\text{A}:\ell}_M (0, c, \nu) \parallel (q, d, \eta)} \quad \text{[M-FailA]}$$

$$\frac{(d = [] \wedge \nu + \delta \notin \mathbf{rdy}(p)) \vee d \neq []}{(p, c, \nu) \parallel (q, d, \eta) \xrightarrow{\delta}_M (0, c, \nu + \delta) \parallel (q, d, \eta + \delta)} \quad \text{[M-FailD]}$$

**Fig. 4.** Monitoring semantics (symmetric rules omitted)

$p$ is either a TST or $0$, and $c$ is a one-position buffer (either empty or containing an output label). The transition relations $\twoheadrightarrow$ and $\twoheadrightarrow_M$ over monitoring configurations, with labels $\lambda, \lambda', \ldots \in (\{\mathsf{A}, \mathsf{B}\} \times \mathsf{L}) \cup \mathbb{R}_{\geq 0}$, is defined in Figure 4.

In the rules in Figure 4, we always assume that the leftmost TST is governed by A, while the rightmost one is governed by B. In rule [M-$\oplus$], A has an internal choice, and she can fire one of her outputs !a, provided that its buffer is empty, and the guard $g$ is satisfied. When this happens, the message !a is written to the buffer, and the clocks in $R$ are reset. Then, B can read the buffer, by firing ?a in an external choice through rule [M-+]; this requires that the buffer of B is empty, and the guard $g$ of the branch ?a is satisfied. Rule [M-Del] allows time to pass, provided that the delay $\delta$ is permitted for both participants, and both buffers are empty. The last three rules specify the runtime monitor. Rule [M-Ok] says that any move accepted by $\twoheadrightarrow$ is also accepted by the monitor. Rule [M-FailA] is used when participant A attempts to do an action not permitted by $\twoheadrightarrow$: this makes the monitor evolve to a configuration where A is culpable (denoted by the term $0$). Rule [M-FailD] makes A culpable when time passes, in two cases: either A has an internal choice, but the guards are no longer satisfiable; or she has an external choice, and there is an incoming message.

When both participants behave honestly, i.e., they never take [M-Fail*] moves, the monitoring semantics preserves compliance (Theorem 9). The *monitoring compliance* relation $\bowtie_M$ is the straightforward adaptation of that in Definition 6, except that $\twoheadrightarrow$ transitions are used instead of $\rightarrow$ ones (see [5]).

**Theorem 9.** $\bowtie \, = \bowtie_M$.

The following lemma establishes that the monitoring semantics is deterministic: that is, if $\gamma \xrightarrow{\lambda}_M \gamma'$ and $\gamma \xrightarrow{\lambda}_M \gamma''$, then $\gamma' = \gamma''$. Determinism is a very desirable property indeed, because it ensures that the culpability of a participant at any given time is uniquely determined by the past actions. Furthermore, for all finite timed traces $\boldsymbol{\lambda}$ (i.e., sequences of actions $A : \ell$ or time delays $\delta$), there exists some configuration $\gamma$ reachable from the initial one.

**Lemma 2.** *Let $\gamma_0 = (p, [], \nu_0) \| (q, [], \eta_0)$. If $p \bowtie q$, then $(\twoheadrightarrow_M, \gamma_0)$ is deterministic, and for all finite timed traces $\boldsymbol{\lambda}$ there exists (unique) $\gamma$ such that $\gamma_0 \xrightarrow{\lambda}_M \gamma$.*

The goal of the runtime monitor is to detect, at any state of the execution, which of the two participants is culpable (if any). Further, we want to identify who is in charge of the next move. This is formalised by the following definition.

**Definition 12 (Duties & culpability).** *Let $\gamma = (p, c, \nu) \| (q, d, \eta)$. We say that A is culpable in $\gamma$ iff $p = 0$. We say that A is on duty in $\gamma$ if (i) A is not culpable in $\gamma$, and (ii) either $p$ is an internal choice, or $d$ is not empty.*

Lemma 3 guarantees that, in each reachable configuration, only one of the participants can be on duty; and if no one is on duty nor culpable, then both participants have reached success.

**Lemma 3.** *If $p \bowtie q$ and $(p, [], \nu_0) \| (q, [], \eta_0) \twoheadrightarrow^*_M \gamma$, then:*

1. *there exists at most one participant on duty in $\gamma$,*
2. *if there exists some culpable participants in $\gamma$, then no one is on duty in $\gamma$,*
3. *if no one is on duty in $\gamma$, then $\gamma$ is success, or someone is culpable in $\gamma$.*

Note that both participants may be culpable in a configuration. E.g., let $\gamma = (!a\{true\}, [], \eta_0) \| (?a\{true\}, [], \eta_0)$. By applying [M-FailA] twice, we obtain:

$$\gamma \xrightarrow{A:?b}_M (0, [], \nu_0) \| (?a\{true\}, [], \eta_0) \xrightarrow{B:?b}_M (0, [], \nu_0) \| (0, [], \eta_0)$$

and in the final configuration both participants are culpable.

*Example 9.* Let $p = !a\{2 < t < 4\}$ be the TST of participant A, and let $q = ?a\{2 < t < 5\} + ?b\{2 < t < 5\}$ be that of B. We have that $p \bowtie q$. Let $\gamma_0 = (p, [], \nu_0) \| (q, [], \nu_0)$. A correct interaction is given by the timed trace $\eta = \langle 1.2, \text{A} : !a, \text{B} : ?a \rangle$. Indeed, $\gamma_0 \xrightarrow{\eta}_M (1, [], \nu_0) \| (1, [], \nu_0)$. On the contrary, things may go awry in three cases:

(i) a participant does something not permitted. E.g., if A fires a at 1 t.u., by
   [M-FailA]: $\gamma_0 \xrightarrow{1}_M \xrightarrow{A:!a}_M (0, [], \nu_0 + 1) \| (q, [], \eta_0 + 1)$, where A is culpable.
(ii) a participant avoids to do something she is supposed to do. E.g., assume
   that after 6 t.u., A has not yet fired a. By rule [M-FailD], we obtain $\gamma_0 \xrightarrow{6}_M$
   $(0, [], \nu_0 + 6) \| (q, [], \eta_0 + 6)$, where A is culpable.
(iii) a participant does not receive a message as soon as it is sent. For instance,
   after a is sent at 1.2 t.u., at 5.2 t.u. B has not yet fired ?a. By [M-FailD],
   $\gamma_0 \xrightarrow{1.2}_M \xrightarrow{A:!a}_M \xrightarrow{4}_M (1, [!a], \nu_0 + 5.2) \| (0, [], \eta_0 + 5.2)$, where B is culpable.

# 5  Conclusions

We have studied a theory of session types (TSTs), featuring timed synchronous communication between two endpoints. We have defined a decidable notion of compliance between TSTs, a decidable procedure to detect when a TST admits a compliant, a decidable subtyping relation, and a (decidable) runtime monitoring.

All these notions have been exploited in the design and development of a message-oriented middleware which uses TSTs to drive safe interactions among distributed components. The idea is a contract-oriented, bottom-up composition, where only those services with compliant contracts can interact via (binary) sessions. The middleware makes available a global store where services can advertise contracts, in the form of TSTs. Assume that A advertises a contract $p$ to the store (this is only possible if $p$ admits a compliant). A session between A and B can be established if (i) B advertises a contract $q$ compliant with $p$, or (ii) B *accepts* the contract $p$ (in this case, the contract of B is the dual of $p$). When the session is established, A and B can interact by sending/receiving messages through the session. During the interaction, all their actions are monitored (according to Definition 11), and possible misbehaviours are detected (according to Definition 12). The middleware is accessible through a set of public APIs; a suite of tools for developing contract-oriented applications is available at [5].

*Related work.* Compliance between TSTs is loosely related to the notion of compliance between *untimed* session types (in symbols, $\bowtie_u$). Let $u(p)$ be the session type obtained by erasing from $p$ all the timing annotations. It is easy to check that the semantics of $(u(p), \nu_0) \mid (u(q), \nu_0)$ in Section 2 coincides with the semantics of $u(p) \mid u(q)$ in [4]. Therefore, if $u(p) \bowtie u(q)$, then $u(p) \bowtie_u u(q)$. Instead, *semantic conservation* of compliance does not hold, i.e. it is not true in general that if $p \bowtie q$, then $u(p) \bowtie_u u(q)$. E.g., let $p = \ !a\{t < 5\} \oplus \ !b\{t < 0\}$, and let $q = \ ?a\{t < 7\}$. We have that $p \bowtie q$ (because the branch !b can never be chosen), whereas $u(p) = \ !a \oplus \ !b \not\bowtie_u ?a = u(q)$. Note that, for every $p$, $u(\mathrm{co}(p)) = \mathrm{co}(u(p))$.

In the context of session types, time has been originally introduced in [9]. However, the setting is different than ours (multiparty and asynchronous, while ours is bi-party and synchronous), as well as its objectives: while we have focussed on primitives for the bottom-up approach to service composition [6], [9] extends to the timed case the *top-down* approach. There, a *choreography* (expressing the overall communication behaviour of a set of participants) is projected into a set of *session types*, which in turn are refined as processes, to be type-checked against their session type in order to make service composition preserve the properties enjoyed by the choreography.

Our approach is a conservative extension of untimed session types, in the sense that a participant which performs an output action chooses not only the branch, but the time of writing too; dually, when performing an input, one has to passively follow the choice of the other participant. Instead, in [9] external choices can also delay the reading time. The notion of correct interaction studied in [9] is called *feasibility*: a choreography is feasible iff all its reducts can reach the success state. This property implies progress, but it is undecidable in general, as shown by [20] in the context of communicating timed automata (however, feasibility is decidable for the subclass of *infinitely satisfiable* choreographies). The problem of deciding if, given a local type $T$, there exists a choreography $G$ such that $T$ is in the projection of $G$ and $G$ enjoys (global) progress is not being addressed in [9]. We think that it can be solved by adapting our kind system (in particular rule [T-+] must be adjusted).

Another problem not addresses by [9] is that of determinining if a set of session types enjoys progress (which, as feasibility of choreographies, would be undecidable). In our work we have considered this problem, under a synchronous semantics, and with the restriction of two participants. Extending our semantics to an asynchronous one would make compliance undecidable (as it is for untimed asynchronous session types [15]). Note that our progress-based notion of compliance does not imply progress with the semantics of [9] (adapted to the binary case). For instance, let $p = \,?a\{x \leq 2\}.\,!a\{x \leq 1\}$ and $q = \,!a\{y \leq 1\}.\,?a\{y \leq 1\}$. We have that $p \bowtie q$, while in the semantics of [9] $(\nu_0, (p, q, \boldsymbol{w_0})) \rightarrow^*$ $(\nu, (!a\{x \leq 1\}, ?a\{y \leq 1\}, \boldsymbol{w_0}))$ with $\nu(x) = \nu(y) > 1$, which is a deadlock state.

Dynamic verification of timed multiparty session types is addressed by [22], where the top-down approach to service composition is pursued [19]. Our middleware instead composes and monitors services in a bottom-up fashion [6].

In [13] timed specifications are studied in the setting of *timed I/O transition systems* (TIOTS). They feature a notion of correct composition, called *compatibility*, following the *optimistic approach* pursued in [14]: roughly, two systems are compatible whenever there exists an environment which, composed with them, makes "undesirable" states unreachable. A notion of *refinement* is coinductively formalised as an alternating timed simulation. Refinement is a preorder, and it is included in the semantic subtyping relation (using compatibility instead of $\bowtie$). Because of the different assumptions (open systems and broadcast communications in [13], closed binary systems in TSTs), compatibility/refinement seem unrelated to our notions of compliance/subtyping. Despite the main notions in [13] are defined on semantic objects (TIOTS), they can be decided on timed I/O automata, which are finite representations of TIOTS. With respect to TSTs, timed I/O automata are more liberal: e.g., they allow for *mixed choices*, while in TSTs each state is either an input or an output. However, this increased expressiveness does not seem appropriate for our purposes: first, it makes the concept of culpability unclear (and it breaks one of the main properties of ours, i.e. that at most one participant is on duty at each execution step); second, it seems to invalidate any dual construction. This is particularly unwelcome, since this construction is one of the crucial primitives of contract-oriented interactions.

**Acknowledgments.** Work partially supported by Aut. Reg. of Sardinia L.R.7/2007 CRP-17285 (TRICS), P.I.A. 2010 ("Social Glue"), P.O.R. Sardegna F.S.E. Operational Programme of the Aut. Reg. of Sardinia, EU Social Fund 2007-13 – Axis IV Human Resources, Objective l.3, Line of Activity l.3.1), by MIUR PRIN 2010-11 project "Security Horizons", and by EU COST Action IC1201 "Behavioural Types for Reliable Large-Scale Software Systems" (BETTY).

# References

1. PayPal buyer protection, https://www.paypal.com/us/webapps/mpp/ua/useragreement-full#13 (accessed: January 20, 2015)
2. Alur, R., Dill, D.L.: A theory of timed automata. Theor. Comput. Sci. 126(2), 183–235 (1994)
3. Barbanera, F., de'Liguoro, U.: Two notions of sub-behaviour for session-based client/server systems. In: PPDP, pp. 155–164 (2010)
4. Barbanera, F., de'Liguoro, U.: Sub-behaviour relations for session-based client/server systems. Math. Struct. in Comp. Science, 1–43 (January 2015)
5. Bartoletti, M., Cimoli, T., Murgia, M., Podda, A.S., Pompianu, L.: Compliance and subtyping in timed session types. Technical report (2015), http://co2.unica.it
6. Bartoletti, M., Tuosto, E., Zunino, R.: Contract-oriented computing in $CO_2$. Sci. Ann. Comp. Sci. 22(1) (2012)
7. Behrmann, G., David, A., Larsen, K.G.: A tutorial on UPPAAL. In: Bernardo, M., Corradini, F. (eds.) SFM-RT 2004. LNCS, vol. 3185, pp. 200–236. Springer, Heidelberg (2004)
8. Bengtsson, J., Yi, W.: Timed automata: Semantics, algorithms and tools. In: Desel, J., Reisig, W., Rozenberg, G. (eds.) ACPN 2003. LNCS, vol. 3098, pp. 87–124. Springer, Heidelberg (2004)
9. Bocchi, L., Yang, W., Yoshida, N.: Timed multiparty session types. In: Baldan, P., Gorla, D. (eds.) CONCUR 2014. LNCS, vol. 8704, pp. 419–434. Springer, Heidelberg (2014)
10. Castagna, G., Dezani-Ciancaglini, M., Giachino, E., Padovani, L.: Foundations of session types. In: PPDP, pp. 219–230 (2009)
11. Castagna, G., Gesbert, N., Padovani, L.: A theory of contracts for web services. ACM Transactions on Programming Languages and Systems 31(5) (2009)
12. Corin, R., Deniélou, P.-M., Fournet, C., Bhargavan, K., Leifer, J.J.: A secure compiler for session abstractions. Journal of Computer Security 16(5) (2008)
13. David, A., Larsen, K.G., Legay, A., Nyman, U., Traonouez, L., Wasowski, A.: Real-time specifications. STTT 17(1), 17–45 (2015)
14. de Alfaro, L., Henzinger, T.A.: Interface automata. In: ACM SIGSOFT, pp. 109–120 (2001)
15. Deniélou, P.-M., Yoshida, N.: Multiparty compatibility in communicating automata: Characterisation and synthesis of global session types. In: Fomin, F.V., Freivalds, R., Kwiatkowska, M., Peleg, D. (eds.) ICALP 2013, Part II. LNCS, vol. 7966, pp. 174–186. Springer, Heidelberg (2013)
16. Dezani-Ciancaglini, M., de'Liguoro, U.: Sessions and session types: An overview. In: Laneve, C., Su, J. (eds.) WS-FM 2009. LNCS, vol. 6194, pp. 1–28. Springer, Heidelberg (2010)
17. Henzinger, T.A., Nicollin, X., Sifakis, J., Yovine, S.: Symbolic model checking for real-time systems. Inf. Comput. 111(2), 193–244 (1994)
18. Honda, K., Vasconcelos, V.T., Kubo, M.: Language primitives and type discipline for structured communication-based programming. In: Hankin, C. (ed.) ESOP 1998. LNCS, vol. 1381, pp. 122–138. Springer, Heidelberg (1998)
19. Honda, K., Yoshida, N., Carbone, M.: Multiparty asynchronous session types. In: POPL (2008)
20. Krčál, P., Yi, W.: Communicating timed automata: The more synchronous, the more difficult to verify. In: Ball, T., Jones, R.B. (eds.) CAV 2006. LNCS, vol. 4144, pp. 249–262. Springer, Heidelberg (2006)

21. Laneve, C., Padovani, L.: The *must* preorder revisited. In: Caires, L., Vasconcelos, V.T. (eds.) CONCUR 2007. LNCS, vol. 4703, pp. 212–225. Springer, Heidelberg (2007)
22. Neykova, R., Bocchi, L., Yoshida, N.: Timed runtime monitoring for multiparty conversations. In: BEAT, pp. 19–26 (2014)
23. Takeuchi, K., Honda, K., Kubo, M.: An interaction-based language and its typing system. In: Halatsis, C., Maritsas, D., Philokyprou, G., Theodoridis, S. (eds.) PARLE 1994. LNCS, vol. 817, pp. 398–413. Springer, Heidelberg (1994)
24. Yoshida, N., Hu, R., Neykova, R., Ng, N.: The Scribble protocol language. In: Abadi, M., Lluch Lafuente, A. (eds.) TGC 2013. LNCS, vol. 8358, pp. 22–41. Springer, Heidelberg (2014)

# Security

# Type Checking Privacy Policies in the π-calculus

Dimitrios Kouzapas[1(✉)] and Anna Philippou[2]

[1] Department of Computing, Imperial College London and
Department of Computing Science, University of Glasgow, Glasgow, UK
dk208@doc.ic.ac.uk
[2] Department of Computer Science, University of Cyprus, Nicosia, Cyprus
annap@cs.ucy.ac.cy

**Abstract.** In this paper we propose a formal framework for studying privacy. Our framework is based on the π-calculus with groups accompanied by a type system for capturing privacy requirements relating to information collection, information processing and information dissemination. The framework incorporates a privacy policy language. We show that a system respects a privacy policy if the typing of the system is compatible with the policy. We illustrate our methodology via analysis of privacy-aware schemes proposed for electronic traffic pricing.

## 1 Introduction

The notion of privacy is a fundamental notion for society and, as such, it has been an object of study within various scientific disciplines. Recently, its importance is becoming increasingly pronounced as the technological advances and the associated widespread accessibility of personal information is redefining the very essence of the term *privacy*.

A study of the diverse types of privacy, their interplay with technology, and the need for formal methodologies for understanding and protecting privacy is discussed in [19], where the authors follow in their arguments the analysis of David Solove, a legal scholar who has provided a discussion of privacy as a taxonomy of possible privacy violations [18]. According to Solove, privacy violations can be distinguished in four categories: *invasions*, *information collection*, *information processing*, and *information dissemination*. Invasion-related privacy violations are violations that occur on the physical sphere of an individual. The authors of [19] concentrate on the latter three categories and they identify a model for studying them consisting of the *data holder* possessing information about the *data subject* and responsible to protect this information against *unauthorized adversaries* within the environment.

The motivation of this paper stems from the need of developing formal frameworks for reasoning about privacy-related concepts. Such frameworks may provide solid foundations for understanding the notion of privacy and allow to rigorously model and study privacy-related situations. More specifically, our objective is to develop a static method for ensuring that a privacy policy is satisfied by an information system using the π-calculus as the underlying theory.

To achieve this objective, we develop a meta-theory for the π-calculus that captures privacy as policy. Following the model of [19], we create a policy language that enables us to describe privacy requirements for private data over data entities. For each type of

© IFIP International Federation for Information Processing 2015
S. Graf and M. Viswanathan (Eds.): FORTE 2015, LNCS 9039, pp. 181–195, 2015.
DOI: 10.1007/978-3-319-19195-9_12

private data we expect entities to follow different policy requirements. Thus, we define policies as objects that describe a hierarchical nesting of entities where each node/entity of the hierarchy is associated with a set of privacy permissions. The choice of permissions encapsulated within a policy language is an important issue because identification of these permissions constitutes, in a sense, a characterization of the notion of privacy. In this work, we make a first attempt of identifying some such permissions, our choice emanating from the more obvious privacy violations of Solove's taxonomy which we refine by considering some common applications where privacy plays a central role.

As an example consider a medical system obligated to protect patient's data. Inside the system a nurse may access patient files to disseminate them to doctors. Doctors are able to process the data without any right to disseminate them. Overall, the data cannot be disclosed outside the hospital. We formalize this policy as follows:

$$t \gg \text{Hospital} : \{\text{nondisclose}\}[\text{ Nurse} : \{\text{access}, \text{disclose Hospital}1\},$$
$$\text{Doctor} : \{\text{access}, \text{read}, \text{write}\}]$$

where t is the type of the patient's data. The policy describes the existence of the Hospital entity at the higher level of the hierarchy associated with the nondisclose permission signifying that patient data should not be disclosed outside the system. Within this structure, a nurse may access (but not read) a patient file and disseminate the file once (disclose Hospital1). Similarly a doctor may be given access to a patient file but is also allowed to read and write data within the files (permissions access, read and write).

Moving on to the framework underlying our study, we employ the $\pi$-calculus with groups [5]. This calculus extends the $\pi$-calculus with the notion of *groups* and an associated type system in a way that controls how data is being disseminated inside a system. It turns out that groups give a natural abstraction for the representation of entities in a system. Thus, we build on the notion of a group of the calculus of [5], and we use the group memberships of processes to distinguish their roles within systems. Information processing issues can be analysed through the use of names of the calculus in input, output and object position to identify when a channel is reading or writing private data or when links to private data are being communicated between groups.

An implementation of the hospital scenario in the $\pi$-calculus with groups would be

$$(v \text{ Hospital})((v \text{ Nurse})(\overline{a}\langle l \rangle.\mathbf{0}) \mid (v \text{ Doctor})(a(x).x(y).\overline{x}\langle d \rangle.\mathbf{0}))$$

In this system, ($v$Hospital) creates a new group that is known to the two processes of the subsequent parallel composition while (Nurse) and (Doctor) are groups nested within the Hospital group and available to processes $\overline{a}\langle l \rangle.\mathbf{0}$ and $a(x).x(y).\overline{x}\langle d \rangle.\mathbf{0}$, respectively. The group memberships of the two processes characterize their nature while reflecting the entity hierarchy expressed in the privacy policy defined above.

The types of the names in the above process are defined as $y : t, d : t$, that is $y$ and $d$ are values of sensitive data, while $l : \text{Hospital}[t]$ signifies that $l$ is a channel that can be used only by processes which belong to group Hospital to carry data of type t. Similarly, $a : \text{Hospital}[\text{Hospital}[t]]$ states that $a$ is a channel that can be used by members of group Hospital, to carry objects of type Hospital[t]. Intuitively, we may see that this system conforms to the defined policy, both in terms of the group structure as well as the permissions exercised by the processes. Instead, if the nurse were able to engage in a $\bar{l}\langle d \rangle$ action then the defined policy would be violated as it would be the case if the type of $a$ was defined as $a :$ Other[Hospital[t]] for some distinct group Other. Thus, the encompassing group is essential for capturing requirements of non-disclosure.

Using these building blocks, our methodology is applied as follows: Given a system and a typing we perform type checking to confirm that the system is well-typed while we infer a permission interface. This interface captures the permissions exercised by the system. To check that the system complies with a privacy policy we provide a correspondence between policies and permission interfaces the intention being that: a permission interface satisfies a policy if and only if the system exercises a subset of the allowed permissions of the policy. With this machinery at hand, we state and prove a safety theorem according to which, if a system $Sys$ type-checks against a typing $\Gamma$ and produces an interface $\Theta$, and $\Theta$ satisfies a privacy policy $\mathscr{P}$, then $Sys$ respects $\mathscr{P}$.

## 2 The Calculus

Our study of privacy is based on the $\pi$-calculus with groups proposed by Cardelli et al. [5]. This calculus is an extension of the $\pi$-calculus with the notion of a group and an operation of group creation where a group is a type for channels. In [5] the authors establish a close connection between group creation and secrecy as they show that a secret belonging to a certain group cannot be communicated outside the initial scope of the group. This is related to the fact that groups can never be communicated between processes. Our calculus is based on the $\pi$-calculus with groups with some modifications.

We assume the existence of two basic entities: $\mathscr{G}$, ranged over by $G, G_1, \ldots$ is the set of groups and $\mathscr{N}$, ranged over by $a, b, x, y, \ldots$, is the set of names. Furthermore, we assume a set of basic types $D$, ranged over by $t_i$, which refer to the basic data of our calculus on which privacy requirements should be enforced. Specifically, we assign each name in $\mathscr{N}$ a type such that a name may either be of some base type t or of type $G[T]$, where $G$ is the group of the name and $T$ the type of value that can be carried on the name. Given the above, a type is constructed via the following BNF.

$$T ::= t \mid G[T]$$

Then the syntax of the calculus is defined at two levels. At the process level, $P$, we have the standard $\pi$-calculus syntax. At the system level, $S$, we include the group construct, applied both at the level of processes $(v\, G)P$, and at the level of systems, $(v\, G)S$, the name restriction construct as well as parallel composition for systems.

$$P ::= x(y{:}T).P \mid \bar{x}\langle z \rangle.P \mid (v\, a{:}T)P \mid P_1 \mid P_2 \mid !P \mid \mathbf{0}$$
$$S ::= (v\, G)P \mid (v\, G)S \mid (v\, a{:}T)S \mid S_1 \mid S_2 \mid \mathbf{0}$$

In $(v\, a{:}T)P$ and $(v\, a{:}T)S$, name $a$ is bound in $P$ and $S$, respectively, and in process $x(y{:}T).P$, name $y$ is bound in $P$. In $(v\, G)P$ and $(v\, G)S$, the group $G$ is bound in $P$ and $S$. We write $\mathtt{fn}(P)$ and $\mathtt{fn}(S)$ for the sets of names free in a process $P$ and a system $S$, and $\mathtt{fg}(S)$ and $\mathtt{fg}(T)$, for the free groups in a system $S$ and a type $T$, respectively. Note that free occurrences of groups occur within the types $T$ of a process/system.

We now turn to defining a labelled transition semantics for the calculus. We define a labelled transition semantics instead of a reduction semantics due to a characteristic of the intended structural congruence in our calculus. In particular, the definition of such a congruence would omit the axiom $(v\ G)(S_1 \mid S_2) \equiv (v\ G)S_1 \mid S_2$ if $G \notin \mathtt{fg}(S_2)$ as it was used in [5]. This is due to our intended semantics of the group concept which is considered to assign capabilities to processes. Thus, nesting of a process $P$ within some group $G$, as in $(v\ G)P$, cannot be lost even if $G \notin \mathtt{fg}(P)$, since the $(v\ G)$ construct has the additional meaning of group membership in our calculus and it instills $P$ with privacy-related permissions as we will discuss in the sequel. The absence of this law renders a reduction semantics rule of parallel composition rather complex.

To define a labelled transition semantics we first define a set of labels:

$$\ell ::= \tau \mid x(y) \mid \bar{x}\langle y\rangle \mid (v\ y)\bar{x}\langle y\rangle$$

Label $\tau$ is the internal action whereas labels $x(y)$ and $\bar{x}\langle y\rangle$ are the input and output actions, respectively. Label $(v\ y)\bar{x}\langle y\rangle$ is the restricted output where the object $y$ of the action is restricted. Functions $\mathtt{fn}(\ell)$ and $\mathtt{bn}(\ell)$ return the set of the free and bound names of $\ell$, respectively. We also define the relation $\mathrm{dual}(\ell, \ell')$ which relates dual actions as

$$\mathrm{dual}(\ell, \ell') \text{ if and only if } \{\ell, \ell'\} = \{x(y), \bar{x}\langle y\rangle\} \text{ or } \{\ell, \ell'\} = \{x(y), (v\ y)\bar{x}\langle y\rangle\}.$$

We use the meta-notation $(F ::= P \mid S)$ to define the labelled transition semantics.

$$x(y : T).P \xrightarrow{x(z)} P\{z/y\} \text{ (In)} \qquad\qquad \bar{x}\langle z\rangle.P \xrightarrow{\bar{x}\langle z\rangle} P \text{ (Out)}$$

$$\frac{F_1 \xrightarrow{\ell} F_1' \quad \mathtt{bn}(\ell) \cap \mathtt{fn}(F_2) = \emptyset}{F_1 \mid F_2 \xrightarrow{\ell} F_1' \mid F_2} \text{ (ParL)} \qquad \frac{F_2 \xrightarrow{\ell} F_2' \quad \mathtt{bn}(\ell) \cap \mathtt{fn}(F_1) = \emptyset}{F_1 \mid F_2 \xrightarrow{\ell} F_1 \mid F_2'} \text{ (ParR)}$$

$$\frac{F \xrightarrow{\ell} F' \quad x \notin \mathtt{fn}(\ell)}{(v\ x : T)F \xrightarrow{\ell} (v\ x : T)F'} \text{ (ResN)} \qquad \frac{F \xrightarrow{\bar{x}\langle y\rangle} F'}{(v\ y : T)F \xrightarrow{(v\ y)\bar{x}\langle y\rangle} F'} \text{ (Scope)}$$

$$\frac{F \xrightarrow{\ell} F'}{(v\ G)F \xrightarrow{\ell} (v\ G)F'} \text{ (ResG)} \qquad \frac{F \equiv_\alpha F'' \quad F'' \xrightarrow{\ell} F'}{F \xrightarrow{\ell} F'} \text{ (Alpha)}$$

$$\frac{P \xrightarrow{\ell} P'}{!P \xrightarrow{\ell} P' \mid !P} \text{ (Repl)} \qquad \frac{F_1 \xrightarrow{\ell_1} F_1' \quad F_2 \xrightarrow{\ell_2} F_2' \quad \mathrm{dual}(\ell_1, \ell_2)}{F_1 \mid F_2 \xrightarrow{\tau} (v\ \mathtt{bn}(\ell_1) \cup \mathtt{bn}(\ell_2))(F_1' \mid F_2')} \text{ (Com)}$$

**Fig. 1.** The labelled transition system

The labelled transition semantics follows along the lines of standard $\pi$-calculus semantics where $\equiv_\alpha$ denotes $\alpha$-equivalence and the rule for the group-creation construct, (ResG), captures that transitions are closed under group restriction.

## 3   Policies and Types

In this section we define a policy language and the appropriate type machinery to enforce policies over processes.

### 3.1 Policies

Typically, privacy policy languages express positive and negative norms that are expected to hold in a system. These norms distinguish what *may* happen, in the case of a positive norm, and what may not happen, in the case of a negative norm on *data attributes* which are types of sensitive data within a system, and, in particular, how the various agents, who are referred to by their *roles*, may/may not handle this data.

The notions of an attribute and a role are reflected in our framework via the notions of base types and groups, respectively. Thus, our policy language is defined in such a way as to specify the allowed and disallowed permissions associated with the various groups for each base type (sensitive data). This is achieved via the following entities:

| | | |
|---|---|---|
| (Linearities) | $\lambda$ | $::=$ 1 \| 2 \| $\ldots$ \| $*$ |
| (Permissions) | P | $::=$ read \| write \| access \| disclose $G\lambda$ \| nondisclose |
| (Hierarchies) | $H$ | $::=$ $\varepsilon$ \| $G : \tilde{p}[H_j]_{j \in J}$ |
| (Policies) | $\mathscr{P}$ | $::=$ $\mathsf{t} \gg H$ \| $\mathscr{P}; \mathscr{P}$ |

Specifically, we define the set of *policy permissions* P: they express that data may be read (read) and written (write), that links to data may be accessed (access) or disclosed within some group $G$ up to $\lambda$ times (disclose $G\lambda$). Notation $\lambda$ is either a natural number or equal to $*$ which denotes an infinite number. While the above are positive permissions, permission nondisclose is a negative permission and, when associated with a group and a base type, expresses that the base type cannot be disclosed to any participant who is not a member of the group.

In turn, a policy has the form $\mathsf{t}_1 \gg H_1; \ldots; \mathsf{t}_n \gg H_n$ assigning a structure $H_i$ to each type of sensitive data $\mathsf{t}_i$. The components $H_i$, which we refer to as *permission hierarchies*, specify the group-permission associations for each base type. A permission hierarchy $H$ has the form $G:\tilde{p}[H_1, \ldots, H_m]$, and expresses that an entity belonging to group $G$ has rights $\tilde{p}$ to the data in question and if additionally it is a member of some group $G_i$ where $H_i = G_i:\tilde{p}_i[\ldots]$, then it also has the rights $\tilde{p}_i$, and so on.

We define the auxiliary functions groups($H$) and perms($H$) so as to gather the sets of groups and the set of permissions, respectively, inside a hierarchy structure:

$$\text{groups}(H) = \begin{cases} \{G\} \cup (\bigcup_{j \in J} \text{groups}(H_j)) & \text{if } H = G : \tilde{p}[H_j]_{j \in J} \\ \emptyset & \text{if } H = \varepsilon \end{cases}$$

$$\text{perms}(H) = \begin{cases} \tilde{p} \cup (\bigcup_{j \in J} \text{perms}(H_j)) & \text{if } H = G : \tilde{p}[H_j]_{j \in J} \\ \emptyset & \text{if } H = \varepsilon \end{cases}$$

We say that a policy $\mathscr{P} = \mathsf{t}_1 \gg H_1; \ldots; \mathsf{t}_n \gg H_n$ is *well formed*, written $\mathscr{P} : \diamond$, if it satisfies the following:

1. The $\mathsf{t}_i$ are distinct.
2. If $H = G : \tilde{p}[H_j]_{j \in J}$ occurs within some $H_i$ then $G \notin \text{groups}(H_j)$ for all $j \in J$, that is, the group hierarchy is acyclic.
3. If $H = G : \tilde{p}[H_j]_{j \in J}$ occurs within some $H_i$, nondisclose $\in \tilde{p}$ and disclose $G'\lambda \in \text{perms}(H_j)$ for some $j \in J$, then $G' \in \text{groups}(H)$. In words, no non-disclosure requirement imposed at some level of a hierarchy is in conflict with a disclosure requirement granted in its sub-hierarchy.

Hereafter, we assume that policies are well-formed policies. As a shorthand, we write $G : \tilde{p}$ for $G : \tilde{p}[\varepsilon]$ and we abbreviate $G$ for $G : \emptyset$.

As an example, consider a hospital containing the departments of surgery (Surgery), cardiology (Cardiology), and psychotherapy (Psychotherapy), where cardiologists of group Cardio belong to the cardiology department, surgeons of group Surgeon belong to the surgery department, psychiatrists of group Psy belong to the psychotherapy department, and CarSurgeon refers to doctors who may have a joint appointment with the surgery and cardiology departments. Further, let us assume the existence of data of type MedFile which (1) should not be disclosed to any participant outside the Hospital group, (2) may be read, written, accessed and disclosed freely within both the surgery and the cardiology departments and (3) may be read, written and accessed but not disclosed outside the psychotherapy department. We capture these requirements via policy $\mathscr{P} = \mathsf{MedFile} \gg H$ where $p_{cd} = \{\mathsf{read}, \mathsf{access}, \mathsf{write}, \mathsf{disclose\ Cardiology} *\}$, $p_{sd} = \{\mathsf{read}, \mathsf{access}, \mathsf{write}, \mathsf{disclose\ Surgery} *\}$, $p_{pd} = \{\mathsf{nondisclose}, \mathsf{read}, \mathsf{access}, \mathsf{write}\}$,

$$H = \mathsf{Hospital}{:}\{\mathsf{nondisclose}\}\,[\mathsf{Cardiology}{:}p_{cd}[\mathsf{Cardio}, \mathsf{CarSurgeon}],$$
$$\mathsf{Surgery}{:}p_{sd}[\mathsf{Surgeon}, \mathsf{CarSurgeon}],$$
$$\mathsf{Psychotherapy}{:}p_{pd}[\mathsf{Psy}]]$$

At this point we note that, as illustrated in the above policy, hierarchies need not be tree-structured: group CarSurgeon may be reached via both the Hospital, Cardiology path as well as the Hospital, Surgery path. In effect this allows to define a process $(\nu\ \mathsf{Hospital})(\nu\ \mathsf{Cardiology})(\nu\ \mathsf{SD})(\nu\ \mathsf{CarSurgeon})P$ belonging to four groups and inheriting the permissions of each one of them.

## 3.2 The Type System

We proceed to define a typing system for the calculus.

*Typing Judgements.* The environment on which type checking is carried out consists of the component $\Gamma$. During type checking we infer the two additional structures of $\Delta$-environments and $\Theta$-interfaces as follows

$$\Gamma \ ::= \ \emptyset \ | \ \Gamma \cdot x : T \ | \ \Gamma \cdot G$$
$$\Delta \ ::= \ \emptyset \ | \ \mathsf{t} : \tilde{p} \cdot \Delta$$
$$\Theta \ ::= \ \mathsf{t} \gg H^\theta ; \Theta \ | \ \mathsf{t} \gg H^\theta$$

with $H^\theta \ ::= \ G[H^\theta] \ | \ G[\tilde{p}]$. Note that $H^\theta$ captures a special type of hierarchies where the nesting of groups is linear. We refer to $H^\theta$ as interface hierarchies. The domain of environment $\Gamma$, $\mathrm{dom}(\Gamma)$, contains all groups and names recorded in $\Gamma$. Environment $\Delta$ assigns permissions to sensitive data types t. When associated with a base type t, permissions read and write express that it is possible to read/write data of type t along channels of type $G[\mathsf{t}]$ for any group $G$. Permission access, when associated with a type t, expresses that it is possible to receive a channel of type $G[\mathsf{t}]$ for any $G$ and, finally, if permission disclose $G\lambda$ is associated with t then it is possible to send channels of type $G[\mathsf{t}]$ for up to $\lambda$ times. Thus, while permissions read and write are related to manipulating sensitive data, permissions access and disclose are related to manipulating links to sensitive data. Finally, interface $\Theta$ associates a sensitive type with a linear hierarchy of groups and a set of permissions, namely, an entity of the form $G_1[G_2[\ldots G_n[\tilde{p}]\ldots]]$.

We define three typing judgements: $\Gamma \vdash x \triangleright T$, $\Gamma \vdash P \triangleright \Delta$ and $\Gamma \vdash S \triangleright \Theta$. Judgement $\Gamma \vdash x \triangleright T$ says that under typing environment $\Gamma$, name $x$ has type $T$. Judgement $\Gamma \vdash P \triangleright \Delta$ stipulates that process $P$ is well typed under the environment $\Gamma$ and produces a permission environment $\Delta$. In this judgement, $\Gamma$ records the types of the names of $P$ and $\Delta$ records the permissions exercised by the names in $P$ for each base type. Finally, judgement $\Gamma \vdash S \triangleright \Theta$ defines that system $S$ is well typed under the environment $\Gamma$ and produces interface $\Theta$ which records the group memberships of all components of $S$ as well as the permissions exercised by each component.

*Typing System.* We now move on to our typing system. We begin with some useful notation. We write:

$$\Delta_T^r = \begin{cases} \mathsf{t : read} & \text{if } T = \mathsf{t} \\ \mathsf{t : access} & \text{if } T = G[\mathsf{t}] \\ \emptyset & \text{otherwise} \end{cases} \qquad \Delta_T^w = \begin{cases} \mathsf{t : write} & \text{if } T = \mathsf{t} \\ \mathsf{t : disclose}\, G1 & \text{if } T = G[\mathsf{t}] \\ \emptyset & \text{otherwise} \end{cases}$$

Furthermore, we define the $\uplus$ operator over permissions:

$$\begin{aligned}
\tilde{p}_1 \uplus \tilde{p}_2 = {} & \{p \mid p \in \tilde{p}_1 \cup \tilde{p}_2 \wedge p \neq \mathsf{disclose}\, G\lambda \wedge p \neq \mathsf{nondisclose}\} \\
& \cup \{\mathsf{disclose}\, G\,(\lambda_1 + \lambda_2) \mid \mathsf{disclose}\, G\lambda_1 \in \tilde{p}_1 \wedge \mathsf{disclose}\, G\lambda_2 \in \tilde{p}_2\} \\
& \cup \{\mathsf{disclose}\, G\lambda \mid \mathsf{disclose}\, G\lambda \in \tilde{p}_1 \wedge \mathsf{disclose}\, G\lambda' \notin \tilde{p}_2\} \\
& \cup \{\mathsf{disclose}\, G\lambda \mid \mathsf{disclose}\, G\lambda' \notin \tilde{p}_1 \wedge \mathsf{disclose}\, G\lambda \in \tilde{p}_2\}
\end{aligned}$$

Operator $\uplus$ adds two permission sets by taking the union of the non nondisclose permissions modulo adding the linearities of the disclose $G\lambda$ permissions. We extend the $\uplus$ operator for $\Delta$-environments: assuming $\mathsf{t} : \emptyset \in \Delta$ if $\mathsf{t} : \tilde{p} \notin \Delta$, we define $\Delta_1 \uplus \Delta_2 = \{\mathsf{t} : \tilde{p}_1 \uplus \tilde{p}_2 \mid \mathsf{t} : \tilde{p}_1 \in \Delta_1, \mathsf{t} : \tilde{p}_2 \in \Delta_2\}$.

Finally, we define the $\oplus$ operator as:

$$\begin{aligned}
G \oplus (\mathsf{t}_1 : \tilde{p}_1, \ldots, \mathsf{t}_m : \tilde{p}_m) &= \mathsf{t}_1 \gg G[\tilde{p}_1], \ldots, \mathsf{t}_m \gg G[\tilde{p}_m] \\
G \oplus (\mathsf{t}_1 \gg H_1^\theta, \ldots, \mathsf{t}_m \gg H_m^\theta) &= (\mathsf{t}_1 \gg G[H_1^\theta], \ldots, \mathsf{t}_m \gg G[H_m^\theta])
\end{aligned}$$

Operator $\oplus$ when applied to a group $G$ and an interface $\Delta$ attaches $G$ to all permission sets of $\Delta$, thus yielding a $\Theta$ interface, whereas, when applied to a group $G$ and an interface $\Theta$, it attaches group $G$ to all interface hierarchies of $\Theta$.

The typing system is defined in Fig. 2. Rule (Name) is used to type names: in name typing we require that all group names of the type are present in $\Gamma$. Process $\mathbf{0}$ can be typed under any typing environment (axiom (Nil)) to infer the empty $\Delta$-interface.

Rule (In) types the input-prefixed process. If environment $\Gamma$ extended with the type of $y$ produces $\Delta$ as an interface of $P$, we conclude that the process $x(y).P$ produces an interface where the type of $T$ is extended with the permissions $\Delta_T^r$, where (i) if $T$ is base type $\mathsf{t}$ then $\Delta$ is extended by $\mathsf{t} : \mathsf{read}$ since the process is reading an object of type $\mathsf{t}$, (ii) if $T = T'[\mathsf{t}]$ then $\Delta$ is extended by $\mathsf{t} : \mathsf{access}$, since the process has obtained access to a link for base type $\mathsf{t}$ and (iii) $\Delta$ remains unaffected otherwise.

$$\text{(Name)} \quad \frac{\mathtt{fg}(T) \subseteq \Gamma}{\Gamma \cdot x : T \vdash x \triangleright T} \qquad\qquad \text{(Nil)} \quad \Gamma \vdash \mathbf{0} \triangleright \emptyset$$

$$\text{(In)} \quad \frac{\Gamma \cdot y : T \vdash P \triangleright \Delta \quad \Gamma \vdash x \triangleright G[T]}{\Gamma \vdash x(y : T).P \triangleright \Delta \uplus \Delta_T^r} \qquad \text{(Out)} \quad \frac{\Gamma \vdash P \triangleright \Delta \quad \Gamma \vdash x \triangleright G[T] \quad \Gamma \vdash y \triangleright T}{\Gamma \vdash \bar{x}\langle y \rangle.P \triangleright \Delta \uplus \Delta_T^w}$$

$$\text{(ParP)} \quad \frac{\Gamma \vdash P_1 \triangleright \Delta_1 \quad \Gamma \vdash P_2 \triangleright \Delta_2}{\Gamma \vdash P_1 \mid P_2 \triangleright \Delta_1 \uplus \Delta_2} \qquad \text{(ParS)} \quad \frac{\Gamma \vdash S_1 \triangleright \Theta_1 \quad \Gamma \vdash S_2 \triangleright \Theta_2}{\Gamma \vdash S_1 \mid S_2 \triangleright \Theta_1 \cdot \Theta_2}$$

$$\text{(ResNP)} \quad \frac{\Gamma \cdot x : T \vdash P \triangleright \Delta}{\Gamma \vdash (\nu \, x : T)P \triangleright \Delta} \qquad \text{(ResNS)} \quad \frac{\Gamma \cdot x : T \vdash S \triangleright \Theta}{\Gamma \vdash (\nu \, x : T)S \triangleright \Theta}$$

$$\text{(ResGP)} \quad \frac{\Gamma \cdot G \vdash P \triangleright \Delta}{\Gamma \vdash (\nu \, G)P \triangleright G \oplus \Delta} \qquad \text{(ResGS)} \quad \frac{\Gamma \cdot G \vdash S \triangleright \Theta}{\Gamma \vdash (\nu \, G)S \triangleright G \oplus \Theta}$$

$$\text{(Rep)} \quad \frac{\Gamma \vdash P \triangleright \Delta}{\Gamma \vdash !P \triangleright \Delta^!}$$

**Fig. 2.** The Typing System

Rule (Out) is similar: If $y$ is of type $T$, $x$ of type $G[T]$ and $\Delta$ is the permission interface for $P$, then, $\bar{x}\langle y \rangle.P$ produces an interface which extends $\Delta$ with permissions $\Delta_T^w$. These permissions are (i) $\{t : \text{write}\}$ if $T = t$ since the process is writing data of type $t$, (ii) $\{\text{disclose } G1\}$ if $T = G[t]$, since the process is disclosing once a link to private data via a channel of group $G$, and (iii) the empty set of permissions otherwise.

Rule (ParP) uses the $\uplus$ operator to compose the process interfaces of $P_1$ and $P_2$. Parallel composition of systems, rule (ParS), concatenates the system interfaces of $S_1$ and $S_2$. For name restriction, (ResNP) specifies that if $P$ type checks within an environment $\Gamma \cdot x : T$, then $(\nu x)P$ type checks in environment $\Gamma$. (ResNS) is defined similarly. Moving on to group creation, for rule (ResGP) we have that, if $P$ produces a typing $\Delta$, then system $(\nu \, G)P$ produces the $\Theta$-interface $G \oplus \Delta$ whereas for rule (ResGS), we have that if $S$ produces a typing interface $\Theta$ then process $(\nu \, G)S$ produces interface $G \oplus \Theta$ Thus, enclosing a system within an $(\nu \, G)$ operator results in adding $G$ to the group memberships of each of the components.

Finally, for replication, axiom (Rep) states that if $P$ produces an interface $\Delta$ then $!P$ produces an interface $\Delta^!$, where $\Delta^!$ is such that if a type is disclosed $\lambda > 1$ in $\Delta$ then it is disclosed for an unlimited number of times in $\Delta^!$. That is, $\Delta^! = \{t : \tilde{p}^! \mid t : \tilde{p} \in \Delta\}$, where $\tilde{p}^! = \{p \in \tilde{p} \mid p \neq \text{disclose } G\lambda\} \cup \{\text{disclose } G * \mid \text{disclose } G\lambda \in \Delta\}$. Note that the type system never assigns the nondisclose permissions, thus interfaces are never inferred on the nondisclose permission. This is the reason the nondisclose permission is ignored in the definition of the $\uplus$ operator.

As an example consider $S = (\nu \, G_1)(\nu \, G_2)P$ where $P = !get(loc : T_l).\overline{put}\langle loc \rangle.\mathbf{0}$. Further, suppose the existence of a base type Loc and types $T_l = G_1[\text{Loc}]$, $T_r = G_2[T_l]$ and $T_s = G_1[T_l]$. Let us write $\Gamma = get : T_r \cdot put : T_s \cdot loc : T_l$. Then we have:

$$\Gamma \vdash \mathbf{0} \triangleright \emptyset \qquad\qquad\qquad\qquad\qquad \text{by (Nil)}$$
$$\Gamma \vdash \overline{put}\langle loc \rangle.\mathbf{0} \triangleright \{\text{Loc} : \{\text{disclose } G_1 1\} \qquad\qquad \text{by (Out)}$$

$$\Gamma \vdash get(loc:T_l).\overline{put}\langle loc\rangle.\mathbf{0} \rhd \{\mathsf{Loc}:\{\text{disclose }G_1\,1,\text{access}\} \qquad \text{by (In)}$$
$$\Gamma \vdash !get(loc:T_l).\overline{put}\langle loc\rangle.\mathbf{0} \rhd \{\mathsf{Loc}:\{\text{disclose }G_1\,*,\text{access}\} \qquad \text{by (Rep)}$$
$$\Gamma \vdash (v\,G_2)P \rhd \mathsf{Loc} \gg G_2 : [\{\text{disclose }G_1\,*,\text{access}\}] \qquad \text{by (ResNP)}$$
$$\Gamma \vdash S \rhd \mathsf{Loc} \gg G_1 : [G_2 : [\{\text{disclose }G_1\,*,\text{access}\}]] \qquad \text{by (ResNS)}$$

## 4   Soundness and Safety

In this section we establish soundness and safety results for our framework. Missing proofs of results can be found in the appendix. First, we establish that typing is preserved under substitution.

**Lemma 1 (Substitution).** If $\Gamma \cdot x : T \vdash P \rhd \Delta$ then $\Gamma \cdot y : T \vdash P\{y/x\} \rhd \Delta$.

The next definition defines an operator that captures the changes on the interface environment when a process executes an action.

**Definition 1** $(\Theta_1 \preceq \Theta_2)$.

1. $\tilde{p}_1 \preceq \tilde{p}_2$ if (i) for all $p \in \tilde{p}_1$ and $p \neq$ disclose $G\lambda$ implies $p \in \tilde{p}_2$, and (ii) for all disclose $G\lambda \in \tilde{p}_1$ implies disclose $\lambda' G \in \tilde{p}_2$ and $\lambda' \geq \lambda$ or $\lambda' = *$.
2. $\Delta_1 \preceq \Delta_2$ if $\forall t, t : \tilde{p}_1 \in \Delta_1$ implies that $t : \tilde{p}_2 \in \Delta_2$ and $\tilde{p}_1 \preceq \tilde{p}_2$.
3. (i) $G[\tilde{p}_1] \preceq G[\tilde{p}_2]$ if $\tilde{p}_1 \preceq \tilde{p}_2$, and (ii) $G[H_1] \preceq G[H_2]$ if $H_1 \preceq H_2$.
4. $\Theta_1 \preceq \Theta_2$ if (i) $\text{dom}(\Theta_1) = \text{dom}(\Theta_2)$, and (ii) for all t, $t \gg H_1 \in \Theta_1$ implies that $t \gg H_2 \in \Theta_2$ and $H_1 \succeq H_2$.

Specifically, when a process executes an action we expect a name to maintain or lose its interface capabilities that are expressed through the typing of the name.

We are now ready to define the notion of *satisfaction* of a policy $\mathscr{P}$ by a permission interface $\Theta$ thus connecting our type system with policy compliance.

**Definition 2.**

- Consider a policy hierarchy $H = G : \tilde{p}[H_j]_{j\in J}$ and an interface hierarchy $H^\theta$. We say that $H^\theta$ *satisfies* $H$, written $H \Vdash H^\theta$, if:

$$\frac{\mathsf{groups}(H^\theta) = G \cup \bigcup_{j\in J}\mathsf{groups}(H_j^\theta) \qquad \forall j \in J, H_j \Vdash H_j^\theta}{\mathsf{perms}(H^\theta) \preceq (\uplus_{j\in J}\mathsf{perms}(H_j^\theta)) \uplus \tilde{p}}{G : \tilde{p}[H_j]_{j\in J} \Vdash H^\theta}$$

- Consider a policy $\mathscr{P}$ and an interface $\Theta$. $\Theta$ *satisfies* $\mathscr{P}$, written $\mathscr{P} \Vdash \Theta$, if:

$$\frac{H \Vdash H^\theta}{t \gg H; \mathscr{P} \Vdash t \gg H^\theta} \qquad\qquad \frac{H \Vdash H^\theta \qquad \mathscr{P} \Vdash \Theta}{t \gg H; \mathscr{P} \Vdash t \gg H^\theta; \Theta}$$

According to the definition of $H \Vdash H^\theta$, an interface hierarchy $H^\theta$ satisfies a policy hierarchy $H$, if its groups can be decomposed into a partition $\{G\} \cup \bigcup_{j\in J} G_j$, such that there exist interface hierarchies $H_j^\theta$ referring to groups $G_j$, each satisfying hierarchy $H_j$ and where the union of the assigned permissions $H_j^\theta$ with permissions $\tilde{p}$ is a superset of the permissions of $H^\theta$, that is, $\text{perms}(H^\theta) \preceq (\uplus_{j \in J} \text{perms}(H_j^\theta)) \uplus \tilde{p}$. Similarly, a $\Theta$-interface satisfies a policy, $\mathscr{P} \Vdash \Theta$, if for each component $t \gg H^\theta$ of $\Theta$, there exists a component $t \gg H$ of $\mathscr{P}$ such that $H^\theta$ satisfies $H$. A direct corollary of the definition is the preservation of the $\preceq$ operator over the satisfiability relation:

**Corollary 1.** If $\mathscr{P} \Vdash \Theta_1$ and $\Theta_2 \preceq \Theta_1$ then $\mathscr{P} \Vdash \Theta_2$.

The next definition formalises when a system satisfies a policy:

**Definition 3 (Policy Satisfaction).** Let $\mathscr{P} : \diamond$. We say that $S$ satisfies $\mathscr{P}$, written $\mathscr{P} \vdash S$, if $\Gamma \vdash S \triangleright \Theta$ for some $\Gamma$ and $\Theta$ such that $\mathscr{P} \Vdash \Theta$.

We may now state our result on type preservation by action execution of processes.

**Theorem 1 (Type Preservation).**

1. Let $\Gamma \vdash P \triangleright \Delta$ and $P \xrightarrow{\ell} P'$ then $\Gamma \vdash P' \triangleright \Delta'$ and $\Delta' \preceq \Delta$.
2. Let $\Gamma \vdash S \triangleright \Theta$ and $S \xrightarrow{\ell} S'$ then $\Gamma \vdash S' \triangleright \Theta'$ and $\Theta' \preceq \Theta$.

**Corollary 2.** Let $\mathscr{P} \vdash S$ and $S \xrightarrow{\ell} S'$ then $\mathscr{P} \vdash S'$.

Let $\text{countLnk}(P, \Gamma, G[t])$ count the number of output prefixes of the form $\bar{x}\langle y \rangle$ in process $P$ where $x : G[t]$ for some base type t. (This can be defined inductively on the structure of $P$.) Moreover, given a policy hierarchy $H$ and a set of groups $\widetilde{G}$, let us write $H_{\widetilde{G}}$ for the interface hierarchy such that (i) $\text{groups}(H_{\widetilde{G}}) = \widetilde{G}$, (ii) $H \Vdash H_{\widetilde{G}}$ and, (iii) for all $H^\theta$ such that $\text{groups}(H^\theta) = \widetilde{G}$ and $H \Vdash H^\theta$, then $\text{perms}(H^\theta) \preceq \text{perms}(H_{\widetilde{G}})$. Intuitively, $H_{\widetilde{G}}$ captures an interface hierarchy with the maximum possible permissions for groups $\widetilde{G}$ as determined by $H$. We may now define the notion of the *error process* which clarifies the satisfiability relation between the policies and processes.

**Definition 4 (Error Process).** Consider a policy $\mathscr{P}$, an environment $\Gamma$ and a system

$$S \equiv (\nu\, G_1)(\nu\, \tilde{x}_1 : \tilde{T}_1)((\nu\, G_2)(\nu\, \tilde{x}_2 : \tilde{T}_2)(\ldots((\nu\, G_n)(\nu\, \tilde{x}_n : \tilde{T}_n)P \mid Q \mid S_n)\ldots) \mid S_1)$$

System $S$ is an *error process* with respect to $\mathscr{P}$ and $\Gamma$, if there exists t such that $\mathscr{P} = t \gg H; \mathscr{P}'$ and at least one of the following holds, where $\widetilde{G} = \langle G_1, \ldots, G_n \rangle$:

1. $\text{read} \notin \text{perms}(H_{\widetilde{G}})$ and $\exists x$ such that $\Gamma \vdash x \triangleright G[t]$ and $P = x(y).P'$.
2. $\text{write} \notin \text{perms}(H_{\widetilde{G}})$ and $\exists x$ such that $\Gamma \vdash x \triangleright G[t]$ and $P = \bar{x}\langle y \rangle.P'$.
3. $\text{access} \notin \text{perms}(H_{\widetilde{G}})$ and $\exists x$ such that $\Gamma \vdash x \triangleright G[t]$ and $P = y(x).P'$.
4. $\text{disclose } G'\, \lambda \notin \text{perms}(H_{\widetilde{G}})$ and $\exists x, y$ such that $\Gamma \vdash x \triangleright G[t]$, $\Gamma \vdash y \triangleright G'[G[t]]$ and $P = \bar{y}\langle x \rangle.P'$.
5. $\text{disclose } G\, \lambda \in \text{perms}(H_{\widetilde{G}})$, $\lambda \neq *$ and $\text{countLnk}(P, \Gamma, G[t]) > \lambda$
6. there exists a sub-hierarchy of $H$, $H' = G_k : \tilde{p}[H_i]_{i \in I}, 1 \leq k \leq n$ with nondisclose $\in \tilde{p}$ and $\exists, x, y$ such that $\Gamma \vdash x \triangleright G[t]$, $\Gamma \vdash y \triangleright G'[G[t]]$ and $P = \bar{y}\langle x \rangle.P'$ with $G' \notin \text{groups}(H')$.

The first two error processes expect that a process with no read or write permissions on a certain level of the hierarchy should not have, respectively, a prefix receiving or sending an object typed with the private data. Similarly an error process with no access permission on a certain level of the hierarchy should not have an input-prefixed subject with object a link to private data. An output-prefixed process that send links through a channel of sort $G'$ is an error process if it is found in a specific group hierarchy with no disclose $G'\lambda$ permission. In the fifth clause, a process is an error if the number of output prefixes to links in its definition (counted with the $\mathrm{countLnk}(P,\Gamma,t)$ function) are more than the $\lambda$ in the disclose $G\lambda$ permission of the process's hierarchy. Finally, if a policy specifies that no data should be disclosed outside some group $G$, then a process should not be able to send private data links to groups that are not contained within the hierarchy of $G$.

As expected, if a process is an error with respect to a policy $\mathscr{P}$ and an environment $\Gamma$ its $\Theta$-interface does not satisfy $\mathscr{P}$:

**Lemma 2.** Let system $S$ be an error process with respect to well formed policy $\mathscr{P}$ and sort $\Gamma$. If $\Gamma \vdash S \triangleright \Theta$ then $\mathscr{P} \not\Vdash \Theta$.

By Corollary 2 and Lemma 2 we conclude with our safety theorem which verifies that the satisfiability of a policy by a typed process is preserved by the semantics.

**Theorem 2 (Safety).** If $\Gamma \vdash S \triangleright \Theta$, $\mathscr{P} \Vdash \Theta$ and $S \xrightarrow{\ell}{}^{*} S'$ then $S'$ is not an error with respect to policy $\mathscr{P}$.

## 5 Example

Electronic Traffic Pricing (ETP) is an electronic toll collection scheme in which the fee to be paid by drivers depends on the road usage of their vehicles where factors such as the type of roads used and the times of the usage determine the toll. To achieve this, for each vehicle detailed time and location information must be collected and processed and the due amount can be calculated with the help of a digital tariff and a road map. A number of possible implementation schemes may be considered for this system [8]. In the centralized approach, all location information is communicated to the pricing authority which computes the fee to be paid based on the received information. In the decentralized approach the fee is computed locally on the car via the use of a third trusted entity such as a smart card. In the following subsections we consider these approaches and their associated privacy characteristics.

### 5.1 The Centralized Approach

This approach makes use of on-board equipment (OBE) which computes regularly the geographical position of the car and forwards it to the Pricing Authority (PA). To avoid drivers tampering with their OBE and communicating false information, the authorities may perform checks on the spot to confirm that the OBE is reliable.

We may model this system with the aid of five groups: ETP corresponds to the entirety of the ETP system, Car refers to the car and is divided into the OBE and the GPS subgroups, and PA refers to the pricing authority. As far as types are concerned, we assume the existence of two base types: Loc referring to the attribute of locations and Fee referring to the attribute of fees. We write $T_l = \mathrm{ETP}[\mathrm{Loc}]$, $T_r = \mathrm{Car}[T_l]$, $T_{pa} = \mathrm{ETP}[T_l]$, $T_x = \mathrm{ETP}[T_l]$ and $T_{sc} = \mathrm{ETP}[T_x]$.

$$O = !read(loc : T_l).\overline{topa}\langle loc\rangle.\mathbf{0}$$
$$| \ !spotcheck(s : T_x).read(ls : T_l).\overline{s}\langle ls\rangle.\mathbf{0}$$
$$L = !(\nu\ newl : T_l)\overline{read}\langle newl\rangle.\mathbf{0}$$
$$A = !topa(z : T_l).z(l : \mathsf{Loc}).\mathbf{0}$$
$$| \ !\overline{send}\langle fee\rangle.\mathbf{0}$$
$$| \ !(\nu\ x : T_x)\overline{spotcheck}\langle x\rangle.x(y : T_l).y(l_s : \mathsf{Loc}).\mathbf{0}$$
$$\mathsf{System} = (\nu\ \mathsf{ETP})(\nu\ spotcheck : T_{sc})(\nu\ topa : T_{pa})$$
$$[\,(\nu\ \mathsf{PA})A \ | \ (\nu\ \mathsf{Car})((\nu\ read : T_r)((\nu\ \mathsf{OBE})O\ |\ (\nu\ \mathsf{GPS})L))\,]$$

In the above model we have the component of the OBE, $O$, belonging to group OBE, and the component responsible for computing the current location, $L$, belonging to group GPS. These two components are nested within the Car group and share the private name $read$ on which it is possible for $L$ to pass to $O$ a name via which the current location may be read. The OBE $O$ may spontaneously read on name $read$ or it may enquire the current location for the purposes of a spot check. Such a check is initiated by the pricing authority $A$ who may engage in three different activities: Firstly, it may receive a name $z$ from the OBE via channel $topa$ and then use $z$ for reading the car location (action $z(l)$). Secondly, it may periodically compute the fee to be paid and communicate the link ($fee : \mathsf{ETP}[\mathsf{Fee}]$) via name $send : \mathsf{ETP}[\mathsf{ETP}[\mathsf{Fee}]]$. Thirdly, it may initiate a spot check, during which it creates and sends the OBE a new channel via which the OBE is expected to return the current location for a verification check.

By applying the rules of our type system we may show that $\Gamma \vdash \mathsf{System} \triangleright \Theta$, where $\Gamma = \{fee : \mathsf{ETP}[\mathsf{Fee}], send : \mathsf{ETP}[\mathsf{ETP}[\mathsf{Fee}]]\}$ and where

$$\Theta = \mathsf{Fee} \gg \mathsf{ETP}[\mathsf{PA}[\{\mathsf{disclose\ ETP}*\}]];\ \ \mathsf{Loc} \gg \mathsf{ETP}[\mathsf{PA}[\{\mathsf{access}, \mathsf{read}\}]];$$
$$\mathsf{Loc} \gg \mathsf{ETP}[\mathsf{Car}[\mathsf{OBE}[\{\mathsf{access}, \mathsf{disclose\ ETP}*\}]]];\ \ \mathsf{Loc} \gg \mathsf{ETP}[\mathsf{Car}[\mathsf{GPS}[\{\mathsf{disclose\ Car}*\}]]]$$

A possible privacy policy for the system might be one that states that locations may be freely forwarded by the OBE. We may define this by $\mathscr{P} = \mathsf{Loc} \gg H$ where

$$H = \mathsf{ETP} : \mathsf{nondisclose}\ [\mathsf{Car} : [\mathsf{OBE} : \{\mathsf{access}, \mathsf{disclose\ ETP}*\},$$
$$\mathsf{GPS} : \{\mathsf{disclose\ Car}*\}],$$
$$\mathsf{PA} : \{\mathsf{access}, \mathsf{read}\}]$$

We have that $\mathscr{P} \Vdash \mathsf{Loc} \gg \mathsf{ETP}[\mathsf{PA}[\{\mathsf{access}, \mathsf{read}\}]]$, since the permissions assigned to groups ETP and PA by the policy are equal to $\{\mathsf{access}, \mathsf{read}\} \preceq \{\mathsf{access}, \mathsf{read}\} = \mathsf{perms}(\mathsf{ETP}[\mathsf{PA}[\{\mathsf{access}, \mathsf{read}\}]])$. Similarly, $\mathscr{P} \Vdash \mathsf{Loc} \gg \mathsf{ETP}[\mathsf{Car}[\mathsf{OBE}[\{\mathsf{access}, \mathsf{disclose\ ETP}*\}]]]$ and $\mathscr{P} \Vdash \mathsf{Loc} \gg \mathsf{ETP}[\mathsf{Car}[\mathsf{GPS}[\{\mathsf{disclose\ Car}*\}]]]$. Thus, we conclude that System satisfies $\mathscr{P}$.

This architecture is simple but also very weak in protecting the privacy of individuals: the fact that the PA gets detailed travel information about every vehicle constitutes a privacy and security threat. An alternative implementation that limits the transmission of locations is presented in the second implementation proposal presented below.

## 5.2  The Decentralized Approach

To avoid the disclosure of the complete travel logs of a system this solution employs a third trusted entity (e.g. smart card) to make computations of the fee locally on the car and send its value to the authority which in turn may make spot checks to obtain evidence on the correctness of the calculation.

The policy here would require that locations can be communicated for at most a small fixed amount of times and that the OBE may read the fee computed by the smart card but not change its value. Precisely, the new privacy policy might be:

Loc $\gg$ ETP : nondisclose [
    Car : [
        OBE : {access, disclose ETP 2},
        GPS : {disclose Car∗},
        SC : {access, read}],
    PA : {access, read}]

Fee $\gg$ ETP : nondisclose [
    Car : [
        OBE : {},
        GPS : {},
        SC : {write, disclose ETP ∗}],
    PA : {access, read}]

The new system as described above may be modelled as follows, where we have a new group SC and a new component $S$, a smart card, belonging to this group:

$$S = !read(loc : T_l).loc(l : \mathsf{Loc}).(v\ newval : Fee)\overline{fee}\langle newval \rangle.\overline{send}\langle fee \rangle.\mathbf{0}$$

$$O = spotcheck(s_1 : T_x).read(ls_1 : T_l).\overline{s_1}\langle ls_1 \rangle.spotcheck(s_2 : T_x).read(ls_2 : T_l).\overline{s_2}\langle ls_2 \rangle.\mathbf{0}$$

$$L = !(v\ newl : T_l)\overline{read}\langle newl \rangle.\mathbf{0}$$

$$A = !(v\ x : T_x)\overline{spotcheck}\langle x \rangle.x(y : T_l).y(l_s : \mathsf{Loc}).\mathbf{0}$$
$$\quad\ |\ send(fee).fee(v : \mathsf{Fee}).\mathbf{0}$$

$$\mathsf{System} = (v\ \mathsf{ETP})(v\ spotcheck : T_{sc})(v\ topa : T_{pa})$$
$$[\,(v\ \mathsf{PA})A\ \ |\ \ (v\ \mathsf{Car})((v\ read : T_r)((v\ \mathsf{OBE})O\ |\ (v\ \mathsf{GPS})L)\ |\ (v\ \mathsf{SC})S)\,]$$

We may verify that $\Gamma \vdash \mathsf{System} \triangleright \Theta$, where $\Gamma = \{fee : \mathsf{ETP}[\mathsf{Fee}], send : \mathsf{ETP}[\mathsf{ETP}[\mathsf{Fee}]]\}$ and interface $\Theta$ satisfies the enunciated policy.

# 6  Related Work

There exists a large body of literature concerned with formally reasoning about privacy. To begin with, a number of languages have been proposed to express privacy policies [16,15] and can be used to verify the consistency of policies or to check whether a system complies with a certain policy via static techniques such as model checking [15,13], on-the-fly using monitoring, or through audit procedures [7,2].

Related to the privacy properties we are considering in this paper is the notion of Contextual Integrity [2]. Aspects of this notion have been formalized in a logical framework and were used for specifying privacy regulations while notions of compliance of policies by systems were considered. Also related to our work is [17] where a family of models named P-RBAC (Privacy-aware Role Based Access Control) is presented that extends the traditional role-based access control to support specification of complex privacy policies. In particular, the variation thereby introduced called Hierarchical P-RBAC introduces, amongst others, the notion of role hierarchies which is reminiscent of our policy hierarchies. However, the methodology proposed is mostly geared towards expressing policies and checking for conflicts within policies as opposed to assessing the satisfaction of policies by systems, which is the goal of our work.

Also related to our work is the research line on typed-based security in process calculi. Among these works, numerous studies have focused on access control which is closely related to privacy. For instance the work on the D$\pi$ calculus has introduced sophisticated type systems for controlling the access to distributed resources [11,12]. Furthermore, discretionary access control has been considered in [4] which similarly to our work employs the $\pi$-calculus with groups, while role-based access control (RBAC) has been considered in [3,9,6]. In addition, authorization policies and their analysis via type checking has been considered in a number of papers including [10,1]. While adopting a similar approach, our work departs from these works in the following respects: To begin with we note that role-based access control is insufficient for reasoning about certain privacy violations. While in RBAC it is possible to express that a doctor may read patient's data and send emails, it is not possible to detect the privacy violation breach executed when the doctor sends an email with the sensitive patient data. In our framework, we may control such information dissemination by distinguishing between different types of data and how these can be manipulated. Furthermore, a novelty of our approach is the concept of hierarchies within policies which allow to arrange the system into a hierarchical arrangement of disclosure zones while allowing the inheritance of permissions between groups within the hierarchy.

To conclude, we mention our previous work of [14]. In that work we employed the $\pi$-calculus with groups accompanied by a type system based on i/o and linear types for capturing privacy-related notions. In the present work, the type system is reconstructed and simplified using the notions of groups to distinguish between different entities and introducing permissions inference during type checking. Most importantly, a contribution of this work in comparison to [14] is that we introduce a policy language and prove a safety criterion that establishes policy satisfaction by typing.

# 7    Conclusions

In this paper we have presented a formal framework based on the $\pi$-calculus with groups for studying privacy. Our framework is accompanied by a type system for capturing privacy-related notions and a privacy language for expressing privacy policies. We have proved a type preservation theorem and a safety theorem which establishes sufficient conditions for a system to satisfy a policy.

The policy language we have proposed is a simple language that constructs a hierarchical structure of the entities composing a system and assigning permissions for accessing sensitive data to each of the entities while allowing to reason about some simple privacy violations. These permissions are certainly not intended to capture every possible privacy issue, but rather to demonstrate a method of how one might formalize privacy rights. Identifying an appropriate and complete set of permissions for providing foundations for the notion of privacy in the general context should be the result of intensive and probably interdisciplinary research that justifies each choice. To this effect, Solove's taxonomy of privacy violations forms a promising context in which these efforts can be based and it provides various directions for future work.

Other possible directions for future work can be inspired by privacy approaches such as contextual integrity and P-RBAC. We are currently extending our work to reason about more complex privacy policies that include *conditional* permissions and the concepts of *purpose* and *obligation* as in P-RBAC. Finally, it would be interesting to explore more dynamic settings where the roles evolve over time.

# References

1. Backes, M., Hritcu, C., Maffei, M.: Type-checking zero-knowledge. In: Proceedings of CCS 2008, pp. 357–370 (2008)
2. Barth, A., Datta, A., Mitchell, J.C., Nissenbaum, H.: Privacy and contextual integrity: Framework and applications. In: Proceedings of S&P 2006, pp. 184–198 (2006)
3. Braghin, C., Gorla, D., Sassone, V.: Role-based access control for a distributed calculus. Journal of Computer Security 14(2), 113–155 (2006)
4. Bugliesi, M., Colazzo, D., Crafa, S., Macedonio, D.: A type system for discretionary access control. Mathematical Structures in Computer Science 19(4), 839–875 (2009)
5. Cardelli, L., Ghelli, G., Gordon, A.D.: Secrecy and group creation. Information and Computation 196(2), 127–155 (2005)
6. Compagnoni, A.B., Gunter, E.L., Bidinger, P.: Role-based access control for boxed ambients. Theoretical Computer Science 398(1-3), 203–216 (2008)
7. Datta, A., Blocki, J., Christin, N., DeYoung, H., Garg, D., Jia, L., Kaynar, D., Sinha, A.: Understanding and protecting privacy: Formal semantics and principled audit mechanisms. In: Jajodia, S., Mazumdar, C. (eds.) ICISS 2011. LNCS, vol. 7093, pp. 1–27. Springer, Heidelberg (2011)
8. de Jonge, W., Jacobs, B.: Privacy-friendly electronic traffic pricing via commits. In: Degano, P., Guttman, J., Martinelli, F. (eds.) FAST 2008. LNCS, vol. 5491, pp. 143–161. Springer, Heidelberg (2009)
9. Dezani-Ciancaglini, M., Ghilezan, S., Jakšić, S., Pantović, J.: Types for role-based access control of dynamic web data. In: Mariño, J. (ed.) WFLP 2010. LNCS, vol. 6559, pp. 1–29. Springer, Heidelberg (2011)
10. Fournet, C., Gordon, A., Maffeis, S.: A type discipline for authorization in distributed systems. In: Proceedings of CSF 2007, pp. 31–48 (2007)
11. Hennessy, M., Rathke, J., Yoshida, N.: safedpi: A language for controlling mobile code. Acta Informatica 42(4-5), 227–290 (2005)
12. Hennessy, M., Riely, J.: Resource access control in systems of mobile agents. Information and Computation 173(1), 82–120 (2002)
13. Koleini, M., Ritter, E., Ryan, M.: Model checking agent knowledge in dynamic access control policies. In: Piterman, N., Smolka, S.A. (eds.) TACAS 2013. LNCS, vol. 7795, pp. 448–462. Springer, Heidelberg (2013)
14. Kouzapas, D., Philippou, A.: A typing system for privacy. In: Counsell, S., Núñez, M. (eds.) SEFM 2013. LNCS, vol. 8368, pp. 56–68. Springer, Heidelberg (2014)
15. Liu, Y., Müller, S., Xu, K.: A static compliance-checking framework for business process models. IBM Systems Journal 46(2), 335–362 (2007)
16. May, M.J., Gunter, C.A., Lee, I.: Privacy APIs: Access control techniques to analyze and verify legal privacy policies. In: Proceedings of CSFW 2006, pp. 85–97 (2006)
17. Ni, Q., Bertino, E., Lobo, J., Brodie, C., Karat, C., Karat, J., Trombetta, A.: Privacy-aware role-based access control. ACM Trans. on Information and System Security 13(3) (2010)
18. Solove, D.J.: A Taxonomy of Privacy. University of Pennsylvania Law Review 154(3), 477–560 (2006)
19. Tschantz, M.C., Wing, J.M.: Formal methods for privacy. In: Cavalcanti, A., Dams, D.R. (eds.) FM 2009. LNCS, vol. 5850, pp. 1–15. Springer, Heidelberg (2009)

# Extending Testing Automata to All LTL

Ala Eddine Ben Salem[✉]

LRDE, EPITA, Le Kremlin-Bicêtre, France
ala@lrde.epita.fr

**Abstract.** An alternative to the traditional Büchi Automata (BA), called Testing Automata (TA) was proposed by Hansen et al. [8, 6] to improve the automata-theoretic approach to LTL model checking. In previous work [2], we proposed an improvement of this alternative approach called TGTA (Generalized Testing Automata). TGTA mixes features from both TA and TGBA (Generalized Büchi Automata), without the disadvantage of TA, which is the second pass of the emptiness check algorithm. We have shown that TGTA outperform TA, BA and TGBA for explicit and symbolic LTL model checking. However, TA and TGTA are less expressive than Büchi Automata since they are able to represent only stutter-invariant LTL properties $(LTL\backslash X)$ [13]. In this paper, we show how to extend Generalized Testing Automata (TGTA) to represent any LTL property. This allows to extend the model checking approach based on this new form of testing automata to check other kinds of properties and also other kinds of models (such as Timed models). Implementation and experimentation of this extended TGTA approach show that it is statistically more efficient than the Büchi Automata approaches (BA and TGBA), for the explicit model checking of LTL properties.

## 1  Introduction

The model checking of a behavioral property on a finite-state system is an automatic procedure that requires many phases. The first step is to formally represent the system and the property to be checked. The formalization of the system produces a model $M$ that formally describes all the possible executions of the system. The property to be checked is formally described using a specification language such as Linear-time Temporal Logic (LTL). The next step is to run a model checking algorithm that takes as inputs the model $M$ and the LTL property $\varphi$. This algorithm exhaustively checks that all the executions of the model $M$ satisfy $\varphi$. When the property is not satisfied, the model checker returns a *counterexample*, i.e., an execution of $M$ invalidating $\varphi$, this counterexample is particularly useful to find subtle errors in complex systems.

The *automata-theoretic approach* [16] to LTL model checking represents the state-space of $M$ and the property $\varphi$ using variants of $\omega$-automata, i.e., an extension of the classical finite automata to recognize words having infinite length (called $\omega$-words).

The *automata-theoretic approach* splits the verification process into four operations:

1. Computation of the state-space of $M$. This state-space can be represented by a variant of $\omega$-automaton, called Kripke structure $\mathcal{K}_M$, whose language $\mathcal{L}(\mathcal{K}_M)$, represents all possible infinite executions of $M$.
2. Translation of the negation of the LTL property $\varphi$ into an $\omega$-automaton $A_{\neg\varphi}$ whose language, $\mathcal{L}(A_{\neg\varphi})$, is the set of all infinite executions that would invalidate $\varphi$.

© IFIP International Federation for Information Processing 2015
S. Graf and M. Viswanathan (Eds.): FORTE 2015, LNCS 9039, pp. 196–210, 2015.
DOI: 10.1007/978-3-319-19195-9_13

3. Synchronization of these automata. This constructs a synchronous product automaton $\mathcal{K}_M \otimes A_{\neg\varphi}$ whose language, $\mathscr{L}(\mathcal{K}_M \otimes A_{\neg\varphi}) = \mathscr{L}(\mathcal{K}_M) \cap \mathscr{L}(A_{\neg\varphi})$, is the set of executions of $M$ invalidating $\varphi$.

4. Emptiness check of this product. This operation tells whether $\mathcal{K}_M \otimes A_{\neg\varphi}$ accepts an infinite word, and can return such a word (a counterexample) if it does. The model $M$ verifies $\varphi$ *iff* $\mathscr{L}(\mathcal{K}_M \otimes A_{\neg\varphi}) = \emptyset$.

The main difficulty of the LTL model checking is the state-space explosion problem. In particular, in the automata-theoretic approach, the product automaton $\mathcal{K}_M \otimes A_{\neg\varphi}$ is often too large to be emptiness checked in a reasonable run time and memory. Indeed, the performance of the automata-theoretic approach mainly depends on the size of the explored part of $\mathcal{K}_M \otimes A_{\neg\varphi}$ during the emptiness check. This explored part itself depends on three parameters: the automaton $A_{\neg\varphi}$ obtained from the LTL property $\varphi$, the Kripke structure $\mathcal{K}_M$ representing the state-space of $M$, and the emptiness check algorithm: the fact that this algorithm is performed "on-the-fly" potentially avoids building the entire product automaton. The states of this product that are not visited by the emptiness check are not generated at all.

Different kinds of ω-automata have been used to represent $A_{\neg\varphi}$. In the most common case, the negation of $\varphi$ is converted into a *Büchi automaton* (BA) with state-based accepting. *Transition-based Generalized Büchi Automata* (TGBA) represent the LTL properties using *generalized* (i.e., multiple) Büchi acceptance conditions *on transitions* rather than on states. TGBA allow to have a smaller [7, 4] property automaton than BA.

Unfortunately, having a smaller property automaton $A_{\neg\varphi}$ does not always imply a smaller product $(A_M \otimes A_{\neg\varphi})$. Thus, instead of targeting smaller property automata, some people have attempted to build automata that are *more deterministic* [14].

Hansen et al. [8, 6] introduced an alternative type of ω-automata called *Testing Automata* (TA) that only observe changes on the atomic propositions. TA are often larger than their equivalent BA, but according to Geldenhuys and Hansen [6], thanks to their high degree of determinism [8], the TA allow to obtain a smaller product and thus improve the performance of model checking. As a back-side, TA have two different modes of acceptance (Büchi-accepting or livelock-accepting), and consequently their emptiness check requires two passes [6], mitigating the benefits of a having a smaller product.

In previous work [2], we propose an improvement of TA called *Transition-based Generalized Testing Automata* (TGTA) that combine the advantages of both TA and TGBA, and without the disadvantages of TA (without introducing a second mode of acceptance and without the second pass of the emptiness check).

Unfortunately, the two variants of testing automata TA and TGTA are less expressive than Büchi automata (BA and TGBA) since they are tailored to represent *stutter-invariant* properties.

The goal of this paper is to extend TGTA in order to obtain a new form of testing automata that represent any LTL property, and therefore extend the model checking approach based on this alternative kind of automata to check other kinds of properties and also other kinds of models.

In order to remove the constraint that TGTA only represent stutter-invariant properties, one solution would be to change the construction of TGTA to take into account the "sub-parts" of the automata corresponding to the "sub-formulas" that are not insensitive to stuttering. Indeed, during the transformation of a TGBA into a TGTA, only the second step exploits the fact that the LTL property is stutter-invariant (this step allows to remove the useless stuttering-transitions). The idea is to apply this second step only for the parts of the automata that are insensitive to stuttering and to apply only the first step of the construction for the other parts (that are sensitive to stuttering).

We have run benchmarks to compare the new form of TGTA against BA and TGBA. Experiments reported that, in most cases, TGTA produce the smallest products ($A_M \otimes A_{\neg\varphi}$) and TGTA outperform BA and TGBA when no counterexample is found (i.e., the property is satisfied), but they are comparable when the property is violated, because in this case the on-the-fly algorithm stops as soon as it finds a counterexample without exploring the entire product.

## 2  Preliminaries

Let $AP$ a finite set of atomic propositions, a valuation $\ell$ over $AP$ is represented by a function $\ell : AP \mapsto \{\bot, \top\}$. We denote by $\Sigma = 2^{AP}$ the set of all valuations over $AP$, where a valuation $\ell \in \Sigma$ is interpreted either as the set of atomic propositions that are true, or as a Boolean conjunction. For instance if $AP = \{a, b\}$, then $\Sigma = 2^{AP} = \{\{a,b\}, \{a\}, \{b\}, \emptyset\}$ or equivalently $\Sigma = \{ab, a\bar{b}, \bar{a}b, \bar{a}\bar{b}\}$.

The state-space of a system can be represented by a directed graph, called Kripke structure, where vertices represent the states of the system and edges are the transitions between these states. In addition, each vertex is labeled by a valuation that represents the set of atomic propositions that are true in the corresponding state.

**Definition 1 (Kripke Structure).** *A* Kripke structure *over the set of atomic propositions AP is a tuple* $\mathcal{K} = \langle S, S_0, \mathcal{R}, l \rangle$*, where:*

- *$S$ is a finite set of states,*
- *$S_0 \subseteq S$ is the set of initial states,*
- *$\mathcal{R} \subseteq S \times S$ is the transition relation,*
- *$l : S \rightarrow \Sigma$ is a labeling function that maps each state $s$ to a valuation that represents the set of atomic propositions that are true in $s$.*

The automata-theoretic approach is based on the transformation of the negation of the LTL property to be checked into an $\omega$-automaton that accepts the same executions. Büchi Automata (BA) are $\omega$-automata with labels on transitions and acceptance conditions on states. Büchi Automata are commonly used for LTL model checking (we use the abbreviation BA for the standard variant of Büchi Automata). The following section present TGBA [7]: a generalized variant of BA that allow a more compact representation of LTL properties [4].

### 2.1  Transition-Based Generalized Büchi Automata (TGBA)

A Transition-based Generalized Büchi Automaton (TGBA) [7] is a variant of a Büchi automaton that has multiple acceptance conditions on transitions.

**Definition 2 (TGBA).** *A TGBA over the alphabet* $\Sigma = 2^{AP}$ *is a tuple* $G = \langle Q, I, \delta, \mathcal{F} \rangle$ *where:*

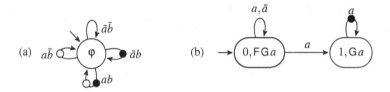

**Fig. 1.** (a) A TGBA recognizing the LTL property $\varphi = \mathsf{G}\mathsf{F}a \wedge \mathsf{G}\mathsf{F}b$ with acceptance conditions $\mathcal{F} = \{\bullet, \circ\}$. (b) A TGBA recognizing the LTL property $\varphi = \mathsf{F}\mathsf{G}a$ with $\mathcal{F} = \{\bullet\}$.

- *Q is a finite set of states,*
- *$I \subseteq Q$ is a set of initial states,*
- *$\mathcal{F}$ is a finite set of acceptance conditions,*
- *$\delta \subseteq Q \times \Sigma \times 2^{\mathcal{F}} \times Q$ is the transition relation, where each element $(q, \ell, F, q') \in \delta$ represents a transition from state $q$ to state $q'$ labeled by a valuation $\ell \in 2^{AP}$, and a set of acceptance conditions $F \in 2^{\mathcal{F}}$.*

*An infinite word $\sigma = \ell_0 \ell_1 \ell_2 \ldots \in \Sigma^{\omega}$ is accepted by $\mathcal{G}$ if there exists an infinite run $r = (q_0, \ell_0, F_0, q_1)(q_1, \ell_1, F_1, q_2)(q_2, \ell_2, F_2, q_3) \ldots \in \delta^{\omega}$ where:*
- *$q_0 \in I$ (the infinite word is recognized by the run),*
- *$\forall f \in \mathcal{F}, \forall i \in \mathbb{N}, \exists j \geq i, f \in F_j$ (each acceptance condition is visited infinitely often).*

*The language of $\mathcal{G}$ is the set $\mathscr{L}(\mathcal{G}) \subseteq \Sigma^{\omega}$ of infinite words it accepts.*

Any LTL formula $\varphi$ can be converted into a TGBA whose language is the set of executions that satisfy $\varphi$ [4].

Figure 1 shows two examples of LTL properties expressed as TGBA. The Boolean expression over $AP = \{a, b\}$ that labels each transition represents the valuation of atomic propositions that hold in this transition. A run in these TGBA is accepted if it visits infinitely often all acceptance conditions (represented by colored dots $\circ$ and $\bullet$ on transitions). It is important to note that the LTL formulas labeling each state represent the property accepted starting from this state of the automaton. These labels are generated by our LTL-to-TGBA translator (Spot [12]), they are shown for the reader's convenience but not used for model checking.

Figure 1(a) is a TGBA recognizing the LTL formula $(\mathsf{G}\mathsf{F}a \wedge \mathsf{G}\mathsf{F}b)$, i.e., recognizing the runs where $a$ is true infinitely often and $b$ is true infinitely often. An accepting run in this TGBA has to visit infinitely often the two acceptance conditions indicated by $\circ$ and $\bullet$. Therefore, it must explore infinitely often the transitions where $a$ is true (i.e., transitions labeled by $ab$ or $a\bar{b}$) and infinitely often the transitions where $b$ is true (i.e., transitions labeled by $ab$ or $\bar{a}b$).

Figure 1(b) shows a TGBA derived from the LTL formula $\mathsf{F}\mathsf{G}a$. Any infinite run in this example is accepted if it visits infinitely often the only acceptance condition $\bullet$ on transition $(1, a, 1)$. Therefore, an accepting run in this TGBA must stay on state 1 by executing infinitely $a$.

The product of a TGBA with a Kripke structure is a TGBA whose language is the intersection of both languages.

**Definition 3 (Product using TGBA).** *For a Kripke structure* $\mathcal{K} = \langle S, S_0, \mathcal{R}, l \rangle$ *and a TGBA* $\mathcal{G} = \langle Q, I, \delta, \mathcal{F} \rangle$ *the product* $\mathcal{K} \otimes \mathcal{G}$ *is the TGBA* $\langle S_\otimes, I_\otimes, \delta_\otimes, \mathcal{F} \rangle$ *where*

- $S_\otimes = S \times Q,$
- $I_\otimes = S_0 \times I,$
- $\delta_\otimes = \{((s,q), \ell, F, (s', q')) \mid (s, s') \in \mathcal{R}, (q, \ell, F, q') \in \delta, l(s) = \ell\}$

**Property 1.** *We have* $\mathscr{L}(\mathcal{K} \otimes \mathcal{G}) = \mathscr{L}(\mathcal{K}) \cap \mathscr{L}(\mathcal{G})$ *by construction.*

The goal of the emptiness check algorithm is to determine if the product automaton accepts an execution or not. In other words, it checks if the language of the product automaton is empty or not. Testing the TGBA (representing the product automaton) for emptiness amounts to the search of an accepting cycle that contains at least one occurrence of each acceptance condition. This can be done in different ways: either with a variation of Tarjan or Dijkstra algorithm [3] or using several Nested Depth-First Searches (NDFS) [15]. The product automaton that has to be explored during the emptiness check is generally very large, its size can reach the value obtained by multiplying the the sizes of the model and formula automata, which are synchronized to build this product. Therefore, building the entire product must be avoided. "On-the-fly" emptiness check algorithms allow the product automaton to be constructed lazily during its exploration. These on-the-fly algorithms are more efficient because they stop as soon as they find a counterexample and therefore possibly before building the entire product.

## 3   Transition-Based Generalized Testing Automata (TGTA)

Another kind of ω-automaton called *Testing Automaton (TA)* was introduced by Hansen et al. [8]. Instead of observing the valuations on states or transitions, the TA transitions only record the changes between these valuations. However, TA are less expressive than Büchi automata since they are able to represent only stutter-invariant LTL properties. Also they are often a lot larger than their equivalent Büchi automaton, but their high degree of determinism [8] often leads to a smaller product size [6].

In previous work [1], we evaluate the efficiency of LTL model checking approach using TA. We have shown that TA are better than Büchi automata (BA and TGBA) when the formula to be verified is violated (i.e., a counterexample is found), but this is not the case when the property is verified since the entire product have to be visited twice to check for each acceptance mode of a TA. Then, in order to improve the TA approach, we proposed in [2] a new ω-automata for stutter-invariant properties, called Transition-based Generalized Testing Automata (TGTA) [2], that mixes features from both TA and TGBA.

The basic idea of TGTA is to build an improved form of testing automata with generalized acceptance conditions on transitions, which allows us to modify the automata construction in order to remove the second pass of the emptiness check of the product.

Another advantage of TGTA compared to TA, is that the implementation of TGTA approach does not require a dedicated emptiness check, it reuses the same algorithm used for Büchi automata, and the counterexample constructed by this algorithm is also reported as a counterexample for the TGTA approach.

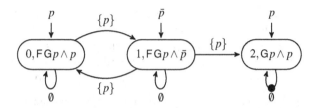

**Fig. 2.** TGTA recognizing the LTL property $\varphi = \mathsf{F}\,\mathsf{G}\,p$ with acceptance conditions $\mathcal{F} = \{\bullet\}$

In [2], we compared the LTL model checking approach using TGTA with the "traditional" approaches using BA, TGBA and TA. The results of these experimental comparisons show that TGTA compete well: the TGTA approach was statistically more efficient than the other evaluated approaches, especially when no counterexample is found (i.e., the property is verified) because it does not require a second pass. Unfortunately, the TGTA constructed in [2] only represent stutter-invariant properties (LTL\X [13]).

This section shows how to adapt the TGTA construction to obtain a TGTA that can represent all LTL properties.

Before presenting this new construction of TGTA, we first recall the definition of this improved variant of testing automata.

While Büchi automata observe the values of the atomic propositions of *AP*, the basic idea of testing automata (TA and TGTA) is to only detect the *changes* in these values; if the values of the atomic propositions do not change between two consecutive valuations of an execution, this transition is called stuttering-transition.

If $A$ and $B$ are two valuations, $A \oplus B$ denotes the symmetric set difference, i.e., the set of atomic propositions that differ (e.g., $\bar{a}b \oplus ab = \{b\}$). Technically, this is implemented with an XOR operation (also denoted by the symbol $\oplus$).

**Definition 4 (TGTA).** *A TGTA over the alphabet* $\Sigma$ *is a tuple* $\mathcal{T} = \langle Q, I, U, \delta, \mathcal{F} \rangle$ *where:*

- *$Q$ is a finite set of states,*
- *$I \subseteq Q$ is a set of initial states,*
- *$U : I \rightarrow 2^{\Sigma}$ is a function mapping each initial state to a set of symbols of $\Sigma$,*
- *$\mathcal{F}$ is a finite set of acceptance conditions,*
- *$\delta \subseteq Q \times \Sigma \times 2^{\mathcal{F}} \times Q$ is the transition relation, where each element $(q, k, F, q')$ represents a transition from state $q$ to state $q'$ labeled by a* changeset $k$ *interpreted as a (possibly empty) set of atomic propositions whose values change between $q$ and $q'$, and the set of acceptance conditions $F \in 2^{\mathcal{F}}$,*

*An infinite word* $\sigma = \ell_0 \ell_1 \ell_2 \ldots \in \Sigma^{\omega}$ *is accepted by* $\mathcal{T}$ *if there exists an infinite run* $r = (q_0, \ell_0 \oplus \ell_1, F_0, q_1)(q_1, \ell_1 \oplus \ell_2, F_1, q_2)(q_2, \ell_2 \oplus \ell_3, F_2, q_3) \ldots \in \delta^{\omega}$ *where:*

- *$q_0 \in I$ with $\ell_0 \in U(q_0)$ (the infinite word is recognized by the run),*
- *$\forall f \in \mathcal{F}, \forall i \in \mathbb{N}, \exists j \geq i, f \in F_j$ (each acceptance condition is visited infinitely often).*

*The language accepted by* $\mathcal{T}$ *is the set* $\mathscr{L}(\mathcal{T}) \subseteq \Sigma^{\omega}$ *of infinite words it accepts.*

Figure 2 shows a TGTA recognizing the LTL formula $\mathsf{F}\,\mathsf{G}\,p$. Acceptance conditions are represented using dots as in TGBAs. Transitions are labeled by changesets: e.g., the transition $(0, \{p\}, 1)$ means that the value of $p$ changes between states 0 and 1. Initial valuations are shown above initial arrows: $U(0) = \{p\}$, $U(1) = \{\bar{p}\}$ and $U(2) = \{p\}$. Any infinite run in this example is accepted if it visits infinitely often, the acceptance transition indicated by the black dot ●: i.e., the stuttering self-loop $(2, \emptyset, ●, 2)$.

As an illustration, the infinite word $\bar{p}; p; p; p; \ldots$ is accepted by the run:

 because the value $p$ only changes between the first two steps. Indeed, a run recognizing such an infinite word must start in state 1 (because only $U(1) = \{\bar{p}\}$), then it changes the value of $p$, so it has to take transitions labeled by $\{p\}$, i.e., $(1, \{p\}, 0)$ or $(1, \{p\}, 2)$. To be accepted, it must move to state 2 (rather than state 0), and finally stay on state 2 by executing infinitely the accepting stuttering self-loop $(2, \emptyset, ●, 2)$.

In the next section, we present in detail the formalization of the different steps used to build a TGTA that represent any LTL property.

## 4   TGTA Construction

Let us now describe how to build a TGTA starting from a TGBA. The TGTA construction is inspired by the one presented in [2], with some changes introduced in the second step of this construction. Indeed, a TGTA is built in two steps as illustrated in Figure 3. The first step transforms a TGBA into an intermediate TGTA by labeling transitions with changesets. Then, the second step builds the final form of TGTA by removing the useless stuttering transitions. In this work, this simplification of stuttering transitions does not require the hypothesis that the LTL property is stutter-invariant (this represents a crucial difference compared to the TGTA construction presented in [2]). For example, Figure 4d shows a TGTA constructed for $\varphi = X p \wedge F G p$ which is not stutter-invariant. In the following, we will detail the successive steps to build this TGTA.

| TGBA | Labeling transitions with "changesets" → | Intermediate TGTA | Elimination of useless stuttering transitions ($\emptyset$) → | TGTA |

**Fig. 3.** The two steps of the construction of a TGTA from a TGBA

### 4.1   First Step: Construction of an Intermediate TGTA from a TGBA

Geldenhuys and Hansen [6] have shown how to convert a Büchi Automaton (BA) into a Testing Automtaton (TA) by first converting the BA into an automaton with valuations on the states (called State-Labeled Büchi Automaton (SLBA)), and then converting this SLBA into an intermediate form of TA by computing the difference between the labels of the source and destination states of each transition.

The first step of the TGTA construction is similar to the first step of the TA construction [6, 2]. We construct an intermediate TGTA from a TGBA by moving labels to states, and labeling each transition by the set difference between the labels of its source and destination states. While doing so, we keep the generalized acceptance conditions on the transitions. The next proposition implements these first steps.

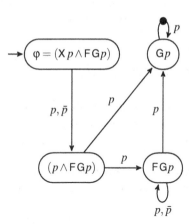

(a) TGBA for $\varphi = Xp \wedge FGp$.

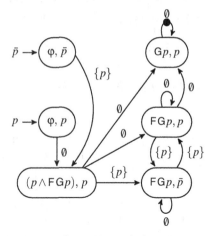

(b) Intermediate TGTA obtained by property 2.

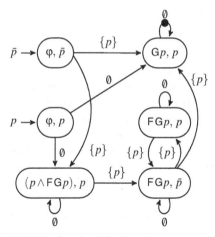

(c) TGTA after simplifications by property 3.

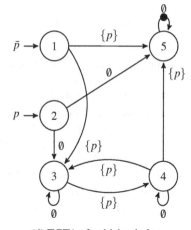

(d) TGTA after bisimulation.

**Fig. 4.** TGTA obtained after various steps while translating the TGBA representing $\varphi = Xp \wedge FGp$, into a TGTA with $\mathcal{F} = \{\bullet\}$

**Property 2 (Converting TGBA into an intermediate TGTA).** *Given any TGBA* $\mathcal{G} = \langle Q_{\mathcal{G}}, I_{\mathcal{G}}, \delta_{\mathcal{G}}, \mathcal{F} \rangle$ *over the alphabet* $\Sigma$*, let us build the TGTA* $\mathcal{T} = \langle Q_{\mathcal{T}}, I_{\mathcal{T}}, U_{\mathcal{T}}, \delta_{\mathcal{T}}, \mathcal{F} \rangle$ *with* $Q_{\mathcal{T}} = Q_{\mathcal{G}} \times \Sigma$, $I_{\mathcal{T}} = I_{\mathcal{G}} \times \Sigma$ *and*
*(i)* $\forall (q, \ell) \in I_{\mathcal{T}}, U_{\mathcal{T}}((q, \ell)) = \{\ell\}$
*(ii)* $\forall (q, \ell) \in Q_{\mathcal{T}}, \forall (q', \ell') \in Q_{\mathcal{T}}, ((q, \ell), \ell \oplus \ell', F, (q', \ell')) \in \delta_{\mathcal{T}} \iff ((q, \ell, F, q') \in \delta_{\mathcal{G}})$
*Then* $\mathscr{L}(\mathcal{G}) = \mathscr{L}(\mathcal{T})$. (The proof of this property. 2 is given in [2].)

An example of an intermediate TGTA is shown on Figure 4b. It is the result of applying the construction of property. 2 to the example of TGBA for $\varphi = X p \wedge F G p$ (shown in Figure 4a). The next property shows how to remove the useless stuttering-transitions (labeled by $\emptyset$) in TGTA.

### 4.2   Second Step: Elimination of Useless Stuttering-Transitions ($\emptyset$)

In the following, we say that a language $\mathscr{L}$ is *stutter-invariant* if the number of the successive repetitions of any letter of a word $\sigma \in \mathscr{L}$ does not affect the membership of $\sigma$ to $\mathscr{L}$ [5]. In other words, $\mathscr{L}$ is stutter-invariant *iff* for any finite sequence $u \in \Sigma^*$, any element $\ell \in \Sigma$, and any infinite sequence $v \in \Sigma^\omega$ we have $u\ell v \in \mathscr{L} \iff u\ell\ell v \in \mathscr{L}$.

We begin by defining the concept of a *language recognized starting from a state* in a TGTA. This definition will be very useful for the formalization of the second step of the TGTA construction presented below.

**Definition 5** ($\mathscr{L}(\mathcal{T}, q)$). *Given a TGTA $\mathcal{T}$ and a state $q$ of $\mathcal{T}$, we say that an infinite word $\sigma = \ell_0 \ell_1 \ell_2 \ldots \in \Sigma^\omega$ is accepted by $\mathcal{T}$ starting from the state $q$ if there exists an infinite run $r = (q, \ell_0 \oplus \ell_1, F_0, q_1)(q_1, \ell_1 \oplus \ell_2, F_1, q_2)(q_2, \ell_2 \oplus \ell_3, F_2, q_3) \ldots \in \delta^\omega$ where: $\forall f \in \mathcal{F}, \forall i \in \mathbb{N}, \exists j \geq i, f \in F_j$ (each acceptance condition is visited infinitely often). The language $\mathscr{L}(\mathcal{T}, q) \subseteq \Sigma^\omega$ is the set of infinite words accepted by $\mathcal{T}$ starting from the state $q$.*

In the following, we will exploit the fact that in a TGTA, the language recognized starting from certain states of a TGTA can be stutter-invariant, although the overall TGTA language (recognized from the initial states) is not stutter-invariant. For example, in the intermediate TGTA shown on Figure 4b, the language recognized starting from the two initial states (labeled by the formula $\varphi = X p \wedge F G p$) is not stutter-invariant. However, the languages recognized starting form the other states (labeled by the formulas $(p \wedge F G p)$, $(F G p)$ and $(G p)$) are stutter-invariants. Indeed, similar to the original TGBA $\mathcal{G}$, in an intermediate TGTA $\mathcal{T}$ obtained by property 2, if the LTL formula labeling a state $q$ is stutter-invariant, then the language recognized starting from this state $q$ is also stutter-invariant (Figure 4b). This can easily be deduced from the proof [2] of property 2.

The next property allow to simplify the intermediate TGTA by removing the useless stuttering transitions and thus obtain the final TGTA. The intuition behind this simplification is illustrated in Figure 5a: In a TGTA $\mathcal{T}$, we have that the language recognized starting from a state $q_0$ is stutter-invariant and $q_0$ can reach an accepting stuttering-cycle by following only stuttering transitions. In the context of TA we would have to declare $q_0$ as being a livelock-accepting state. For TGTA, we replace the accepting stuttering-cycle by adding a self-loop labeled by all acceptance conditions on $q_n$, then the predecessors of $q_0$ are connected to $q_n$ as in Figure 5b. In the last step of the following construction, for each state $q$ such that $\mathscr{L}(\mathcal{T}, q)$ is stutter-invariant, we add a stuttering self-loop to $q$ and we remove all stuttering transitions from $q$ to other states. Figure 4c shows how the automaton from Figure 4b is simplified.

**Property 3 (Elimination of useless stuttering transitions to build a TGTA).** *Given a TGTA $\mathcal{T} = \langle Q, I, U, \delta, \mathcal{F} \rangle$. By combining the first three of the following operations,*

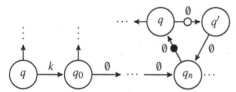 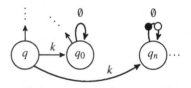

(a) TGTA $\mathcal{T}$ before reduction of stuttering transitions ($\emptyset$). $\mathscr{L}(\mathcal{T},q_0)$ is stutter-invariant.

(b) $\mathcal{T}$ after reduction of stuttering transitions ($\emptyset$).

**Fig. 5.** Elimination of useless stuttering transitions in TGTA

*we can remove the useless stuttering-transitions in this TGTA (Figure 5). The fourth operation can be performed along the way for further (classical) simplifications.*

1. *If $Q \subseteq Q$ is a SCC such that for any state $q \in Q$ we have $\mathscr{L}(\mathcal{T},q)$ is stutter-invariant and any two states $q,q' \in Q$ can be connected using a sequence of stuttering transitions $(q,\emptyset,F_0,r_1)(r_1,\emptyset,F_1,r_2)\cdots(r_n,\emptyset,F_n,q') \in \delta^*$ with $F_0 \cup F_1 \cup \cdots \cup F_n = \mathcal{F}$, then we can add an accepting stuttering self-loop $(q,\emptyset,\mathcal{F},q)$ on each state $q \in Q$. I.e., the TGTA $\mathcal{T}' = \langle Q, I, U, \delta \cup \{(q,\emptyset,\mathcal{F},q) \mid q \in Q\}, \mathcal{F} \rangle$ is such that $\mathscr{L}(\mathcal{T}') = \mathscr{L}(\mathcal{T})$. Let us call such a component $Q$ an **accepting Stuttering-SCC**.*

2. *Let $q_0$ is a state of $\mathcal{T}$ such that $\mathscr{L}(\mathcal{T},q_0)$ is stutter-invariant. If there exists an accepting Stuttering-SCC $Q$ and a sequence of stuttering-transitions:*
   *$(q_0,\emptyset,F_1,q_1)(q_1,\emptyset,F_2,q_2)\cdots(q_{n-1},\emptyset,F_n,q_n) \in \delta^*$ such that $q_n \in Q$ and $q_0, q_1,\ldots q_{n-1} \notin Q$ (as shown in Figure 5a), then:*
   - *For any transition $(q,k,F,q_0) \in \delta$ going to $q_0$ (with $(q,k,F,q_n) \notin \delta$), the TGTA $\mathcal{T}'' = \langle Q, I, U, \delta \cup \{(q,k,F,q_n)\}, \mathcal{F} \rangle$ is such that $\mathscr{L}(\mathcal{T}'') = \mathscr{L}(\mathcal{T})$ (Figure 5b).*
   - *If $q_0 \in I$, the TGTA $\mathcal{T}'' = \langle Q, I \cup \{q_n\}, U'', \delta, \mathcal{F} \rangle$ with $\forall q \neq q_n, U''(q) = U(q)$ and $U''(q_n) = U(q_n) \cup U(q_0)$, is such that $\mathscr{L}(\mathcal{T}'') = \mathscr{L}(\mathcal{T})$.*

3. *Let $\mathcal{T}^\dagger = \langle Q, I^\dagger, U^\dagger, \delta^\dagger, \mathcal{F} \rangle$ be the TGTA obtained after repeating the previous two operations as much as possible (i.e., $\mathcal{T}^\dagger$ contains all the transitions and initial states that can be added by the above two operations. Then, we add a non-accepting stuttering self-loop $(q,\emptyset,\emptyset,q)$ to any state $q$ that did not have an accepting stuttering self-loop and such that $\mathscr{L}(\mathcal{T},q)$ is stutter-invariant. Also we remove all stuttering transitions from $q$ that are not self-loops since stuttering can be captured by self-loops after the previous two operations. After this last reduction of stuttering transitions, we obtain the final TGTA (Figure 4c).*
   *More formally, the TGTA $\mathcal{T}''' = \langle Q, I^\dagger, U^\dagger, \delta''', \mathcal{F} \rangle$ with $\delta''' = \{(q,k,F,q') \in \delta^\dagger \mid \mathscr{L}(\mathcal{T},q)$ is **not stutter-invariant** $\} \cup \{(q,k,F,q') \in \delta^\dagger \mid k \neq \emptyset \vee (q = q' \wedge F = \mathcal{F})\} \cup \{(q,\emptyset,\emptyset,q) \mid \mathscr{L}(\mathcal{T},q)$ is stutter-invariant $\wedge (q,\emptyset,\mathcal{F},q) \notin \delta^\dagger\}$ is such that: $\mathscr{L}(\mathcal{T}''') = \mathscr{L}(\mathcal{T}^\dagger) = \mathscr{L}(\mathcal{T})$.*

4. *Any state from which one cannot reach a Büchi-accepting cycle can be removed from the automaton without changing its language.*

The proof of Property 3 is similar to the proof of the second step of TGTA construction given in [2].

Figure 4c shows how the TGTA from Figure 2 is simplified by the above Property 3.

Similar to the TA construction [2], the resulting TGTA can be further simplified by merging bisimilar states (two states $q$ and $q'$ are bisimilar if the automaton $\mathcal{T}$ can accept the same infinite words starting from either of these states, i.e., $\mathscr{L}(\mathcal{T}, q) = \mathscr{L}(\mathcal{T}, q')$). This optimization can be achieved using any algorithm based on partition refinement, the same as for Büchi automata, taking $\{\mathcal{F} \cap \mathcal{G}, \mathcal{F} \setminus \mathcal{G}, \mathcal{G} \setminus \mathcal{F}, \mathcal{Q} \setminus (\mathcal{F} \cup \mathcal{G})\}$ as initial partition and taking into account the acceptance conditions of the outgoing transitions. The final TGTA obtained after all these steps is shown in Figure 4.

As for the other variants of ω-automata, the automata-theoretic approach using TGTA has two important operations: the construction of a TGTA $\mathcal{T}$ recognizing the negation of the LTL property $\varphi$ and the emptiness check of the product $(\mathcal{K} \otimes \mathcal{T})$ of the Kripke structure $\mathcal{K}$ with $\mathcal{T}$.

**Definition 6 (Product using TGTA).** *For a Kripke structure $\mathcal{K} = \langle S, S_0, \mathcal{R}, l \rangle$ and a TGTA $\mathcal{T} = \langle \mathcal{Q}, I, U, \delta, \mathcal{F} \rangle$, the product $\mathcal{K} \otimes \mathcal{T}$ is a TGTA $\langle S_\otimes, I_\otimes, U_\otimes, \delta_\otimes, \mathcal{F}_\otimes \rangle$ where*
- *$S_\otimes = S \times \mathcal{Q}$,*
- *$I_\otimes = \{(s,q) \in S_0 \times I \mid l(s) \in U(q)\}$,*
- *$\forall (s,q) \in I_\otimes, U_\otimes((s,q)) = \{l(s)\}$,*
- *$\delta_\otimes = \{((s,q), k, F, (s', q')) \mid (s, s') \in \mathcal{R}, (q, k, F, q') \in \delta, k = (l(s) \oplus l(s'))\}$,*
- *$\mathcal{F}_\otimes = \mathcal{F}$.*

**Property 4.** *We have $\mathscr{L}(\mathcal{K} \otimes \mathcal{T}) = \mathscr{L}(\mathcal{K}) \cap \mathscr{L}(\mathcal{T})$ by construction.*

Since a product of a TGTA with a Kripke structure is a TGTA, we only need an emptiness check algorithm for a TGTA automaton. A TGTA can be seen as a TGBA whose transitions are labeled by changesets instead of valuations of atomic propositions. When checking a TGBA for emptiness, we are looking for an accepting cycle that is reachable from an initial state. When checking a TGTA for emptiness, we are looking exactly for the same thing. Therefore, because emptiness check algorithms do not look at transitions labels, the same emptiness check algorithm used for the product using TGBA can also be used for the product using TGTA.

## 5   Experimental Evaluation of TGTA

In order to evaluate the TGTA approach against the TGBA and BA approaches, an experimentation was conducted under the same conditions as our previous work [1], i.e., within the same CheckPN tool on top of Spot [12] and using the same benchmark Inputs (formulas and models) used in the experimental comparison [1] of BA, TGBA and TA. The models are from the Petri net literature [11], we selected two instances of each of the following models: the Flexible Manufacturing System (4/5), the Kanban system (4/5), the Peterson algorithm (4/5), the slotted-ring system (6/5), the dining philosophers (9/10) and the Round-robin mutex (14/15). We also used two models from actual case studies: **PolyORB** [10] and **MAPK** [9]. For each selected model instance, we generated 200 verified formulas (no counterexample in the product) and 200 violated formulas (a counterexample exists): 100 random (length 15) and 100 weak-fairness [1] (length 30) of the two cases of formulas. Since generated formulas are very often trivial to verify (the emptiness check needs to explore only a handful of states), we selected only those formulas requiring more than one second of CPU for the emptiness check in all approaches.

## 5.1  Implementation

Figure 6 shows the building blocks we used to implement the three approaches. The automaton used to represent the property to check has to be synchronized with a Kripke structure representing the model. Depending on the kind of automaton, this synchronous product is implemented differently. The TGBA and BA approaches can share the same product implementation. The TGTA approach require a dedicated product computation. The TGBA, BA, and TGTA approaches share the same emptiness check.

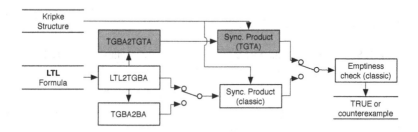

**Fig. 6.** The experiment's architecture in Spot. Three command-line switches control which one of the approaches is used to verify an LTL formula on a Kripke structure. The new components required by the TGTA approach are outlined in Gray.

## 5.2  Results

Figure 7 compares the sizes of the products automata (in terms of number of states) and Figure 8 compares the number of visited transitions when running the emptiness check; plotting TGTA against BA and TGBA. This gives an idea of their relative performance. Indeed, in order to protect the results against the influence of various optimizations, implementation tricks, and the central processor and memory architecture, Geldenhuys and Hansen [6] found that the number of states gives a reliable indication of the memory required, and, similarly, the number of transitions a reliable indication of the time consumption. Each point of the scatter plots corresponds to one of the 5600 evaluated formulas (2800 violated with counterexample as black circles, and 2800 verified having no counterexample as green crosses). Each point below the diagonal is in favor of TGTA while others are in favor of the other approach. Axes are displayed using a logarithmic scale. All these experiments were run on a 64bit Linux system running on an Intel(R) 64-bit Xeon(R) @2.00GHz, with 10GB of RAM.

## 5.3  Discussion

**On verified properties** (green crosses), the results are very straightforward to interpret. On the scatter plots of Figure 7, the cases where the TGTA approach is better than BA and TGBA approaches, appear as green crosses below the diagonal. In these cases,

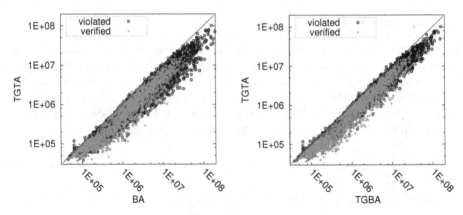

**Fig. 7.** Size of products (number of states) using TGTA against BA and TGBA

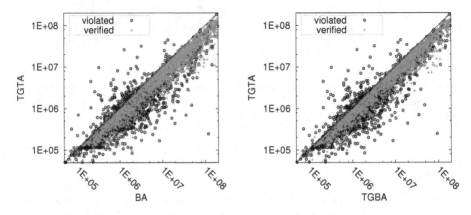

**Fig. 8.** Performance (number of transitions explored by the emptiness check) using TGTA against BA and TGBA

The TGTA approach is a clear improvement because the products automata are smaller using TGTA. The same result is observed for the scatter plots of Figure 8, when looking at the number of transitions explored by the emptiness check, the TGTA approach also outperforms TGBA and BA approaches for verified properties.

**On violated properties** (black circles), for the number of transitions explored by the emptiness check, it is difficult to interpret the scatter plots of Figure 8 because the emptiness check is an on-the-fly algorithm. It stops as soon as it finds a counterexample without exploring the entire product. Thus, for violated properties, the exploration order of non-deterministic transitions of TGBA, BA and TGTA changes the number of transitions explored in the product before a counterexample is found.

However, if we analyze the scatter plots of Figure 7, we observe that the TGTA approach produces the smallest products. This allows the TGTA approach to seek a counterexample in a smaller product and therefore have a better chance to find it faster.

## 6    Conclusion

In previous work [2], we have shown that *Transition-based Generalized Testing Automata* (TGTA) are a way to improve the model checking approach when verifying stutter-invariant properties. In this work, we propose a construction of a TGTA that allow to check any LTL property (stutter-invariant or not). This TGTA is constructed in two steps. The first one builds an intermediate TGTA from a TGBA (*Transition-based Generalized Büchi Automata*). The second step transforms an intermediate TGTA into a TGTA by removing the useless stuttering-transitions that are not self-loops (this reduction does not need the restriction to stutter-invariant properties as in our previous work [2]).

The constructed TGTA combines advantages observed on both Testing Automata (TA) and TGBA:

- From TA, it reuses the labeling of transitions with changesets, and the elimination of the useless stuttering-transitions, but without requiring a second pass in the emptiness check of the product.
- From TGBA, it inherits the use of generalized acceptance conditions on transitions.

TGTA have been implemented in Spot easily, because only two new algorithms are required: the conversion of a TGBA into a TGTA, and a new definition of a product between a TGTA and a Kripke structure.

We have run benchmarks to compare TGTA against BA and TGBA. Experiments reported that TGTA produce the smallest products automata and therefore TGTA outperform BA and TGBA when no counterexample is found in these products (i.e., the property is satisfied), but they are comparable when the property is violated, because in this case the on-the-fly algorithm stops as soon as it finds a counterexample without exploring the entire product.

We conclude that there is nothing to lose by using TGTA to verify any LTL property, since they are always at least as good as BA and TGBA and we believe that TGTA are better thanks to the elimination of the useless stuttering-transitions during the TGTA construction.

As a future work, an idea would be to provide a direct conversion of LTL to TGTA, without the intermediate TGBA step. We believe a tableau construction such as the one of Couvreur [3] could be easily adapted to produce TGTA. Another important optimization is to build on-the-fly the TGTA during the construction of the synchronous product. Especially when the number of atomic propositions (*AP*) is very large, because this may lead to build a TGTA with a large number of unnecessary initial states, that are not synchronized with the initial state(s) of the Kripke structure.

## References

1. Ben Salem, A.E., Duret-Lutz, A., Kordon, F.: Generalized Büchi automata versus testing automata for model checking. In: Proc. of SUMo 2011, vol. 726, pp. 65–79. CEUR (2011)
2. Ben Salem, A.-E., Duret-Lutz, A., Kordon, F.: Model Checking Using Generalized Testing Automata. In: Jensen, K., van der Aalst, W.M., Ajmone Marsan, M., Franceschinis, G., Kleijn, J., Kristensen, L.M. (eds.) ToPNoC VI. LNCS, vol. 7400, pp. 94–122. Springer, Heidelberg (2012)

3. Couvreur, J.-M.: On-the-fly verification of linear temporal logic. In: Wing, J.M., Woodcock, J. (eds.) FM 1999. LNCS, vol. 1708, pp. 253–271. Springer, Heidelberg (1999)

4. Duret-Lutz, A., Poitrenaud, D.: SPOT: an extensible model checking library using transition-based generalized Büchi automata. In: Proc. of MASCOTS 2004, pp. 76–83. IEEE Computer Society Press (2004)

5. Etessami, K.: Stutter-invariant languages, ω-automata, and temporal logic. In: Halbwachs, N., Peled, D.A. (eds.) CAV 1999. LNCS, vol. 1633, pp. 236–248. Springer, Heidelberg (1999)

6. Geldenhuys, J., Hansen, H.: Larger automata and less work for LTL model checking. In: Valmari, A. (ed.) SPIN 2006. LNCS, vol. 3925, pp. 53–70. Springer, Heidelberg (2006)

7. Giannakopoulou, D., Lerda, F.: From states to transitions: Improving translation of LTL formulæ to Büchi automata. In: Peled, D.A., Vardi, M.Y. (eds.) FORTE 2002. LNCS, vol. 2529, pp. 308–326. Springer, Heidelberg (2002)

8. Hansen, H., Penczek, W., Valmari, A.: Stuttering-insensitive automata for on-the-fly detection of livelock properties. In: Proc. of FMICS 2002. ENTCS, vol. 66(2). Elsevier (2002)

9. Heiner, M., Gilbert, D., Donaldson, R.: Petri nets for systems and synthetic biology. In: Bernardo, M., Degano, P., Zavattaro, G. (eds.) SFM 2008. LNCS, vol. 5016, pp. 215–264. Springer, Heidelberg (2008)

10. Hugues, J., Thierry-Mieg, Y., Kordon, F., Pautet, L., Barrir, S., Vergnaud, T.: On the formal verification of middleware behavioral properties. In: Proc. of FMICS 2004. ENTCS, vol. 133, pp. 139–157. Elsevier (2004)

11. Kordon, F., et al.: Report on the model checking contest at petri nets 2011. In: Jensen, K., van der Aalst, W.M., Ajmone Marsan, M., Franceschinis, G., Kleijn, J., Kristensen, L.M. (eds.) ToPNoC VI. LNCS, vol. 7400, pp. 169–196. Springer, Heidelberg (2012)

12. MoVe/LRDE. The Spot home page: http://spot.lip6.fr (2014)

13. Peled, D., Wilke, T.: Stutter-invariant temporal properties are expressible without the next-time operator. Information Processing Letters 63(5), 243–246 (1995)

14. Sebastiani, R., Tonetta, S.: "More deterministic" vs. "Smaller" Büchi automata for efficient LTL model checking. In: Geist, D., Tronci, E. (eds.) CHARME 2003. LNCS, vol. 2860, pp. 126–140. Springer, Heidelberg (2003)

15. Tauriainen, H.: Automata and Linear Temporal Logic: Translation with Transition-based Acceptance. PhD thesis, Helsinki University of Technology, Espoo, Finland (September 2006)

16. Vardi, M.Y.: Automata-theoretic model checking revisited. In: Cook, B., Podelski, A. (eds.) VMCAI 2007. LNCS, vol. 4349, pp. 137–150. Springer, Heidelberg (2007)

# Efficient Verification Techniques

# Simple Isolation for an Actor Abstract Machine

Benoit Claudel[1], Quentin Sabah[2], and Jean-Bernard Stefani[3(✉)]

[1] The MathWorks, Grenoble, France
[2] Mentor Graphics, Grenoble, France
[3] INRIA Grenoble-Rhône-Alpes, Valbonne, France

**Abstract.** The actor model is an old but compelling concurrent programming model in this age of multicore architectures and distributed services. In this paper we study an as yet unexplored region of the actor design space in the context of concurrent object-oriented programming. Specifically, we show that a purely run-time, annotation-free approach to actor state isolation with reference passing of arbitrary object graphs is perfectly viable. In addition, we show, via a formal proof using the Coq proof assistant, that our approach indeed enforces actor isolation.

## 1 Introduction

*Motivations.* The actor model of concurrency [1], where isolated sequential threads of execution communicate via buffered asynchronous message-passing, is an attractive alternative to the model of concurrency adopted e.g. for Java, based on threads communicating via shared memory. The actor model is both more congruent to the constraints of increasingly distributed hardware architectures – be they local as in multicore chips, or global as in the world-wide web –, and more adapted to the construction of long-lived dynamic systems, including dealing with hardware and software faults, or supporting dynamic update and reconfiguration, as illustrated by the Erlang system [2]. Because of this, we have seen in the recent years renewed interest in implementing the actor model, be that at the level of experimental operating systems as in e.g. Singularity [9], or in language libraries as in e.g. Java [24] and Scala [13].

When combining the actor model with an object-oriented programming model, two key questions to consider are the exact semantics of message passing, and its efficient implementation, in particular on multiprocessor architectures with shared physical memory. To be efficient, an implementation of message passing on a shared memory architecture ought to use data transfer by reference, where the only data exchanged is a pointer to the part of the memory that contains the message. However, with data transfer by reference, enforcing the share-nothing semantics of actors becomes problematic: once an arbitrary memory reference is exchanged between sender and receiver, how do you ensure the sender can no longer access the referenced data ? Usual responses to this question, typically involve restricting the shape of messages, and controlling references (usually through a reference uniqueness scheme [19]) by various means, including run-time support, type systems and other static analyses, as in Singularity [9], Kilim [24], Scala actors [14], and SOTER [21].

© IFIP International Federation for Information Processing 2015
S. Graf and M. Viswanathan (Eds.): FORTE 2015, LNCS 9039, pp. 213–227, 2015.
DOI: 10.1007/978-3-319-19195-9_14

*Contributions.* In this paper, we study a point in the actor model design space which, despite its simplicity, has never, to our knowledge, been explored before. It features a very simple programming model that places *no restriction* on the shape and type of messages, and *does not require* special types or annotations for references, yet still enforces the share nothing semantics of the actor model. Specifically, we introduce an actor abstract machine, called Siaam. Siaam is layered on top of a sequential object-oriented abstract machine, has actors running concurrently using a shared heap, and enforces strict actor isolation by means of run-time barriers that prevent an actor from accessing objects that belong to a different actor. The contributions of this paper can be summarized as follows. We formally specify the Siaam model, building on the Jinja specification of a Java-like sequential language [18]. We formally prove, using the Coq proof assistant, the strong isolation property of the Siaam model. We describe our implementation of the Siaam model as a modified Jikes RVM [16]. We present a novel static analysis, based on a combination of points-to, alias and liveness analyses, which is used both for improving the run-time performance of Siaam programs, and for providing useful debugging support for programmers. Finally, we evaluate the performance of our implementation and of our static analysis.

*Outline.* The paper is organized as follows. Section 2 presents the Siaam machine and its formal specification. Section 3 presents the formal proof of its isolation property. Section 4 describes the implementation of the Siaam machine. Section 5 presents the Siaam static analysis. Section 6 presents an evaluation of the Siaam implementation and of the Siaam analysis. Section 7 discusses related work and concludes the paper. Because of space limitations, we present only some highlights of the different developments. Interested readers can find all the details in the second author's PhD thesis [22], which is available online along with the Coq code [25].

## 2    Siaam: Model and Formal Specification

*Informal presentation.* Siaam combines actors and objects in a programming model with a single shared heap. Actors are instances of a special class. Each actor is equipped with at least one mailbox for queued communication with other actors, and has its own logical thread of execution that runs concurrently with other actor threads. Every object in Siaam belongs to an actor, we call its *owner.* An object has a unique owner. Each actor is its own owner. At any point in time the ownership relation forms a partition of the set of objects. A newly created object has its owner set to that of the actor of the creating thread.

Siaam places absolutely *no restriction* on the references between objects, including actors. In particular objects with different owners may reference each other. Siaam also places *no constraint* on what can be exchanged via messages: the contents of a message can be an arbitrary object graph, defined as the graph of objects reachable (following object references in object fields) from a root object specified when sending a message. Message passing in Siaam has a zero-copy semantics, meaning that the object graph of a message is not copied from

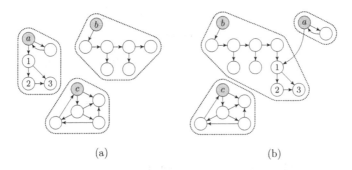

(a)                                              (b)

**Fig. 1.** Ownership and ownership transfer in Siaam

the sender actor to the receiver actor, only the reference to the root object of a message is communicated. An actor is only allowed to send objects it owns[1], and it cannot send itself as part of a message content.

Figure 1 illustrates ownership and ownership transfer in Siaam. On the left side (a) is a configuration of the heap and the ownership relation where each actor, presented in gray, owns the objects that are part of the same dotted convex hull. Directed edges are heap references. On the right side (b), the objects 1, 2, 3 have been transferred from $a$ to $b$, and object 1 has been attached to the data structure maintained in $b$'s local state. The reference from $a$ to 1 has been preserved, but actor $a$ is no longer allowed to access the fields of 1, 2, 3.

To ensure isolation, Siaam enforces the following invariant: an object $o$ (in fact an executing thread) can only access fields of an object that has the same owner than $o$; any attempt to access the fields of an object of a different owner than the caller raises a run-time exception. To enforce this invariant, message exchange in Siaam involves twice changing the owner of all objects in a message contents graph: when a message is enqueued in a receiver mailbox, the owner of objects in the message contents is changed atomically to a null owner ID that is never assigned to any actor ; when the message is dequeued by the receiver actor, the owner of objects in the message contents is changed atomically to the receiver actor. This scheme prevents pathological situations where an object passed in a message $m$ may be sent in another message $m'$ by the receiver actor without the latter having dequeued (and hence actually received) message $m$. Since Siaam does not modify object references in any way, the sender actor can still have references to objects that have been sent, but any attempt from this sender actor to access them will raise an exception.

---

[1] Siaam enforces the constraint that all objects reachable from a message root object have the same owner – the sending actor. If the constraint is not met, sending the message fails. However, this constraint, which makes for a simple design, is just a design option. An alternative would be to consider that a message contents consist of all the objects reachable from the root object which have the sending actor as their owner. This alternate semantics would not change the actual mechanics of the model and the strong isolation enforced by it.

$$\text{READ} \quad \frac{hp\ s\ a = \text{Some}\ (C, fs) \qquad fs(F, D) = \text{Some}\ v}{P, w \vdash \langle a.F\{D\}, s\rangle - \text{OwnerCheck}\ a\ True \rightarrow \langle \text{Val}\ v, s\rangle}$$

$$\text{READX}\ P, w \vdash \langle a.F\{D\}, s\rangle - \text{OwnerCheck}\ a\ False \rightarrow \langle \text{Throw}\ OwnerMismatch, s\rangle$$

$$\text{GLOBAL} \quad \frac{acs\ s\ w = \text{Some}\ x \qquad P, w \vdash \langle x, shp\ s\rangle - wa \rightarrow \langle x', h'\rangle \qquad \text{ok\_act}\ P\ s\ w\ wa}{\text{upd\_act}\ P\ s\ w\ wa = (xs', ws', ms', \_) \qquad s' = (xs'[w \mapsto x'], ws', ms', h')}{P \vdash s \rightarrow s'}$$

**Fig. 2.** Siaam operational semantics: sample rules

*Siaam: model and formal specification.* The formal specification of the Siaam model defines an operational semantics for the Siaam language, in the form of a reduction semantics. The Siaam language is a Java-like language, for its sequential part, extended with special classes with native methods corresponding to operations of the actor model, e.g. sending and receiving messages. The semantics is organized in two layers, the *single-actor* semantics and the *global* semantics. The single-actor semantics deals with evolutions of individual actors, and reduces actor-local state. The global semantics maintains a global state not directly accessible from the single-actor semantics. In particular, the effect of reading or updating object fields by actors belongs to the single-actor semantics, but whether it is allowed is controlled by the global semantics. Communications are handled by the global semantics.

The single actor semantics extends the Jinja formal specification in HOL of the reduction semantics of a (purely sequential) Java-like language [18] [2]. Jinja gives a reduction semantics for its Java-like language via judgments of the form $P \vdash \langle e, (lv, h)\rangle \rightarrow \langle e', (lv', h')\rangle$, which means that in presence of program $P$ (a list of class declarations), expression $e$ with a set of local variables $lv$ and a heap $h$ reduces to expression $e'$ with local variables $lv'$ and heap $h'$.

We extend Jinja judgments for our single-actor semantics to take the form $P, w \vdash \langle e, (lv, h)\rangle - wa \rightarrow \langle e', (lv', h')\rangle$ where $\langle e, lv\rangle$ corresponds to the local actor state, $h$ is the global heap, $w$ is the identifier of the current actor (owner), and $wa$ is the actor action requested by the reduction. Actor actions embody the Siaam model per se. They include creating new objects (with their initial owner), including actors and mailboxes, checking the owner of an object, sending and receiving messages. For instance, succesfully accessing an object field is governed by rule READ in Figure 2. Jinja objects are pairs $(C, fs)$ of the object class name $C$ and the field table $fs$. A field table is a map holding a value for each field of an object, where fields are identified by pairs $(F, D)$ of the field name $F$ and the name $D$ of the declaring class. The premises of rule READ retrieve the object referenced by $a$ from the heap ($hp\ s\ a = \text{Some}\ (C, fs)$ – where $hp$

---

[2] Jinja, as described in [18], only covers a subset of the Java language. It does not have class member qualifiers, interfaces, generics, or concurrency.

is the projection function that retrieves the heap component of a local actor state, and the heap itself is an association table modelled as a function that given an object reference returns an object), and the value $v$ held in field $F$. In the conclusion of rule READ, reading the field $F$ from $a$ returns the value $v$, with the local state $s$ (local variables and heap) unchanged. The actor action OwnerCheck $a$ $True$ indicates that object $a$ has the current actor as its owner. Apart from the addition of the actor action label, rule READ is directly lifted from the small step semantics of Jinja in [18]. In the case of field access, the rule READ is naturally complemented with rule READX, that raises an exception if the owner check fails, and which is specific to Siaam. Actor actions also include a special *silent* action, that corresponds to single-actor reductions (including exception handling) that require no access to the global state. Non silent actor actions are triggered by object creation, object field access, and *native calls*, i.e. method calls on the special actor and mailbox classes.

The global semantics is defined by the rule GLOBAL in Figure 2. The judgment, written $P \vdash s \rightarrow s'$, means in presence of program $P$, global state $s$ reduces to global state $s'$. The global state $(xs, ws, ms, h)$ of a Siaam program execution comprises four components: the actor table $xs$, an ownership relation $ws$, the mailbox table $ms$, and a shared heap $h$. The projection functions $acs$, $ows$, $mbs$, $shp$ return respectively the actor table, the ownerships relation, the mailbox table, and the shared heap component of the global state. The actor table associates an actor identifier to an actor local state consisting of a pair $\langle e, lv \rangle$ of expression and local variables. The rule GLOBAL reduces the global state by applying a single step of the single-actor semantics for actor $w$. In the premises of the rule, the shared heap $shp$ $s$ and the current local state $x$ (expression and local variables) for $w$ are retrieved from the global state. The actor can reduce to $x'$ with new shared heap $h'$ and perform the action $wa$. ok_act tests the actor action precondition against $s$. If it is satisfiable, upd_act applies the effects of $wa$ to the global state, yielding the new tuple of state components $(xs', ws', ms', \_)$ where the heap is left unchanged. The new state $s'$ is assembled from the new mailbox table, the new ownership relation, the new heap from the single actor reduction and the new actor table where the state for actor $w$ is updated with its new local state $x'$. We illustrate the effect of actor actions in the next section.

## 3 Siaam: Proof of Isolation

The key property we expect the Siaam model to uphold is the strong isolation (or share nothing) property of the actor model, meaning actors can only exchange information via message passing. We have formalized this property and proved it using the Coq proof assistant (v8.4) [8]. We present in this section some key elements of the formalization and proof, using excerpts from the Coq code. The formalization uses an abstraction of the operational semantics presented in the previous section. Specifically, we abstract away from the single-actor semantics. The local state of an actor is abstracted as being just a table of local variables (no expression), which may change in obvious ways: adding or removing a local variable, changing the value held by a local variable. The formalization (which we call Abstract Siaam) is thus a generalization of the Siaam operational semantics.

*Abstract Siaam: Types.* The key data structure in Abstract Siaam is the *configuration*, defined as an abstraction of the global state in the previous section. A configuration `conf` is a tuple comprising an actor table, an ownership relation, a mailbox table and a shared heap. In Coq:

```
Record conf : Type := mkcf { acs : actors; ows : owners; mbs : mailboxes; shp : heap }.
```

Actor table, ownership relation, mailbox table and heap are all defined as simple association tables, i.e. lists of pairs $\langle i, d \rangle$ of identifiers $i$ and data $d$:

```
Definition actors := table aid locals.          Definition actor := prod aid locals.
Definition owners := table addr (option aid).    Definition mailboxes := table mid mbox.
Definition heap := table addr object.
```

Identifiers `aid`, `addr`, and `mid` correspond to actor identifiers, object references, and mailbox identifiers, respectively. The data `locals` is a table of local variables (with identifier type `vid`), an actor is just a pair associating an actor identifier with a table of local variables, and a mailbox `mbox` is a list of messages associated with an actor identifier (the actor receiving messages via the mailbox):

```
Definition locals := table vid value.    Definition message := prod msgid addr.
Definition queue := list message.        Record mbox : Type := mkmb { own : aid ; msgs : queue}.
```

A message is just a pair consisting of a message identifier and a reference to a root object. A value can be either the null value (`vnull`), the *mark* value (`vmark`), an integer (`vnat`), a boolean (`vbool`), an object reference, an actor id or a mailbox id. The special *mark* value is simply a distinct value used to formalize the isolation property.

*Abstract Siaam: Transition rules.* Evolution of a Siaam system are modeled in Abstract Siaam as transitions between configurations, which are in turn governed by transition rules. Each transition rule in Abstract Siaam corresponds to an an instance of the GLOBAL rule in the Siaam operational semantics, specialized for dealing with a given actor action. For instance, the rule governing field access, which abstracts the global semantics reduction picking the `OwnerCheck` a *True* action offered by a READ reduction of the single-actor semantics (cf. Figure 2) carrying the identifier of actor $e$, and accessing field $f$ of object $o$ referenced by $a$ is defined as follows:

```
Inductive redfr : conf → aid → conf → Prop :=
| redfr_step : ∀ (c1 c2 : conf)(e : aid)(l1 l2 : locals)(i j : vid)(v w : value)(a: addr)
                 (o : object)(f: fid),
    set_In (e,l1) (acs c1) → set_In (i, w) l1 → set_In (j,vadd a) l1 →
       set_In (a,o) (shp c1) → set_In (f,v) o → set_In (a, Some e) (ows c1) →
         v_compat w v → l2 = up_locals i v l1 →
            c2 = mkcf (up_actors e l2 (acs c1)) (ows c1) (mbs c1) (shp c1) →
               c1 =fr e ⇒ c2
where " t '=fr' a '⇒' t' " := (redfr t a t').
```

The conclusion of the rule, `c1 =fr e ⇒ c2`, states that configuration `c1` can evolve into configuration `c2` by actor `e` doing a field access `fr`. The premises of the rule are the obvious ones: `e` must designate an actor of `c1`; the table `l1` of local variables of actor e must have two local variables i and j, one holding a reference a to the accessed object (set_In (j,vadd a) l1), the other some value w (set_In ( i, w) l1) compatible with that read in the accessed object field (v_compat w v); a must point to an object o in the heap of c1 (set_In (a,o) (shp c1) ), which must have a field f, holding some value v (set_In (f,v) o) ; and actor e must be the owner of object o for the field access to succeed (set_In (a, Some e) (ows c1)). The final configuration c2 has the same ownership relation, mailbox table and shared heap than the initial one c1, but its actor table is updated with new local state of actor e (c2 = mkcf (up_actors e l2 (acs c1)) (ows c1) (mbs c1) (shp c1)), where variable i now holds the read value v (l2 = up_locals i v l1).

Another key instance of the Abstract Siaam transition rules is the rule presiding over message send:

```
Inductive redsnd : conf → aid → conf → Prop :=
| redsnd_step : ∀ (c1 c2 : conf)(e : aid) (a : addr) (l : locals) (ms: msgid)(mi: mid)
               (mb mb': mbox)(owns : owners),
    set_In (e,l) (acs c1) →
    set_In (vadd a) (values_from_locals l) →
    trans_owner_check (shp c1) (ows c1) (Some e) a = true →
    set_In (mi,mb) (mbs c1) →
    not (set_In ms (msgids_from_mbox mb)) →
    Some owns = trans_owner_update (shp c1) (ows c1) None a →
    mb' = mkmb (own mb) ((ms,a)::(msgs mb)) →
    c2 = mkcf (acs c1) owns (up_mboxes mi mb' (mbs c1)) (shp c1) →
    c1 =snd e ⇒ c2
where " t '=snd' a '⇒' t' " := (redsnd t a t').
```

The conclusion of the rule, c1 =snd e ⇒ c2, states that configuration c1 can evolve into configuration c2 by actor e doing a message send snd. The premises of the rule expects the owner of the objects reachable from the root object (referenced by a) of the message to be e; this is checked with function trans_owner_check : trans_owner_check (shp c1) (ows c1) (Some e) a = true. When placing the message in the mailbox mb of the receiver actor, the owner of all the objects reachable is set to None; this is done with function trans_owner_update: Some owns = trans_owner_update (shp c1) (ows c1) None a. Placing the message with id ms and root object referenced by a in the mailbox is just a matter of queuing it in the mailbox message queue: mb' = mkmb (own mb) ((ms,a)::(msgs mb)).

The transition rules of Abstract Siaam also include a rule governing silent transitions, i.e. transitions that abstract from local actor state reductions that elicit *no* change on other elements of a configuration (shared heap, mailboxes, ownership relation, other actors). The latter are just modelled as transitions arbitrarily modifying a given actor local variables, with no acquisition of object references that were previously unknown to the actor.

*Isolation proof.* The Siaam model ensures that the only means of information transfer between actors is message exchange. We can formalize this isolation property using mark values. We call an actor a *clean* if its local variables do not hold a mark, and if all objects *reachable* from a and belonging to a hold no mark in their fields. An object o is reachable from an actor a if a has a local variable holding o's reference, or if, recursively, an object o' is reachable from a which holds o's reference in one of its fields. The isolation property can now be characterized as follows: a clean actor in any configuration remains clean during an evolution of the configuration if it never receives any message. In Coq:

```
Theorem ac_isolation : ∀ (c1 c2 : conf) (a1 a2: actor),
    wf_conf c1 → set_In a1 (acs c1) → ac_clean (shp c1) a1 (ows c1) →
    c1 =@ (fst a1) ⇒* c2 → Some a2 = lookup_actor (acs c2) (fst a1) →
    ac_clean (shp c2) a2 (ows c2).
```

The theorem states that, in any well-formed configuration c1, an actor a1 which is clean (ac_clean (shp c1) a1 (ows c1)), remains clean in any evolution of c1 that does not involve a reception by a1. This is expressed as c1 =@ (fst a1) ⇒* c2 and ac_clean (shp c2) a2 (ows c2), where fst a1 just extracts the identifier of actor a1, and a2 is the descendant of actor a1 in the evolution (it has the same actor identifier than a1: Some a2 = lookup_actor (acs c2) (fst a1)). The relation =@ a ⇒*, which represents evolutions not involving a message receipt by actor a, is defined as the reflexive and transitive closure of relation =@ a ⇒, which is a one step evolution not involving a receipt by a. The isolation theorem is really about transfer of information between actors, the mark denoting a distinguished bit of information held by an actor. At first sight it appears to say nothing about about ownership, but notice that a clean actor $a$ is one such that all objects that belong to $a$ are clean, i.e. hold no mark in their fields. Thus a corollary of the theorem is that, in absence of message receipt, actor $a$ cannot acquire an object from another actor (if that was the case, transferring the ownership of an unclean object would result in actor $a$ becoming unclean).

A well-formed configuration is a configuration where each object in the heap has a single owner, all identifiers are indeed unique, where mailboxes hold messages sent by actors in the actor table, and all objects referenced by actors (directly or indirectly, through references in object fields) belong to the heap. To prove theorem ac_isolation, we first prove that well-formedness is an invariant in any configuration evolution:

```
Theorem red_preserves_wf : ∀ (c1 c2 : conf), c1 ⇒ c2 → wf_conf c1 → wf_conf c2.
```

The theorem red_preserves_wf is proved by induction on the derivation of the assertion c1 ⇒ c2. To prove the different cases, we rely mostly on simple reasoning with sets, and a few lemmas characterizing the correctness of table manipulation functions, of the trans_owner_check function which verifies that all objects reachable from the root object in a message have the same owner, and of the trans_owner_update function which updates the ownership table during message transfers. Using the invariance of well-formedness, theorem ac_isolation is proved by induction on the derivation of the assertion c1 =@ (fst a1) ⇒* c2. To prove the different cases, we rely on several lemmas dealing with reachability and cleanliness.

The last theorem, live_mark, is a liveness property that shows that the isolation property is not vacuously true. It states that marks *can* flow between actors during execution. In Coq:

```
Theorem live_mark : ∃ (c1 c2 : conf)(ac1 ac2 : actor),
    c1 ⇒* c2 ∧ set_In ac1 (acs c1) ∧ ac_clean (shp c1) ac1 (ows c1)
        ∧ Some ac2 = lookup_actor (acs c2) (fst ac1) ∧ ac_mark (shp c2) ac2 (ows c2).
```

# 4   Siaam: Implementation

We have implemented the Siaam abstract machine as a modified Jikes RVM [16]. Specifically, we extended the Jikes RVM bytecode and added a set of core primitives supporting the ownership machinery, which are used to build trusted APIs implementing particular programming models. The Siaam programming model is available as a trusted API that implements the formal specification presented in Section 2. On top of the Siaam programming model, we implemented the ActorFoundry API as described in [17], which we used for some of our evaluation. Finally we implemented a trusted event-based actor programming model on top of the core primitives, which can dispatch thousand of lightweight actors over pools of threads, and enables to build high-level APIs similar to Kilim with Siaam's ownership-based isolation.

**Bytecode.** The standard Java VM instructions are extended to include: a modified object creation instruction `New`, which creates an object on the heap and sets its owner to that of the creating thread; modified field read and write acess instructions `getfield` and `putfield` with owner check; modified instructions load and store array instructions `aload` and `astore` with owner check.

**Virtual Machine Core.** Each heap object and each thread of execution have an owner reference, which points to an object implementing the special `Owner` interface. A thread can only access objects belonging to the `Owner` instance referenced by its owner reference. Core primitives include operations to retrieve and set the owner of the current thread, to retrieve the owner of an object, to withdraw and acquire ownership over objects reachable from a given root object. In the Jikes RVM, objects are represented in memory by a sequence of bytes organized into a leading header section and the trailing scalar object's fields or array's length and elements. We extended the object header with two reference-sized words, `OWNER` and `LINK`. The `OWNER` word stores a reference to the object owner, whereas the `LINK` word is introduced to optimize the performance of object graph traversal operations.

**Contexts.** Since the JikesRVM is fully written in Java, threads seamlessly execute application bytecode and the virtual machine internal bytecode. We have introduced a notion of execution context in the VM to avoid subjecting VM bytecode to the owner-checking mechanisms. A method in the *application context* is instrumented with all the isolation mechanisms whereas methods in the *VM context* are not. If a method can be in both context, it must be compiled in two versions, one for both contexts. When a method is invoked, the context of the caller is used to deduce which version of the method should be called. The decision is taken statically when the invoke instruction is compiled.

**Owernship Transfer.** Central to the performance of the Siaam virtual machine are operations implementing ownership transfer, `withdraw` and `acquire`. In the formal specification, owner-checking an object graph and updating the owner of objects in the graph is done atomically (see e.g. the message send transition rule in Section 3). However implementing the `withdraw` operation as an atomic operation would be costly. Furthermore, an implementation of ownership transfer

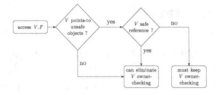

**Fig. 3.** Owner-check elimination decision diagram

must minimize graph traversals. We have implemented an iterative algorithm for `withdraw` that chains objects that are part of a message through their `LINK` word. The list thus obtained is maintained as long as the message exists so that the `acquire` operation can efficiently traverse the objects of the message. The algorithm leverages specialized techniques, initially introduced in the Jikes RVM to optimize the reference scanning phase during garbage collection [10], to efficiently enumerate the reference offsets for a given base object.

## 5   Siaam: Static Analysis

We describe in this section some elements of Siaam static analysis to optimize away owner-checking on field read and write instructions. The analysis is based on the observation that an instruction accessing an object's field does not need an owner-checking if the object accessed belongs to the executing actor. Any object that has been allocated or received by an actor and has not been passed to another actor ever since, belongs to that actor. The algorithm returns an under-approximation of the owner-checking removal opportunities in the analyzed program.

Considering a point in the program, we say an object (or a reference to an object) is *safe* when it always belongs to the actor executing that point, regardless of the execution history. By opposition, we say an object is *unsafe* when sometimes it doesn't belong to the current actor. We extend the denomination to instructions that would respectively access a safe object or an unsafe object. A safe instruction will never throw an `OwnerException`, whereas an unsafe instruction might.

**Analysis.** The Siaam analysis is structured in two phases. First the safe dynamic references analysis employs a local must-alias analysis to propagate owner-checked references along the control-flow edges. It is optionally refined with an inter-procedural pass propagating safe references through method arguments and returned values. Then the safe objects analysis tracks safe runtime objects along call-graph and method control-flow edges by combining an inter-procedural points-to analysis and an intra-procedural live variable analysis. Both phases depend on the transfered abstract objects analysis that propagates unsafe abstract objects from the communication sites downward the call graph edges.

By combining results from the two phases, the algorithm computes conservative approximations of unsafe runtime objects and safe variables at any control-flow point in the program. The owner-check elimination for a given instruction $s$ accessing the reference in variable $V$ proceeds as illustrated in Figure 3. First the unsafe objects analysis is queried to know whether $V$ may points-to an unsafe runtime object at $s$. If not, the instruction can skip the owner-check for $V$. Otherwise, the safe reference analysis is consulted to know whether the reference in variable $V$ is considered safe at $s$, thanks to dominant owner-checks of the reference in the control-flow graph.

The Siaam analysis makes use of several standard intra and inter-prodedural program analyses: a call-graph representation, an inter-procedural points-to analysis, an intra-procedural liveness analysis, and an intra-procedural must-alias analysis. Each of these analyses exists in many different variants offering various tradeoffs of results accuracy and algorithmic complexity, but regardless of the implementation, they provide a rather standard querying interface. Our analysis is implemented as a framework that can make use of different instances of these analyses.

**Implementations.** The intra-procedural safe reference analysis which is part of the Siaam analysis has been included in the Jikes RVM optimizing compiler. Despite its relative simplicity and its very conservative assumptions, it efficiently eliminates about half of the owner-check barriers introduced by application bytecode and the standard library for the benchmarks we have tested (see Section 6). The safe reference analysis and the safe object analyses from the Siaam analysis have been implemented in their inter-procedural versions as an offline tool written in Java. The tool interfaces with the Soot analysis framework [23], that provides the program representation, the call graph, the inter-procedural pointer analysis, the must-alias analysis and the liveness analysis we use.

**Programming Assistant.** The Siaam programming model is quite simple, requiring no programmer annotation, and placing no constraint on messages. However, it may generate hard to understand runtime exceptions due to failed owner-checks. The Siaam analysis is therefore used as the basis of a programming assistant that helps application developers understand why a given program statement is potentially unsafe and may throw an owernship exception at runtime. The Siaam analysis guarantees that there will be no false negative, but to limit the amount of false positives it is necessary to use a combination of the most accurate standard (points-to, must-alias and liveness) analyses. The programming assistant tracks a program $P$ backward, starting from an unsafe statement $s$ with a non-empty set of unverified ownerhip preconditions (as given by the ok_act function in Section 2), trying to find every program points that may explain why a given precondition is not met at $s$. For each unsatisfied precondition, the assistant can exhibit the shortest execution paths that result in an exception being raised at $s$. An ownership precondition may comprise requirements that a variable or an object be safe. When a requirement is not satisfied before $s$, it raises one or several questions of the form "why is $x$ unsafe before $s$?". The assistant traverses the control-flow backward, looks for immediate answers at each statement reached, and propagates the questions further if necessary, until all questions have found an answer.

# 6   Evaluation

**Siaam Implementation.** We present first an evaluation of the overall performance of our Siaam implementation based on the DaCapo benchmark suite [3], representative of various real industrial workloads. These applications use regular Java. The bytecode is instrumented with Siaam's owner-checks and all threads share the same owner. With this benchmark we measure the overhead of the dynamic ownership machinery, encompassing the object owner initialization and the owner-checking barriers, plus the allocation and collection costs linked to the object header modifications.

We benchmarked five configurations. `no siaam` is the reference Jikes RVM without modifications. `opt` designates the modified Jikes RVM with JIT owner-checks elimination. `noopt` designates the modified Jikes RVM without JIT owner-checks elimination. `sopt` is the same as `opt` but the application bytecode has safety annotations issued by the offline Siaam static analysis tool. Finally `soptnc` is the same as `sopt` without owner-check barriers for the standard library bytecode. We executed the 2010-MR2 version of the DaCapo benchamrks, with two workloads, the `default` and the `large`. Table 1 shows the results for the Dacapo 2010-MR2 runs. The results were obtained using a machine equipped with an Intel Xeon W3520 2.67Ghz processor. The execution time results are normalized with respect to the `no-siaam` configuration for each program of the suite: *lower is better*. The geometric mean summarizes the typical overhead for each configuration. The `opt` figures in Table 1 show that the modified virtual machine including JIT barrier elimination has an overhead of about 30% compared to the not-isolated reference. The JIT elimination improves the performances by about 20% compared to the `noopt` configuration. When the bytecode is annotated by the whole-program static analysis the performance is 10% to 20% better than with the runtime-only optimization. However, the DaCapo benchmarks use the Java reflection API to load classes and invoke methods, meaning our static analysis was not able to process all the bytecode with the best precision. We can expect better results with other programs for which the call graph can be entirely built with precision. Moreover we used for the benchmarks a context-insensitive, flow-insensitive pointer analysis, meaning the Siaam analysis could be even more accurate with sensitive standard analyses. Finally the standard library bytecode is not annotated by our tool, it is only treated by the JIT elimination optimization. The `soptnc` configuration provides a good indication of what the full optimization would yield. The results show an overhead (w.r.t. application) with a mean of 15%, which can be considered as an acceptable price to pay for the simplicity of developing isolated programs with Siaam.

The Siaam virtual machine consumes more heap space than the unmodified Jikes RVM due to the duplication of the standard library used by both the virtual machine and the application, and because of the two words we add in every object's header. The average object size in the DaCapo benchmarks is 62 bytes, so our implementations increases it by 13%. We have measured a 13% increase in the full garbage collection time, which accounts for the tracing of the two additional references and the memory compaction.

**Table 1.** DaCapo benchmarks

| Benchmark | opt | noopt | sopt | soptnc | opt | noopt | sopt | soptnc |
|---|---|---|---|---|---|---|---|---|
| workload | | *default* | | | | *large* | | |
| antlr | 1.20 | 1.32 | 1.09 | 1.11 | 1.21 | 1.33 | 1.11 | 1.10 |
| bloat | 1.24 | 1.41 | 1.17 | 1.05 | 1.40 | 1.59 | 1.14 | 0.96 |
| hsqldb | 1.24 | 1.36 | 1.09 | 1.06 | 1.45 | 1.60 | 1.29 | 1.10 |
| jython | 1.52 | 1.73 | 1.41 | 1.24 | 1.45 | 1.70 | 1.45 | 1.15 |
| luindex | 1.25 | 1.46 | 1.09 | 1.05 | 1.25 | 1.43 | 1.09 | 1.03 |
| lusearch | 1.31 | 1.45 | 1.17 | 1.18 | 1.33 | 1.49 | 1.21 | 1.21 |
| pmd | 1.32 | 1.37 | 1.29 | 1.24 | 1.34 | 1.44 | 1.39 | 1.30 |
| xalan | 1.24 | 1.39 | 1.33 | 1.35 | 1.29 | 1.41 | 1.38 | 1.40 |
| *geometric mean* | 1.28 | 1.43 | 1.20 | 1.16 | 1.34 | 1.50 | 1.25 | 1.15 |

**Table 2.** ActorFoundry analyses

| | Ownercheck | | | Message Passing | | | Time | ratio to Ideal | |
|---|---|---|---|---|---|---|---|---|---|
| | | Ideal | Siaam | | Ideal | Siaam | | | |
| | Sites | safe | safe | Sites | safe | safe | (sec) | Siaam | SOTER |
| ActorFoundry | | | | | | | | | |
| threadring | 24 | 24 | 24 | 8 | 8 | 8 | 0.1 | 100% | 100% |
| [1] concurrent | 99 | 99 | 99 | 15 | 12 | 10 | 0.1 | 98% | 58% |
| [2] copymessages | 89 | 89 | 84 | 22 | 20 | 15 | 0.1 | 91% | 56% |
| performance | 54 | 54 | 54 | 14 | 14 | 14 | 0.2 | 100% | 86% |
| pingpong | 28 | 28 | 28 | 13 | 13 | 13 | 0.1 | 100% | 89% |
| refmessages | 4 | 4 | 4 | 6 | 6 | 6 | 0.1 | 100% | 67% |
| Benchmarks | | | | | | | | | |
| chameneos | 75 | 75 | 75 | 10 | 10 | 10 | 0.1 | 100% | 33% |
| fibonacci | 46 | 46 | 46 | 13 | 13 | 13 | 0.2 | 100% | 86% |
| leader | 50 | 50 | 50 | 10 | 10 | 10 | 0.1 | 100% | 17% |
| philosophers | 35 | 35 | 35 | 10 | 10 | 10 | 0.2 | 100% | 100% |
| pi | 31 | 31 | 31 | 8 | 8 | 8 | 0.1 | 100% | 67% |
| shortestpath | 147 | 147 | 147 | 34 | 34 | 34 | 1.2 | 100% | 88% |
| Synthetic | | | | | | | | | |
| quicksortCopy | 24 | 24 | 24 | 8 | 8 | 8 | 0.2 | 100% | 100% |
| [3] quicksortCopy2 | 56 | 56 | 51 | 10 | 10 | 5 | 0.1 | 85% | 75% |
| Real world | | | | | | | | | |
| clownfish | 245 | 245 | 245 | 102 | 102 | 102 | 2.2 | 100% | 68% |
| [4] rainbow_fish | 143 | 143 | 143 | 83 | 82 | 82 | 0.2 | 99% | 99% |
| swordfish | 181 | 181 | 181 | 136 | 136 | 136 | 1.7 | 100% | 97% |

**Siaam Analysis.** We compare the efficiency of the Siaam whole-program analysis to the SOTER algorithm, which is closest to ours. Table 2 contains the results that we obtained for the benchmarks reported in [21], that use Actor-Foundry programs. For each analyzed application we give the total number of owner-checking barriers and the total number of message passing sites in the bytecode. The columns "Ideal safe" show the expected number of safe sites for each criteria. The column " Siaam safe" gives the result obtained with the Siaam analysis. The analysis execution time is given in the third main colum. The last column compares the result ratio to ideal for both SOTER and Siaam. Our analysis outperforms SOTER significantly. SOTER relies on an inter-procedural live-analysis and a points-to analysis to infer message passing sites where a by-reference semantics can applies safely. Given an argument $a_i$ of a message passing site $s$ in the program, SOTER computes the set of objects passed by $a_i$ and the set of objects transitively reachable from the variables live after $s$. If the inter-section of these two sets is empty, SOTER marks $a_i$ as eligible for by-reference argument passing, otherwise it must use the default by-value semantic. The weakness to this pessimistic approach is that among the live objects, a significant part won't actually be accessed in the control-flow after $s$. On the other hand, Siaam do care about objects being actually accessed, which is a stronger evidence criterion to incriminate message passing sites. Although Siaam's algorithm wasn't designed to optimize-out by-value message passing, it is perfectly adapted for that task. For each unsafe instruction detected by the algorithm, there is one or several guilty dominating message passing sites. Our diagnosis algorithm tracks back the application control-flow from the unsafe instruction to the incriminated message passing sites. These sites represent a subset of the sites where SOTER cannot optimize-out by-value argument passing.

# 7    Related Work and Conclusion

Enforcing isolation between different groups of objects, programs or threads in presence of a shared memory has been much studied in the past two decades. Although we cannot give here a full survey of the state of the art (a more in depth analysis is available in [22]), we can point out three different kinds of related works: those relying on type annotations to ensure isolation, those relying on run-time mechanisms, and those relying on static analyses.

Much work has been done on controlling aliasing and encapsulation in object-oriented languages and systems, in a concurrent context or not. Much of the works in these areas rely on some sort of reference uniqueness, that eliminates object sharing by making sure that there is only one reference to an object at any time, e.g. [5,14,15,19,20]. All these systems restrict the shape of object graphs or the use of references in some way. In contrast, Siaam makes no such restriction. A number of systems rely on run-time mechanisms for achieving isolation, most using either deep-copy or special message heaps for communication, e.g. [7,9,11,12]. Of these, O-Kilim [12], which builds directly on the PhD work of the first author of this paper [6], is the closest to Siaam: it places no constraint on transferred object graphs, but at the expense of a complex programming model and no programmer support, in contrast to Siaam. Finally several works develop static analyses for efficient concurrency or ownership transfer, e.g. [4,21,24]. Kilim [24] relies in addition on type annotations to ensure tree-shaped messages. The SOTER [21] analysis is closest to the Siaam analysis and has been discussed in the previous section.

With its annotation-free programming model, which places no restriction on object references and message shape, we believe Siaam to be really unique compared to other approaches in the literature. In addition, we have not found an equivalent of the formal proof of isolation we have conducted for Siaam. Our evaluations demonstrate that the Siaam approach to isolation is perfectly viable: it suffers only from a limited overhead in performance and memory consumption, and our static analysis can significantly improve the situation. The one drawback of our programming model, raising possibly hard to understand runtime exceptions, is greatly alleviated by the use of the Siaam analysis in a programming assistant.

# References

1. Agha, G.A.: Actors: A Model of Concurrent Computation in Distributed Systems. The MIT Press (1986)
2. Armstrong, J.: Erlang. Commun. ACM 53(9) (2010)
3. Blackburn, S.M., Garner, R., Hoffman, C., et al.: The DaCapo benchmarks: Java benchmarking development and analysis. In: OOPSLA 2006. ACM (2006)
4. Carlsson, R., Sagonas, K.F., Wilhelmsson, J.: Message analysis for concurrent programs using message passing. ACM Trans. Program. Lang. Syst. 28(4) (2006)
5. Clarke, D., Wrigstad, T.: External uniqueness is unique enough. In: Cardelli, L. (ed.) ECOOP 2003. LNCS, vol. 2743, pp. 176–200. Springer, Heidelberg (2003)
6. Claudel, B.: Mécanismes logiciels de protection mémoire. PhD thesis, Université de Grenoble (2009)
7. Czajkowski, G., Daynès, L.: Multitasking without compromise: A virtual machine evolution. In: OOPSLA 2001. ACM (2001)
8. Coq development team, http://coq.inria.fr
9. Fahndrich, M., Aiken, M., et al.: Language Support for Fast and Reliable Message-based Communication in Singularity OS. In: 1st EuroSys Conference. ACM (2006)
10. Garner, R.J., Blackburn, S.M., Frampton, D.: A comprehensive evaluation of object scanning techniques. In: 10th ISMM. ACM (2011)
11. Geoffray, N., Thomas, G., Muller, G., et al.: I-JVM: a java virtual machine for component isolation in osgi. In: DSN 2009. IEEE (2009)
12. Gruber, O., Boyer, F.: Ownership-based isolation for concurrent actors on multi-core machines. In: Castagna, G. (ed.) ECOOP 2013. LNCS, vol. 7920, pp. 281–301. Springer, Heidelberg (2013)
13. Haller, P., Odersky, M.: Actors that unify threads and events. In: Murphy, A.L., Vitek, J. (eds.) COORDINATION 2007. LNCS, vol. 4467, pp. 171–190. Springer, Heidelberg (2007)
14. Haller, P., Odersky, M.: Capabilities for uniqueness and borrowing. In: D'Hondt, T. (ed.) ECOOP 2010. LNCS, vol. 6183, pp. 354–378. Springer, Heidelberg (2010)
15. Hogg, J.: Islands: aliasing protection in object-oriented languages. SIGPLAN Not. 26(11) (1991)
16. http://jikesrvm.org
17. Karmani, R.K., Shali, A., Agha, G.: Actor frameworks for the JVM platform: a comparative analysis. In: 7th PPPJ. ACM (2009)
18. Klein, G., Nipkow, T.: A machine-checked model for a java-like language, virtual machine, and compiler. ACM Trans. Program. Lang. Syst. 28(4) (2006)
19. Minsky, N.H.: Towards alias-free pointers. In: Cointe, P. (ed.) ECOOP 1996. LNCS, vol. 1098, pp. 189–209. Springer, Heidelberg (1996)
20. Müller, P., Rudich, A.: Ownership transfer in universe types. SIGPLAN Not. 42(10) (2007)
21. Negara, S., Karmani, R.K., Agha, G.A.: Inferring ownership transfer for efficient message passing. In: 16th PPOPP. ACM (2011)
22. Sabah, Q.: SIAAM: Simple Isolation for an Abstract Actor Machine. PhD thesis, Université de Grenoble (December 2013)
23. http://sable.github.io/soot/
24. Srinivasan, S., Mycroft, A.: Kilim: Isolation-Typed Actors for Java. In: Vitek, J. (ed.) ECOOP 2008. LNCS, vol. 5142, pp. 104–128. Springer, Heidelberg (2008)
25. https://team.inria.fr/spades/siaam/

# Sliced Path Prefixes:
# An Effective Method to Enable
# Refinement Selection

Dirk Beyer, Stefan Löwe[(✉)], and Philipp Wendler

University of Passau, Passau, Germany
loewe@fim.uni-passau.de

**Abstract.** Automatic software verification relies on constructing, for a given program, an abstract model that is (1) abstract enough to avoid state-space explosion and (2) precise enough to reason about the specification. Counterexample-guided abstraction refinement is a standard technique that suggests to extract information from infeasible error paths, in order to refine the abstract model if it is too imprecise. Existing approaches —including our previous work— do not choose the refinement for a given path systematically. We present a method that generates alternative refinements and allows to systematically choose a suited one. The method takes as input one given infeasible error path and applies a slicing technique to obtain a set of new error paths that are more abstract than the original error path but still infeasible, each for a different reason. The (more abstract) constraints of the new paths can be passed to a standard refinement procedure, in order to obtain a set of possible refinements, one for each new path. Our technique is completely independent from the abstract domain that is used in the program analysis, and does not rely on a certain proof technique, such as SMT solving. We implemented the new algorithm in the verification framework CPACHECKER and made our extension publicly available. The experimental evaluation of our technique indicates that there is a wide range of possibilities on how to refine the abstract model for a given error path, and we demonstrate that the choice of which refinement to apply to the abstract model has a significant impact on the verification effectiveness and efficiency.

## 1 Introduction

In the field of automatic software verification, abstraction is a well-understood and widely-used technique, enabling the successful verification of real-world, industrial programs (cf. [4, 13, 14]). Abstraction makes it possible to omit certain aspects of the concrete semantics that are not necessary to prove or disprove the program's correctness. This may lead to a massive reduction of a program's state space, such that verification becomes feasible within reasonable time and resource limits. For example, SLAM [5] uses predicate abstraction [18] for creating an abstract model of the software. One of the current research

---

A preliminary version of this article appeared as technical report [12].

© IFIP International Federation for Information Processing 2015
S. Graf and M. Viswanathan (Eds.): FORTE 2015, LNCS 9039, pp. 228–243, 2015.
DOI: 10.1007/978-3-319-19195-9_15

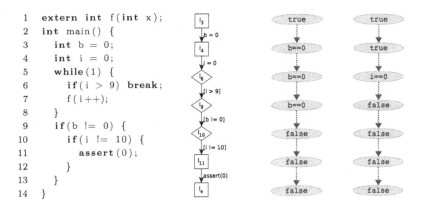

```
1    extern int f(int x);
2    int main() {
3        int b = 0;
4        int i = 0;
5        while(1) {
6            if(i > 9) break;
7            f(i++);
8        }
9        if(b != 0) {
10           if(i != 10) {
11               assert(0);
12           }
13       }
14   }
```

**Fig. 1.** From left to right, the input program, an infeasible error path, and a "good" and a "bad" interpolant sequence for the infeasible error path

directions is to invent techniques to automatically find suitable abstractions. An ideal model is abstract enough to avoid state-space explosion and still contains enough detail to verify the property. Counterexample-guided abstraction refinement (CEGAR) [15] is an automatic technique that starts with a coarse abstraction and iteratively refines an abstract model using *infeasible* error paths. If the analysis does not find an error path in the abstract model, the analysis terminates with the result TRUE. If the analysis finds an error path, the path is checked for feasibility. If this error path is feasible according to the concrete program semantics, then it represents a bug, and the analysis terminates with the result FALSE. However, if the error path is infeasible, then the abstract model was too coarse. In this case, the infeasible error path can be passed to an interpolation engine, which identifies information that is needed to refine the current abstraction, such that the same infeasible error path is excluded in the next CEGAR iterations. CEGAR is successfully used, for example, by the tools SLAM [5], BLAST [7], CPACHECKER [10], and UFO [1].

Craig interpolation [16] is a technique that yields for two contradicting formulas an interpolant formula that contains less information than the first formula, but is still expressive enough to contradict the second formula. In software verification, interpolation was first used for the domain of predicate abstraction [19], and later for value-analysis domains [11]. Independent of the analysis domain, interpolants for path constraints of infeasible error paths can be used to refine abstract models and to eliminate the infeasible error paths in subsequent CEGAR iterations. In this context, it is important to point out that the choice of interpolants is crucial for the performance of the analysis. Figure 1 gives an example: In this program, the analysis will typically find the shown error path, which is infeasible for two different reasons: both the value of i and the value of b can be used to find a contradiction. In general, it is now beneficial for the verifier to track the value of the boolean variable b, and not to track the value of the loop-counter variable i, because the latter has many more possible values, and tracking it would usually lead to an expensive unrolling of the loop. Instead, if only variable b is tracked, the verifier can conclude the safety of the program without unrolling the loop. Thus, we would like to use for refinement the interpolant sequence shown on the left (with only the boolean variable) and not the right one (with the loop-counter variable). However, interpolation engines typically do not allow to guide the interpolation process towards "good", or away from "bad", interpolant sequences. The interpolation engines inherently cannot do a better job here: they do not have access to information such as whether a specific variable is a loop counter and should be avoided in the interpolant. Instead, which interpolant is returned depends solely on the internal algorithms of the interpolation engine. This is especially true if the model checker uses an off-the-shelf interpolation engine, which normally cannot be controlled on such a fine-grained level. In this case, the model checker is stuck to what the interpolation engine returns, be it good or bad for the verification process.

Therefore, we present an approach that allows to *guide* the interpolation engine to produce different interpolants, without changing the interpolation engine. To achieve this, we extract from one infeasible error path a set of infeasible sliced paths, each infeasible for a different reason. Each of these sliced paths can be used for interpolation, yielding different interpolant sequences that are all expressive enough to eliminate the original infeasible error path. Our approach fits well into CEGAR (with or without lazy abstraction [20]), because only the refinement component needs customization, and the new approach remains compatible with off-the-shelf interpolation engines.

**Contributions.** We make the following key contributions: (1) we introduce a domain- and analysis-independent method to extract a set of infeasible sliced paths from infeasible error paths, (2) we prove that interpolants for such a sliced path are also interpolants for the original infeasible error path, (3) we explain that —and how— it is possible to obtain, given a set of infeasible sliced paths, different precisions (interpolants) for the same infeasible error path, and that the choice of the precision makes a significant difference for CEGAR, (4) we implement the presented concepts in the open-source framework for software verification CPACHECKER, and (5) we show experimentally that the novel approach to obtain different precisions significantly impacts the effectiveness and efficiency.

While we use interpolation to compute the refined precisions, our method is not bound to interpolation: invariant-generation techniques for refinement such as *path invariants* [8] can equally benefit from the new possibility of choice.

**Related Work.** The desire to control which interpolants an interpolation engine produces, and trying to make the verification process more efficient by finding good interpolants, is not new. Our goal is to contribute a technique that is independent from the abstract domain that a program analysis uses, and independent from specific properties of interpolation engines.

The first work in this direction suggested to control the *interpolant strength* [17] such that the user can choose between strong and weak interpolants. This approach is unfortunately not implemented in standard interpolation engines. The technique of interpolation abstractions [22], a generalization of term abstraction [2], can be used to guide solvers to pick good interpolants. This is achieved by extending the concrete interpolation problem by so called templates (e.g., terms, formulas, uninterpreted functions with free variables) to obtain a more abstract interpolation problem. An interpolant for the abstract interpolation problem is also a solution to the concrete interpolation problem. Suitable interpolants can be chosen using a cost function, because these interpolation abstractions form a lattice. In contrast to interpolation abstractions, our approach does not rely on SMT solving and is independent from the interpolation engine and abstract domain, so it is also applicable to, e.g., value and octagon domains.

Path slicing [21] is a technique that was introduced to reduce the burden of the interpolation engine: Before the constraints of the path are given to the interpolation engine, the constraints are weakened by removing facts that are not important for the infeasibility of the error path, i.e., a more abstract error path is constructed. We also make the error path more abstract, but in different directions to obtain different interpolant sequences, from which we can choose one that yields a suitable abstract model. While path slicing is interested in reducing the run time of the *interpolation engine* (by omitting some facts), we are interested in reducing the run time of the *verification engine* (by spending more time on interpolation and selection but creating a better abstract model).

## 2   Background

Our approach is based on several existing concepts, and in this section we remind the reader of some basic definitions and our previous work in this field [11].

**Programs, Control-Flow Automata, States, Paths, Precisions.** We restrict the presentation to a simple imperative programming language, where all operations are either assignments or assume operations, and all variables range over integers.[1] A program is represented by a control-flow automaton (CFA). A CFA $A = (L, l_0, G)$ consists of a set $L$ of program locations, which model the program counter, an initial program location $l_0 \in L$, which models the program entry, and a set $G \subseteq L \times Ops \times L$ of control-flow edges, which model the operations that are executed when control flows from one program location to the next. The set of program variables that occur in operations from $Ops$ is denoted by $X$. A *verification problem* $P = (A, l_e)$ consists of a CFA $A$, representing the program, and a target program location $l_e \in L$, which represents the specification, i.e., "the program must not reach location $l_e$".

A *concrete data state* of a program is a variable assignment $cd : X \to \mathbb{Z}$, which assigns to each program variable an integer value; the set of integer values is denoted as $\mathbb{Z}$. A *concrete state* of a program is a pair $(l, cd)$, where $l \in L$ is a program location and $cd$ is a concrete data state. The set of all concrete states of a program is denoted by $\mathcal{C}$, a subset $r \subseteq \mathcal{C}$ is called *region*. Each edge $g \in G$ defines a labeled transition relation $\overset{g}{\to} \subseteq \mathcal{C} \times \{g\} \times \mathcal{C}$. The complete transition

---

[1] Our implementation is based on CPACHECKER, which operates on C programs; non-recursive function calls are supported.

relation $\rightarrow$ is the union over all control-flow edges: $\rightarrow = \bigcup_{g \in G} \xrightarrow{g}$. We write $c \xrightarrow{g} c'$ if $(c, g, c') \in \rightarrow$, and $c \rightarrow c'$ if there exists a $g$ with $c \xrightarrow{g} c'$.

An *abstract data state* represents a region of concrete data states, formally defined as abstract variable assignment. An *abstract variable assignment* is either a partial function $v : X \rightharpoonup \mathbb{Z}$ mapping variables in its definition range to integer values, or $\bot$, which represents no variable assignment (i.e., no value is possible, similar to the predicate *false* in logic). The special abstract variable assignment $\top = \{\}$ does not map any variable to a value and is used as initial abstract variable assignment in a program analysis. Variables that do not occur in the definition range of an abstract variable assignment are either omitted by purpose for abstraction in the analysis, or the analysis is not able to determine a concrete value (e.g., resulting from an uninitialized variable declaration or from an external function call). For two partial functions $f$ and $f'$, we write $f(x) = y$ for the predicate $(x, y) \in f$, and $f(x) = f'(x)$ for the predicate $\exists c : (f(x) = c) \wedge (f'(x) = c)$. We denote the *definition range* for a partial function $f$ as $\mathrm{def}(f) = \{x \mid \exists y : f(x) = y\}$, and the *restriction* of a partial function $f$ to a new definition range $Y$ as $f_{|Y} = f \cap (Y \times \mathbb{Z})$. An abstract variable assignment $v$ represents the set $\llbracket v \rrbracket$ of all concrete data states $cd$ for which $v$ is valid, formally: $\llbracket \bot \rrbracket = \{\}$ and for all $v \neq \bot$, $\llbracket v \rrbracket = \{cd \mid \forall x \in \mathrm{def}(v) : v(x) = cd(x)\}$. The abstract variable assignment $\bot$ is called *contradicting*. The *implication* for abstract variable assignments is defined as follows: $v$ implies $v'$ (written $v \Rightarrow v'$) if $v = \bot$, or for all variables $x \in \mathrm{def}(v')$ we have $v(x) = v'(x)$. The *conjunction* for abstract variable assignments $v$ and $v'$ is defined as:

$$v \wedge v' = \begin{cases} \bot & \text{if } v = \bot \text{ or } v' = \bot \text{ or } (\exists x \in \mathrm{def}(v) \cap \mathrm{def}(v') : \neg\, v(x) = v'(x)) \\ v \cup v' & \text{otherwise} \end{cases}$$

The *semantics of an operation* $op \in Ops$ is defined by the strongest-post operator $\mathsf{SP}_{op}(\cdot)$: given an abstract variable assignment $v$, $\mathsf{SP}_{op}(v)$ represents the set of concrete data states that are reachable from the concrete data states in the set $\llbracket v \rrbracket$ by executing $op$. Formally, given an abstract variable assignment $v$ and an assignment operation $x := exp$, we have $\mathsf{SP}_{x:=exp}(v) = \bot$ if $v = \bot$, or $\mathsf{SP}_{x:=exp}(v) = v_{|X \setminus \{x\}} \wedge v_x$ with

$$v_x = \begin{cases} \{(x, c)\} & \text{if } c \in \mathbb{Z} \text{ is the result of the arith. evaluation of expression } exp_{/v} \\ \{\} & \text{otherwise (if } exp_{/v} \text{ cannot be evaluated)} \end{cases}$$

where $exp_{/v}$ denotes the interpretation of expression $exp$ for the abstract variable assignment $v$. Given an abstract variable assignment $v$ and an assume operation $[p]$, we have $\mathsf{SP}_{[p]}(v) = \bot$ if $v = \bot$ or the predicate $p_{/v}$ is unsatisfiable, or we have $\mathsf{SP}_{[p]}(v) = v \wedge v_p$, with $v_p = \{(x, c) \in (X \setminus \mathrm{def}(v) \times \mathbb{Z}) \mid p_{/v} \Rightarrow (x = c)\}$ and $p_{/v} = p \wedge \bigwedge_{y \in \mathrm{def}(v)} y = v(y)$.

A *path* $\sigma$ is a sequence $\langle (op_1, l_1), \ldots, (op_n, l_n) \rangle$ of pairs of an operation and a location. The path $\sigma$ is called *program path* if for every $i$ with $1 \leq i \leq n$ there exists a CFA edge $g = (l_{i-1}, op_i, l_i)$ and $l_0$ is the initial program location, i.e., the path $\sigma$ represents a syntactic walk through the CFA. The result of appending the pair $(op_n, l_n)$ to a path $\sigma = \langle (op_1, l_1), \ldots, (op_m, l_m) \rangle$ is defined as $\sigma \wedge (op_n, l_n) = \langle (op_1, l_1), \ldots, (op_m, l_m), (op_n, l_n) \rangle$.

Every path $\sigma = \langle (op_1, l_1), \ldots, (op_n, l_n) \rangle$ defines a *constraint sequence* $\gamma_\sigma = \langle op_1, \ldots, op_n \rangle$. The *conjunction* $\gamma \wedge \gamma'$ of two constraint sequences $\gamma = \langle op_1, \ldots, op_n \rangle$ and $\gamma' = \langle op'_1, \ldots, op'_m \rangle$ is defined as their concatenation, i.e., $\gamma \wedge \gamma' = \langle op_1, \ldots, op_n, op'_1, \ldots, op'_m \rangle$, the *implication* of $\gamma$ and $\gamma'$ (denoted by $\gamma \Rightarrow \gamma'$) as the implication of their strongest-post assignments $\mathsf{SP}_\gamma(\top) \Rightarrow \mathsf{SP}_{\gamma'}(\top)$, and $\gamma$ is *contradicting* if $\mathsf{SP}_\gamma(\top) = \bot$. The *semantics of a path* $\sigma = \langle (op_1, l_1), \ldots, (op_n, l_n) \rangle$ is defined as the successive application of the strongest-post operator to each operation of the corresponding constraint sequence $\gamma_\sigma$: $\mathsf{SP}_{\gamma_\sigma}(v) = \mathsf{SP}_{op_n}(\ldots \mathsf{SP}_{op_1}(v) \ldots)$. The set of concrete program states that result from running a program path $\sigma$ is represented by the pair $(l_n, \mathsf{SP}_{\gamma_\sigma}(\top))$, where $\top$ is the initial abstract variable assignment. A path $\sigma$ is *feasible* if $\mathsf{SP}_{\gamma_\sigma}(\top)$ is not contradicting, i.e., $\mathsf{SP}_{\gamma_\sigma}(\top) \neq \bot$. A concrete state $(l_n, cd_n)$ is *reachable*, denoted by $(l_n, cd_n) \in Reach$, if there exists a feasible program path $\sigma = \langle (op_1, l_1), \ldots, (op_n, l_n) \rangle$ with $cd_n \in [\![\mathsf{SP}_{\gamma_\sigma}(\top)]\!]$. A location $l$ is reachable if there exists a concrete data state $cd$ such that $(l, cd)$ is reachable. A program is *safe* (the specification is satisfied) if $l_e$ is not reachable. A program path $\sigma = \langle (op_1, l_1), \ldots, (op_n, l_e) \rangle$, which ends in $l_e$, is called *error path*.

The *precision* is a function $\pi : L \to 2^\Pi$, where $\Pi$ depends on the abstract domain that is used by the analysis. It assigns to each program location some analysis-dependent information that defines the level of abstraction of the analysis. For example, if using predicate abstraction, the set $\Pi$ is a set of predicates over program variables. If using a value domain, the set $\Pi$ is the set $X$ of program variables, and a precision defines which program variables should be tracked by the analysis at which program location.

**Counterexample-Guided Abstraction Refinement (CEGAR).** CEGAR, a technique for automatic iterative refinement of an abstract model [15], is based on three concepts: (1) a *precision*, which determines the current level of abstraction, (2) a *feasibility check*, which decides if an error path (counterexample) is feasible, and (3) a *refinement* procedure, which takes as input an infeasible error path and extracts a precision to refine the abstract model such that the infeasible error path is eliminated from further exploration. Algorithm 1 shows an instantiation of the CEGAR algorithm. It uses the CPA algorithm [9, 11] for program analysis with dynamic precision adjustment and an abstract domain that is formalized as a configurable program analysis (CPA) with dynamic precision adjustment $\mathbb{D}$. The CPA uses a set $E$ of abstract states and a set $L \to 2^\Pi$ of precisions. The analysis algorithm computes the sets reached and waitlist, which represent the current reachable abstract states with precisions and the frontier, respectively. The analysis algorithm is run first with $\pi_0$ as coarse initial precision (usually $\pi_0(l) = \{\}$ for all $l \in L$). If all program states have been exhaustively checked, indicated by an empty waitlist, and no error was reached then the CEGAR algorithm terminates and reports TRUE (program is safe). If the CPA algorithm finds an error in the abstract state space, then it stops and returns the yet incomplete sets reached and waitlist. Now the corresponding abstract error path is extracted from the set reached, using the procedure ExtractErrorPath, and passed to the procedure IsFeasible for the *feasibility check*.

---

**Algorithm 1** CEGAR($\mathbb{D}, e_0, \pi_0$), cf. [11]

---

**Input:** a CPA with dynamic precision adjustment $\mathbb{D}$ and
    an initial abstract state $e_0 \in E$ with precision $\pi_0 \in (L \to 2^\Pi)$
**Output:** verification result TRUE (property holds) or FALSE
**Variables:** a set reached of elements of $E \times (L \to 2^\Pi)$,
    a set waitlist of elements of $E \times (L \to 2^\Pi)$, and
    an error path $\sigma = \langle (op_1, l_1), \ldots, (op_n, l_n) \rangle$
1:   reached := $\{(e_0, \pi_0)\}$; waitlist := $\{(e_0, \pi_0)\}$; $\pi := \pi_0$
2:   **while** *true* **do**
3:      (reached, waitlist) := CPA($\mathbb{D}$, reached, waitlist)
4:      **if** waitlist = $\{\}$ **then**
5:          **return** TRUE
6:      **else**
7:          $\sigma :=$ ExtractErrorPath(reached)
8:          **if** IsFeasible($\sigma$) **then**    // error path is feasible: report bug
9:              **return** FALSE
10:      **else**    // error path is infeasible: refine and restart
11:          $\pi(l) := \pi(l) \cup$ Refine($\sigma$)($l$), for all program locations $l$
12:          reached := $\{(e_0, \pi)\}$; waitlist := $\{(e_0, \pi)\}$

---

**Algorithm 2** Refine($\sigma$)

---

**Input:** an infeasible error path $\sigma = \langle (op_1, l_1), \ldots, (op_n, l_n) \rangle$
**Output:** a precision $\pi \in L \to 2^\Pi$
**Variables:** a constraint sequence $\Gamma$
1:   $\Gamma := \langle \rangle$
2:   $\pi(l) := \{\}$, for all program locations $l$
3:   **for** $i := 1$ to $n - 1$ **do**
4:      $\gamma^+ := \langle op_{i+1}, \ldots, op_n \rangle$
5:      $\Gamma :=$ Interpolate($\Gamma \wedge \langle op_i \rangle, \gamma^+$)    // inductive interpolation
6:      $\pi(l_i) :=$ ExtractPrecision($\Gamma$)    // create precision based on $\Gamma$
7:   **return** $\pi$

---

If the abstract error path is feasible, meaning there exists a corresponding concrete error path, then this error path represents a violation of the specification and the algorithm terminates, reporting FALSE. If the error path is infeasible, i.e., is not corresponding to a concrete program path, then the precision was too coarse and needs to be refined. The *refinement* step is performed by procedure Refine (cf. Alg. 2) which returns a precision $\pi$ that makes the analysis strong enough to exclude the infeasible error path from future state-space explorations. This returned precision is used to extend the current precision of the CPA algorithm, which is started in CEGAR's next iteration and re-computes the sets reached and waitlist based on the new, refined precision. CEGAR is often used with lazy abstraction [20] so that after refining, instead of the whole state space, only some parts of reached and waitlist are removed, and re-explored with the new precision.

**Interpolation for Constraint Sequences.** An *interpolant* for two constraint sequences $\gamma^-$ and $\gamma^+$, such that $\gamma^- \wedge \gamma^+$ is contradicting, is a constraint sequence $\Gamma$ for which 1) the implication $\gamma^- \Rightarrow \Gamma$ holds, 2) the conjunction $\Gamma \wedge \gamma^+$ is contradicting, and 3) the interpolant $\Gamma$ contains in its constraints only variables that occur in both $\gamma^-$ and $\gamma^+$ [11].

Next, we introduce our novel approach, which extracts from one infeasible error path a set of infeasible sliced path prefixes. Sect. 4 then uses this method to extend the procedure Refine to perform precision extraction on a set of infeasible sliced prefixes, offering to select the most suitable precision from several choices.

## 3   Sliced Prefixes

**Infeasible Sliced Prefixes.** A CEGAR-based analysis encounters an infeasible error path if the precision is too coarse. An infeasible error path contains at least one assume operation for which the reachability algorithm computes a non-contradicting *abstract* successor based on the current precision, but computes a contradicting successor if the *concrete* semantics of the program is used. Every infeasible error path contains at least one such contradicting assume operation, but often, there exist several independently contradicting assume operations in an infeasible error path, which leads to the notion of infeasible sliced prefixes: A path $\phi = \langle (op_1, l_1), \ldots, (op_w, l_w) \rangle$ is a *sliced prefix* for a program path $\sigma = \langle (op_1, l_1), \ldots, (op_n, l_n) \rangle$ if $w \le n$ and for all $1 \le i \le w$, we have $\phi.l_i = \sigma.l_i$ and $(\phi.op_i = \sigma.op_i$ or $(\phi.op_i = [true]$ and $\sigma.op_i$ is assume op$))$, i.e., a sliced prefix results from a program path by omitting pairs of operations and locations from the end, and possibly replacing some assume operations by no-op operations. If a sliced prefix for $\sigma$ is infeasible, then $\sigma$ is infeasible.

**Extracting Infeasible Sliced Prefixes from an Infeasible Error Path.** Algorithm 3 extracts from an infeasible error path a set of infeasible sliced prefixes. The algorithm iterates through the given infeasible error path $\sigma$. It keeps incrementing a feasible sliced prefix $\sigma_f$ that contains all operations from $\sigma$ that were seen so far, except contradicting assume operations, which were replaced by no-op operations. Thus, $\sigma_f$ is always feasible. For every element $(op, l)$ from the original path $\sigma$ (iterating in order from the first to the last pair), it is checked

---

**Algorithm 3** ExtractSlicedPrefixes($\sigma$)

---

**Input:** an infeasible path $\sigma = \langle (op_1, l_1), \ldots, (op_n, l_n) \rangle$
**Output:** a non-empty set $\Sigma = \{\sigma_1, \ldots, \sigma_n\}$ of infeasible sliced prefixes of $\sigma$
**Variables:** a path $\sigma_f$ that is always feasible
1: $\Sigma := \{\}$
2: $\sigma_f := \langle \rangle$
3: **for each** $(op, l) \in \sigma$ **do**
4:     **if** $\mathsf{SP}_{\sigma_f \wedge (op, l)}(\top) = \bot$ **then**
5:         // add $\sigma_f \wedge (op, l)$ to the set of infeasible sliced prefixes
6:         $\Sigma := \Sigma \cup \{\sigma_f \wedge (op, l)\}$
7:         $\sigma_f := \sigma_f \wedge ([true], l)$     // append no-op
8:     **else**
9:         $\sigma_f := \sigma_f \wedge (op, l)$     // append original pair
10: **return** $\Sigma$

---

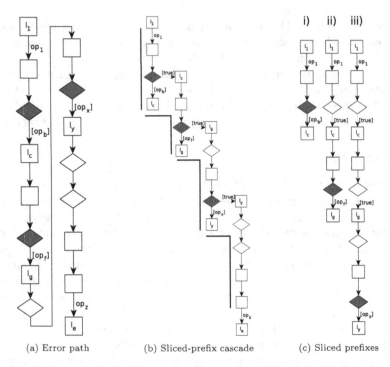

(a) Error path          (b) Sliced-prefix cascade          (c) Sliced prefixes

**Fig. 2.** From one infeasible error path to a set of infeasible sliced prefixes

whether it contradicts $\sigma_f$, which is the case if the result of the strongest-post operator for the path $\sigma_f \wedge (op, l)$ is contradicting (denoted by $\bot$). If so, the algorithm has found a new infeasible sliced prefix, which is collected in the set $\Sigma$ of infeasible sliced prefixes. The feasible sliced prefix $\sigma_f$ is extended either by a no-op operation (Line 7) or by the current operation (Line 9). When the algorithm terminates, which is guaranteed because $\sigma$ is finite, the set $\Sigma$ contains infeasible sliced prefixes of $\sigma$, one for each 'reason' of infeasibility. There is always at least one infeasible sliced prefix because $\sigma$ is infeasible.

The sliced prefixes that Alg. 3 returns have some interesting characteristics: (1) Each sliced prefix $\phi$ starts with the initial operation $op_1$, and ends with an assume operation that contradicts the previous operations of $\phi$, i.e., $\mathsf{SP}_\phi(\top) = \bot$. (2) The $i$-th sliced prefix, excluding its (final and only) contradicting assume operation and location, is a prefix of the $(i + 1)$-st sliced prefix. (3) All sliced prefixes differ from a prefix of the original infeasible error path $\sigma$ only in their no-op operations.

The visualizations in Fig. 2 capture the details of this process. Figure 2a shows the original error path. Nodes represent program locations and edges represent operations between these locations (assignments to variables or assume operations over variables, the latter denoted with brackets). To allow easier distinction, program locations that are followed by assume operations are drawn as diamonds, while other program locations are drawn as squares. Program locations before contradicting assume operations are drawn with a filled background.

The sequence of operations ends in the error state, denoted by $l_e$. Figure 2b depicts the cascade-like sliced prefixes that the algorithm encounters during its progress. Figure 2c shows the three infeasible sliced prefixes that Alg. 3 returns for this example.

The refinement procedure can now use any of these infeasible sliced prefixes to create interpolation problems, and is not bound to a single, specific interpolant sequence for the original infeasible error path: a refinement selection from different precisions is now possible. The following proposition states that this is a valid refinement process.

***Proposition.*** Let $\sigma$ be an infeasible error path and $\phi$ be the $i$-th infeasible sliced prefix for $\sigma$ that is extracted by Alg. 3, then all interpolant sequences for $\phi$ are also interpolant sequences for $\sigma$.

***Proof.*** Let $\sigma = \langle (op_1, l_1), \ldots, (op_n, l_n) \rangle$ and $\phi = \langle (op_1, l_1), \ldots, (op_w, l_w) \rangle$. Let $\Gamma_{\phi^j}$ be the $j$-th interpolant of an interpolant sequence for $\phi$, i.e., for the two constraint sequences $\gamma_{\phi^j}^- = \langle op_1, \ldots, op_j \rangle$ and $\gamma_{\phi^j}^+ = \langle op_{j+1}, \ldots, op_w \rangle$, with $1 \leq j < w$. Because $\phi$ is infeasible, the two constraint sequences $\gamma_{\phi^j}^-$ and $\gamma_{\phi^j}^+$ are contradicting, and therefore, $\Gamma_{\phi^j}$ exists [11]. The interpolant $\Gamma_{\phi^j}$ is also an interpolant for $\gamma_{\sigma^j}^- = \langle op_1, \ldots, op_j \rangle$ and $\gamma_{\sigma^j}^+ = \langle op_{j+1}, \ldots, op_n \rangle$, if (1) the implication $\gamma_{\sigma^j}^- \Rightarrow \Gamma_{\phi^j}$ holds, (2) the conjunction $\Gamma_{\phi^j} \wedge \gamma_{\sigma^j}^+$ is contradicting, and (3) the interpolant $\Gamma_{\phi^j}$ contains only variables that occur in both $\gamma_{\sigma^j}^-$ and $\gamma_{\sigma^j}^+$. Consider that $\gamma_{\phi^j}^-$ was created from $\gamma_{\sigma^j}^-$ by replacing some assume operations by no-op operations, and that $\gamma_{\phi^j}^+$ was created from $\gamma_{\sigma^j}^+$ by replacing some assume operations by no-op operations and by removing the operations $\langle op_{w+1}, \ldots, op_n \rangle$ at the end. Thus, both $\gamma_{\phi^j}^-$ and $\gamma_{\phi^j}^+$ do not contain any additional constraints (except for no-op operations) than $\gamma_{\sigma^j}^-$ and $\gamma_{\sigma^j}^+$, respectively.

Because $\Gamma_{\phi^j}$ is an interpolant for $\gamma_{\phi^j}^-$ and $\gamma_{\phi^j}^+$, we know that $\gamma_{\phi^j}^- \Rightarrow \Gamma_{\phi^j}$ holds, and because $\gamma_{\sigma^j}^-$ can only be stronger than $\gamma_{\phi^j}^-$, Claim (1) follows. The conjunction $\Gamma_{\phi^j} \wedge \gamma_{\phi^j}^+$ is contradicting, and $\gamma_{\sigma^j}^+$ can only be stronger than $\gamma_{\phi^j}^+$. Thus, Claim (2) holds. Because $\Gamma_{\phi^j}$ references only variables that occur in both $\gamma_{\phi^j}^-$ and $\gamma_{\phi^j}^+$, which do not contain more variables than $\gamma_{\sigma^j}^-$ and $\gamma_{\sigma^j}^+$, resp., Claim (3) holds.

## 4    Slice-Based Refinement Selection

Extracting good precisions from the infeasible error paths is key to the CEGAR technique, and the choice of interpolants influences the quality of the precision, and thus, the effectiveness of the analysis algorithm. By using the results introduced in the previous section, the refinement procedure can now be improved by selecting a precision that is derived via interpolation from a selected infeasible sliced prefix.

*Slice-based refinement selection* extracts from a given infeasible error path not only one single interpolation problem for obtaining a refined precision, but a set of (more abstract) infeasible sliced prefixes and thus, a set of interpolation problems, from which a refined precision can be extracted. The interpolation

---

**Algorithm 4** Refine$^+(\sigma)$

---

**Input:** an infeasible error path $\sigma = \langle (op_1, l_1), \ldots, (op_n, l_n) \rangle$
**Output:** a precision $\pi \in L \rightarrow 2^\Pi$
**Variables:** a constraint sequence $\Gamma$,
    a set $\Sigma$ of infeasible sliced prefixes of $\sigma$,
    a mapping $\tau$ from infeasible sliced prefixes and program locations to precisions
1: $\Sigma :=$ ExtractSlicedPrefixes$(\sigma)$
2: // compute precisions for each infeasible sliced prefix
3: **for each** $\phi_j \in \Sigma$ **do**
4:    $\tau(\phi_j) :=$ Refine$(\phi_j)$   // Alg. 2
5: // select suitable sliced prefix (based on the sliced prefixes and their precisions)
6: $\phi_{selected} :=$ SelectSlicedPrefix$(\tau)$
7: // return precision for CEGAR based on selected sliced prefix
8: **return** $\tau(\phi_{selected})$

---

problems for the extracted paths can be given, one by one, to the interpolation engine, in order to derive interpolants for each sliced prefix individually. Hence, the abstraction refinement of the analysis is no longer dependent on what the interpolation engine produces, but instead it is free to choose from a set of interpolant sequences the one that it finds most suitable. The move from solving a single interpolation problem to solving multiple interpolation problems, and understanding refinement selection as an optimization problem, is a key insight of our novel approach.

Algorithm 4 shows the algorithm for slice-based refinement selection, which is an extension of Alg. 2 in the CEGAR algorithm, allowing *to choose a suitable precision* during the refinement step. First, this algorithm calls ExtractSlicedPrefixes to extract a set of infeasible sliced prefixes. Second, it computes precisions for the sliced prefixes and stores them in the mapping $\tau$. Third, one sliced prefix is chosen by a heuristic (in function SelectSlicedPrefix), and fourth, the precision of the chosen sliced prefix is selected for refinement of the abstract model. The heuristic can decide based on the information contained in the sliced prefixes as well as in the precisions, e.g., which variables are referenced.

**Refinement-Selection Heuristics.** We regard the problem of finding and selecting a preferable refinement as an independent direction for further research, and here, we restrict ourselves to presenting some ideas for a few refinement-selection heuristics. There are two obvious options for refinement selection that are independent of the actual interpolants. Using the interpolant sequence derived from the very first, i.e., the shortest, infeasible prefix may rule out many similar infeasible error paths. The downside of this choice is that the analysis may have to track information rather early, possibly blowing up the state-space and making the analysis less efficient. The other straight-forward option (similar to counterexample minimization [2]) is to use the longest infeasible sliced prefix (containing the last contradicting assume operation) for computing an interpolant sequence. This may lead to a precision that is local to the error location and does not require refining large parts of the state space at the beginning of the error path. However, it may also lead to a larger number of refinements if many error paths with a common prefix exist. A more advanced strategy is to analyze the domain types [3] of the variables that are referenced in the extracted precision. Each precision can be assigned a score that depends on the domain types of the variables in the precision such that the score of the infeasible sliced prefix is better if its extracted precision references only 'easy' types of variables, e.g., boolean variables, and no integer variables or even loop counters. This allows to focus on variables that are inexpensive to analyze, avoiding loop unrolling where possible, and keeping the size of the abstract state space as small as possible.

As future work, we plan to systematically investigate many different refinement heuristics; such heuristics can be integrated without changing the overall algorithm, by replacing only the function SelectSlicedPrefix in Alg. 4 accordingly.

## 5  Experiments

We implemented our approach in the open-source verification framework CPACHECKER [10], which is available online [2] under the Apache 2.0 license. CPACHECKER already provides several abstract domains that can be used for program analysis with CEGAR. We only extended the refinement process to work according to Alg. 4 (Refine$^+$), and did neither change the abstract domains nor the interpolation engines. Our implementation is available in the source-code repository of CPACHECKER. The tool, the benchmark programs, the configuration files, and the complete results are available on the supplementary web page [3].

**Setup.** For benchmarking, we used machines with two Intel Xeon E5-2650v2 eight-core CPUs with 2.6 GHz and 135 GB of memory. We limited each verification run to two CPU cores, 15 min of CPU time, and 15 GB of memory. We measured CPU time and report it rounded to two significant digits. BENCHEXEC [4] was used as benchmarking framework to ensure precise and reproducible results.

**Configurations.** Out of the several abstract domains that are supported by CPACHECKER, we choose the value analysis with refinement [11] for our experiments. We use CPACHECKER, tag `cpachecker-1.4.2-slicedPathPrefixes`.

In order to evaluate the potential of our approach, we compare four different heuristics for refinement selection (function SelectSlicedPrefix in Alg. 4): (1) shortest sliced prefix, (2) longest sliced prefix, (3) sliced prefix with best domain-type score, and (4) sliced prefix with worst domain-type score. The domain-type score of a sliced prefix is computed based on the domain types [3] of the variables that occur in the precisions, i.e., variables with a boolean character are preferred over loop counters and other integer variables.

**Benchmarks.** To present a thorough evaluation of our approach, we need a large number of verification tasks, and thus, we use the repository of SV-COMP [6] as a source of verification tasks. We select all verification tasks that fulfill the following characteristics, which are necessary for a valid evaluation of our approach: (1) the verification tasks relate to reachability properties, because the

---

[2]  http://cpachecker.sosy-lab.org/

[3]  http://www.sosy-lab.org/~dbeyer/cpa-ref-sel/

[4]  https://github.com/dbeyer/benchexec

**Table 1.** Number of solved verification tasks for different heuristics for slice-based refinement selection on different subsets of benchmarks

| Heuristic | | Sliced-Prefix Length | | Score | | Oracle | | |
|---|---|---|---|---|---|---|---|---|
| | # Tasks | Shortest | Longest | Best | Worst | Best | Worst | Diff |
| DeviceDrivers64 | 619 | 326 | 395 | 399 | 319 | 403 | 315 | 88 |
| ECA | 1 140 | 489 | 512 | 570 | 478 | 611 | 410 | 201 |
| ProductLines | 597 | 456 | 361 | 402 | 360 | 463 | 353 | 110 |
| Sequentialized | 234 | 29 | 22 | 30 | 27 | 30 | 19 | 11 |
| All Tasks | 2 696 | 1 369 | 1 359 | 1 470 | 1 252 | 1 577 | 1 165 | 412 |

analysis that we use does not support other properties; (2) the reachability property of the verification tasks does not rely on concurrency, recursion, dynamic data structures or pointers, because the analysis that we use does not support these features; and (3) there is at least one refinement during the analysis with more than one infeasible sliced prefix, i.e., in at least one refinement iteration, a refinement selection is possible. More restrictions are not necessary because our goal is to show that there *exists* a significant difference in effectiveness and efficiency, depending on the choice of which sliced prefix is used for precision refinement. The scope of our experiments is not to evaluate *which* refinement selection is the best. The set of all verification tasks in our experiments contains a total of 2 696 verification tasks.

**Results.** Table 1 shows the number of verification tasks that the analysis could solve using refinement selection with one of the four heuristics described above. We also show hypothetical results of a fictional heuristic "Oracle", which, for a given program, always selects the best (or the worst) of the four basic heuristics. In other words, the column "Oracle Best" shows how many tasks could be solved by at least one of the heuristics, and the column "Oracle Worst" shows how many tasks could be solved by all of the heuristics. The difference between these numbers (column "Diff") gives an approximation of the potential of our approach and provides evidence how important refinement selection is. We list the results for the full set of 2 696 verification tasks as well as for several subsets (categories of SV-COMP'15). We consider these categories to be especially interesting because they contain larger programs than the remaining categories and our approach focuses on improving refinements in large programs (with long and complex error paths, and many contradicting assume operations per error path).

The results show that selecting the right refinement can have a significant impact on the effectiveness of an analysis. In our benchmark set there are more than 400 verification tasks for which the choice of the refinement-selection heuristic makes the difference between being able to solve the task and running into a timeout. Without our refinement-selection approach, the choice of the refinement depends solely on the internal algorithm of the interpolation engine, and this potential for improving the analysis would be lost. The results show that none of the presented heuristics is clearly the best. The heuristic that uses the

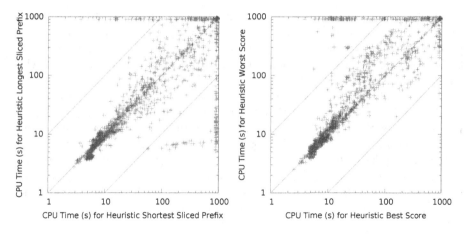

(a) Heuristic "Shortest" vs. "Longest"    (b) Heuristic "Best Score" vs. "Worst Score"

**Fig. 3.** Scatter plots comparing the CPU time of the analysis with different heuristics for slice-based refinement selection for all 2 696 verification tasks

refinement with the best score regarding the domain types of the variables that are contained in the precisions is the best overall (as expected, because it is the only one that systematically tries to select a refinement that hopefully makes it easier for the analysis). However, there are still verification tasks that cannot be solved with this heuristic but with one of the others (as witnessed by the difference between columns "Score Best" and "Oracle Best"). Thus, finding a better refinement-selection heuristics is promising future work.

Figure 3 shows scatter plots for comparing the CPU times of the analysis with two of the four heuristics for slice-based refinement selection. The large number of data points at the top and right borders of the boxes show those results that were solved using one of the heuristics but not by the other. In addition, one can see that the choice of the refinement-selection heuristic can also have a performance impact of factor more than 10 even for those programs that can be solved by both heuristics (witnessed by the data points in the upper left and lower right corners). This effect also results in a huge performance difference in total: the CPU time for those 1 165 verification tasks that could be solved with all heuristics varies between 110 h (heuristic "Score Worst") and 57 h (heuristic "Score Best"), a potential improvement due to refinement selection of almost 50 %.

## 6   Conclusion

This paper presents our novel approach of *sliced prefixes* of program paths, which extracts several infeasible sliced prefixes from one single infeasible error path. From any of these infeasible sliced prefixes, an independent interpolation problem can be derived that can be solved by a standard interpolation engine, and the refinement procedure can choose from the resulting interpolant sequences the one that it considers best for the verification. Our novel approach is independent from the abstract domain (in particular, does not depend on using an SMT solver) and can be combined with any analysis that is based on CEGAR, while previous work on guided interpolation [22] is applicable only to SMT-based approaches. Finally, we demonstrated on a large experimental evaluation on standard verification tasks that the choice, which sliced prefix to take for precision extraction, has a significant impact on the effectiveness and efficiency of the program analysis. In future work, we plan to systematically explore more criteria for ranking sliced prefixes, and then investigate guided techniques for automatically selecting a preferable refinement. Furthermore, we plan to extend our experiments to other abstract domains, such as predicate abstraction and octagons; preliminary results already look promising.

# References

1. Albarghouthi, A., Li, Y., Gurfinkel, A., Chechik, M.: UFO: A framework for abstraction- and interpolation-based software verification. In: Madhusudan, P., Seshia, S.A. (eds.) CAV 2012. LNCS, vol. 7358, pp. 672–678. Springer, Heidelberg (2012)

2. Alberti, F., Bruttomesso, R., Ghilardi, S., Ranise, S., Sharygina, N.: An extension of lazy abstraction with interpolation for programs with arrays. Formal Methods in System Design 45(1), 63–109 (2014)

3. Apel, S., Beyer, D., Friedberger, K., Raimondi, F., von Rhein, A.: Domain types: Abstract-domain selection based on variable usage. In: Bertacco, V., Legay, A. (eds.) HVC 2013. LNCS, vol. 8244, pp. 262–278. Springer, Heidelberg (2013)

4. Ball, T., Cook, B., Levin, V., Rajamani, S.K.: SLAM and Static Driver Verifier: Technology transfer of formal methods inside Microsoft. In: Boiten, E.A., Derrick, J., Smith, G.P. (eds.) IFM 2004. LNCS, vol. 2999, pp. 1–20. Springer, Heidelberg (2004)

5. Ball, T., Rajamani, S.K.: The SLAM project: Debugging system software via static analysis. In: Launchbury, J., Mitchell, J.C. (eds.) POPL, pp. 1–3. ACM, New York (2002)

6. Beyer, D.: Software verification and verifiable witnesses (Report on SV-COMP 2015). In: Baier, C., Tinelli, C. (eds.) TACAS 2015. LNCS, vol. 9035, pp. 401–416. Springer, Heidelberg (2015)

7. Beyer, D., Henzinger, T.A., Jhala, R., Majumdar, R.: The software model checker Blast. Int. J. Softw. Tools Technol. Transfer 9(5-6), 505–525 (2007)

8. Beyer, D., Henzinger, T.A., Majumdar, R., Rybalchenko, A.: Path invariants. In: Ferrante, J., McKinley, K.S. (eds.) PLDI, pp. 300–309. ACM, New York (2007)

9. Beyer, D., Henzinger, T.A., Théoduloz, G.: Program analysis with dynamic precision adjustment. In: ASE, pp. 29–38. IEEE, Washington, DC (2008)

10. Beyer, D., Keremoglu, M.E.: CPACHECKER: A tool for configurable software verification. In: Gopalakrishnan, G., Qadeer, S. (eds.) CAV 2011. LNCS, vol. 6806, pp. 184–190. Springer, Heidelberg (2011)

11. Beyer, D., Löwe, S.: Explicit-state software model checking based on CEGAR and interpolation. In: Cortellessa, V., Varró, D. (eds.) FASE 2013. LNCS, vol. 7793, pp. 146–162. Springer, Heidelberg (2013)

12. Beyer, D., Löwe, S., Wendler, P.: Domain-type-guided refinement selection based on sliced path prefixes. Technical Report MIP-1501, University of Passau (January 2015), arXiv:1502.00045

13. Beyer, D., Petrenko, A.K.: Linux driver verification. In: Margaria, T., Steffen, B. (eds.) ISoLA 2012, Part II. LNCS, vol. 7610, pp. 1–6. Springer, Heidelberg (2012)

14. Blanchet, B., Cousot, P., Cousot, R., Feret, J., Mauborgne, L., Miné, A., Monniaux, D., Rival, X.: A static analyzer for large safety-critical software. In: Cytron, R., Gupta, R. (eds.) PLDI, pp. 196–207. ACM, New York (2003)

15. Clarke, E.M., Grumberg, O., Jha, S., Lu, Y., Veith, H.: Counterexample-guided abstraction refinement for symbolic model checking. J. ACM 50(5), 752–794 (2003)

16. Craig, W.: Linear reasoning. A new form of the Herbrand-Gentzen theorem. J. Symb. Log. 22(3), 250–268 (1957)

17. D'Silva, V., Kröning, D., Purandare, M., Weissenbacher, G.: Interpolant strength. In: Barthe, G., Hermenegildo, M. (eds.) VMCAI 2010. LNCS, vol. 5944, pp. 129–145. Springer, Heidelberg (2010)

18. Graf, S., Saïdi, H.: Construction of abstract state graphs with PVS. In: Grumberg, O. (ed.) CAV 1997. LNCS, vol. 1254, pp. 72–83. Springer, Heidelberg (1997)

19. Henzinger, T.A., Jhala, R., Majumdar, R., McMillan, K.L.: Abstractions from proofs. In: Jones, N.D., Leroy, X. (eds.) POPL, pp. 232–244. ACM, New York (2004)

20. Henzinger, T.A., Jhala, R., Majumdar, R., Sutre, G.: Lazy abstraction. In: Launchbury, J., Mitchell, J.C. (eds.) POPL, pp. 58–70. ACM, New York (2002)

21. Jhala, R., Majumdar, R.: Path slicing. In: Sarkar, V., Hall, M. (eds.) PLDI, pp. 38–47. ACM, New York (2005)

22. Rümmer, P., Subotic, P.: Exploring interpolants. In: Jobstmann, B., Ray, S. (eds.) FMCAD, pp. 69–76. IEEE, Washington, DC (2013)

# Author Index

Printed in the United States
By Bookmasters